HERSELF DEFINED

Books by Barbara Guest

HERSELF DEFINED The Poet H.D. and Her World
ROBERT GOODNOUGH, ARTIST (*with B. H. Friedman*)
SEEKING AIR (*A Novel*)

POETRY
BIOGRAPHY
THE TÜRLER LOSSES
THE COUNTESS FROM MINNEAPOLIS
MOSCOW MANSIONS
THE BLUE STAIRS
POEMS
THE LOCATION OF THINGS

HERSELF
DEFINED
THE POET H.D. AND HER WORLD

BARBARA GUEST

QUILL

New York

Library of Congress Cataloging in Publication Data

Guest, Barbara.
Herself defined.

Bibliography: p.
Includes index.
1. H. D. (Hilda Doolittle), 1886–1961—Biography.
2. Poets, American—20th century—Biography.   I. Title.
PS3507.O726Z68   1985   811'.52 [B]   84–24886
ISBN 0-688-04709-2

Printed in the United States of America

First Quill Edition

1 2 3 4 5 6 7 8 9 10

by Kenneth Fields. Reprinted by permission of David R. Godine, Publisher, Boston; and Carcanet Press Limited, Publisher, *Tribute to Freud* by H.D., Carcanet Press Limited, England, 1971.

The Estate of Frances Gregg and Laurence Pollinger, Ltd., agents, for permission to quote extracts from "The Apartment" and "The Unknown Face," by Frances Gregg, and for permission to quote extracts from unpublished letters of Frances Gregg to H.D.

John Shaffner Associates, Inc., N.Y., for permission to quote extracts from *The Heart to Artemis* by Bryher. Copyright © 1962 by Winifred Bryher.

Holt, Rinehart and Winston, Publishers, for permission to quote extracts from *The House on Jefferson Street* by Horace Gregory. Copyright © 1971 by Horace Gregory. Reprinted by permission of Holt, Rinehart and Winston, Publishers.

Little, Brown and Company, for permission to quote an extract from "Helen" from *Poems* by George Seferis. English translation copyright © 1960 by Rex Warner. Reprinted by permission of Little, Brown and Company in association with the Atlantic Monthly Press; and The Bodley Head, London, for permission to quote an extract from "Helen" from *Poems* by George Seferis, translated by Rex Warner.

Mr. Islay Lyons for permission to quote from unpublished letters of Kenneth Macpherson.

Macmillan Publishing Co. for permission to quote extracts from "The Lover Mourns for the Loss of Love" from *Collected Poems of William Butler Yeats* (New York: Macmillan, 1956); and Michael Yeats and Macmillan London Limited for permission to quote extracts from "The Lover Mourns for the Loss of Love" by W. B. Yeats.

Mrs. Grace McAlmon Marissael for permission to quote extracts from unpublished letters and manuscripts of Robert McAlmon.

Alfred W. Satterthwaite for permission to quote extracts from *Miranda Masters* by John Cournos (New York: Alfred A. Knopf, 1926); from *Autobiography* by John Cournos (New York: G. P. Putnam's Sons, 1935); and from unpublished material by John Cournos.

Viking Penguin Inc., for excerpts from *Kangaroo* by D. H. Lawrence. Copyright 1923 by Thomas Seltzer, Inc. Copyright renewed 1951 by Frieda Lawrence. Reprinted by permission of Viking Penguin Inc. Excerpts from *Aaron's Rod* by D. H. Lawrence. Copyright 1922 by Thomas Seltzer, Inc. Copyright renewed 1951 by Frieda Lawrence. Reprinted by permission of Viking Penguin Inc. Excerpts from *The Collected Letters of D. H. Lawrence*, edited by Harry T. Moore. Copyright 1932 by the Estate of D. H. Lawrence, and 1934 by Frieda Lawrence; copyright 1933, 1948, 1953, 1954, and each year 1956–62 by Angelo Ravagli and C. Montegue Weekley, Executors of the Estate of Frieda Lawrence Ravagli. Reprinted by permission of Viking Penguin Inc.; and Laurence Pollinger Limited and The Estate of Mrs. Frieda Lawrence Ravagli.

The Estate of Louis Wilkinson and Laurence Pollinger, Ltd., agents, for permission to quote extracts from *The Buffoon* by Louis Wilkinson (New York: Alfred A. Knopf, 1916; London: Village Press, 1975). Copyright © 1975 by Oliver Wilkinson.

The following libraries for permission to quote from unpublished material in their collections:

The Beinecke Rare Book and Manuscript Library, Yale University;

The Henry W. and Albert A. Berg Collection, the New York Public Library, Astor, Lennox and Tilden Foundations;

Bryn Mawr College Library;

The Houghton Library, Harvard University;

The Rosenbach Museum & Library;

The Poetry/Rare Books Collections of the University Libraries, State University of New York at Buffalo;

Richard Aldington Papers, Special Collections, Morris Library, Southern Illinois University at Carbondale.

The British Library, Department of Manuscripts, for permission to quote from Add. MS 57784, letter of Hilda Doolittle to Cecil Gray dated December 15 (no year), and Add. MS 57794, extract from a letter of Philip Heseltine to Cecil Gray, n.d. (attributed date 1918).

All photos credited to Beinecke are from the Beinecke Rare Book and Manuscript Library, Yale University.

Preface

I began with the initials, H.D. As a schoolgirl they gazed back at me from anthologies of poetry. There was a surprisingly early, certainly premature edition of the *Collected Poems,* and then the blue wartime editions of what came to be called *Trilogy;* this was all of the work of H.D. with which I was acquainted. It was sufficient to convert me to Imagism, to tempt me into feeble, complimentary imitations of H.D. I was never successful. No one ever has been.

Stephen Guest was much older than I when we met in the sort of apartment H.D. might have frequented. It was a combination of manuscripts, clutter, worn furniture, dried flower petals, foreign languages—a bohemia of tastes and circumstance. It may have been this background that encouraged Stephen immediately after we were introduced to speak of H.D. He showed no surprise when I told him how much I revered many of her poems. He rather took it for granted that this American young woman should have responded to an impeccable poetry.

As our friendship progressed, he wove into it the story of H.D., which she relates in her autobiographical novel *Bid Me to Live,* then unpublished. In particular I was moved by the episode in Cornwall, the flight of the swallow, the mysterious father of the unborn daughter, who Stephen confided was a composer whose name was Cecil Gray. An aura of "romance" now surrounded the initials. (In London, H.D. had told her daughter, Perdita, about "Cornwall," adding that "some people found the story romantic." So we did.)

I was never privileged to know the late Norman Holmes Pearson, H.D.'s friend, confidant, and literary executor. He was persistent in obtaining much of the literary relevancies of H.D., which included the entire correspondence of H.D. with her friend Bryher, for the Beinecke Library archives at Yale University. The position he assumed in the life of H.D. began during the Second World War when an earlier friendship formed in New York City warmed, and continued until her death, fifteen years before his own. We are indebted to him for recognizing the need to establish H.D. as a poet of shared eminence along with the friends of her youth, Marianne Moore, William Carlos Williams, and Ezra Pound. During Pearson's lifetime he was dedicated in his efforts to promote the career of H.D., and to formalize her position among the powerful circles of critics and guardians of literary awards.

Next to her daughter, Perdita Schaffner, the person of most consequence in the life of H.D. was her friend and companion, the writer Bryher. When I began this book I assumed in my precarious innocence that I would be writing a biography of H.D. After I had reached the first encounter of Bryher and

H.D., which was in 1918, I realized that within the chambers of the life I was examining lay another nautilus, Bryher. It was impossible to proceed with my labors without considering on each step of the way a presiding "elf," as H.D. in happier moments called Bryher, or "Napoleon," which was Thornton Wilder's drier tribute. I began to think of her as a difficult "genius," this person who had been born Annie Winifred Ellerman, and who, in an exceptional decision to remove herself from the dominance of her parents, chose to take by deed poll a name from one of the Scilly Isles, Bryher.

H.D. remained Bryher's heroine, her "star," for forty-three years. It was at Bryher's home in Switzerland in 1978 that I first entered an atmosphere once filled by the excitant presence of H.D. Where friends and lovers had shed their memories, I was showed now into a cranky, book-filled room whose furniture dated from the 1930s, when the Bauhaus-style house, Kenwin, was built. Surrounding the oddly shaped room in which we sat were other geometric rooms and narrow passageways that I was permitted to walk through as Bryher led me on a house tour. Featured on the tour, with only a hasty glance at her remarkable collection of Elizabethans, was Kenwin's only contemporary addition, Bryher's pride, a glistening furnace room. Beyond were the Alps, below was Lake Geneva. Kenwin was not so much haunted, as it was *empty*. Built for the needs of creative, indulgent people, and during one chaotic span the home for a menagerie of dogs and monkeys, Kenwin with its austere architecture must have been disordered by arguments, literary shapes, animal howls, camera noises—now there were dusty answers.

Bryher, an aged warrior in her double-breasted wool jacket and tailored skirt, her short, brusquely cut white hair, did not give off any hint of sadness, or melancholy. She concealed her loneliness under an autocratic manner. Her politeness was intellectual; she was not then, nor could she ever have been, genial. Those "frightening blue eyes, the eyes of a child," as H.D. once described them, closed over memories of H.D. She talked about travel, yes. About Kenwin, whose name combined that of her second husband, Kenneth Macpherson, with her given name, Winifred. She spoke perceptfully about war, politics, education. The person who dominated the conversation was her remarkable father, Sir John Ellerman, once owner of the world's largest shipping fleet. It was Bryher's pleasure to refer to his skills as an Alpinist: "my mountaineer father."

In her eighties, Bryher would give only an oblique substance to the Lady of the Lake, who once had reigned alongside her over Kenwin. A careful listener can, of course, catch the invisible throw. And once or twice I did so. But there was no major revelation about H.D. or herself. I do not know what she believed she was shielding. I wish she had talked openly to me. This book might have been different spelled from her own lips. It was necessary to paste the H.D.-Bryher story together with the dry ink and typewritten letters and a dubious reliance on intuition. I expect Bryher was by nature secretive, and probably suspicious of any intruder on her history. It was evident she liked to control; a verbal slip or allusion once escaped, she would examine its loss.

It was what Bryher withheld that lent my research its determination. From then on I entered into her conspiracy. Beyond those sharp eyes lay much experience and a shrewd guess at a world she spent her life trying to place into focus. I discovered scraps of her knowledge within her correspondence with H.D., which began in 1918 and ended with H.D.'s death in 1961. More than scraps, whole tablecloths. I dwell at length on Bryher, because I wish to prepare the reader to find encapsulated within this biography of H.D., without any formal sentiment of mine, the story of Bryher.

I have not proposed to add to the literary criticism of H.D.'s work, such as it is in its still early stages, beyond consulting her writing at appropriate moments. As this biography has progressed, more of her unpublished work has become accessible. In particular there is the carefully collated and definitive edition of her *Collected Poems*. Within the literary remnants lies for me the fascination of a woman who developed in a few years, let us say between 1912 and 1920, into the Imagist poet H.D. With only the frailest education in the classics, or more bluntly, with "small Latin and less Greek," armed with Denis George Mackail's prose translations and the *Greek Anthology*, she determined to begin with selections from Euripides as the basis of her translations. She went further. Her instinctual rendering of Greek classical poetry would be the point of departure for her own poetry.

How did this transformation take place, wherein the girlish "dryad" of Ezra Pound's fantasy became the poet known not as Hilda Doolittle—daughter of a respected astronomer at the University of Pennsylvania, and a kindly, discreet mother from the seclusive Moravians of Bethlehem, Pennsylvania—but as H.D., "pagan mystic" of Imagism? The immediate answer is Ezra Pound. Pound invented his poetics and he invented the people who would occupy the place settings at his banquets. His first celebration in his role as an entrepreneur of poetry was in honor of his fiancée, his Galatea, "H.D. Imagiste." Ezra Pound was only the first of an interesting list of what H.D. called her "initiators," literary men, a psychoanalyst, journalist, husband, composer, academic. These "initiators," as she listed them, were all men. Freud is not included in her list. That would have been too presumptuous, although drawing from her memories of her relatively brief analysis with Freud, she wrote a book about him and H.D.

H.D.'s life was directed, assisted, shared by men who recognized the conflicting elements that tormented women whom they regarded as "stars." She suffered and was fragmented by her dependencies. Nothing supports this statement so much as the photographs of H.D. in her early beauty and then the ravaged image revealed in her late pictures. Yet she was in unexpected ways a most fortunate person. Not only did she have her "initiators," but in most cases in her relations with women the psychic intimacy she demanded was duly returned. With a few exceptions, the women for whom she cared admired her in her role of priestess, poetess, Egeria; they loved her for being H.D. She gave without stint, with even a mania to those whom she loved. Beginning with Frances Gregg, her first and strongest love, the Fayne Rabb of *HERmione*, she was cherished and even adulated by the women of her circle, her lovers and friends. A lonely woman, H.D. was surrounded by a court, if at times provincial and limited.

The title of this biography, I believe, has the sound of H.D., and the challenge it implies was a responsibility H.D. accepted. The definition of self, the penetration into self, was H.D.'s preoccupation and obsession. Her prose writing is always autobiographical; so is much of her poetry. From her private loneliness she views herself at a literary angle. In her prose she is like the woman on a Japanese scroll painting who holds back the curtain in order to watch the couple there on the pillows; she is the third person, who winks at us, saying, "Regard them, if you will, but look also at me, although hidden, I am necessary."

Neither social pressures, political issues, lovers, or a child hindered H.D. in her dutiful pursuit of herself. And it was an exotic, estranged, even sophisticated life she found for herself. She traveled to Vienna to see Freud. She went to Egypt, Greece, England, the Continent. She was in not only permanent, but willing exile all her life. And yet she was separated by a kind of homelessness of self, from the self who hypnotized her.

Unlike her contemporaries, Eliot, Pound, and Stevens, who used historical fragments in their efforts to construe an impersonal and, to them, necessary order, H.D. assembled those compulsive word associations, hieratic images, hallucinatory landscapes as frames for the documentation of her own history. I emphasize H.D.'s need to define herself, because of her surfacing narcissism, the bloodline of a poet. She declared that she had "a very intense inner life." She left many clues, shells upon the strand, idols among the veils. Her presence has had its effect on me. I succumbed to the physical beauty, the witchery, tact, gaiety. She has been an example of discipline and a scrupulous dedication to work.

I should like to apologize for errors of fact and judgment (mistakes made by a writer unaccustomed to the strict overtures of research). I do promise that whenever tempted, I have willingly exchanged fantasy for fact. H.D. was capable of creating her own legend. I want only to exorcize, within my limits, the myths that have been promulgated upon her.

What is offered here is mere encaustic. I have passed hours listening to the H.D. spells (perfect pitch)—transfixed in the poems by her delicacy of mind and touch, her quickness to seize temporal, as well as spiritual, beauty. And I am grateful for those moments when H.D. with a blithe generosity permitted me to stumble on her rituals, her magic stones.

New York City, 1977
Southampton, New York, 1982

Acknowledgments

I wish to thank Perdita Schaffner, H.D.'s daughter, for her kindness and continuing presence during the writing of this book. The work has been enlivened by her remarks, which have contributed vitality to the obscurities of the past. During the lean times of writing, her tact and thoughtfulness have been sustaining. She permitted me to examine the unpublished correspondence between H.D. and Bryher. She has read the typescript and provided useful suggestions.

I also wish to thank John Schaffner for his advice, support, and careful reading of the manuscript, followed by helpful emendations.

The late Bryher Macpherson, H.D.'s companion for over forty years, was kind enough to permit me to visit her home, Kenwin, near Montreux, Switzerland, on several important occasions.

I would like to thank the following people: Professor Miriam Benkovitz for generously providing the Dorothy Yorke interview; Mrs. Gemma d'Auria for showing me letters written to her by H.D., and providing glimpses of an early H.D.; Silvia Dobson—whose kindness, advice, and unremitting support throughout the writing of this book is partially equaled by the valuable information she provided about her friendship with H.D.—for showing me letters written to her by H.D. and the letters from Frances Gregg to H.D.; Laetitia Cerio for her memories of Cecil Gray on Capri; H. P. Collins for his valuable "Memoir" of H.D.; Anne Friedberg for her perceptive comments on *Borderline* and other films made by Kenneth Macpherson; the H.D. scholar Susan Friedman, whose research and kindness were consulted and appreciated; the late Horace Gregory and his late wife, Marya Zaturenska, for their friendly advice and shared memories of H.D. and Bryher; Dr. Erich Heydt, whose memories of his association with H.D at Küsnacht, and his recollections and reconstruction of Dr. Brunner's Klinik at Küsnacht, Switzerland, were of inestimable value in writing of the late years of H.D.; Kenneth Hopkins, whose consistent support, which began with the photograph of the young Frances Gregg and continued through his recollections of the Powys brothers; Maria Jolas for vividly reconstructing the Paris of the 1920s and 1930s and stories of *Transition;* Professor François Lafitte for generously providing me with copies of H.D.'s letters to Havelock Ellis that were in his possession; Kermit Lansner for his admirable and unfailing editorial advice and friendship; James Laughlin for his careful reading of the typescript and for his creative suggestions and support; Islay Lyons for permission to use photographs of H.D. and Bryher; Grace McAlmon Marissael for recollections of her brother, Robert McAlmon, and her generosity in sending unsolicited photographs of McAlmon; Helena

Morley for recollections of H.D. in London; the late scholar Harry T. Moore
for generously sharing details in his possession of the H.D.-Aldington relationship; May Sarton for her recollections of her friendship with H.D.; Professor Alfred Satterthwaite for intimate recollections of his stepfather, John
Cournos, and the photographs of Cournos, Brigit Patmore, and Dorothy Yorke
in his possession; Dr. Melitta Schmideberg for kindly sending me her memoir
of H.D.; Oliver Wilkinson for his perceptive memories of his mother, Frances
Gregg, so generously shared, and his permission to quote from his mother's
journal and her letters to H.D.; Henry Williams of the Moravian Library for
introducing me to the Francis Wolle manuscript; Helen Wolff for her kindness
in discussing her relations with H.D. and Bryher, and her editorial suggestions; Richard Wellish for his sensitive translations of Goethe and Eduard
Möricke; Professor A. Walton Litz, Pound scholar, for his illuminative information regarding the 1912 episodes of H.D. in Paris and Venice.

This book could not have been written without the cooperation of many libraries and librarians, and I would like to thank all of them, especially the following:

Donald Gallup, former Curator of the Yale Collection of American Literature, Beinecke Library, who, with the permission of Perdita Schaffner, made
the unpublished writings of H.D. and her correspondence with Bryher available to me, and whose friendly guidance was a persuasive influence to complete a book whose beginning he had encouraged.

Also at the Beinecke Library, I want to thank Louis Silverstein for his help
in locating material, his suggestions on the completed typescript; Aldo Cupo
and Steven Jones and the entire Reading Room staff for their able assistance.
David Schoonover, present Curator of American Literature, and Marjorie
Wynne, Research Librarian, were also helpful in their various fields.

At Bryn Mawr College Library, I would like to thank Leo Dolenski for his
help and encouragement; at the Houghton Library, Harvard University, F.
Thomas Noonan; Patricia Willis at the Rosenbach Museum and Library for
her friendly assistance and Dr. Clive Driver for his kind permission to use the
Marianne Moore papers, and the photograph of Marianne Moore; at the Rogers
Memorial Library, Southampton, New York, Vivian Murray and Thomas Boyle
for unremitting assistance; Dr. Lola Szladits, Curator of the Berg collection of
New York Public Library, for permission to use the May Sinclair letters and
correspondence from H.D. and Bryher to May Sarton; the British Library,
London; the Huntington Library, San Marino, California; the Pasadena Public
Library; Southern Illinois University Library; the State University of New
York at Buffalo Library; and the New York Society Library, were all helpful.

The Alumni Office of Friends' Central School in Philadelphia, Pennsylvania,
generously searched their files for records of the class of 1905.

I should like to express my gratitude to: Peter Ackroyd, Frank and Margaret
Allen, Louise Beckman, Edward Butscher, Jimmy Daniels, Guy Davenport,
Robert Duncan, Hugh Ford, Terry Frost, Jane Gaitenby, Mary Anne Gauger,
Hadley Haden-Guest, the late Lady Hannay, Trumbull Higgins, Alister Ker-
shaw, Ann Dunn, the late Professor James E. Phillips, Anthony Powell, Anthony

Quinton, Mary de Rachewiltz, David Rattray, Anthony Rota, Nancy Ryan, Toni Scott, Gaby Stuart, Tony Ullyatt, Joan Wilentz.

My gratitude for the constancy of Kate Medina, my editor, whose noble face across the desk never frowned on muddled efforts . . . whose continuing professionalism brought this book to its close . . . and whose joy at our mutual perseverance I shall cherish.

To Katherine Tiddens, Mrs. Medina's assistant, who with a gentle touch wrought a respectable order among the paragraphs . . . whose delicacy of manner midst the clamor of deadlines reserved time for laughter, my grateful thanks.

Also at my publishers, to Stephanie von Hirschberg for the very special attention she gave my book, and to Elizabeth Murphy for her help.

Finally, for thoughtfulness, care, perspicacity, competence . . . and her accomplished maneuvers in libraries, combined with a delight at a shared conspiracy among the strategies of literary detection for nearly five years . . . the most replete of assistants, my affectionate gratitude to Virginia L. Smyers.

ENVOI

She rewarded with small mirrors. They fell
unpierced through the thistles of woven things.

Brazen tears.

She found a trunk and filled it with stones.
Cornish stones.

In the snows searching
I found a coarse, crepe rune:

"Save me the waltz."

Goodbye. Initials.

CONTENTS

List of Illustrations

For *my* "initiators"
Dr. Charles Hiram Richards
and
Ted Wilentz

PART ONE

The world is yet unspoiled for you,
you wait, expectant—
you are like the children
who haunt their own steps
for chance bits—a comb
that may have slipped,
a gold tassle, unravelled,
plucked from your scarf,
twirled by your slight fingers
into the street—
a flower dropped.

       "The Gift" (*Sea Garden*)

CHAPTER ONE

"A Pink Moth in the Shrubbery"

"He drags me out of the shadows," wrote Hilda Doolittle of Ezra Pound. When she first met him in 1901 she was fifteen, a schoolgirl in Upper Darby, a suburb of Philadelphia. It was a Halloween party, and Pound, a student at the University of Pennsylvania, was dressed as a Tunisian princeling. Their real intimacy began in 1905. Hilda was living at home and commuting to Bryn Mawr. In retrospect, she told her mother, it would have been much better if, like the other girls, she had been permitted to live at the college. A day pupil, she thought of herself as separated from her classmates with their shared activities that took place after she had left for home. Had she been secured within the protective atmosphere of Bryn Mawr's "ivy-clad" walls, her romance with Ezra might have ripened more slowly, if ever. But an impulsive, overly sensitive young woman in a household stuffy with relatives and domesticity would welcome the extravagant Mr. Pound.

William Carlos Williams, also a student at the university, called Hilda a "bizarre beauty." He noted her strong jaw, light hair, and blue eyes. She leaped over stiles in the fields, a hoyden, careless of her dress. Upper Darby, then all fields and countryside, wild flowers and hidden paths, had made Hilda a country girl. She ran out into the rain, calling it to fall down on her; she plunged into the dangerous surf at Watch Hill, New Jersey, frightening everyone until she was rescued. This would be her life's description: her bizarre beauty, her attraction to danger, and the need for a rescuer. Bryn Mawr with its sedate rules and restrictions might have tamed her, spared her the excitement Ezra sparked with his gallimaufry, his intellect reaching out like burning straw.

Williams—who went on to become an internist at the French Hospital in New York City, attracted to her as he was—taking her to dances and writing letters equally discreet and confessional, still kept a certain distance. Not so Pound. "Before meeting Pound is like B.C. and A.D.," said Williams. Pound was unlike anyone else in what Henry James called the "goodliest village," Philadelphia.

Separated by his intellectual curiosity, the early maturing of an original mind, Pound needed a disciple. Williams was one; he was joined by Hilda. "Dryad," Ezra called her. Her early history—growing up among a separatist religious sect, annoyance with a household of brothers, a hint of the wistful, above all a spiritedness—was no preparation for her initiation by Ezra Pound.

Only a freshman when Pound became her mentor, she knew nothing of literature or art, except fairy tales, myths, music, Moravian legends. Suddenly she was listening to Pound's eloquent mockery of the nineteenth-century American poets all of whom he disliked, especially the poet of "the forest primeval." Pound didn't want to have anything to do with primeval or the pioneer. It was bad enough having been born in Hailey, Idaho. He sang of the troubadours, Provence, William Morris, Algernon Swinburne. Who in Philadelphia knew, or cared, about Provence, except Ezra. And now Hilda. He forced an education on her that included the classics—Latin and Greek poets; Henrik Ibsen, Count Maurice Maeterlinck, even Yoga, whatever his greedy mind had picked up. Her indoctrination had now become so sophisticated that Bryn Mawr with its slower and more realistic demands could not keep pace. Pound took her to see *Peer Gynt* at the Philadelphia Academy of Music. He also brought a fancy French cheese, called Brie, none of them had ever heard of, much less tasted, to one of their simple picnics. Hideous taste! "You have no palates," stormed Pound. "Palate," another word Hilda had never heard.

She did make two friends at Bryn Mawr with whom she would correspond all her life—Marianne Moore and Mary Herr. Marianne was tall with shining thick braids, reflective eyes, an alert, at times caustic, mind that early appraised the human measure. Even as unconfessed poets she and Hilda found one another sympathetic. In 1921 Marianne Moore, replying to Bryher's eager questions, wrote to her:

My first impression of Hilda is very clear. There is a forsythia bush on the campus at Bryn Mawr near Taylor Hall, the central building on the campus (an office building and lecture-hall combined) and a main campus path passes along the side of the building. I remember Hilda passing this bush in a great hurry on the path heading from Rockefeller Hall—and the Bryn Mawr village to Dalton Hall, the science building. She struck me as being extremely humanitarian and detached, as if she would not insult you by coldness in the necessary and at longest, brief moment of mutual inspection but I felt that she was not interested in the life of the moment. I remember her eyes which glittered and gave me an impression of great acuteness and were, as I said, sunny and genial at the same time. I remember her seeming to lean forward as if resisting a high wind and have the impression of the toe of one foot turning in a little and giving an effect of positiveness and wilfulness. I thought of her as an athlete, I believe. Hilda's being a non-resident was very much to the loss of the resident members of the class . . . Katherine Ecob . . . has a great affection for her and has chiefly the impression of her social charm and bed-rock reliability.

Hilda possessed the gift of friendship. Mary Herr, who became a librarian, was her lifelong friend. Their letters release images of H.D., particularly during the Second World War, she rarely allowed to show elsewhere. We find distant reflections of the Hilda of Bryn Mawr days, and a later, homesick H.D.

The reason Hilda gave for dropping out of Bryn Mawr was that she had become ill. She hinted at a nervous breakdown. This was untrue. Inexplicably, she failed English. "I loved *Beowulf!*" she wept. She also did badly in her other classes. She left Bryn Mawr because she had one failing mark, and the others were low passing. This was enough to discourage her in her mid-sophomore year, and possibly the administration as well. The truth was that she was facing dual worlds: an authoritarian institute of learning, and an equally authoritarian poet. It was either Ezra Pound or Bryn Mawr. "Remember," wrote Hilda about her abrupt departure, "I was an outcast." Pound, an outcast himself, was responsible for this.

In 1938, writing of her daughter, whom she found in "such an odd state at nineteen," she recalled: "I was still at Bryn Mawr at her age—I know I should make no comparisons but I had such a dreary time getting away and paid so heavily for my 'glamour.'" She never ceased to chastise herself for having left college, and just as consistently, she praised her decision. Weren't her ancestors dissenters?

Williams wrote in *Imaginations:* "Hilda Doolittle before she began to write poetry or at least before she began to show it to anyone would say: 'You're not satisfied with me, are you Billy? There's something lacking isn't there?' When I was with her my feet always seemed to be sticking to the ground while she would be walking on the tips of the grass stems."

Hilda had been writing to Williams at the French Hospital, lively, flirtatious letters, always asking about his writing. She had first told him that she would "so like to know *two* of the rising young poets of the age." One of her letters to Williams is signed with her initials, H.D. The letters stare out from the page. She would confess to him that she was more in sympathy with the odd and lonely, "with those people that feel themselves apart from the whole—that are somehow lost and torn and inclined to become embittered by that very loneliness." Here without probing she would recognize her lifelong attraction to people who, whether creatively, socially, or sexually, were troubled by the barriers placed by society.

William Carlos Williams remained an observer; he may have been a disappointed suitor, although he always said that he thought of Hilda as "Pound's girl." He sent her an acrostic for her birthday, although neglecting the actual birthdate!

Hark Hilda! heptachordian hymns
Invoke the year's initial idea
Like liquid lutes low languishings.
Dim dawn defeated dusk derides.
Awake for Aurora's advent angel anthemings arise!

Williams, who in later years might well have been embarrassed by his effort, reported that "she only laughed at me." She wrote: "You say you slaved over it! It should have burst from your lips as a song!"

Had the poem been composed ten years later, Hilda would never have criticized the slavery of the author. By then her own method had become deliberate and careful. The inspiration may have "burst" upon her, but her method of composition was slow.

One day Williams received a letter declaring that Hilda was going to dedicate her life and love "to one who has been, beyond all others, torn and lonely—and ready to crucify himself yet more for the sake of helping all—I mean that I have promised to marry Ezra." Williams' role was to be that of a very dear friend. "For you are to me, Billy, nearer and dearer than many—than most."

While they were engaged, formally, as Pound had given her a ring, the Pound family was entertained at Upper Darby. The Doolittles, especially Hilda's father, then the director of the Flower Astronomical Observatory of the University of Pennsylvania, had disapproved from the very first of her choice, and that disapproval included the family of such an audacious young man. Francis Wolle, Hilda's cousin, who seems to have been ubiquitous in the Doolittle home, visiting his boy cousins, describes the dinner with the Pounds. Ezra had appeared with no hat over his leonine mass of hair, and "while ties were absolute standard of dress for men, he wore none, but had his shirt open at the neck in true Byronic fashion." He was also the first person Wolle had ever seen wear tortoiseshell spectacles. It was one of those staid Sunday dinners that regulated the lives of the American middle class. This dinner, designedly usurped by Ezra, turned out to be a somewhat different affair, according to Wolle. "After the meal he [Pound] read his poems to his adoring parents and Hilda, while the rest of us listened in confused wonderment." For once, even the Professor was upstaged. The Doolittles eventually were impressed by Mr. Pound, assayer of the Philadelphia Mint, and his well-bred wife, so ambitious for her son, and to all appearances, approving of Hilda.

But soon after, Williams received a letter announcing the engagement was broken. Hilda wrote that she was "happy now as I was before—and I know that God is good." God may have appeared in the person of Mary Moore of Trenton, New Jersey, whom he had been seeing at the same time as his engagement to H.D., and to whom Pound dedicated his book *Personae*. She also received a ring. Williams had noted that Pound was shifty and secretive in his relations with women. Though Pound may have "betrayed" Hilda, become interested in another lady of tapestries (the Irish Bride Scratton, whom he met in London), married Dorothy Shakespear, and invested his life in Olga Rudge, in spirit he never ceased to care for H.D. The calls he heeded, and which interrupted his love affairs, were those that promised an extenuation of his own already overwhelming personality. It was an eagerness for the new in his personal as well as his artistic life that was his undoing in private matters. Again in life as in art he usually gave more than he received. In Hilda's case it was he who gave her "the jolt that got me out of the University groove, set me with my face toward Europe, eventually led to my staying on in London."

Ezra dedicated to her the "Is-Hilda Book," or "Hilda's Book." It was a book of poems composed between 1905 and 1907.[1] There are lovely images of the youthful Hilda in this book where she appears as a "Lady tall and fair to see" with her long fingers and her "tree-born spirit of the wood." In a lyric, sweet as silk, he calls her "Saint Hilda," and as in his late cantos, he invokes her blessing: "Saint Hilda pray for me / Lay on my forehead / Cool hands of thy blessing / Out of thy purity / Lay on my forehead / White hands of thy blessing . . ."

There was another Hilda who would flit in and out of the woods, her face changing in the mist, her moods altering with each dryad challenge, just as his troubadour self might appear fickle as it searched the world: they were alike. Once they had been two excellent actors in a brief charade called "being in love."

In *End to Torment*, one of her last books, H.D. found the release she needed from the bondages of family and Ezra Pound. She told her story with wistfulness and love. But it remains her story. She had been writing it in one form or another all her life—fifty years of remembering, of going over the details of a garden scene in Upper Darby. She and Ezra in a tree house. Kisses. Papa's warning voice. The last streetcar back to Philadelphia, which Ezra, or "Ray," as he was called, would race to catch. H.D. would write of embraces in Dr. Snively's study (at an Episcopal school nearby), and the embarrassment of being "caught out" by his students, daughters of clergymen. She believed that she had given herself to Pound, emotionally, if not, as she put it, "biologically." She remained a passionate "demi-vierge." She had, without realizing it, expected too much from him: intellectual contacts, a proper engagement, literary instruction, marriage. No matter that she declared herself thankful she had not married Ezra, because "he would have destroyed me and the center they call 'Air and Crystal' of my poetry." An afterthought. Despite her moth wings, the young Hilda would have married Pound.

---

[1] Included in H.D.'s *End to Torment* (see bibliography).

More important than any presumptive legal tie was her awakening by
him as a poet. She always acknowledged her debt to Pound, and in return remained loyal to their past and his difficult present. She awaited
his letters from St. Elizabeth's "with the intense apprehension with
which I waited almost fifty years ago, when Ezra left finally for Europe."
She even forgave him the brevity of their charade, for it was he who had
first recognized the beauty of the flitting moth. Pound has left a poem,
"Au Jardin," that summons the time of their wooing:

> And I loved a love once,
> Over beyond the moon there,
> I loved a love once,
> And, may be, more times,
>
> But she danced like a pink moth in the shrubbery.

CHAPTER TWO

Moravian Heritage

Hilda Doolittle was born September 10, 1886, in Bethlehem, Pennsylvania. Her childhood was spent among the Moravian community in Bethlehem, the sect to which her mother's family belonged, and it was in this spirit of Moravianism that Hilda grew up. Any biography must first take into account the influence of this church upon her.

Bethlehem was founded in the winter of 1741 by the Moravian Brethren who had come from Saxony to America. Persecuted in their native Moravia, which like Bohemia was occupied by Slavonic tribes, persecuted by Catholics and Lutherans and Hussites alike, the Moravian Brethren had originally taken refuge in Saxony under the protection of Count Nikolaus von Zinzendorf in the early eighteenth century. He was considered a heretic by the Catholics and Lutherans for his belief that God was the very essence of Love. The Moravians were given property on his lands, and there they built a settlement called Herrnhut, "Watched over by the Lord." The Brethren, or Unitas Fratrum, were bound to exercise constant love to one another and also to other religious sects. They were not to pass judgment by uttering a word against those who differed from themselves. Theirs was a doctrine of purity and grace. There was no ornament to the dress. Mourning was never worn. Death was not a subject for sorrow.

At Herrnhut they had practiced a doctrine of Pietism to which H.D. added her own mystical beliefs. She wrote: "I must have the absolutely pure, mystical Moravian pietism or poetism or hard-boiled Freudian facts." There could be no truer summation of her attitude toward life or poetry. She always sought out the world of the beyond, whether through table tipping, Tarot cards, crystal gazing, astrology, or numerology.

The Moravian doctrine teaches that faith is a direct and supernatural illumination from God. ("Supernatural" could here be defined as "above the natural order of things.") It assures us that once this illumination, which is the recognition of the love of Christ, has been experienced, we are saved. There is no morality, piety, or orthodoxy existent, unless it has been touched by this "sufficient, sovereign, saving grace."

The church is based on sharing the love of Christ, who is recognized by the Moravians as God, the fountainhead of all love. Once a Moravian brother had been overwhelmed by this joyous revelation, it was his duty to share his grace with others. This explains the church's missionary zeal. The Moravians have spread their religion throughout the world. In the eighteenth century they began to send missionaries (Hilda's direct ancestors) to the West Indies, and have continued to do so to this day. The mother of Samuel Beckett was educated in Ireland at a Moravian school!

At Herrnhut they had kept a night watch. Each hour of the night was announced by singing a verse of a hymn to suggest holy thoughts to those who might be awake. In a sanatorium near Zurich, H.D. would keep the night watch while she lay sleepless and ecstatic, writing the poems that appear in her last book, *Hermetic Definition*. In these poems each hour of night and morning is ritualistically announced by its Angel. Although influenced by her other esoteric reading, this ritual evolved naturally from stories she had heard of the earlier Moravian practices. These Angels or Stars that enter into her late poetry, together with the religious entreaties in her war poems of the *Trilogy*, were always present in an unconscious nourished from childhood on Moravian history and doctrines.

What would become a well-known brother-and-sister trio—Laura, William Rose, and Stephen Benét—were living in Bethlehem while Hilda was growing up, although she did not then meet them. The Benéts were not Moravians. Their father, a military man, had been posted to Bethlehem and the Benét children, as outsiders, did not attend the Moravian school. When, as published poets, H.D. and William Rose Benét met in New York, they reminisced about the Moravian Christmas, where after the service a Sister gave each person a lit candle. In her memoirs Laura Benét wrote that "the legend was that if you could reach home with your candle you would have good fortune in the new year." But H.D. described the Christmas service as of a "ferocity not to be imagined." She always observed the ritual of the lighted candles at Christmas; for years there was a standing order with the Moravians to supply her brothers with the special beeswax candles made by the Brethren.

In Bethlehem, in the Moravian Church, men and women sat separated from one another; they entered by different doors, the women wearing little white caps, as did H.D.'s grandmother, who even wore hers at home. Industrious, the pioneer Moravians made their own furniture, farmed their own produce; they even sent their own merchant ships forth to carry their manufactures. In this productiveness, and in other aspects, they resemble the Quakers.

It is the emphasis on industry implicit in the doctrine that may have contributed to H.D.'s insistence on the value of her own work, even at the expense of others around her. She was a hard worker, even, it has been suggested, a compulsive one. Her poems were written and rewritten. Her prose suffered constant redrafting. Throughout her life, whether crippled or ill, she managed to write. Her life was one long, rigorous discipline. And this same dedication to work ran through her family, from great-grandparents to the grandchildren. Her surviving brothers were dedicated to their careers. Melvin and Harold became wealthy and respected businessmen. (Even Eric, the beloved half brother, is said to have died from the strain of overwork.) Gilbert, with a surplus of energy, left his wife and children to enlist in the army during the Great War. Selected from the ranks, he became an officer and was one of the early killed at Thiaucourt, France, in 1918. The hardships of the first Moravian settlers challenged their descendants.

Moravianism, unlike the Puritan societies of New England, and even the nearby Quakers, was so uncommon that its adherents might find themselves separated from the more usual orthodoxies of their friends. There was constantly with H.D., in addition to the natural immunity of an artist, a feeling of "apartness" of custom, and even of language. Later that separateness would be a geographical one, and the customs and language would be a real barrier. A discontinuity in her youth, together with her adult years of exile, would explain some of the tensions that shaped her life.

Walking the streets of Bethlehem today, with the buildings so closely set to one another, one feels a suffocation begin to obtrude, a claustrophobia. There carefully preserved are the original stone buildings of the Gemein House, the Bell House, and the Sisters' house. The seminary buildings extend down to the creek. Along Church Street, where the Doolittles and Wolles lived at 110, each house seems to eye the other— the house of the sister-in-law, of nephews, of the uncle. At the same time, this fraternal and paternal closeness could lend a security, the sheltering noise of wings surrounding one, as if all was directed from the center, the Church itself, by a central protective eye. The sense of the "love" of Christ dwelling within each house may have been for H.D. a private source of strength.

In the 1950s H.D. wrote a historical novella about Count Zinzendorf and his followers, which she called "The Mystery." Nestling among her papers is a poem she calls a "Hymn" for Count Zinzendorf. In this hymn the voice of the early Imagist H.D. and the ancestral hermetic commingle. She speaks of "the wound of grace," and "the wound of love."

H.D.'s grandfather on her mother's side, Francis Wolle, whose family roots had originated in Poznán, Poland (midway between Berlin and Warsaw, with a mixed German and Polish population), was a Moravian minister and principal of the Young Ladies' Seminary in Bethlehem until he retired in 1881. (Before the Civil War young girls from the South had been sent to this seminary for their education; during the war it was used to house the wounded.) Although born in a nearby Moravian town in 1820, Francis Wolle had lived in Bethlehem since childhood. He was an

exceptional person, known as "Papalie" by his family; to a larger public
interested in botany he was considered a world specialist in desmids and
published a book on them. (Amy Lowell's grandfather, John Amory
Lowell, was a well-known botanist, giving his botanical library and herbarium to Harvard. Did the two Imagists discuss their grandfathers?) By
1876 his botanical experiments were an amusement to the family, as they
were when H.D. was a girl, setting out to the Sisters with botanical plates
to be watercolored by the careful old ladies for her grandfather's book. In
1906 Wolle's herbarium was presented by his widow to the University of
Pennsylvania.

Francis Wolle had five children for whom he needed to provide. With
that same ingenuity expressed by so many members of isolated com-
munities, he proceeded in 1852, a year before H.D.'s mother's birth, to
invent a machine to manufacture paper bags! He sent salesmen out to
talk the small stores into using paper bags and it was a difficult task. But
the business prospered and Wolle's brothers took it over and expanded
it. Presumably after the pleasures of his invention, Wolle was no longer
interested in paper bags; he departed for a six-month tour of Europe.
This journey was the beginning of a Wolle tradition that extended from
H.D.'s Uncle Fred, who went to Munich to study music, to H.D. herself.
H.D.'s immediate family, despite their involvement in a provincial community, were not insular.

After Francis' return a decline in his fortunes (although helped by the
sale of land, jointly owned by the brothers, to the Bethlehem Steel Cor-
poration) decided him to become a Moravian reverend and principal of
the seminary. He is an odd, sympathetic, eccentric, playful figure. H.D.
grew up alongside a crocodile her grandfather had been sent from Florida. He could be dictatorial as well. Helen Wolle declined what was for
her his frightening suggestion of going to the West Indies as a missionary, a career selected by her father, who believed she had taught at the
seminary long enough and should go forth and spread the gospel, and
while doing so, find herself a husband. Instead she decided to marry the
stranger in their midst, Charles Doolittle, whom she at first had refused,
because he was a widower with two children. "Very well," had rejoined
Wolle, "on the condition you and your husband buy part of my property
on Church Street and build your house next to mine!"

"Mamalie," Francis' wife, had been a daughter of a Jedidiah Weiss,
whose family had originated in Germany but had settled as Moravian
ministers in the West Indies. She was born in 1824 in Bethlehem, and
like her husband is buried on Nisky Hill. She often took the Doolittle children to the old cemetery, known as "God's Acre," a block
from where they lived and showed them the graves of the earlier Moravians and even an Indian grave of the warrior Chingachgook, whom
James Fenimore Cooper wrote about in *The Pioneers*. Then they would

go to the new cemetery on Nisky (named after a Moravian settlement.in Saxony) Hill and look from its height across to the industrial mills of a new Bethlehem. In *The Gift*, a memoir H.D. wrote during World War II, Mamalie is the little widow lady with a child, who then married Papalie, Francis Wolle. But she is also a mysterious figure. Just as there was for the young Hilda a mystery about that other child of her father's whose birth had caused the death of his first wife—child and mother buried on Nisky Hill—so was Mamalie's past endowed with secrets. Dead children with unused names. Former husbands and wives. They disturbed Hilda. They belonged to a private family history she could not enter.

Her grandparents had a son, Fred, born ten years after Hilda's mother, Helen, in 1863, who was one of the rare ones of the Wolle family. After returning from Munich, he taught music at the seminary. This was his first step. J. Fred Wolle founded the Bach choir at Bethlehem. This choir has developed into a Bach festival held each year. Wolle's interpretation of Bach has been much praised, but it was his devotion to Bach, even to the point of quarreling with the church elders, that drew him close to H.D. In 1905 he left Bethlehem to head the music department at the University of California. Teaching music was never satisfying to Wolle and he returned to Bethlehem, to his beloved and ultimately famous choir. Helen Wolle Doolittle explained to the young Hilda that it was Fred who had "the gift." This "gift," which the Moravians believed was passed from generation to generation, was one of vision, of wisdom of the Holy Spirit, however it manifested itself. Hearing so often of Uncle Fred's "gift," Hilda was fascinated. Was it possible that this gift had passed to her? In war-struck London, while she wrote these impressions of her childhood and youth, often there must have passed through her mind the certainty that her poetry was an expression of "the gift." Never except during those critical days of bombardment and possible death had she felt so close to her Moravian ancestors.

The Doolittle family had come originally from England. "Their quaint name, then spelled Doolittel, runs back to the reign of Queen Elizabeth and perhaps before," wrote H.D. She learned that another ancestor had been a preacher in London who was persecuted when he "in defiance of the law, erected preaching places when churches were lying in ruins after the great fire." He was, she wrote, "One of the last of the rejected clergy." The "quaintness" of the name was to cause Hilda a certain discomfort and may have been responsible for the brilliant suggestion of Ezra Pound's—that she reduce it to initials.

Thus both sides of H.D.'s family were dissenters: the Moravian Wolles and the Puritan Doolittles. The Doolittles had first settled in Connecticut, where several were noted patriots during the Revolutionary War. A branch of the family went out to Indiana, where Hilda's father, Charles

Leander Doolittle, was born in 1843. The Civil War interrupted his studies in astronomy at the University of Michigan. After losing a brother in
the war, he enlisted and was appointed a government surveyor. Charles
returned to the university when the war ended and received his degree
in civil engineering in 1874. (Four of his sons would receive similar degrees.) He married Martha Farrand from Indiana and they had two sons,
Alfred and Eric. (Alfred disappears from the story early, as he left soon
after his father had moved to Bethlehem and upon the death of his
mother; the last trace given is his departure for Washington, D.C.)

Appointed professor of astronomy and mathematics at Lehigh University in 1875, Charles Doolittle took his family with him to Bethlehem,
where his wife died in childbirth only a year later.

In 1882 Helen Wolle married this tall, alien, bearded stranger from Indiana who had fought in the Civil War. From all evidence it proved to
be a good marriage. There were, as usual, secret losses on each side. For
Helen there proved to be a lack of sympathy toward her music and her
church. For Charles there was the continual reminder that he was an
outsider.[1]

The Doolittles had four children born between 1884 and 1894: Gilbert,
Hilda, Harold, and Charles Melvin (known as "Melvin"). Eric, who was
H.D.'s much-loved half brother, assumed the role of reliable eldest
brother and son. Despite Eric's relieving his father, and eventually becoming his assistant at the observatory, the Professor claimed that his
"one girl was worth all her brothers." This claim, in turn, placed an emotional burden on Hilda. She must, despite her own inclinations, please
her father. And this sense of duty makes her early escape from the family
and her father all the more remarkable.

In "Advent" (a section of *Tribute to Freud*) she wrote: "I am on the
fringes or in the penumbra of the light of my father's science and my
mother's art . . . the house in some indescribable way depends upon
father-mother. At the point of integration or regeneration, there is no
conflict over rival loyalties."

Hilda, with her long feet and hands, her luminous probing eyes, most
resembled her father. Her separateness as the only girl matched his
separateness from the Wolles. There was an undefined, natural linkage
between the two. "Not one day went by," said her friend Bryher, that
she did not mention "my father, the Astronomer."

The *Dictionary of American Biography* summarizes Charles Doolittle's
achievements:

> His contribution was to make research observations on the stellar coordi-
> nates, constant aberration and on the variations of latitude upon the

[1] Surprisingly, all of Helen's generation of cousins married outside the Moravian sect.
By 1930 only one Wolle, an unmarried woman, remained in Bethlehem.

earth . . . probably no single contribution to the problem of latitude variation was of greater value than the results he obtained at the Flower Observatory. He retired from the chair of astronomy at that University and
in 1912 becoming emeritus professor received the honorary degree of
L.D.D. from Lehigh University . . . He was a fellow of the American Association for the Advancement of Science and a member of the American
Philosophical Society, and from 1899 to 1912 treasurer of the American
Astronomical Society.

His was an intense, all-embracing career, far removed from the tidy,
cloistered streets of Bethlehem. He even shocked the Wolles in 1890 by
becoming a Democrat! His son Eric, who would succeed his father as
professor of astronomy at the University of Pennsylvania, a position he
would hold until his early death in 1920, alone seems to have recognized
his father's eminence and could forgive the abstract lapses in his concentration and conversation. The Professor's daughter substituted pride for
understanding. She allowed a mystery to surround her father, a preserv-
ing halo she never dared penetrate.

In *The Gift* H.D. at last reveals her admiration for her father:

> He came from another world, another country. He looked at the sky as
> the sons of the sea must always look. His text book on Practical Astron-
> omy was used for many years I believe at the Naval College of Annapolis.
> This book is called *Practical Astronomy as Applied to Geodesy and Navi-
> gation* . . . He gave thirty years of observation to this work . . . Here
> was cold and absolute beauty, here was mathematics as applied to the
> revolution of the earth around the sun . . . "The earth does not go round
> and round in perfect circles," he would say, "it wobbles like a ship at
> sea."

His book was written in 1885, in the early years of his marriage and before the birth of Hilda.

The Professor showed the same dedication to work his daughter later
displayed. And the loneliness of the occupation, of being in a world of
earth and sky, alone in the dark, an acceptance of solitude his daughter
would share.

In Bethlehem he had gone out each night to his "transit house" in
back of the Church Street house to watch the changes of the earth. He
slept during the day. Sometimes during the winter nights his wife would
bring hot water to melt the icicles from his beard.

Doolittle remained at Lehigh for twenty years, until 1895. He was next
asked to take a similar position at the University of Pennsylvania and in
1896 became Flower Professor of Astronomy, first director of the famous
observatory (named after its donor) at the university. Here he constructed another transit house, and Eric, now his assistant, would go out

to the big observatory itself, which rotated. The Professor preferred to
make his nightly observations from a Zenith telescope that had a fixed
position.

This advancement in his career also meant that the family would have
to leave Bethlehem. Hilda was then nine, and she was both resentful and
frightened of the move. This displacement from the guardian Moravians
would initiate a lifetime's shuttling back and forth from one country to
another, from cottages to hotels, to flats, and finally to a sanatorium. The
house at 110 Church Street represented her last formal home, the farewell from her strict, yet kindly, ancestors.* The move would only be to
Upper Darby, where the Flower Observatory was located, five miles
west of Philadelphia. Yet the Moravian community would mourn them as
emigrants to another land.

The new house sat on a knoll on three acres. It was surrounded by
working farms. There were two large maple trees and they and the
shrubs made a shade for summer picnics. A sizable porch fronted the
house. And it was a large house, L-shaped. A parlor, sitting room, dining
room, and kitchen on the first floor. Upstairs on the second floor were five
bedrooms and a bath. On the third floor were three bedrooms for the
younger boys and their visiting cousins. The other ell was given over to
the business of the observatory. It was here the Professor had his study
and worked with his son Eric and another assistant. At first these young
men lived above the study, later when Eric was married, he and his wife
lived above. The drawing of the "Venus de Milo," brought back from the
honeymoon trip to Europe, once more hung in the parlor. Here was an
old-fashioned Emersonian American home with an empty, yet produc-
tive, countryside surrounding it, and intellectual labors taking place inside.

There was another less idealistic view of the American home and that
was usually seen by the women of the household. Although the Doolittles were able to hire a cook, selected from that horde of new immigrants
who rushed to the mills of Bethlehem, the tasks of Mrs. Doolittle remained unending. A streetcar passed below the house on its way back
and forth from Philadelphia. It was necessary for her to take the streetcar into town in the morning and shop for groceries and household
needs, returning in the afternoon. She would probably make the trip several times a week. If she was going to Wanamaker's, she would take
Hilda with her. The amount of provisions brought into the house must
have been astounding. By farm or manor standards, setting a table for
seven at breakfast and nine at dinner would scarcely count. But all the
details, except the actual cooking, fell on the mother's shoulders, aside
from the demands of her children, and an undoubtedly catered-to husband.

It is small wonder that Hilda felt separated from her mother by the

*A Pennsylvania State historical marker has recently been placed at this site to indicate
that "Hilda Doolittle (H.D.) the renowned poet was born here on September 10, 1886."

demands of a large family, university assistants, relatives, who constantly visited—all of whom consumed so much of her mother's time. Freud told H.D. that her life was a search for her mother. In her analysis she learned that "an empty house with no boys and a piano is apparently my UNK [unconscious] ideal." Reality had handed her a withdrawn father and a mother stranded in domesticity. Nor is it any wonder that Hilda in later life could never be charmed by the lures of the homely life. Except when forced to during the Second World War, there is no evidence that she ever cooked a "proper" meal.

William Carlos Williams, a frequent guest at Upper Darby, gives a description of the household that suggests a combination of rigidity and confusion dominated by Professor Doolittle. Williams describes the house with its flower garden capably tended by Mrs. Doolittle, who "led a harassed life and showed it: with her hair drawn tightly back like all capable women." He goes on to say that "the five children were all over the house, and no doubt, their friends as well. When they were at dinner and Mrs. Doolittle noticed that the Professor wished to speak, she would quickly announce: Your father is about to speak! Silence immediately ensued. Then in a slow and deep voice, and with his eyes fixed on nothing, as Ezra Pound said, just above, nothing nearer than the moon, he said what he had to say. It was a disheartening process." Also a sad one, as it illustrated an exceptional man ill-suited to join carelessly into the family banter.

H.D. writes that when her father laughed he made a sort of neighing sound, like a horse. When as a little girl, she came across a drawing called "Nightmare," she asked her mother what it was because she was frightened by the drawing. "What is a nightmare? Is it a sort of horse?" Her mother tore the picture out of the book and threw it away. Here H.D. wants the reader to believe that her mother was fearful of the parallel the daughter drew between a nightmare and her father's laugh. That her mother suspected that her husband's going out at night to his observatory might have frightened the girl may be the hidden suggestion behind H.D.'s need to tell the story. (Inadvertently H.D. also gives an early illustration of the word association she would employ in her poetry.)

Their nearest neighbors, luckily as it turned out, were the Snively family. The father, an Episcopal priest, was the warden of the Burd School, an orphanage for the daughters of clergymen. Their chapel was now the Doolittles' nearest church. The daughter, Margaret, was Hilda's age, and became her best friend. The two girls, along with Matilda Wells, who lived nearby, would ride around the countryside in Margaret's pony trap. It was now "Margaret, Matilda, and Hilda," a girlish threesome, as opposed to the infernal house of boys. As the girls grew older they invented picnics, dances, and walking clubs. They used to spend several weeks

with Matilda at Bailey Island in Casco Bay, Maine. And Hilda stayed
with Margaret every summer at the Snively cottage at Watch Hill,
New Jersey. H.D. celebrates her summer visits in *Palimpsest:*

> Somewhere behind them the moon had fallen down perpendicular,
> slipped off the flat stretch of sand where hillocks marked drift and sand
> hill, where following sand hill and sand crest and hollow of sand trough,
> it seemed eventually one must surely reach a sea, the rim of a New Jersey
> seacoast; where inland cut apart from the inwash of sea, were fresh pools,
> where dragon-flies opened iridescent petal of frail wing, where hovering
> dragon-fly perched on the ivory, out-rayed petal of New Jersey lotus . . .
> A Graeco-Egyptian was wandering across New Jersey marshes in search
> of those famous (even in Egypt) ivory pointed, saffron-scented lily lo-
> tuses.

Margaret assumed a necessary role in Hilda's life. Also resident in England, she appeared at significant intervals during Hilda's early years
there. It was her brother, DeForrest, who had introduced H.D. to Ezra
Pound. Margaret appears as a sensible, intelligent woman, not given to
Hilda's emotional flights, nor, as with other women, would she fall under
Hilda's domination. Her own later life was made difficult by financial
problems, and then Bryher, in gratitude for her past support of H.D.,
stepped in with financial aid. In 1969 Margaret Snively Pratt, now living
in New Zealand, after receiving a copy of *Tribute to Freud* Pearson had
sent her, contributed further information on an episode H.D. relates both
in her book on Freud and in *The Gift.*

This incident came to have a disproportionate meaning in H.D.'s life,
so much so that she tends to give several variations on it. It seems that
one evening her father had returned home, incoherent and fainting from
a wound in his head. Hilda first discovered him and proceeded to wipe
the blood from his forehead. She insisted that it was she who had first
come to his aid. But then came the older brothers and she was sent
away. "Why," she continued to ask. "Why didn't they give me credit for
being the first to help him? Why was I pushed aside?" For years she was
traumatized by this event. She spoke of it to her various analysts, including Freud and Havelock Ellis, and the episode returned in her dreams.
What, indeed, had happened to Papa?

Writing in 1933 to Robert McAlmon, who had told her of his nightmares stemming from the beatings his father had given him as a child,
H.D. replied that she, too, had nightmares. They dated from the time her
father had arrived home with a bleeding head. She told McAlmon that
they had learned he had been struck by the streetcar that passed their
house in Upper Darby. Here she makes the first acknowledgment she
had ever made of the cause of the blow. Over the years she had deliberately chosen to regard the episode as one of insoluble mystery. That now,

in 1933, she was able to describe more literally what had happened, she attributes to her sessions with the psychiatrist Dr. Hanns Sachs. She would always place an emphasis on any unusual or untoward event in her life, an occurrence that someone else might take much more lightly, or even forget. Yet all her life H.D. feared a taxicab would strike her. (In her exchange with McAlmon, H.D. reveals that she does not acknowledge a discrepancy between the very real and terrible beatings McAlmon was given, and the fact that it was her father, not herself, who had received a blow.)

In Margaret's commonsensical version the plot now thins:

> One night when I was staying at Hilda's her parents had gone into the city to some affair. About 10 P.M. we heard someone at the door. When we opened it we saw the professor with his beard dark from blood. He was very dazed and all he could say was "Mama, Mama." Later he was able to say that she had stayed on for a bit so she wasn't with him. He had signalled to the conductor to stop, but he hadn't seen the signal and the professor never noticed that the car hadn't stopped so he just stepped off into space. Luckily he wasn't badly hurt . . .

In *The Gift* he suffers from a severe concussion. The plot thickens in a letter she wrote to Havelock Ellis in 1933 describing the incident, with her flair for melodrama, and adding that her father's "life was despaired of for some time." She emphasizes in this letter that after the grown-ups, who would be her mother and the older brother, Eric, arrived on the scene, "*they simply ignored us all* and sent us to bed. We were never told how dangerous it was . . . did not know if he was to die in the night . . . but *somehow we were shunted aside.*" (my italics) Then she goes on to remark that children were "too proud and too deeply tender to mention, themselves, any heroics of the sort of first-aid." She tells Ellis that she had "terrible phobias after my father's death." And then more surprisingly, as this is her only known admission, she tells Ellis: "The worst of all this is that I repressed it all; nature I suppose, as I would no doubt not have had the child if I had given way to some sure knowledge of my loss, and earlier memories." She did not mourn the death of her father, as she learned in her work with Freud, because she expected to join him when she died in childbirth.

When Hilda was sent to Miss Gordon's School in West Philadelphia, Dr. Snively was persuaded to send Margaret. Despite her favorite girl friends, Hilda was unhappy—she probably had been spoiled at the Moravian Girls' Seminary—and in 1902 she was transferred to the Friends' Central School in Philadelphia, where she was a student until 1905, when she left for her disastrous year at Bryn Mawr.

The yearbook describes her as she was when she first met Pound, as someone "with a face with gladness overspread / Soft smiles by human kindness bred." Her tastes were literary and leaned toward the classics. She was a fiend at basketball, her height there was an asset. She was five feet eleven inches. Her height embarrassed her when she and her mother shopped at the new Philadelphia Wanamaker's, or Bonwit Teller, where her mother, a normal height in that era of shorter women, frequently wished that dresses would fit her daughter "the way they did other girls." Hilda eyed those ranks of simple, washable frocks longingly. Nothing fit her outsize Doolittle frame. The later H.D. would seldom shop in stores for ready-made clothes. There would be an occasional exotic choice, but as a rule her dresses, suits, and even coats were made up for her by excellent seamstresses, whether in London or Switzerland.

An irresistible quotation from the yearbook tells us:

> In the yard at recess every day
> Tall Hilda at "pass-ball" did play,
> While the D's all did stand
> And say, "Isn't she grand!
> Let's buy her some cake right away!"

From the "Girl's Prophecy" we read: "Hilda is studying astronomy principally because she found it so convenient to look right into the stars without using a telescope." An accurate forecast of the later H.D.

The favorite child, Hilda, begged for her father's wandering attention. Professor Doolittle did his best to offer his daughter the cultural opportunities of Philadelphia. He took her with him to the scientific and philosophical societies to which he belonged. Once H.D. described Philadelphia to Bryher as "the Bath-Boston of the States unconscious . . . Go to The Philadelphia Academy of Music, it is pure Wien . . ."

Beginning in the early 1950s, H.D. began to correspond with Gemma d'Auria, who, although younger than she, had attended the Friends' School at the same time. Gemma, a writer and sculptor, then living in Los Angeles, was the daughter of a physics professor at the university, an associate of Professor Doolittle. H.D. recalled the senior class of the university performing *Iphigenia in Aulis*. (A production in which Pound had taken part.) H.D. wrote to Gemma: ". . . I felt I had heard Greek at last."

She had been "awakened," a word she used further on in her letter to Gemma, to Greek drama by the Messenger who appears at the end. (Iphigenia was to be sacrificed so that her father, Agamemnon, might win the war against the Trojans.) This Messenger announces that the life of Iphigenia has been spared. A slain deer has been substituted at the altar by the Goddess Artemis. To the mother of Iphigenia, Clytemnestra, the Messenger says, "Your daughter has been wafted to the gods." When Agamemnon enters he enjoins his wife to be happy, their daughter lives. He tells her, "Our daughter, truly, possesses fellowship with the gods."[2]

[2] *Iphigenia in Aulis,* written by Euripides, may explain why H.D., after her "awakening," selected Euripides for her future adaptations and translations, above the other Greek dramatists. (Bryher used *The Heart to Artemis* as the title of her autobiography!)

CHAPTER THREE

"Wee Witches"

An awakening to Greek drama with an assurance of a domicile among the gods was of less consequence to her family than a daughter's failure at Bryn Mawr. The Doolittle household had rigid scholastic standards. H.D. was the only one of their progeny not to graduate from college. Her status as a prodigal daughter was made clear to her, and she never forgot this lowering of her self-respect.

"She was a disappointment to her father, an odd duckling to her mother, an importunate overgrown unincarnated entity that had no place here" was H.D.'s melancholy description of herself in 1909.

Ezra was in faraway Europe. She first turned to her half brother Eric, always her favorite, for consolation. He was married and living at home in the wing reserved for assistants from the university. His wife, whom Hilda disliked, soon put a stop to Hilda's notion that she and her brother should become soul mates.

Next Hilda decided that what she really needed was a girl her own age, a twin sister. She had always had a "curious desperate yearning" for a baby sister. Enter Frances Gregg, introduced by Nan Hoyt, a mutual friend. Hoyt appears in *HERmione* as Nellie Thorpe.

Frances Gregg—christened Fanny Josepha (after a Spanish ancestress, she said)—was born in 1884 and was thus two years older than Hilda. She lived with her widowed mother in a small apartment in Philadelphia. According to Frances' son, Oliver Wilkinson, she had come from pioneering American stock. The Greggs were connected with the Roosevelts, and Frances' grandmother, Gertrude Heart, had been a noted speaker on women's rights, on drink and venereal disease, and a "most respected pillar of the Church." (An American Josephine Butler.) When Frances was a young girl she "gave herself to God at a Camp Meeting." Much later she would adopt a more sophisticated approach to religion. Just as Hilda had her Moravianism, so Frances had a sincere desire for a religious belief, provincial as it may have been. "She contributed her understanding to benefit mankind," wrote her admiring son (in a letter to the author), whereas "Hilda chose an opposite philosophy, that of art being a discipline that transcended the ordinary commerce of life."

An intense friendship formed between the two young women in their early twenties. They talked, they laughed, they kissed. Each became the other's confidante. Their pet names were "twigs" and "flower." They discussed what were for them important subjects—literature, myth, magic, intuition, love. There they were, two prophetesses, absorbed with one another, sitting side by side on the sofa, holding hands, their heads bent toward each other, whispering. Hilda had found her twin—and her love.

> O hyacinth of the swamp-lands
>   Blue lily of the marshes,
> How could I know,
>   Being but a foolish shepherd
>   That you would laugh at me?

Hilda dedicated the poem to Frances (Theocritus, thanks to Pound's influence, firmly in mind).

H.D. wrote their story in 1922, entwining it with the drama of her wooing by Ezra Pound. She called the story "Her."[1] H.D. was Her (short for "Hermione") Gart, (Pound, incidentally, gave his mother this name in his book *Indiscretions,* published in 1923), which Hilda had then adopted because, encouraged by Pound, she identified herself with the Queen from *The Winter's Tale.* Frances she named Fayne Rabb; and Pound, George Lowndes. (H.D.'s tendency was to give her characters assumed names that especially rankled on the ear.)

Hilda in a letter told Frances she must realize that "no one will ever love you as I loved you." H.D., continually haunted by her girl-love, described Frances in "Paint It Today," a story (unpublished) she wrote shortly before "Her": "She was not attractive. Spotted face. Grey raincoat. It was her eyes set in the unwholesome face; it was the shoulders, marble splendour, unspoiled by the severe draping of the rain proof. It was her hand, small unbending still with archaic grandeur; it was her eyes, an unholy splendour . . . Her eyes were the blue eyes, it is said one sees in heaven; eyes, Angel . . ."

Frances was Hilda's first girl-love, although previously Hilda had been flirtatious (an adjective particularly suited to her) with her cousin, Gretchen Wolle (Baker). For a short while she had hoped Gretchen, although much younger, would be that "sister"; the family hadn't particularly cared for Hilda's usurpation of Gretchen. Frances, the girl who finally became the object of this love, must indeed have been someone very special; her image would never leave H.D. Both women would live with men, have other lovers, produce children, but this first girl-love was an excitement that eclipsed any other.

There is no doubt that Frances answered Hilda's unspoken need to dominate. In "Her," Fayne-Frances would say, "But you are iron. Where

---

[1] "Her" was published by New Directions in 1981 and entitled *HERmione.*

do you get your strength, Hermione?" H.D., despite her deliberately cultivated frailty, was and would remain iron; an iron vein ran in her that she poetically termed "crystal."

It was characteristic of H.D. to place undue demands of affection upon those close to her, or those to whom she felt particularly drawn. As a consequence, she suffered from imagined slights and disappointments. She also considered it her requisite to withdraw from a relationship when she chose, no matter how insistent her earlier demands had been upon the person involved. A behavior not unusual, but in each case emphasized by the impetuousness of her original demand. This complexity was at work in her marriage with Richard Aldington, whom she never actually forgave for having an affair with another woman in the early years of their marriage, even though it had been Hilda who with her emotional and sexual ambivalence created the situation. She demanded a kind of emotional subjugation and idealized relationship from her first deep love, Frances Gregg, while at the same time Frances would be exposed to the most candid criticism and arbitrary desertion.

Frances made exits and entrances in H.D.'s life until her own death during the Second World War. She was the will-o'-the-wisp woman. John Cowper and Llewelyn Powys, both of whom were in love with her, thought of her as half androgynous, half sad, "like Doña Rita," in Joseph Conrad's *The Arrow of Gold*.[2]

Frances' son, Oliver Wilkinson, has described his mother's relationship with Hilda as "deep, bitter-sweet."

Privately, Hilda and Frances referred to themselves as "wee witches," but it was Pound who had first spotted Hilda and Frances as "witches." "If you had lived in Salem," he said, "you would have been burned." In his conversations with Hilda, whenever she would begin to cast her mystic spell and wander into the abstract, the vague, he would interrupt her with "Oh don't talk such rot."

By the same romantic firelight where she wooed Frances, sitting on the same sofa that held their confidences, Hilda would read the letters Ezra sent her from London. Suddenly in 1910 he announced, "I'm coming back to gawd's own god damn country." He would be in New York. Well, so would she.

She told her parents she wished to go to New York to look for literary work. They may have been relieved to have her away for a time, the family tensions having increased, and the presence of Frances having

2 Dr. Bernard Meyer, a Conrad scholar, in a discussion of Conrad's androgynous heroines has written that although Conrad attempts with Doña Rita to paint her as "mysteriously feminine," he refers to her head as "delicately masculine," and he described her body as "statuesque, gleaming, cold like a block of marble." Doña Rita in love "conveys rather a mood of melancholy and an atmosphere of neurotic suffering."

been no help; quite the contrary. They disliked Frances more than they disliked Pound, and he up to then had seemed the most suspect of all.

She arranged to stay with a friend who lived in Patchin Place in Greenwich Village. Pound would be staying nearby at Waverly Place, also in the Village.

Although Hilda was only at Patchin Place for a short time, she detested it and this was an unhappy period. The bitterly cold city was unfamiliar. How could she anticipate that Patchin Place would become a famous address because of its occupants, Djuna Barnes and E. E. Cummings, writers with whom H.D. later would be associated. What mainly preoccupied her in 1910 was Pound's neglect.

Not realizing that Pound was now a recognized poet and man of letters, she had expected him to remain her province, the same suitor of Upper Darby, the dweller in her tree house. But by 1910 Pound's *Personae* and *Exultations* (published in London) were being noticed and, importantly, in the United States, read by Harriet Monroe, the doyenne of Chicago, the founder of *Poetry* magazine. In 1910 he would publish *The Spirit of Romance,* and by 1912 two more books of poems would be in print. He was the friend of William Butler Yeats and Ford Madox Ford. He was an arrivé in London. He wished an international reputation; New York and the rest of America had yet to accept him. He was, as a consequence, busy in New York politicking his credos with William Carlos Williams, announcing his presence to the poets whom Williams had gathered. He had no time for Hilda. When Pound was "on the job" he permitted himself no distractions.

Hilda left New York and returned home. She had made no contacts, had found no work. She comforted herself with the thought that now she was more herself "in a nice house and surroundings," in other words within a situation she could dominate.

Halley's Comet had recently appeared, causing great excitement among the astronomers and press; the Flower Observatory was a gathering place for reporters. Pound might shoot his own comet into the stars, but Hilda was consoled with the attention that was being paid to Professor Doolittle and his household. She was also, to her father's dismay, reading Camille Flammarion, whom the Professor considered "unreliable and sensational." Hilda may have been doing her homework to impress Pound, who now abruptly announced that he would visit her while staying with his parents in nearby Wyncote.

Pound did, when it was convenient, take an almost obsessive interest in Hilda. She has described their conversation and lovemaking in "Her," the same story that tells of her love for Frances. She contrasts Fayne and George as spirits Hermione is wooed by. And incidentally, neither of them escapes the criticism of Hermione Gart; H.D. succeeds in permitting Hermione to appear, with minor blemishes, a goddess.

In "Her" there are reported conversations between Pound and Hilda, all of which reveal Hilda as she would prefer to be seen. George says in very Poundian tones, "You are fey with the only wildness . . . You never manage to look decently like other people. You look like a Greek Goddess or a coal-scuttle." She is annoyed at him because he calls her "Diana," not the Greek "Artemis." He also makes the mistake of using "Queen of Love," instead of "Aphrodite."

"What she really wanted was for George to say, 'God, you must give up this sort of putrid megalomania, get out of this place' . . . She wanted George to make one of his drastic statements that would dynamite her world away for her . . . she saw that her two hands reached toward George like the hands of a drowned girl."

Unfortunately he only mended his mistakes by telling her she was a Greek and a goddess. He kissed her and quoted Swinburne. "The hounds of spring are on winter's traces . . ." This was not enough. What remained were carnations a guilty Pound sent to her. And Fayne-Frances.

Yet he had returned to her, had he not? True, he was leaving her for Europe directly, but her witch's intuition told her there would be another act in the drama. One that she herself would initiate.

In "Her," Hilda's mother is given the last word. She is made to say:

"She's done it."

"Done what, Mama?"

"Made you hate him."

"I don't hate as you say George Lowndes. I don't love him."

"This thing called Fayne Rabb. What is it Fayne Rabb does to everybody?"

Then, to an astonished Her, Fayne admits she loves George. George had indeed admired her poems. The story of Her ends with a hysterical and near-delirious Her being packed off to bed.

That H.D.'s emotional prose is based on fact is corroborated by the journal, or diary, Frances kept of her life, which has survived. She has written: "Two girls in love with each other, and each in love with the same man. Hilda, Ezra, Frances." She records that it was from Ezra she received her first kiss.

A plan now emerged for Hilda to accompany Frances and Mrs. Gregg to Europe. Her parents had probably tired of the drama unsettling the household and had given their weary consent. They would allow her to be away for four months. The solicitous, troubled parents could not know that the four months would extend themselves into a lifetime.

William Carlos Williams, who came to see Hilda off, has described the scene at the dock; only he and Professor Doolittle were present that spring of 1911. He could not have guessed that Hilda, seemingly so victorious and proud, saw herself as a prodigal leaving home. H.D. confessed that "she felt instinctively that she had failed by all the conventional and scholarly standards. She had failed in her college career; she had failed as a social asset with her family and the indiscriminate mob of relatives and relays of communal friends that surrounded it. She had burned her candle of rebellion at both ends and she was left unequipped for the simplest dealings with the world." Her confession is like that of Virginia Woolf, the memoir writer of *Moments of Being,* in which Woolf tells of her guilt for having failed her stepbrother socially and degrading the family's Victorian standards, then further betraying them by escaping Hyde Park Gate for Bloomsbury.

Williams has written: "The picture of Professor Doolittle at the pier on the departure of his daughter for England to meet Ezra Pound (as he well knew) impressed me deeply. He was alone with her, aside from myself. He was sitting on a trunk, completely silent. No word to me or to anyone."

The crossing on the *Floride* was so rough that ever after Hilda claimed she had a terror of sinking, although this "terror" might well have concealed her joy at escape, and her fear of a return to Philadelphia. But she was terrified; the ship was threatened. What was hurt was her pride. The Greggs rode out the storm gleefully. Frances proved herself braver than H.D.!

At the beginning of the voyage H.D. had held Frances in her arms in an empty lifeboat, secure from the eyes of Mrs. Gregg, whispering over and over that "Hermione" loved her. "Men and women will come and say I love you. Men will say I love you Hermione, but will anyone ever say I love you Fayne as I say it? I don't want to be (as they say crudely) a boy. Nor do I want to be a girl. What is all this trash of Sappho? None of that seems real . . . to matter. I see you. I feel you. My pulse runs swiftly . . ."

They disembarked at Le Havre a week late due to the storm and went on to Paris, where Hilda found their lodgings too far from the center of Paris and unattractive (a variation on the refrain of Patchin Place).

She was further annoyed that the Louvre was closed because of the theft of art objects. Paris was enjoying a *scandale!* Apollinaire had been apprehended; Picasso was involved. A mad young poet, a friend of Apollinaire, was found to be the thief. The Prince of Poets was released from custody and Picasso learned a lesson about contraband art. H.D. left Paris without having seen the Louvre.

Ezra Pound had been interested in the troubadours and lesser contemporary French poets. Curiously, neither he nor H.D. ever mentioned Apollinaire. It was Symbolism and Imagism without Gallicism or Surrealism that interested them.

Throughout their travels, Hilda and Mrs. Gregg had been in furious

combat over Frances. Mrs. Gregg accusing Hilda of robbing the widow
of her orphan, of destroying her morals. Hilda shouting back that Mrs.
Gregg was battening upon Frances' soul, denying her a life of her own.
("Hilda was quite right, too," wrote Oliver Wilkinson to the author.)

During their brief stay in Paris, Hilda met Walter Morse Rummel, the
pianist friend of Ezra's whom Hilda had heard play in Philadelphia. Of
the meeting with Rummel, Hilda remarked, "His grandfather invented
the Morse Code. My father, an astronomer, is the establisher of the variation of latitude." Hilda was impressed by Rummel. Later she would
meet him on another visit to Paris and, as would Ezra, be attracted to the
elegant and accomplished young man. Rummel, obviously intrigued by
Hilda, gave a party in honor of the visiting Americans. Frances, remembering her role of a neglected bystander, reported: "Any party that included Hilda was prone to end in deepening gloom and a general pur-
ple physical and emotional haze."

But now she was eager to continue to London. H.D. was an Anglophile; there was no equivocation in her love for London. Yet over and
over she would question, "Does London like me?"

From "Paint It Today":

Americans especially were gently and whimsically derided now and again
in her presence for intensity and earnestness. She insinuated in their
midst, tall and shy in the manner of their own people, would feel an im-
poster, almost an eavesdropper. Was it better to blurt forth that there was
a stranger at the gates or to sink further and shyer into the soft recesses of
the chintz covered Chesterfield?

At first she was surprised, because of the shared language and traditions, that she and Frances were so separated from the people whom
they longed to know: "the elite, the artist, the musician at least from all
the artists and literary people."

Ezra was reassuring. "You're odd here, you're a great success." Finally
she reasoned that she had been "taken up," but that Frances was too impetuous and forthright for the British. Despite her secretly sworn love
for Frances, she was relieved when the Greggs decided to return home.
Hilda would be on her own, and with the help of Ezra, heaven knew
what she might accomplish.

She was quite beautiful. The only fault the English found with her
face was her nose, which they considered too short for elegance. A short
nose was also thought to be "American." Her height, which had embarrassed her at home, was here an asset. She could be refreshing and
charming and in her snobbishness knew toward whom to direct her
charm.

In 1911 Hilda wrote to Mrs. Homer Pound that Ezra "has been so good
to me introducing me to celebrities and lesser oddities—he always has

some underdog on hand." For instance, there was "a derelict poet named Flint who had made the fatal mistake of marrying his landlady's daughter, a hopeless little Cockney." She might have here been contrasting herself as an auspicious choice of a wife for Ezra. Little did Hilda suspect that this "derelict" would be of the utmost importance in the founding of the Imagist movement, which would launch her own career.

She told Mrs. Pound that Ezra had taken her to tea with Harold Monro, the alert editor of the *Poetry Review*. Ezra had introduced her to May Sinclair, Ernest Rhys, Viola Meynell, Galsworthy's sister, Yeats, and a Mrs. Shakespear. In short, on the arm of Ezra she was making a debut into London's literary world—at last. When she asked Ezra if they were engaged, he had answered, "Gawd forbid," but the tenor of her letters to Mrs. Pound is that of a fiancée. After all, Ezra had given her a pearl ring that Katherine Heyman, the musician for whom he had been an advance agent in Europe, had given him. Heyman had been the "older woman" who had introduced Pound to Freud, Swedenborg, Balzac's *Séraphîta*, Yoga, all the "culture" Pound had brought back to Hilda. The ring was considered Hilda's engagement ring. So much for the powers of Katherine Heyman, of whom the elder Pounds so much disapproved. And so much for the nebulous engagement of Hilda; Pound had other plans for her.

Before those plans could be advanced, he took her to May Sinclair's studio in Kensington, the quarter of London Pound had selected for himself. There, with the consent of Miss Sinclair, "the only gentleman among us," he and Hilda were permitted to be alone. Ezra could follow up his formal kindnesses with kisses; "pressured ones," she called them.

May Sinclair was a prolific novelist whose books sold well. Gentle, shy, and philanthropic, she befriended Ezra, and, although she was at first shocked by Hilda, who was determined to play the role of the adventuress, May would become a reliable friend. Later she would also accept Aldington. After Ezra had introduced Sinclair to these younger poets and lectured her on Imagism, she wrote to Charlotte Mew, one of the finest, if not the most obscure, poets of her time (though much praised by Thomas Hardy, her benefactor), that she was going to help these young people. She would uphold Imagism as a legitimate movement. She regretted that Imagism was opposed to the poetry of her dear friend Miss Mew.

By June of 1915 she was again writing to Charlotte Mew:

I'm not so stupid really as I seem . . . H.D. is the best of the Imagists (you'll observe that I don't say very much about the others) . . . A lot of the Victorian passion was *hair-tearing*. The precise criticism I could have applied to the Imagists [in a review she wrote]—if I'd been out that day for criticism is that they lack strong human passion . . . In writing to

Richard A. I said, "some of you will have an emotion that the 'image' will not carry; then where are you?"

She consistently defended H.D. She may have been a bit bedazzled by her and the legend that was thickening around her. At one point May wrote to the drab and impoverished Charlotte Mew that "I'm getting on with my H.D. (She is glorious!)"

Promotion by May Sinclair meant a good deal in the years when Imagism was first being introduced, and afterward, when it was in need of a public reminder. She was a central figure among the older group of Wells, Arnold Bennett, Hugh Walpole, and Galsworthy. She was much respected, and a word from her had a ring in it. She took on Imagism with the same stalworthy air with which she espoused suffragism. She was the first notable literary woman Hilda met; when May Sinclair died in 1946, she remembered Hilda with fifty pounds and books from her personal library.

CHAPTER FOUR

"There Was a Helen Before There Was a War"

"My emotions are pre-War. My body exceedingly Post." So H.D. drama-
tized herself. What was this pre-World War I atmosphere like for Hilda?
She spent her days at the British Museum. Not one to explore unknown
London by herself, she once ventured alone to Golders Green and the excursion was duly noted in a letter. Mostly she roamed her own boroughs
of Bloomsbury and Kensington, relying on Pound and close friends to
lead the way.

In the evenings there were Soho restaurants, walks on the Chelsea Em-
bankment, parties at the homes of literary hostesses to whom Pound had
introduced her. Perhaps somewhere Pound was lecturing in a ladies'
drawing room. Yeats was reading at his flat at 18 Woburn Buildings, or
talking about his mystical experiences. Yeats and spiritualism, H.D. approved of both. There were meetings of the poets in Pound's crowded
rooms at Church Walk; afterward they gathered at the Poetry Book
Shop, presided over by Harold Monro. There was the new cabaret, the
Cave of the Golden Calf, decorated by an artist named Wyndham Lewis,
and owned by a former wife of the famed playwright August Strindberg.

There were frequent meetings at tea shops with Pound and Brigit Patmore. Secretly impressed, her new friends forgave Brigit her marriage to
the grandson of the poet Coventry Patmore, and her connections with his
circle. These figures of a past decade were scorned by Ezra and his
friends: Alice Meynell with her delicate Catholicism, her friendship and
solicitude for the superior, if wretched poet Francis Thompson; Coventry, his erotic verse and knightly obeisance to Mrs. Meynell. Their time
had passed; once the Meynells had been arbitrators of the literary scene.
Brigit was contemporary, beautiful, red-haired, rebellious. Badly treated
by her husband and devoted to her sons, she was contemptuous of her
husband and preferred "les jeunes," as Ford Madox Ford called Ezra's
group.

Brigit has described her first meeting with Hilda, from which issued a
friendship of many years. It was Ezra who suggested that Brigit ask his
friend from Philadelphia to tea. He had told her the friend was called
Hilda Doolittle and that she was shy of her name and that she was staying then near Russell Square. Brigit asked Ezra if he could imagine that

she would joke about anyone's name. She chided him, "Not so much American contempt for the English please!"

Brigit and Hilda had tea at a club near Piccadilly. Brigit found Hilda too frail for her height, and noticed that Hilda stooped, attempting to conceal that height, which spoiled her appearance. (This was a complaint of all Hilda's friends; she appeared to be ashamed of her large frame.) "But no goddess ever showed such extreme vulnerability in her face, nor so wild and wincing a look in her deep-set eyes. She had soft brownish hair, a pallid complexion and a pouting sensitive mouth, but a magnificent line of jaw and chin gave a reassuring strength. Her voice was high, light and musical, with even less trans-Atlantic intonation than that of Ezra's."

Then took place the scene in which the naive Hilda asked Brigit if Brigit was her real name—adding that only servants in America were called Brigit! Brigit replied she was always called Brigit, although her real name was Ethel Elizabeth Morrison-Scott.

The entrancing, unhappily married Mrs. Patmore with her ties to the literary sets of London began to succumb to the charm of this young woman from overseas. Brigit, when asked, would say that it was difficult to analyze H.D.'s charm: either one saw it or one didn't. For years Brigit would attempt to shelter the vulnerable H.D. and would prove a dependable friend in tight circumstances; she may have been her lover. Eventually, however, Brigit would behave as was natural for her, finding men charming also; she found one so fatally attractive that she ran away with him, abandoning H.D.

Tea shops became a place where Hilda could dream, or read a book. They were splendid for long conversations; she could question Brigit about "storied" England, about Rye, where Henry James lived, about Winchelsea. Brigit was an adornment on the landscape; she was wise and filled with treasures.

Hilda was not lonely; she was still too young to be haunted, and too excited to be bored. And she was protected by her "nearest male relative," as Ezra called himself, the leading poet in London, at least among his group. She was admired. She was in the land of Shakespeare, toward whom she would always feel a particular reverence. There was so much in the air. She was writing poetry. In such a short while she had become herself; she was no longer Professor Doolittle's difficult daughter. Her father was nonetheless contributing two hundred pounds a year, and would continue to do so. (Two hundred pounds was the equivalent of one thousand dollars in 1912, and would have the value of ten thousand dollars today.)

In 1928 H.D. would write to Ezra from Switzerland: "I admit I am at times very lonely . . . I was made by that pre-war London atmosphere and style, you, Brigit, Rummel, all the in and out and mellow strength one got in those days from London." Pound would agree. He wrote: "It has never been the same." And what H.D. wrote in late middle age, as she reviewed her life, applied to Pound as well as to herself: "They liked me in Pre-War London. I believe it was because they thought I was *different.*"

She was also in fashion. *Greekness* was everywhere. People, not only those just down from university, were quoting Samuel Butcher and Andrew Lang's Homer. Sculpture by contemporaries was made with Greek curls. Sandaled or bare feet marked a complete break from buttoned boots. Gone were the curves and boned collars. Fashion switched to Poiret of France and Fortuny of Venice. Fortuny dresses were cut straight from the shoulder to flow unimpeded, with just a hint of chiton. Poiret, the new French dressmaker everyone took up, introduced dresses cut to resemble the maidens on Greek vases, a loose overblouse falling over a long skirt. Hair was also loosely knotted and worn with a band across the forehead à la grecque. The body should be long, lean and willowy—very Hildaish. This had all begun around 1907 and there is the question whether Pound with his genius for the modern had not scented this in the air of London and transported this Greekness back to Philadelphia. Hilda's earlier attempts at classical verse may have originated from this. The classics were no longer considered an agony to be endured for a university degree, but were actually found to be readable and applicable to the contemporary world. Many an Achilles, considering himself blessed by the gods, set forth for the trenches of the Great War.

Translations now were more frequent in America as well as England. The translations were mostly horrendous, nineteenth-century versifications, stale and florid. There was an audience waiting for the freshness of the "pure Greek," as H.D. would define it. Anemones freshly gathered. Laurel unwithered.

Best of all, Hilda Doolittle *looked* the part. She could be seen either as a Greek maiden or a Greek god. Hermes or Aphrodite; Artemis, especially. She was able, with theatrical clairvoyance, to assume the reality of the role she chose to play. People enjoyed long conversations about purity and simplicity, their eyes fastened on the heavens where dwelt the Greek constellations.

Then at a party Brigit Patmore introduced Hilda to Richard Aldington. "Not our kind" was what that mistress of the pejorative, Virginia Woolf, concealed under her comment on Richard Aldington when he had come to her asking her to contribute to a fund that was being gathered for T. S. Eliot to permit him to leave the bank where he was employed so that he could give more of his time to poetry. She wrote in her diary in 1927, long after Aldington and H.D. had separated: "A bluff, powerful, rather greasy eyed, nice downright man, who will make

his way in the world, which I don't much like people to do." She also
wrote to Eliot himself that she thought Aldington belonged to the
"Murry [John Middleton Murry] world, where dog eats dog."

H.D. was six years older than Aldington when she met him in 1912.
(Although she declared to Bryher that she was *five* years his elder.) He
was twenty. Born in 1892, he came from a mixed background. His father
was from the middle class, well educated and a lawyer. His mother was,
in his words, "a country wench. She copped the old fellow down hunting. I was born six months after. One's people are one's damned ruin." He
was intelligent, educated through his father's library and later at the
University of London. Now he had a job on Fleet Street, covering, of all
things, sports events. He had "copped" what was offered. He was even
selling his poetry quite frequently to newspapers.

He early evidenced a knack for obtaining free-lance work. He was
clever, if never the literary genius he wished to be. Unfortunately, the
work he took on to support himself and others—translations, anthology
compilations—took time away from his creative work. When he met
Hilda, he was trying to keep himself going by hard work, yet at the same
time, like any young man, he wanted to enjoy himself. He was well
aware of the need for advancement in the world. He realized that to do
this he would have to rely on his wits, not having the advantages of family, money, or position. He had made a precocious beginning. Among the
many acquaintances he had made in London was Brigit Patmore. She
took him to a party and there introduced him to Hilda.

The early Aldington-H.D. relationship is revealed mainly in her unpublished book "Asphodel," written in 1921–22. She had intended to tell
the story of her life in four books: "Paint It Today," "Asphodel," "Her,"
and "Madrigal." The original scheme was dropped; "Madrigal" emerged
as her autobiography, entitled *Bid Me to Live*. "Asphodel" was written
during a bitter and sometimes distraught period of her life, after the
marriage to Aldington had broken up. (Aldington is called Darrington.)
He is sometimes a sympathetic, albeit worshipful, character. He calls
Hilda Astraea which is a constellation in the heavens, shining as the
Virgin with scales and crown: this is to be translated into Virgo, the zodiac sign under which Hilda was born. She would always believe in
zodiacal revelation.

In "Asphodel" Hilda writes that one of the things she liked about Darrington was his understanding of her need to look at Persian manuscripts
and Greek friezes in the British Museum. He doesn't laugh at her for
being American and hence ignorant of foreign culture. He gives her
Greek books to read that aren't too difficult. Although he knows more
Greek than she, he acknowledges that she is nearer the true Greek in
spirit. He is informed by her that he is "late, a sort of Graeco-Roman
overflowering period." Humbly he responds that he is "a bit florid at

times. True British roast beef." Then he cleverly presses his case. "We'll not let this go on much longer darling. You see I'm afraid your bed will suddenly turn into Zeus in the night—you're the sort of thing that would draw God from Heaven—and thwart me."

They actually may have talked like this. H.D. preferred conversation (when it wasn't gossip, in which she also delighted) to be on a high level of intellectual exchange. Brigit had commented on Hilda and Richard's need, which was "almost like a drug," for verbal communication. She had added that "they never understood people who were inarticulate."

Fortunately for Aldington—for indeed he was in love with her—he had one very strong asset. He may not have been authentic fifth-century-B.C. Greek, but he was a twentieth-century Englishman, and she wanted to remain in England. "Everyone said she belonged in England," she wrote.

She showed him her poetry; he formed an opinion, which was to remain with him, of this early, very early work that she was one of the finest poets of their era. He acknowledged her superiority over the other Imagists, and mostly over himself. Further, he was entirely sympathetic with the relationship she had had with Frances. Aldington encouraged freedom among lovers, and no doubt he was surprised to be challenged and chastised when his own path diverged. He could behave like a cad when it suited him; there was indeed a dubious quality in him that Woolf had sensed, and so had the young Hilda. But he was capable of deep love and abiding loyalty and affection. A lover, a cad, a swashbuckler, a highly intelligent and also a gifted man, he possessed qualities that succeeded in making life most complicated and eventually unrewarding for him. There was indeed an element of the self-destructive in Aldington.[1] Like H.D., he was such a hard worker. In one of her books she casts him as a Roman, rather hard and practical, at the same time enamored of an intellectual, sexually ambivalent Greek woman.

They took separate rooms, Aldington on the floor above her, at 6 Church Walk, across a small paved "courtyard" from Ezra Pound in Kensington. (The first street of her childhood had been a Church Street.) It was at Church Walk, interrupted by the many visitors to Pound's room, that the three began to discuss their ideas of poetics. And it is at that time in 1912 that H.D. became directly associated with the Imagist movement.

[1] In his biography of Lawrence, published in 1950, *D. H. Lawrence: Portrait of a Genius But . . .* , Aldington analyzed Lawrence as a "very complex and self-contradictory person, in whom two hostile selves seemed always struggling for mastery." Professor Norman Timmins Gates, Aldington's bibliographer, has remarked that in this way Aldington himself resembled Lawrence. And in fact, when Lawrence read what Aldington had written about him in an earlier essay, he commented that it was more about Richard than about himself. Professor Gates suggests that both Lawrence and Aldington had divided personalities.

TEMPORA

Io! Io! Tamuz:
the Dryad stands in my court-yard
With plaintive, querulous crying.
(Tamuz. Io! Tamuz!)
Oh, no, she is not crying: "Tamuz."
She says, "May my poems be printed this week?
The god Pan is afraid to ask you,
May my poems be printed this week?"

Lustra   Ezra Pound

They were agreed upon three principles: (1) direct treatment of the subject, (2) allow no word that was not essential to the presentation, (3) in their rhythms to follow the musical phrase rather than strict regularity. Those three rules became the skeleton around which Pound would later build his program of Imagism. They were out to free poetry from the fashionable Georgian influence, of Victorians, even of the twilit Celts, with the notable exception of Yeats, whom they idolized and who would show great sympathy for the Imagists, even if it is somewhat doubtful that he understood their program. Importantly, Yeats was a friend of Pound and even consulted Pound about his own poetry. He was one of them, if not "of" them. The important thing was that Pound was presenting to Aldington and Hilda at this early period a program that would launch a new era in poetry.

The principles in their organization and aims were of course more complicated. Pound's object was to manipulate French Symbolism and turn it into Imagism, if he could; if not, he would throw Symbolism out.

Henri Bergson came in, and so did an original thinker, T. E. Hulme, who actually initiated what would be recognized as Pound's revolutionary ideas, at a Poet's Club meeting that had taken place as far back as 1908. More of this later. But at the moment the trio at Church Walk were excitedly laying their plans. Pound, without telling anyone, may have been plotting to tailor the new movement to fit his protégée, Hilda Doolittle.

In 1912 in the midst of poetics and new friendships, Hilda suddenly received a letter from Frances Gregg saying that she was getting married and would be arriving in England. Her husband was an extension course lecturer; they would be going to Brussels. Frances wanted Hilda to come with her to keep her company, as her husband would frequently be absent. She added that this was to be a trial marriage, which would break up if there were no children. It was a situation Hilda appreciated, although she felt sorry that Frances had thrown herself away on a poor lecturer. "Wee witches will grow up," wrote Frances.

The couple duly arrived and Hilda and Richard Aldington met them at the Victoria Station Hotel. Instead of a pitiable, modest lecturer, they found Louis Wilkinson, who was something of a celebrity. He gave lectures on Renaissance art at girls' colleges and various platforms in America. Indeed, Hilda had heard of him at Bryn Mawr. Physically he was attractive: John Cowper Powys had nicknamed him "the archangel."

He immediately recognized Hilda when they met at the hotel: "It could only be she!" Looking around the room at his other friends there to greet them, Hilda guessed that one of them was a baronet! She noticed that the china tea service was quite elegant. The scene was strangely out of focus from what she had expected.

She quickly credited Frances with taste, and it must be admitted, because it seeps through her account, she was jealous. Frances had triumphed over her.

Hilda decided she was willing to accept the invitation now pressed by Louis to accompany the couple to Brussels. It is surprising that Hilda, so involved in the birth of a new poetry movement, should have been willing to drop everything and rush off with the Wilkinsons. It was Pound who stopped this impulsive and ill-judged step.

The trio had gotten as far as Victoria Station, where they were to take the boat train, when Pound arrived and grabbed hold of Hilda. He told her that Frances had a chance of happiness, but that if she went with them, she would spoil it. Hilda obeyed and turned back.

On the way home Hilda must have considered what Frances had said about Aldington, words quoted in "Paint It Today" that may have influenced her impulsive decision to join the Wilkinsons: "He has the manners of an inn-keeper's son. I can see with my brain that he is beautiful . . . He is exactly like a Faun . . . They say he has a talent for verse. I know in some way he is what people say he is . . . I hate him . . . I hated him to open the door for you and brush your shoulder . . . I think him under the surface, unclean." Frances knew instinctively that, although she had been able to write "reams of letters" to Pound, in no furtive way would Aldington be willing to correspond with her. At that point, for him there was only one witch. It had been Aldington, and not Frances, in whom Hilda had confided, who "understood the other half or the explanatory quarter of the sentences I left unsaid." Frances had shot her dart, Hilda had responded, but Pound had prevented the debacle.

Frances and Louis were involved in a unique situation, one neither Hilda nor Pound had known about. Frances was really in love with Llewelyn Powys, whose brother John Cowper Powys was in love with her. As a matter of fact, so was Llewelyn, but he was ill from tuberculosis. All three brothers Powys (Theodore was the third) were well on their way to fame as novelists. The Powys clan was bardic and mesmeric.

Llewelyn and John had caused ladies to swoon when they gave lectures in America. Their literary styles differed, yet each respected the other; they were competitors and companions. Louis Wilkinson was their best friend.

Llewelyn, who had been with Louis at Cambridge, said that Louis had "complete sang-froid." He also "accepted most of humanity." In fact, to his friends Louis was a sort of paragon. Frances had met Louis at a lecture of John's in Philadelphia. Since marriage was not possible for John at that time, he decided that Louis Wilkinson (his best friend) needed a wife and suggested that he become her husband. In his autobiography, *Swan's Milk*, Wilkinson speaks of himself as eager to marry because "his unromantic disjoined sensually spasmodic way of life could not, must not go on."

In the same autobiography, published in 1934, Wilkinson, addressing himself, wrote: "You told me that Hardy, writing about Jude and Arabella, had explained to you why you fooled yourself for so long about your first wife." And then he quotes Hardy: "His *idea* of her was the thing of more consequence, not Arabella." Presumably, Wilkinson's *idea* of Frances was what mattered.

Wilkinson continues: "His mother liked America until he married an American wife." He insists that his wife did all she could "to present herself as innocent and deeply afflicted." He goes on, reluctantly, to admit that he had been in love with her, briefly. The marriage broke up in 1920. An intuitive person might well have predicted this breakup from Wilkinson's eagerness to have Hilda accompany him and his new wife to Brussels so soon after their wedding. Frances had made a mistake about Aldington. He may have thrown a stone or two at H.D.'s pedestal, but she remained where he had once placed her. In contrast, Wilkinson displaced Frances.

But back to Victoria Station and the embarkation for the Continent. The Wilkinsons were to honeymoon in Venice. Who should now accompany them but the Powys brothers!

After they arrived in Venice, Frances dressed up like a boy and the three had a festive time. Their behavior must have been startling, because it even shocked the Venetians, who were going to throw them out. Just in time Louis assumed the role of the correct British gentleman, asserted himself, and said the proper British thing. The four were then permitted to leave without benefit of jail or threatened scandal.

Alyse Gregory, the wife of Llewelyn Powys, has written that "no one is more essentially civilized [than Louis] . . . He has a very high standard of social conduct . . ." The magistrates of Venice were no match for this Englishman, a man of discrimination and enlightenment.

Frances liked her costume so much she wore it all the way to Genoa.

Llewelyn reported in a letter to his sister that Frances was like a person "walking in a trance, her head full of dreams." She is "Our Lady" as a "little girl," "a Hamadryad waiting for a faun." He stresses that she is not thin but "athletic and boyish" and her almost "Tess-like contours" would appeal to Hardy.[2]

After the honeymoon the Wilkinsons continued to live in Italy, with the exception of intervals in America, where Louis was lecturing. From Italy Frances wrote to Hilda that she was expecting a child in January 1915. Enclosed in the letter was a flower. The wee witches were growing up.

[2] A photo of Frances dressed in her Venetian boy's garb, perched on a balustrade, reveals a charming, impish young person enjoying herself immensely as the center of an admiring male group.

CHAPTER FIVE

"H.D. Imagiste"

It is September 1912, a year after Hilda arrived in Europe. She has been at the British Museum studying the Greek friezes and plates of Egyptian figures. She is abstracted, contemplative. And yet there is a purposeful air about her as she hurries down the museum steps to the nearby museum bun shop. Ezra Pound is waiting there for her. He is dressed in his Whistlerian garb, the velvet jacket, the loose tie. Together they are a pictorial couple. She is so tall and lean, beautiful with the squared jaw and the hair falling over her brow. He is certainly no ordinary clerk. His reddish hair is long and tumbled, he has a watchful, impudent look about the eyes. Something of that air of inquisitive fantasy Aubrey Beardsley used to catch in his drawings. Neither at this moment is interested in appearances. There is a more direct reason for the meeting. Hilda has consented to show Ezra Pound her new poems.

She puts her books and gloves onto a chair, takes out a notebook, and hands it to him.

He reads "Hermes of the Ways." Hilda's poem had been suggested by an invocation to Hermes by the poetess Anyte that was in the *Greek Anthology* Pound had first introduced her to.

"Why, Dryad, this is good!"

He takes out a sharp red pencil, changes a word here or there, crosses one out. He rereads the poem, and then the next one, "Acon," another poem based on a translation from a Latin Renaissance book he had also given her. Then there is "Orchard." Pound is really pleased. She is a model pupil. More than that, she is a poet; the scornful, exacting teacher is now certain of this. Selecting "Hermes of the Ways," and giving her one of his catlike looks, he again takes up his pencil and signs the poem: "H.D. Imagiste."

That is the story. The attitudes, the gestures, the theatricality are in character. It is a brilliant coup. Pound has created another poet, acolyte. He has added a disciple to the new *ism* he is about to create and introduce to the market.

Would that today the excised poem with its corrections might rest in the Berg Collection in New York, alongside Pound's similar selective corrections and deletions to "The Waste Land" of Eliot.

For years Pound had been preparing her for this debut. He had found a new name for her, tossing away "Doolittle." She was the first charter member of a new *ism* with which Ezra was preparing to startle London. Unlike Professor Higgins, he had not found his Miss Doolittle selling flowers outside Covent Garden, but he planned to transform her from a dedicated scribbler into the poet, H.D. He succeeded.

But not before much propaganda would ensue and many explanations and apologies and references be recalled. Somehow along the way the *e* would be dropped from *imagisme*. It was a French *ism* meant to show that *imagisme* was replacing *symbolisme*, a cult Pound had come to detest due to its inferior copyists. He was a natural entrepreneur and he intended through H.D. to create a legend. They both enjoyed theater, and each was an uninhibited actor.

Although Pound claimed that he invented Imagism to launch H.D.'s career, the evolution had been in fact more complicated, beginning with the Poet's Club of 1908. A truer explanation had been given by the poet F. S. Flint, who wrote in the May 1, 1915, issue of the magazine *The Egoist:*

> Somewhere in the gloom of the year 1908, Mr. T. E. Hulme proposed to a companion that they should form a poets club. The thing was done there and then. The Club began to dine and members read their verses. At the end of the year they published a small plaquette on the verses, called "For Christmas, MDCCCCVIII." On this plaquette was printed one of the first "Imagist" poems by T. E. Hulme: "Autumn." I think that what brought the real nucleus of this group together was a dissatisfaction with English poetry . . . In all this Hulme was ringleader. He insisted too on absolutely accurate presentation and no verbiage. There was a lot of talk and practice among us with what we called the "Image."

Pound did not invent "the image," he was the publicist of the movement under the word *imagisme*. And no movement got underway with so much celebration, propaganda, and expertise. Pound's interest in Imagism did not last long; it was too narrow a frame for him. But while it lasted, he used his considerable powers to promote it.

Richard Aldington, who was not an original member of Hulme's group, confessed that what he calls "Ezra's Imagism" was forced on both H.D. and himself against their wills. He also claimed that neither he nor H.D. was fully aware that it was "simply advertising bull-dust."

This is Aldington's post reductio ad absurdum; in fact, Imagism became much more than an acrobatic cloud, performing its new techniques. It introduced a few poets who might well have remained unknown to readers and anthologies, and inserted itself into the history of English poetry. With its use of "free" verse, Imagism rid a lame poetry of a musty Georgian Romanticism. Imagism was Pound's early glove tossed at the Georgian heirs of the Victorians. He used Imagism (as later he would direct Vorticism) to attack what he contended was, in cultural terms, a sophistic society. Like the later Eliot of *Tradition and the Individual Talent*, he believed that the *whole existing order can be altered by a new work of art.*

There were to be no muddy abstractions, no superfluous words. This is one explanation of why H.D. came to be known, and rightly so, as the finest Imagist. Her poetry of this period is always concrete, never abstract. This kind of poetry exerts a powerful discipline. What the Symbolists had put in, the Imagists took out. A difficulty was that the poetry was often intellectual, chill, austere. (In *The Green Hat*, the daring novel that caught the "sophistication" of the twenties, Michael Arlen, who had briefly associated with Pound, wrote: "The Imagists, they're short for poetry, like nightie for nightingale.") The brevity it exerted, in H.D.'s case, left the reader tense; there was no relaxation in her poetry. Also—and this is absolutely true of H.D.'s poetry—Imagism obeyed Pound's (or Hulme's) doctrine that the image was the center of meaning and this image would carry the energy of the poem. Pound may have inherited the use of the word "energy," but in any case, he was adamant about its importance. When he turned to Vorticism, "energy" became even more dominant.

Purity! Nothing in excess! Pound sent off his famous letter to courageous Harriet Monroe, at *Poetry* magazine in Chicago. He wanted her to receive her information about Imagism straight from the source:

> Objectivity and again objectivity, and no expression, no hindside beforeness, no Tennysonianness of Speech—nothing, *nothing* that you couldn't in some circumstance, in the stress of some emotion, *actually say.* Every *literaryism*, every book word, fritters away a scrap of the reader's patience, a scrap of his sense of your sincerity. When one really feels and thinks, one stammers with a simple speech. It is only in the flurry, the small frothy excitement of writing, or the inebriety of a metre, that one falls into the easy, easy—oh how easy!—speech of books and poems that one has read.[1]

The unacknowledged shades of William Wordsworth and Samuel Taylor Coleridge may have hovered over Pound as he sent his declaration to the New World.

In his role as foreign correspondent for *Poetry*, Pound proceeded on his audacious way. He told Harriet Monroe: "I've had luck and am sending you some *modern stuff* by an American. I say modern, for it is the laconic speech of the Imagistes, even if the subject is classic. At least H.D.

---

[1] In *Lustra* he gives a more poetic explanation of the devices of Imagism in building a poem:

> Here they stand without quaint devices,
> Here they stand with nothing archaic about them.

has lived with these things since childhood . . . This is the sort of American stuff that I can show here and in Paris without its being ridiculed. Objectivity—no slither; direct—no excessive use of adjectives, no metaphors that won't permit examination. It's straight talk, straight as the Greek!" Cleverly, he added: "And it was only by persistence that I got to see it at all."

H.D.'s first published poems, "Hermes of the Ways," "Orchard," "Epigram," appeared in *Poetry* in January 1913. With the publication of these poems the movement was indeed launched. These poems were a prelude to many more poems by H.D. to be published by *Poetry* over the years. From now on the work of that "pagan mystic," as Harriet Monroe lovingly called H.D., would appear in the most important contemporary magazines in the world and be anthologized countless times.

In setting out to get II.D. published (also William Carlos Williams and, somewhat more reluctantly, Richard Aldington), Pound broadened the outlook of *Poetry* magazine. Monroe's own inclinations had been toward Edgar Lee Masters, Vachel Lindsay, Robert Frost, and Carl Sandburg. Pound had inadvertently divided the magazine into those who believed in native American origins, speech, and subject matter, and those who had been influenced by the French Symbolists, the Imagists, Hellenism, in other words, anything *foreign*.

There is a vignette of H.D. during this period left by John Gould Fletcher, an aspiring Imagist, who in 1913 at the insistence of Pound had visited the Aldingtons. Fletcher was a young poet from Arkansas, a student at Harvard recently come to London. He had a comfortable income and had taken an expensive flat in Adelphi Terrace. Ezra had decided to promote him, too, and get his work published in *Poetry*.

After Pound had vanished from the scene, Fletcher would become friendly with Amy Lowell. In his autobiography, *Life Is My Song*, Fletcher told of meeting H.D. at her flat. To introduce himself he paid her a few necessary compliments on her work. "H.D. nervously assured me that, for her part, she was never sure that anything she had ever written had been good. Ezra encouraged her to write and to go on writing. She simply wrote as she felt." Later, after Fletcher had become a friend of Sara Teasdale, he remarked that Teasdale's fragile appearance and her tendency to seclude herself from society reminded him of H.D.—although she did not have "H.D.'s cultivated archaisms which sometimes seemed to me in H.D.'s presence almost an affectation."

Fletcher's remarks reveal another side of H.D. She wished to discount herself as part of a "movement"; she wanted her poetry to appear as if it had sprung full-blown, to estrange herself from didacticism, to emphasize her reliance on inspiration, and even on automatic writing.

It's probably likely that she didn't follow or understand all of Pound's pronouncements—after all, he had only recently revealed his secrets.

With the instinct of sudden genius, she recognized the form that suited her sensibility, and that form proceeded from Greek drama and Greek poetry.

To show how assured this instinct was, there is a quotation from the late and eminent Greek scholar C. M. Bowra, who wrote:

> Compared with most modern litera ure Greek is surprisingly simple and unadorned, but this simplicity . . . is reached through an omission of anything which seems unessential and by an emphasis on what seems structurally or emotionally important . . . Greek literature achieves its special distinction by omitting everything that is not essential to the plan of the whole and securing its effect by the power given to each part in its place . . . In particular they avoided the sentimental and purely decorative.

H.D. set out to achieve this distinction Bowra attributes to the Greeks.

After her first successful publications, H.D. came to be considered the Goddess of Imagism, and until Amy Lowell came along she was the sole woman connected with this startlingly new *ism*. There are earlier warnings of the theatricality of both Pound and H.D.; they were fond of dress-up and playacting. Pound was never as violent as D. H. Lawrence, but he was quite capable of knocking tea cups off of tables with his cane; like the later Surrealists, he epatéd the bourgeois, nibbling floral bouquets (but so did the older generation of Ford Madox Ford).

H.D., for her part, was fond of making entrances. She also liked to "elevate" the conversation in a goddesslike fashion, speaking airily of the nearby Mount Olympus. Her rather large feet tended to skim the earth. An enemy would find her a natural target for satire, and she had two rather serious enemies. The first was the husband of Frances Gregg, Louis Wilkinson. H.D., with some assistance from Aldington, may very likely have treated the pair after they had returned from Europe as minor subjects, somehow beneath her. In any event, Wilkinson's novel of 1916, *The Buffoon*, satirizes Americans, Imagists, and their followers, with special attention to H.D. and Ezra Pound. Its dedication is ambiguous: "dedicated to Frances Gregg in recognition."

In *The Buffoon*, H.D. is called Eunice Dinwiddie. Edward (Wilkinson) has come to a party to meet her and is told that she:

> Queens it in this set—undisputed. . . .
> Her pose was perfect. What could be more fascinating than that studied artlessness—studied, yes, evidently but still so unassailably managing not to give itself away . . . She was just sufficiently over-tall for her epicene figure draped in flowing grey, to give a charming effect of blown mist. Her head, with its little smooth crown and childishly ruffled inexpert roll of hair, was made to be held tenderly and savagely between a lover's

hands. Her features were Greek, they suggested a hamadryad; only one flaw, her nose was insufficient . . . No one greeted the Divinity. Her whim to be the first to speak was always respected. The result was an effective hush into which her rich, low, beautifully modulated voice might break like a note from an organ.

"Your eyes are sad, what are you seeking?" Then after a long silence she asks, "What beautiful thing have you been doing?"

Raoul Root (or Ray-Ray), who is Pound, is made to say, "Imagism abhors imagery. We have nothing to do with image-making. Imagery is one of the worn out decorations that we have scrapped."

In a sense, this book and John Cournos' later one, *Miranda Masters* (a truly brutal satire), are tributes to the power of H.D.'s personality. She had charisma, a special ability to project. It is evident in her photographs, which are more than stills: she makes a subject that convinces.

Hugh Kenner, in his brilliant, nearly hypnotic book *The Pound Era,* does not reveal himself as a consistent admirer of H.D. However, he finds much to praise in "Hermes of the Ways," and he knowingly dissects the poem with the conclusion that:

> We do not mistake the poem for the imagined utterance of some Greek, nor do we hear a modern saying "I feel as if . . ."
> . . . Wherever we turn our attention in the poem we find H.D. thinking through its images, exclusively through them, and presenting no detail not germane to such thinking, no detail obligated merely by pictorial completeness.

When a poet makes such a "breakthrough" as H.D. did when she wrote this poem, when she goes such a distance from ordinary verse, one asks what gave her this start. Although Dr. Kenner does not imply the connection, it seems quite possible that among the poems of Ezra Pound she was influenced by his 1912 poem "The Return."

> See, They return; ah, see the tentative
> Movements, and the slow feet,
> The trouble in the pace and the uncertain
> Wavering!

It is the pace, the tension, and the shift in this poem Dr. Kenner alludes to as exceptional, and this must have inspired H.D. The Pound poem offers nourishment; it is a pioneer poem for the new age of poetry for which Pound would act as an entrepreneur.

"Hermes of the Ways" is not an imitation or a mutation of the Pound poem, yet from his earlier breakthrough, H.D. must have found the impetus to speak in her own voice.

HERMES OF THE WAYS

The hard sand breaks,
and the grains of it
are clear as wine.

Far off over the leagues of it,
the wind,
playing on the wide shore,
piles little ridges,
and the great waves
break over it.

But more than the many-foamed ways
of the sea,
I know him
of the triple path-ways
Hermes
who awaits.

Nearly half a century later, with less innocence and more formal consideration, she shortened the story to read:
"H.D.—Hermes—Hermeticism and all the rest of it."

CHAPTER SIX

Interlude: Travel and Family

Church Walk was deserted by October 1912.

First Aldington and Hilda went off to Paris; Pound followed later. Before leaving London, Hilda and Richard had been introduced to a visitor at Pound's, a young philosopher from the University of Pennsylvania, Henry Slominsky. He was the author of a recently published book, *Heraklit und Parmenides*. The book with its discussion of knowledge based on the perception of the senses and belief in eternal flux had made a great impression on Aldington. Hilda was also enthusiastic.[1] Aldington said that Pound never appreciated Slominsky because he never listened to him. (There is a whisper of Slominsky in Canto LXXVII.)

In Paris, Richard and Hilda came across him in the Luxembourg Garden. From then on, Slominsky would dominate their evenings in Paris. "Noctes Atticae" was Aldington's description of their discussions of Hellas and Hellenism, Pythagoras and Plato, Empedocles, Heraclitus, Homer, Thucydides, Aeschylus, and Theocritus. What a heavy grace for Hilda.

H.D. was always quick to grasp what would be helpful to her work; she had an ability to sift out the necessary and ignore the rest. She wrote only of what interested her, which at times gives her work a one-dimensional quality. This concentration, this shutting out of what she considered irrelevant, also strengthens her work; it is a vital background composed of limited organisms. Hadn't Pound, her "initiator" (a term she would use for the important men in her life), written in 1915: "The essential thing in a poet is that he builds his world."

Just as at Church Walk, Aldington and Hilda took separate rooms. Hilda had first gone to a pension on the Rue Jacob recommended by Louise Skidmore, a former girl friend of both Hilda and Ezra. Later she moved to Aldington's hotel. For the first time she and Richard were alone together in a foreign city; her diary intimates that these were not always happy times. Frequently she was depressed, even despairing, and she realized that sooner or later she would have to come to a decision about Richard.

---

[1] As well she might have been. Heraclitus deposited a philosophic treatise in the Temple of Artemis at Ephesus, his birthplace, prohibiting publication (or exhumation) until after his death.

Aldington had taken a financial risk in coming to Paris. He had thrown up his job on Fleet Street to follow her to the city that would come to mean more to him than any city in the world. Even at that early date he was a Francophile, as opposed to her definite Anglophilia. And it was much easier for her to walk about Paris in his company. She finally did get to the Louvre and at last saw the original of the "Venus de Milo," whose reproduction had hung in the Doolittle house, brought back from her parents' honeymoon in Europe.

There is always a lacuna in Hilda's rendering of the visits she has made to cities. (The notable later exception would be Venice.) She was so self-absorbed that the everyday contact she had with the French as a people left no impression on her. All her paths led to Greece. She would only retain a memory of those hotels she stayed in that inspired her poetry.

On this trip she had no introduction to the writers in Paris who would later come to be important to her. Gertrude Stein was living in Paris then, and just the year before had written her idyllic *Tender Buttons* (published 1914). St. John Perse, who would appear as a mythic figure in H.D.'s late work, had just written *Éloges*, poetry that would influence T. S. Eliot, whom she would also later know. The Symbolists, the Parnassians, influences on Pound (who would nevertheless choose to ignore the significance of Valéry and the Surrealists)—it was all there waiting for her.

She was seeing Pound's expatriate friend Walter Rummel. Rummel had appeared briefly in London earlier that year playing Debussy in a concert. Hilda had introduced him to Olivia Shakespear, the fascinating woman whom Pound so liked, and to her daughter, Dorothy. Hilda developed a slight crush on Walter; his were the intellectual interests of a dilettante, a type who would often attract her. He was more subtle, more of a gentleman than Richard. Then, too, music was necessary to her life. She had wanted to be a musician and was indeed a fairly good pianist. It was music's association with "the gift" that added to it a romantic component. Poetry was basic; antique art or Renaissance art was important visually; but in music she could let herself into the realm of pure pleasure. Rummel also possessed a pleasant home, books, an elegant life, as opposed to the fractious bohemian existence. He doubtless had money. H.D., shot through with certain aspects of bohemianism, nevertheless retained an ambivalence to the bourgeois life with its monetary accompaniment and ease of living. He, in turn, must have liked her poetry, which he was to read later on in a visit to London when he played three pieces of Pound set to music. And later he would compose music for her "Attic" poems.

A mysterious and tragic incident marred the couple's Paris sojourn. Margaret Cravens, a young American woman related, it was believed, to

The Doolittle Family,
a. 1910: Professor Doo-
little, Hilda, Gilbert,
Charles Melvin, Mrs.
Doolittle, Harold, Eric,
Alfred. *(Beinecke)*

The Flower Astronomi-
al Observatory, Uni-
versity of Pennsylvania.
(Beinecke)

The Doolittle home,
Upper Darby, Pennsyl-
vania, where H.D. lived
from 1895 to 1911.
(Beinecke)

Francis Wolle, H.D.'s
grandfather. *(Beinecke)*

Marianne Moore, ca. 1921, "Dactyl."
(*The Rosenbach Museum and Library*)

Ezra Pound, ca. 1903. (*Beinecke*)

"In the corridors of the Diocletian Gallery she saw the little figure. It lay...comfortably asleep. The Hermaphrodite."

Frances Gregg, ca. 1912. (*Courtesy of Oliver Wilkinson*)

git Patmore. *(Courtesy of Professor red Satterthwaite)*

chard Aldington in WWI uniform, 1918. *(Beinecke)*

Corfe Castle, Dorset, where H.D. lived in 1917 when Richard Aldington was in camp nearby. *(Photograph: J. Allan Cash Ltd., Worldwide Photographic Library, London)*

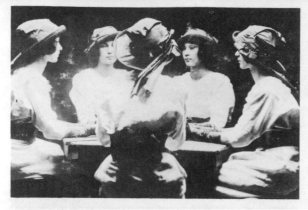

ABOVE LEFT: Dorothy "Arabella" Yorke. *(Courtesy of Professor Alfred Satterthwaite)*

ABOVE RIGHT: John Cournos. *(Courtesy of Professor Alfred Satterthwaite)*

H.D. and Perdita, 1919. *(Beinecke)*

Bosigran, Cornwall. Possibly the house where H.D. lived with Cecil Gray in 1918. *(Photograph by Belinda McKay)*

the Sidney Lanier family, had come to live in Paris. It was she who had originally introduced Rummel to Pound, and now that Hilda and Richard were in Paris, Rummel broke the news to them that Pound was engaged to Dorothy Shakespear. Rummel also told Margaret, and shortly thereafter Margaret committed suicide. It was at first believed that her frustrated love for Rummel had caused her action; she had sent him a posthumous letter. But Rummel disclaimed all, stating that, although she had been taking music lessons from him, there had been no romantic attachment. Rummel declared, "It was Ezra she had cared for."

There was also Thérèse Chaigneau, an even more elegant friend of Rummel. He had introduced Hilda to Thérèse at the charming house near Passy where Thérèse entertained those musicians who, like Rummel, were influenced by the moderns, Claude Debussy and Maurice Ravel. Walter Rummel had married Thérèse Chaigneau quite suddenly. When Hilda met her she had not guessed at a precipitate marriage, nor did Hilda seem to entertain the possibility. Certainly Hilda never made the connection between this marriage and the suicide of Margaret Cravens.

After Margaret's suicide Pound took Hilda walking in Paris. His friends conspired to stay near him so that he would not be alone. Hilda, the closest to him, was worried about the severity of his reaction to Margaret's death. The two friends one evening stood together on a bridge crossing the Seine, near the Île St.-Louis. She drew close to him, as if to share his unhappiness. Ezra was carrying the ebony stick he sometimes affected. With a helpless, despondent gesture he waved it toward the river, the chestnut blossoms, waved it, as Hilda believed, at all his friends and himself. Then he turned and whispered to her, "And the morning stars sang together." This scene, confided in a letter to Ford Madox Ford, who later was gathering reminiscences of the youthful Ezra Pound, was Hilda's recollection of the last few days in Paris in 1912.

In Canto LXVII Pound called the dead woman "Margaret of the seven griefs" and spoke of her, along with her grandmother who had drowned, as a victim of the "doom of Atreus."

The Margaret Cravens incident assumed all sorts of proportions for Hilda, who almost believed that she herself might have been the one to commit suicide, as she had been "dropped" by Pound too. She identified with Margaret, who had appeared to live the kind of life Hilda would wish for herself—an elegant apartment, many friends, independence from her family.

Then Hilda learned from Pound that for years Margaret had slept with a revolver under her pillow. Hilda was to mull over the incident, tied up as it was with her own suicidal inclinations, and with her tortuous relationship with Pound. It also seems possible that this suicide may have helped to persuade Hilda to marry Richard. Finally recognizing that there were many complications in Pound's life, that he could only be an accessory to her maintenance, she now shifted her dependence to Richard, hoping he would be her bulwark, that his would be the strength that would preserve her from a similar despairing fate.

The Paris trip of 1912 was an interlude broken by a letter from the Doolittles asking Hilda to meet them when their ship docked in Genoa.

Aldington hurried back to London to make arrangements so that he could rejoin Hilda when her family got to Rome. She proceeded to Genoa to meet her parents, Dr. Snively, and Margaret. Then the group all traveled to Florence and arrived in Rome, where they stayed through Christmas.

In his autobiography Aldington disingenuously explains his trip to Rome as an assignment from A. R. Orage of *The New Age*, a magazine of much importance to artists and intellectuals in London. This assignment was probably obtained for him by Pound, who had begun writing for *The New Age* in that same year, 1912. Pound, as an editor, would soon see to it that the literary end of the magazine was reserved for the Imagists.

Orage, a fool to some, a genius to others, and certainly one of the least money-conscious of men, carried on his work in the ABC in Chancery Lane, another cheap tea and bun shop. Infrequently he could be found at the plush Café Royal. He was a supporter of the younger, unknown writers—Middleton Murry, Katherine Mansfield, Michael Arlen, and Herbert Read. Also connected with *The New Age* were established writers together with politicos emerging from the socialist Fabians: George Bernard Shaw, Hilaire Belloc, H. G. Wells, Leslie Haden-Guest, Arnold Bennett, Havelock Ellis, and John Galsworthy. It is important to note these "heavyweights," as, prompted by Pound, they would soon be reading the Imagists.

Aldington was quick to take up so useful a connection as Orage. Here his romance with Hilda was of real value, although he did not admit it in his autobiography. In fact in this book, of all places, he withheld the story of his private life with H.D.

With his entrée as a *New Age* correspondent, and presenting himself as an eligible young man, Aldington made some notable contacts, including the much-admired Catholic poet Alice Meynell. (It was a case of mutual dislike.) He settled into an inexpensive pension and adapted himself to the Roman way of life, divided between the tavernas and the British Embassy. H.D., at a hotel with her family, was constricted by their activities. Her reward was to watch the pleasure her father received from his contact with the antique world. He spoke of wanting to go to Greece.

H.D.'s private Roman celebration took place in a discovery she made at the Diocletian Gallery; it was a discovery to which she would always refer. One has a tendency to use the word "always" together with the word "refer" when writing of H.D., because she saw what she needed and retained those same images. She had an assortment of ideas and events that were repetitious; they were thoughts and images that might be embellished by her reading, or actual experiences never to be relinquished. "In the corridors of the Diocletian Gallery she saw the little figure. It lay, not on a pedestal of cold stone, but on a soft black velvet cushion. It lay comfortably asleep. The Hermaphrodite."

This little figure would haunt her future trips to Rome and she would always visit it. How early H.D. was attracted to the physical unification of male and female! She may have suspected, even in her pre-Freud days, the depth of her own bisexuality.

Through Aldington she met Phyllis Bottome in Rome. Hilda only made a note of this meeting, and seems never thereafter to have mentioned her. The introduction had come from Ezra, who liked to throw his women friends together—when he chose. Hilda may have suspected a romance, but this does not seem to have been the case. Phyllis Bottome was one of the more interesting women in a period in which many forceful feminists were beginning to emerge. She was American on her father's side, her mother was English, and her brothers had gone to the University of Pennsylvania with Ezra. She would become a well-known and prolific novelist, a propagandist of Adlerian psychology, and during World War II a lecturer for the British Ministry of Information. Her autobiographies, written with simplicity and honesty, show her to have been a resourceful and vivid person. She and Ezra remained lifelong friends. One associates her somehow with that other forceful woman writer Vera Brittain, mother of Shirley Williams, now prominent in the new Social Democratic Party. H.D., as here with Phyllis Bottome, to her loss tended to be disinterested in women probing political and social reform.

The Doolittles went to Capri. Hilda must have persuaded her parents to go there; one can scarcely imagine any attraction that island would have had for her parents. Ruins, proper ruins they wanted, and so they left soon for Sicily, apprehensively leaving Hilda and Richard on Capri.

No more than Ezra would Aldington have been the choice of the Doolittles for Hilda. At a hazard one guesses they would have preferred a Jamesian character, a Lambert Strether or a Merton Densher. Certainly Walter Rummel would have appealed to them, but not this rather coarse and hearty Englishman with his assorted airs of belonging and of not belonging. They couldn't place him. In America it would have been simpler, for middle-class Americans are just as eager as the English to determine one's social position; here they were off course, they couldn't

judge. Their only clue was that he must be "literary," which in itself
was sufficiently damaging. That he managed to tag along with the family
group is a witness to Hilda's domination over her family, and also probably to the good manners of the Doolittles—Professor Doolittle was enjoying himself more than he had in years.

When Norman Holmes Pearson asked her in 1938 about the composition and locale of her early poems, H.D. answered:

> I let my pencil run riot in those early days of my apprenticeship in an
> old-fashioned school copy book written when I could get one. Then I
> would select from any pages of automatic or pseudo-automatic writing,
> the few lines that satisfied me. I was doing that in my first [it would be
> the second] dark London autumn, 1912 then in Italy where I spent that
> winter, Capri especially where I had some time and space and found the
> actual geographical Greece for the first time, the Syren Isle of the
> Odyssey.

Hilda had only a short time in Capri, as the family had asked her to
meet them in Venice. First she and Richard went to a little hotel in
Naples, recommended by Slominsky. This intimate excursion with Richard was the first radical step in what she called her "rebellion," one she
had certainly delayed. Then they returned to Capri.

Her notes say: "Work on Greek and walks, R. loses watch, rocks, swal-
lows, roses, figs, goat-cheese, pear-blossom, iris. Monte Solario, daisies on
walls, R.A. talks in half frightened manner." She was making notes for
her poems and at the same time chronicling their honeymoon.

It was a tense, emotional period that could be compared to the arches
the sea had dug out of the rocks that appeared cut off from land on the
coast of Capri. Stone, battered, corroded, reminiscent, the arches would
make a prophetic picture of her life. Then there was poetry, sex, the
Siren Island, even Pan! She told Aldington she believed she saw Pan
there, and she claimed that he moved among the wild flowers. When the
woman who would soon be called H.D. was intense, she was *very very*
intense, and islands seemed to heighten this state.

She was both frightened and enchanted by islands. In a poem, "What
Are Islands to Me?" she explained that they were as "an inner region of
defence, escape, these are the poems of escapism." She also mentions
"memory." The first island of memory was a "thickly wooded island in
the Lehigh River, and believe it or not, was named actually Calypso's Island." Add island to her unrelinquished objects. And now Capri, which
was a Mediterranean reminder of her Pennsylvania island.

In 1938 she would write a poem called "Calypso," a bitter poem,
choosing as its targets the human mankind who would never understand
the magic of the goddess world. Here H.D., as she opposes Odysseus to
Calypso, might well have been writing of Pound.

At the time of this first visit to Capri, Hilda must have behaved something like that girl who ran with William Carlos Williams into the rain, or the one on the New Jersey shore who dared the waves. She was also frightened: she was challenging her parents with an uncertain relationship.

To offset her personal problems, there was the physical life of the island. Capri was her first physical brush with the classic world of the Greeks, and it was here that she found space, "space and time," she said. *Sea Garden,* the title of her first book, published in 1916 by the worthy Constable, evokes Capri. One wonders which among these poems was actually written in Capri. "Cliff Temple" seems an obvious choice, although all the poems may have found their moments of inspiration there. In any case, she was on Capri long enough to catch the wind of freedom.

In an essay published in 1924 called "Theocritus in Capri," Aldington wrote about their time there:

> Youth, spring in a Mediterranean island, Greek poetry, idleness . . .
> Those were the days when Greek was an intoxication of delight . . .
> when the white violet was peculiarly sacred . . . because it was the
> flower of Meleager . . . But then we were happy, then we were near the
> gods . . . There were wild pear-trees in blossom, the green silver olive
> gardens . . . little cyclamen flowers . . . purple anemonies, green lizards
> . . . sunny rocks . . . Strangest of all came from close at hand the shrill,
> pure note of a reed-pipe, made by one of the boys who guard the goats. It
> was as if Lacon and Daphnis were not dead, but still making music for
> Pan.

Instead of making straight for Venice, they took a side trip to Florence, and a memento of their visit is a poem H.D. kept in her diary. Written by Aldington, it is interesting, not so much for its literary merit as for the contents, which reveal the conflict between the two lovers. Aldington must have been inspired by Fra Angelico's "The Annunciation" in the Museo di San Marco; a painting that in its luminosity addresses the triumph of the spirit over the physical world. This triumph, which must have caused the painter much personal torment, he expiated through this nearly miraculous painting.

ANGELICO'S CORONATION
To H.D.

But if I loved thee, and thy fragile hands
tenderly touched me as thou crowned her
I would grow weary for the white wild earth
Scurry of satyr-hooves in dewy lands,
Pan-Pipes at noon, the lust, the shaggy fur
White bosoms and swift Dionysiac mirth.

This poem remained with Aldington until 1958, when he sent it to H.D.

The reunion in May of 1913 in Venice was definitely not a success. Hilda's parents were annoyed and suspicious about the delay she and Aldington had caused them by detouring to Florence. Furthermore, Ezra Pound was there to greet them. Hilda was caught between Richard's masculinity and Pound's masterfulness. Pound was possessive, considering her an extension of his family. He was practiced at showing a mother and daughter around Venice, having been there the previous year with Mrs. Shakespear and Dorothy. Here his omnipotence was a threat to her poetry, her "crystal and air." Only Aldington was enchanted with Venice.

H.D. came to love Venice. She returned often and wrote Venice into her poems. Just before she died, she was planning to go there with Gemma d'Auria. And so it is surprising that this first glimpse of the enchantress left her untouched. However, while there she was confronted with conflicting and strong personalities, and the scene got out of her control. Her father, angry, decided to rush off to America "on business." He must have been annoyed to be forced to cope with both Aldington and Pound on this, a special excursion with his daughter. As Williams' account of those evening meals at the Doolittles' has indicated, the Professor was not one who liked to accept a secondary role in his daughter's life.

Pound in his newly assumed familial role must have shared Professor Doolittle's irritation with the delayed arrival of the obviously "honeymooning" Hilda and Aldington. Pound's private feelings seem to have included a dubiety toward the intentions of Aldington, together with a jealousy toward a rival who had infringed upon his former domain. He confined his feelings to a clever poem (later included in *Lustra*) about Aldington, whom he addresses as "the faun." Pound refers to the illicit stay on Capri, where Richard as the faun is called "capriped," or "goat-footed."

THE FAUN

Ha! sir, I have seen you sniffing and snoozling
            about my flowers.
And what, pray, do you know about
            horticulture, you capriped?
"Come Auster, come Apeliota,
And see the faun in our garden.
But if you move or speak
This thing will run at you
And scare itself to spasms."

After her husband had departed, Mrs. Doolittle confided to Hilda that he had burned all of the letters from Pound that Hilda had left at home. Later H.D. pretended that she didn't suppose she "really wanted to keep his letters. There was a great untidy bundle of them written on notepaper he had appropriated from hotels, a sort of grand tour a wealthy aunt had taken him on." This explanation sounds a little too offhand, and surely conceals a hurt. There may have been other Pound letters written from Wabash College also burned by her father. Did Hilda wish, by shrugging it off, to spare her father from a deserved criticism?

In Venice, Hilda fretted about wearing unfashionable dark dresses; later she would remedy this on a side trip to Pound's "magic place," Sirmione. She saw the home of Catullus (where, incidentally, Pound had also taken the Shakespear ladies). And in Sirmione her mother bought Hilda violet crepe she later had made up into dresses in London.

Then, having seen off both Aldington and Pound, Hilda and her mother went on to Innsbruck and other tourist spots. Charles Doolittle had abruptly returned to Europe, where he and his wife continued their travels. Hilda escaped to Paris to meet Aldington.

CHAPTER SEVEN

The Green Baize Door

Hilda and Richard returned to London. On October 18, 1913, at the registry office in the borough of Kensington, witnessed by Professor and Mrs. Doolittle and an avuncular Ezra Pound, they were married. This registry office would be the scene of several other literary marriages: Frieda and D. H. Lawrence, Katherine Mansfield and John Middleton Murry, and Nora and James Joyce.

The Aldingtons moved into Holland Place Chambers, in the "Borough of Imagism," Kensington. Ford Madox Ford said long afterward that "Kensington from 1908 to 1920 offered a pretty useful profile of the life of the literary part of the British mind of that period."

Ford himself had moved to a set of rooms over shops at 84 Holland Park Avenue. The flat became the home and office of the *English Review*. The Pre-Raphaelites lent an advisory air, represented by a portrait of Ford as a child painted by his grandfather, Ford Madox Brown. There were Chippendale chairs and an inlaid Spanish cabinet in which the *English Review* manuscripts were stored, and the desk of the poet Christina Rossetti.[1]

Violet Hunt became a great friend of the Aldingtons. After several misalliances she was then in search of a marriageable man; she was attracted to Ford, who, unfortunately, was already married. After a prolonged affair the two made a quick scramble to Germany, where Ford, by changing his name back to its original Germanic Hueffer, hoped to establish German citizenship, as his father had not completed his British naturalization process. The foregoing sentence is only a hint of the confusion that surrounded the ill-judged actions of Ford and Violet.

As an editor he produced a magazine of the highest quality. In life his inherently romantic temperament destroyed whatever attempt he might make to simplify his situation. The consequence of his flight to Germany was a legal, domestic, and, for the *English Review*, literary scandal. The newspapers were delighted with the pranks of the noble, but muddled, Ford-Hueffers. The publicity did no serious damage to the *English Re-*

[1] A mystery of ownership is attached to the desk. Said to be Christina's, it may originally have belonged to the Empress Eugénie, who spent several years of exile in England. Bryher bought the desk for H.D. at the estate sale of Violet Hunt. H.D. never liked Christina's poetry; it was unfashionable among "les jeunes."

view, and may have helped its sales. The effect on Ford was deleterious; he needed all the support his Imagist friends could give him. Writing about Ford after his death, Pound said that in this period of Ford's life he was surrounded by "gargoyles." Here Pound alludes to the popular novelists of the day, Galsworthy, Bennett, and Wells. Pound went on to remark that until he and other "uncomfortables" came along, Ford had "no one to play with."

The Imagists were attracted to Violet. She represented to all of them, and especially to H.D., a living connection with the Pre-Raphaelites. Violet's father was a well-known watercolorist, and her mother a model for Tennyson's "Margaret"; the Hunt family was well connected, yet sufficiently disengaged from any social stratification not to inhibit H.D.'s romantic need for an attachment to an English family with a literary past. Tennyson, Browning, and Ruskin had been friends of the Hunts.

Iris Barry, who was to become a protégée of Pound and whose short memoir of the period gives a piquant flavor to the various sets and activities, describes Violet as "chattering with sublime disregard for practically everything, dishevelled hair, obviously a beauty of the Edwardian age." Violet was a genuine English eccentric. (She brings to mind Lady Ottoline Morrell of the later Garsington set.[2]) Someone observed that she looked rather like "a handsome witch." At her home in Chelsea she gave many parties, inviting May Sinclair, Pound, Wyndham Lewis, Rebecca West, the Compton Mackenzies, Brigit Patmore, Aldington, H.D., Henry James, and Yeats. Ezra Pound called Violet's poetry "paste jewels in molasses"; yet he was grateful for her hospitality and useful introductions.

The *English Review* had been started in December 1908; there were two schools of contributors. There was an older generation including Conrad, James, W. H. Hudson, Wells, Meredith, Arnold Bennett. To this older group Ford added "les jeunes," whom he called "the haughty and proud generation." These included D. H. Lawrence, Pound, Lewis, Norman Douglas, Flint, Eliot, H.D., and Aldington.

"Les jeunes" would gather at the editorial office at 84 Holland Park or at South Lodge, the house Violet and Ford optimistically shared. Ford was unceasing in his encouragement of this young generation of writers. He described himself as "a sort of half-way house between nonpublishable youth and real money—a sort of green baize swing door that everyone kicks both on entering and leaving." The *English Review* and later the

---

[2] At her country house, Garsington, Lady Morrell entertained the gilded literati in their youth before the Great War, and even later as their fame grew and her health declined, into the postwar era. She early took up the anti-Establishment D. H. Lawrence, who would caricature his hostess and her pleasure dome in his novel *Women in Love*. The film made from this book attempts to reconstruct the imaginative decor of Garsington. Alas, H.D. was never invited to Garsington.

Transatlantic Review were important magazines for H.D. to appear in, and her publication in them was made possible by Ford's openness to the experimental.

In a 1962 interview with Donald Hall, published in the *Paris Review,* Pound was asked if it had been Ford who had helped him toward a "natural language." He answered: "One was hunting for a simple and natural language, and Ford was ten years older, and accelerated the process toward it. It was a continual discussion of that sort of thing. Ford knew the best of the people who were there before him, you see, and he had nobody to play with until Wyndham and I and my generation came along. He was definitely in opposition to the dialect, let us say, of Lionel Johnson and Oxford."[3] Pound then went on to explain that, in opposition to Eliot's relation to Christianity, "the actual outlook of the experimental generation was all a question of the private ethos." (This an attitude with which Ford sympathized.)

From 1908 until the Great War, several influential magazines emerged. The Poet's Club had met in 1908; in 1912 Pound had announced Imagism; Wyndham Lewis and Pound were beginning their discussion of Vorticism in 1913, an outgrowth of which was the short-lived magazine *BLAST.*

The year 1908 marked the beginning of an exceptional renaissance in English letters and politics. The Liberals, ushered in by their great victory of 1906, would be challenged by Sidney and Beatrice Webb's Fabians, and then the Webbs would survive an attempted coup d'état by the younger Fabians, H. G. Wells and Leslie Haden-Guest. Eventually there would emerge the Labour Party, which Haden-Guest would represent for thirty-five years. It should be emphasized that there was throughout this time a close connection between literary and political groups; reformists and literary experimentalists together signaled the end of Victorianism. Pound and Aldington had tunneled into the New Age.

A magazine that would prove to be even more necessary to the Imagists than the *English Review* was *The Egoist,* and it, too, illustrates the connection between art and political design. *The Egoist's* genesis was *The New Freewoman.* (This magazine, in turn, was an offshoot of the One Thousand Club, named after a group of women who had met in America to discuss contemporary issues.) The name came from the Freewoman Discussion Circle meeting at the suffragette quarters. In this

---

[3] The Anglo-Irish Lionel Johnson was a poet of the "Celtic Renaissance (or Twilight)" of the 1890s. He was a member of the Rhymer's Club, associated with Yeats, whose toast sung at their meetings proclaimed their beliefs: "We drink defiance / Tonight to all but Rhyme, / And most of all to Science / And all such skins of lions / That hide the ass of Time." (He was also a cousin of Olivia Shakespear, mother of Pound's future bride.) "Oxford" represents the poets included in *The Oxford Book of English Verse.*

original group there were only eight women. As the group expanded, so the need for more space. The meetings were moved to a vegetarian restaurant! Among their speakers was Mrs. Havelock Ellis, who spoke on eugenics; another speaker discussed divorce reform. We are told that "other subjects were Sex Oppression and the Way Out, Celibacy, Prostitution, and the Abolition of Domestic Drudgery." This was indeed the opening of a new age for women.

The meeting places of the Freewoman Discussion Circle indicate the atmosphere of the times. Eventually the Blavatsky Institute (a theosophical society) "provided a London address for the editorial offices and a room in their publishing offices at Oakley House Bloomsbury, round the corner from the British Museum. Neighbors were Swedenborgians, a missionary society and a Teacher of Memory."

In Virginia Woolf's *Night and Day,* Mary Datchett is a young woman who volunteers her services for Suffragism. Her office is in Bloomsbury, and the building, which had once been a handsome mansion, is rented to various relief causes, "disseminating their views upon the protection of native races, or the value of cereals as foodstuffs."

The staff with the usual reform disinterest in food, lunch at a vegetarian restaurant or take sandwiches to eat beneath the plane trees of Russell Square; when Mary Datchett patronizes a restaurant with naughty red plush chairs, she dines wickedly on roast beef and gravy, a note of gourmandise meant to separate Mary from the usual reform worker. Mary also goes after lunch to the nearby British Museum to look at the Elgin Marbles. It would be such a woman who, after *The New Freewoman* became *The Egoist,* would read Aldington's and Pound's criticism and the poetry of H.D. and Eliot.

The New Freewoman magazine was originally begun as an organ for the philosophy of Dora Marsden, and it was founded by Dora's friend Harriet Weaver. Jane Lidderdale, in her informed and intimate biography of her godmother, Harriet Weaver, has explained that because of her unworldly claim on life, her unselfishness and devotion to causes—some called her a "beautiful nun"—Weaver was able to publish the banned James Joyce: his *Portrait of the Artist as a Young Man* was serialized in *The Egoist.* The name of the magazine had been changed when the intrepid Dora Marsden decided that the best way for underprivileged workers to cure their ills would be for them to learn to think more highly of themselves—in other words, to become egoists; through this revised thinking they would force others to change their views of them. The idea was that workers, by considering themselves victims of society, invited their own victimization. Thus reform, like religion, began from within. Dora Marsden announced in *The New Freewoman* that the "downtrodden must 'GET UP.'" Harriet Weaver had always supported the philosophic essays of Dora Marsden, but this time she found in Marsden's "egoists" an idea that especially fitted in with her own beliefs. "She had read Walt Whitman's 'I celebrate myself, I sing myself' . . . She loved and admired people whose gifts were in some sense or other, for self-celebration." This would indeed explain her attraction to Ezra Pound!

Rebecca West was one of the editors of the magazine. Pound, scenting out, as always, a place where he might publish his friends, offered himself as an editor.

In a relatively short time Dora Marsden, who was really interested in an extremist and a linguistic philosophy, had departed, retaining a title of overseer. Pound immediately called upon his cohorts, and very soon the magazine began to publish T. S. Eliot, Ford Madox Ford, Arthur Waley, Joyce, H.D. *The Egoist* became an excellent propaganda instrument for Imagism, in fact there were complaints about its nepotism, and when Imagism no longer interested Pound, it became a home for Vorticism. After Aldington had gone into the army, H.D. took over his position as assistant editor. She was neither very good at the job, nor much interested in it, so eventually the job passed on to the more competent Eliot.

Importantly for all of them, Harriet Weaver, the benefactress, became their friend. Miss Weaver described H.D. at their first meeting as "tall, thin, pale, rather handsome, dreamy-eyed, pleasant-mannered." They would remain friends for many years, and she published H.D.'s poetry when the magazine matured into the Egoist Press. She also lent her support to a Poets' Translation Series, which was an important outlet for H.D.'s translations from the Greek, and later those of Aldington and friends.

Another magazine published at this time was *Poetry and Drama,* from Harold Monro's bookshop. Monro had represented the Georgian poets, but now he agreeably sponsored the new school of English poetry advertised by Pound.

Marinetti had come to town to advertise Futurism, to the disgust of Pound, quick to note a rival showman, in particular one whom he considered a *farceur.* Roger Fry in 1911 organized the Post-Impressionist Exhibition. Up until 1912, Wyndham Lewis exhibited with the relatively conservative Camden Town Group, until he invented a style he called "Vorticist." His murals on the walls of the Cave of the Golden Calf were closer to Italian Futurism, or Cubism, than the work of his Camden Town Group. The ceiling of the club was supported by columns created by the sculptor Jacob Epstein, noticeably nonclassic. The patrons of the club would dance what were called Vorticist dances: the bunny hug and the turkey trot. It was at this club that H.D. one night smoked a cigarette and was rebuked by the management, more enlightened about decor than female behavior. H.D. never forgot this snub, which was "pointed only at her," she kept repeating, out of a room of smokers.

Ezra Pound had moved into a room across from the Aldingtons at Holland Place Chambers. There was a constant coming and going of Ezra's "discoveries," including Wyndham Lewis and Henri Gaudier-Brzeska.

Pound's instant recognition of natural genius again proved itself in his promotion of Henri Gaudier-Brzeska, a young sculptor from France then residing in England. He may be one of the unrecognized geniuses of his time. To his own name, "Gaudier," he had added that of an emotionally disturbed older woman with whom he lived in absolute poverty and celibacy. To rescue him from this poverty, which limited the materials he could use in his sculpture, Pound sent clients to him and patrons such as Edward Marsh and, indirectly, the Ranee of Sarawak. Among the writers whom Gaudier-Brzeska sculpted were Frank Harris and the enterprising Enid Bagnold. He was also a great friend of T. E. Hulme.

The work that survives are drawings, particularly the ones he executed for the often-reproduced bust of Pound, and several sculptures; aside from Harris and Bagnold, there are an Epstein-like figure of a dancer, and the original and sensitive "Faun." In his Paris period his style was Rodinesque, but in only a few years Gaudier-Brzeska had begun a Vorticist style that is both primitive, and in advance of Cubism. Whatever influence was there, the spirit, for that is the element in his sculpture most present, overcame it. He was a rare one—primitive, yet classical; opposed to Naturalism, yet not abstract. Innocent and sophisticated, he later was to influence Henry Moore, who came across his drawing long after Gaudier-Brzeska, an immediate casualty of the Great War, was dead at twenty-three. This discursion on Gaudier-Brzeska is warranted because of his friendship with Pound, who had introduced him to H.D. and Aldington. The originality of his work illustrates the directions into which the prewar London of H.D. ventured. H.D. would have been more interested in the irrational behavior of his companion and the puzzle of their relationship, as was Katherine Mansfield, than in the genius of his work. H.D.'s narrow visual appreciation failed to include contemporary artists.

Such a discovery as Gaudier-Brzeska began to displace H.D. in Pound's pounderama. As for Wyndham Lewis, few people could compete intellectually with him or his conversation, frequently brutal, especially when he directed his criticism toward the human race. Pound could not fail to respond to Lewis' anarchic brilliance, or to the work of T. S. Eliot and James Joyce. As these people proportionately grew in Pound's esteem, it is no wonder that he dropped the frailer postures of his saltimbanques, *Des Imagistes*.

Pound defined his position quite simply: "Imagism was a point in the curve of my development. Some people remained at that point. I moved on."

His "moving on" may have been hastened by an ill-timed visit by Amy Lowell to London in 1913; she came to meet the Imagists. She had read H.D.'s poems in *Poetry* magazine and decided that her own poetry was also Imagist. Pound had made it known that there was room only for one dictator in the movement and that dictator was himself; he denounced Lowell's poetry as "amygism." Nevertheless, Amy decamped with a batch of Imagist poetry and the resolve to publish her own Imagist anthologies; indeed, she was thinking in terms of a succession of anthologies.

The daughter of Boston merchants, Amy Lowell was bold, authoritative, businesslike—accustomed to dominating any scene. She had talent, education, and money. Extremely stout, and embarrassed about her physical condition (in her hotel rooms she had the mirrors covered), still her carriage remained regal; her place in society was assured. She represented a kind of American royalty. No matter in what strata she found herself, Amy Lowell would determinedly win her way. Though the battle might cost her life, as indeed it did, she would succeed.[4]

Without the apparent sophistication of Gertrude Stein (who would be a near neighbor at the Alfred Whiteheads' when Amy visited England in 1914), she shared Stein's common sense and vigorous belief that whatever she did was right. Both women felt free to experiment in their work without the need of a protector, an explainer. They were in this way very unlike H.D. They were also excellent publicists, comparable to Pound. Amy Lowell could be very generous with those who attached themselves to her and whose work she approved of; she was quick to spot the best. From her first meeting with the Aldingtons in 1913, she took to them, especially to H.D.

At the time of her meeting with Amy, H.D. was indeed in bloom. Richard Aldington describes her in those days:

> I would say of H.D. that she was more distinguished (to use one of Yeats' favourite adjectives) than Ezra, both as a person and as a mind. I have never known anybody, not even Lawrence, with so vivid and aesthetic an apprehension . . . To look at beautiful things with H.D. is a remarkable experience. She has a genius for appreciation, a severe but wholly positive taste. She lives on the heights, and never wastes time on what is inferior or in finding fault with masterpieces. She responds so swiftly, understands so perfectly, re-lives the artist's mood so intensely, that the work of art seems transformed . . .

---

[4] Amy Lowell claimed that writing her biography of Keats did her in. She was fifty-one when she died in 1925. The likely cause was an inoperable hernia. Her normal work schedule of lecturing (even when ill), correspondence, and the production of vast quantities of poems and critical writings would undermine the healthiest of constitutions (not to mention her imbroglios with poets and the press).

If that is the sort of praise H.D. had become accustomed to, particularly from her husband, it is no wonder that the goddess legend might lend itself to satire. Aldington never scaled down his opinion of H.D. or her work. This period from her first entrée into London life until the Great War was probably the happiest and most exciting time of her life. It is small wonder that H.D. sought forever after that lost place and time.

Richard also had an admirer. A description of him exists in the character of Richard Nicholson, the hero of May Sinclair's best-selling novel of 1919, *Mary Olivier*. There had been some gossip that she had been in love with Aldington, but her biographer insists that she would have been too scrupulous to interfere in the life of a married man—such was her innocence. But to take a moderate view, there is an element of idealized love in the splendid Nicholson.

> She knew what she would see: the fine, cross upper lip lifted backwards by the moustache, the small grizzled brown moustache turned up, that made it look crosser. The narrow, pensive lower lip thrust out by its light jaw. His nose—quite a young nose—that wouldn't be Roman . . . it looked out over your head, tilted itself up to sniff the world, obstinate, alert . . . He liked to go clipped and cleaned. You felt that he liked his own tall straight slenderness.
>
> . . . "I want to finish with all my Greek stuff," he said, suddenly. "I want to go on to something else—studies in everything clean and straight in five pages where other people would take fifty . . . I want to go smash through some of the tradition. The tradition of the long, grey paragraph. We might learn things from France . . ."
>
> He discovers that although she is acting as his secretary she also is a poet. "That translation of the Bacche—what made you think of doing it like that?"
>
> "I'd been reading Walt Whitman—It showed me you could do without rhyme. I knew it must sound as if it was all spoken—chanted—that they mustn't sing . . ."
>
> "Yes. Yes. It *is* the way to do it. The only way . . . You see, that's what my Euripides book's about. The very thing I've been trying to ram down people's throats for years."

This could, of course, have been from her memory of conversations between Aldington and H.D. about translation. It does sound very like them—with the eager May Sinclair worshipfully listening in.

Ezra Pound married Dorothy Shakespear on April 20, 1914 at St. Mary Abbots, the parish church of Kensington, the church whose bells had disturbed the peace of the Imagist chambers on Church Walk. In 1924 H.D. wrote to her friend, Viola Jordan, in New Jersey:

> Mrs. Ezra is a tall girl . . . She has fairish hair, not actually "yellow" and greyish eyes, not actually grey, not blue. She used to dress in a very

pretty, rather fussy Gainsboroughish [*sic*] manner—not at all "city" but
picturesque. I don't see her (or him much now . . .) Mrs. E. spends a
few months every year with her mother here in London . . . Yes, Ez is
"married" but there seems to be a pretty general concensus of opinion
that Mrs. E. has not been "awakened" . . . She is very English and
"cold" and I personally like her although she is unbearably critical and
never has been known to make a warm friend with a man or woman. She
loathes (she says) children! However that may be a little pose. She is a
bit addictive to little mannerisms. I don't think she can be poignantly sensitive or she would never have stuck Ezra. Ezra is kind but blustering and
really stupid. He is adolescent. He seems almost "arrested" in development.

Although this was written ten years after the marriage, H.D. may still
have been suffering from the wounds of Pound's desertion, not of her as
a woman, but of the program, the poetry—Imagism—they had shared. By
then, too, she may have considered herself a more worldly and wiser
woman whose youthful anticipations had undergone several tests.[5] According to her current code, Ezra Pound may not have "passed" as an altogether human subject. Her other choices also failed to pass; her relations with men would continue to be ambivalent.

Pound left Imagism for Vorticism. But what was this Vorticism? It centered around the idea that at the Vortex there was the center of Energy;
in Imagism the center of Energy was the Image.

The real difference was that this movement had Wyndham Lewis at its
head. Here is how Lewis explained Vorticism: "You think at once of a
whirlpool, and at the heart of the whirlpool is a great silent place where
all the energy is concentrated. And there at the point of concentration is
the Vorticist." A vortex was a place where energy gathered; the center,
however, was empty, readying itself to be filled by concentrated energy.
One can think of it as a tornado, or an immense Niagara Falls. The city
was also the vortex to which all energy gathered. In this case the city
was London. They even wanted to proclaim a Vortex King! Just as
Imagism contained for some the basic trappings of Symbolism (a coincidence the Frenchman René Taupin would spot, although his evidence
was denied by Pound), so Vorticism was not Futurism or Cubism, but
there were elements of each within it. It seems that Vorticism was primarily for the British.

Just as Dr. Kenner has pointed out that the lines of a Vorticist painting
are diagonal, not horizontal or vertical as in Futurism or Cubism, so did
the movement differ by degrees of direction. F.T. Marinetti and Carlos
Carrà must have had an influence. They admired energy let loose in the

_____

[5] Wyndham Lewis, writing in 1948 of his "Early London Environment," called
Dorothy Pound "hieratically rigid."

world, the energy in certain cases turning into fascism. Fascism certainly did have, as in Vorticism, a nationalistic base. However, Lewis preferred his *ism* because it refused to destroy the past and drew a line from the past to the present to create a connection. He wanted to have it both ways, to destroy the past and at the same time to create a present.

H.D. has never noted what she thought about the Vorticist program, but what she felt about it was another matter. What she felt was deserted. The little clan of Imagists who had been foremost on the stage, the most modern of all poets, were now pushed aside by a movement that was primarily for art and architecture. The exponents, such as Pound and Lewis, appeared at first to be literary men, but literature was not Lewis' main concern at this point. Marinetti had probably already written what could be taken as a Vorticist poem. Who was left now to propagandize the Imagist poets?—H.D., Aldington, Flint, and Fletcher. Williams could be included, but he was off searching for his own form; Alfred Kreymborg for a time figured, but he was following Williams. Lawrence was never primarily an Imagist, nor was Eliot. The core group was only a handful, and its influence had been larger than its number.

H.D. kept to her Greeks. Aldington had persuaded Harriet Weaver to publish translations in a series. This would keep a few of their number occupied.

Despite a crisis, a lull never lasted long among these youthful enthusiasts. There would always be an interruption. (London was, indeed, a vortex.) John Cournos, Russian-born journalist and poet, who had been an art critic on the Philadelphia *Record,* now arrived. He was impoverished, free-lancing as a journalist in London; he had an opportune letter of introduction from Alfred Kreymborg in New Jersey to Ezra Pound. Kreymborg and Man Ray intended publishing a magazine to be called *The Glebe;* Cournos, along with Williams, expected to be published in it. He approached Pound and they became friendly. Pound introduced him to the Aldingtons.

Cournos' inclusion in *Des Imagistes* made him a welcome visitor at the Aldingtons'. In his *Autobiography* Cournos wrote:

> The three of them got along beautifully! they were a small close coterie to which few others adhered. They thought of themselves as reincarnated delegates from a past more poetic and more beautiful than anything that had ever existed; their mission was to rescue literature from more than two thousand years of perversion. They expected to inspire each other and each expected that he and the others would inspire still others until a veritable renaissance would inevitably occur. They did not know what 1914 was to hold for them and the whole world.

A more mundane than archaic incident at this time was related by Cournos when he wrote of an evening spent with the Aldingtons in which they discussed H.D.'s name having been abbreviated to initials. Beneath the goddess mask there hid a real person intimidated by society, yet unquestioning of her art. Cournos jokingly suggested "Hedda Dabler." He notes that "there was more than a little of Hedda Gabler about her."

Kreymborg had found a publisher, Alfred and Charles Boni, proprietors of the Washington Square Bookshop in Greenwich Village. Pound, still on the job, mailed the manuscript of *Des Imagistes* to Kreymborg, who turned it over to the Boni brothers. *Des Imagistes* first appeared as the February 1914 number of *The Glebe* (whose name was inspired by the once fertile Jersey meadows, now a malodorous swamp of factory waste). On the second of March the same sheets bound in blue cloth board were issued as a book by the Bonis. In England *Des Imagistes* was also published by Harold Monro. The poets included were Aldington, H.D., Flint, Skip Cannell, Amy Lowell, Williams, Joyce, Pound, Ford Madox Hueffer, Allen Upward, and John Cournos.

When one reads Christopher Hassall's intensive and fascinating biography of Edward Marsh, the question continually posed is: How did an outsider, an American, Ezra Pound, ever make his mark on the British literary scene? Marsh himself was a friend of those cultivated Souls who lived in houses called the Clouds.[6] Not only were they Establishment politically, through their association with the Prime Minister Herbert Asquith and his wife Margot, but there were among the Souls arbiters of the literary scene.

Edward Marsh, private secretary to Winston Churchill at the Admiralty, was the devoted friend of Rupert Brooke and the poets of what was then called the Georgian Group. From these Georgian poets Marsh culled a Georgian anthology. At first Pound was invited to be represented; later he was dropped, as it was decided to publish only British poets in the anthology.

Marsh was also the friend of D. H. Lawrence, who had managed to force his way through the hedgerows of society into a sort of fashionable acceptance by this group. He would be included in the anthology. Pound was the friend of the uninvited outsiders T. E. Hulme and F. S. Flint. The Establishment moved in sublime ways, and Pound, as one can now review his position, was out to destroy its godly destiny. His aims were very different from those of D. H. Lawrence, who believed that Armageddon, given a sufficient negotiable force of wills, might turn out to form a beatification of the earth.

True, Pound had strong cohorts in Ford Madox Ford and Yeats. But who was Pound? A red-headed Colonial. No wonder he wanted to rid

---

[6] Clouds was the home of the Wyndhams in Wiltshire, the maternal grandparents of Lady Cynthia Asquith—a favored setting for the poets grouped around Eddie Marsh.

poetry of Victorians and Georgians! The anger and contempt he felt formed a vortex of its own, at first called Imagism and then called Vorticism. The New Age contained the Nobs who would conquer the Snobs. *The Egoist* would venture to declare the universal rights of man, not only for fair work and housing, but for the freedom to read whatever print got to their hands, print having always been a preserve of the upper classes.

The Imagists, promoted by an American and assembling poets who were definitely not of the British Establishment, were thus outsiders. Fortunately, there was a tremendous gain in being anti-Establishment. The poets and writers were helped by others who shared the same stigma—Socialists, Liberals, and Fabians. When the new magazines welcomed these outsiders—"les jeunes"—they found they had landed on their feet. This accomplishment took courage and panache on the part of the promoters, and one can understand now that a certain bitterness must have settled quite deeply in Pound while he waged this battle against the opposition and its country. This feeling persisted, despite the numerous influential friends who had supported him.

No British publisher had offered to publish Pound's *Des Imagistes*—it had to come out first in America. American poetry was never popular in Britain and is only slightly more so today, despite the shared language. H.D. was one of the few American poets to be published in Britain, and this may have been due to powerful support. She sold less well there, but her reviews were mostly fair and favorable.

Imagism, of itself, was scarcely considered in America; now Amy Lowell decided that it was up to her to bring this poetry to America and publicize it. As a consequence of the first cautious Boni publication in 1914, she again took ship for England. When her maroon limousine rolled off the ship and proceeded with her to the expensive precincts of the Berkeley Hotel in London, the Imagists were alerted that the merchant from Brookline had arrived to plead their case. From the Berkeley she accepted and directed invitations—which were more like commands.

Pound fired the first salvo by inviting her to a dinner at the Dieudonné, a restaurant popular among artists. Underestimating her antagonist, she accepted with delight, expecting an Imagist welcome in her honor. What she received was a Vorticist celebration. The point was made offensively clear that the assemblage of artists was in the main composed of Vorticists, including Pound, Lewis, Gaudier-Brzeska, and their adherents who were giving a dinner in honor of their magazine *BLAST*. For Amy Lowell the Dieudonné dinner was a personal disaster, but she was able to shrug it off; she had a thick skin.

Pound had just written: "The Vortex is the point of maximum energy. It represents in mechanics the greatest efficiency. We use the words 'greatest efficiency' in the precise sense—as they would be used in a text book of MECHANICS."

A machine is in a greater or less degree a living thing . . .
They are the inventors of this bareness and hardness, and should be the great enemies of Romance.

"Bareness and hardness." "Enemies of Romance." Surely these had formerly been the directives of Imagism. But where were the Greeks; where were the Japanese with their unmechanized haiku and tanka; where was the "pagan mystic," H.D., or Pound himself? Talking machines, she'd be damned if she'd have anything to do with them.

From her transatlantic post Amy Lowell had come to believe that Imagism was the most perfect and exquisite doctrine that could be presented to a grasping materialistic world. It was now forcibly being pointed out to her that she was *derrière-garde*. Nevertheless, she returned from the dinner disheveled, but not confused, consummately sure of a victory in another war. For anyone else that dinner would have meant retreat. For Amy Lowell it was simply a matter of noblesse oblige.

From *The Pisan Cantos:*

CANTO LXXVII

Well, Campari is gone since that day
with Dieudonné and with Voisin
And Gaudier's eye on the telluric mass of Miss Lowell

Amy issued invitations to a special dinner to be held at the Berkeley in her own rooms. The guests would be the Aldingtons, Pound, Ford Madox Hueffer (Ford), Frieda and D. H. Lawrence, Fletcher, Cournos, Flint, Allen Upward, Gaudier-Brzeska. It was a dinner of rude remarks, uncertain speculations, and, for Fletcher, "embarrassed expectancy." The enemy in the midst was Pound; the bearer of bad news was D. H. Lawrence. He made an extravagant entrance, declaring that his friend Eddie Marsh had let out the information that Britain was going to declare war.

What strikes one now is the innocence of Amy Lowell—the monomaniacal innocence that permitted her, if we can believe the evidence, to disregard totally the reality that Europe, the world, was on the eve of a conflagration. This splendid isolation of herself into a literary context, the sole dweller on the shore as the tide washes in, seems very American. So is Pound's equally egomaniacal emphasis on his latest *ism*. Gaudier-Brzeska, who would soon be dead in the war that was preparing itself, represents the true innocence of the infant generis. H.D. and Aldington appear for an uncertain moment like deprived onlookers, ready to pick the leftovers of the Vorticist feast. Only Lawrence seems aware that this dinner party is the entr'acte that will have as its finale the end of civilization as they have known it.

Candles, the park, the handsome room with its long french windows opening onto the soft summer night, Amy's voice beautifully reading French poetry, cliquish power struggles, acid laughter, the cleverness of Pound attacking Amy, whom he rightly, although irrelevantly, saw as his enemy—at first H.D. must have been delighted and soothed by this pleasant scene so richly endowed in decor and gifted guests. She was with her friend, the all-powerful Amy Lowell. Fear may have been in the offing: her brother was due to arrive in London; he would be near a war. And she was not insensitive to the possibility of a war; she simply had never experienced one. None of those people had. Amy represented for H.D. the strength of what had once been—home.

They were all figures in a gaudy scene. Theirs was to taste this "last moment's pause" as if it were the final day of the year, before the guns went off. The group gathered that July of 1914 to celebrate their accomplishments and were, in fact, assembled on the edge of a precipice. And so they clowned, and Pound tried to trick Amy, yet Amy was the victor. With her merchant's expertise she would return to America with the manuscripts of Imagist poems and the promise of the publication of, not one, but three anthologies. She promised the Imagists that there would be a future.

H.D. was always careful and diplomatic in her relations with other poets. There was never a definite break with Pound. If he had ceased to be her protector, there was the worshipful Aldington and the all-powerful Amy Lowell.

A correspondence continued for many years between Lowell and H.D. The Houghton Library at Harvard contains nearly sixty letters written by H.D. until Amy's death in 1925. Amy never exploited H.D. and H.D. never crossed her. H.D. must have recognized Amy's conservatism within a society where one behaved or risked social rejection. She therefore carefully concealed her marriage difficulties from Amy. H.D. must have been aware that Amy was quite capable of saying to her, as she did to Elinor Wylie on the occasion of her marriage to William Rose Benét: "Marry again and I shall cut you dead and I warn you Society will do the same. You will be nobody." H.D. needed Amy Lowell far too much to endanger their relationship with any revelations of marital disorder. She only pointed out to Amy that she wished to keep her career separate from that of Aldington's, that each had a separate identity and they must not be confused as a married couple.

Amy had become so interested in H.D. that she corresponded with Mrs. Doolittle for news of H.D. when she did not hear from Hilda herself. There was a reliance on H.D. as her most sympathetic correspondent in England, although later she and Aldington became closer as

she began to succumb to his flattery. She even confided the details of the
finances of the Imagist anthologies, carefully worked out in a clerk's me-
ticulous script.

The publication of the three anthologies *Some Imagist Poets,* edited by
Amy Lowell and published by Houghton Mifflin in Boston and by Constable in London, appeared in 1915, 1916, and 1917, and gave a strong
impetus to the movement. Magazines began to take Imagism seriously;
The Egoist had a special Imagist number with Flint's "History of
Imagism" included. In America the *New Republic* published an article
by Conrad Aiken, who had not been absorbed in the movement, pointing
out that they were a mutual admiration society. Amy was stomping the
lecture trail, holding high the banner of Imagism. Her lectures were attended by many thousands of people. One, given at St. Mark's in the
Bowery in New York (now housing the New York Poetry project), was
attended by 927 people. By spreading the message of Imagism, she made
H.D. a poet worthy of consideration all over America.

Moreover, Amy Lowell's criticism of H.D.'s work as it appeared in her
book *Tendencies in Modern American Poetry* stamped H.D.'s authenticity—and it was not simply a lyrical appreciation, it was extremely perceptive besides: "H.D. has a strange, faun-like, dryad-like quality, she
seems always as though just startled from a brake of fern.

"Strange paradox! to be the prophet of a renewing art, and to spend
one's life longing for a vanished loveliness.

"The everyday world startles her."

Fortunately for H.D. this is the kind of lyrical description designed to
appeal to the reader's idea of what a poet should be, and would stimu-
late an interest in the poet's work. Amy Lowell goes further:

> There are people who find this poetry cold. In one sense it is, for in it is
> something of the coolness of marble, etc.
>
> How sad the loneliness of it! A poet's poet.
>
> The faults of such poetry are not in its treatment, but in its very texture.
> This is a narrow art, it has no scope, it neither digs deeply nor spreads
> widely . . . "There are more things in Heaven and Earth" than such po-
> etry takes cognizance of. H.D. is not a great poet, but she is a rarely per-
> fect poet. It is true that she employs the same technique throughout her
> work, and that it is perhaps monotonous to those who are not concerned
> with its excellence. It also bears with it the seeds of over-care, of some-
> thing bordering on preciosity. There is a certain thinness of the original
> conception, and only the lustre of its polish saves it. But this is a lustre
> known to no one else.
>
> . . . the tricks of her manner occasionally recall the Greek, but her
> thoughts are perfectly her own.

Lowell has presented H.D. quite masterfully; she has entranced us with
the description of the startled faun, and goes on with a teasing picture

when she says, "Let me liken H.D.'s poetry to the cool flesh of a woman bathing in a fountain—cool to the sight, cool to the touch, but within is a warm beating heart." After our senses are stimulated, Amy then gets down to the serious business of poetics, and there her astuteness shows without the romantic trappings dear to her own imagery. Again, like her contemporary Gertrude Stein, Amy Lowell certainly understood show business, yet she had the intelligence to add seriousness to her presentation. She established H.D. in America.

CHAPTER EIGHT

Crossing the Tightrope

One summer evening in the first week of August 1914, H.D., Aldington, and Cournos, now a firm threesome, gathered with an apprehensive crowd in front of Buckingham Palace. The lights were on in the palace, and soon the royal family came out onto the balcony. The King spoke. War was officially declared.

The three had been dutifully reading classical translations in the British Museum. Once H.D. pointed out the word "freesia" to Cournos as being an example of a beautiful "Greek word." Cournos looked up the word and found it was derived from the name of a Dr. F. H. T. Freese. How Cournos loved telling that story in his later bitter years. Pointing out H.D.'s ignorance of the classic Greece she was so attached to, he liked to add, "Fancy a Bryn Mawr girl knowing Greek!" Their pleasant dilatory schedule would soon end. They were faced with two realities for which they were unprepared: war, and H.D.'s pregnancy.

Hilda had been told of her pregnancy the morning of the day war was declared. The much respected woman doctor whom she had consulted had urged her to go ahead and have the child.

The Aldingtons gave up their rooms in Kensington. This move may have been caused by the new coolness between them and Pound. He was busy pursuing Eliot, then Robert Frost (who now was in England—an event of slight interest to H.D.), to be followed by Conrad Aiken. The Aldingtons moved to Hampstead Heath. As it turned out, this was a fortuitous choice, because their new neighbors were Frieda and D. H. Lawrence, whom they had met at the Amy Lowell dinner at the Berkeley.

Thus began the friendship with D. H. Lawrence, who would be, after Pound and Aldington, one of H.D.'s "initiators." Since neither H.D. nor Lawrence was capable of an ordinary relationship, what was established between them became intense, arbitrary, passionate—ending in disappointment and anger. However inadvertently, Lawrence did succeed in changing her life. H.D. thought often of Lawrence in later years, of the fineness of his early novels, his moods, his heresies, although she came to believe much of his psychological examinations (as in *Fantasia of the Unconscious*) absurd. She outgrew his philosophies, but not his personality; she dreamed about him.

Lawrence was capable of great tenderness and thoughtfulness with someone as highly strung as H.D. Early on he remarked, "She is like a person walking a tight-rope. You wonder if she'll get across." He became protective of her, probably overly so, as he was an accomplished meddler. He considered her one of his disciples, one of his votaries. At this time, in 1914, there may have been a romantic "dalliance"; who knows?

As soon as the war began, they each immediately grasped its horror: without at that time having any personal loss, they seem to have suffered more than their friends. Later, when H.D.'s child was stillborn due, she claimed, to someone breaking the news of the sinking of the *Lusitania* in a rather "cruel" way, it was Lawrence who comforted her. The stillborn child was symbolic, unwanted though it had been; it was the stillborn dream they all had carried of a bright future, of poetic hopes and fulfillment, instead of threat and death. There is little likelihood that the sinking of the *Lusitania* caused this miscarriage, but H.D. chose to place her guilt for not wanting the child on an international episode. It was hysterical thinking, but then, the atmosphere lent itself to emotional decisions and hysteria.

H.D. announced many times that the old world, her world, ended with the war. What both she and Lawrence felt, Lawrence put into his novel *Kangaroo:*

> In 1915, autumn, Hampstead Heath, leaves burning in heaps in the blue air, London still almost pre-war London: but by the pond on the Spaniards Road blue soldiers, wounded soldiers in their bright hospital blue and red, always there: and earth coloured recruits with pale faces drilling near Parliament Hill. The pre-war world still lingering, and some vivid strangeness, glamour thrown in. At night all the great beams of the searchlights, in great straight bars, feeling across the London sky, feeling the clouds, feeling the body of the dark overhead . . .
> It was 1915 the old world ended. In winter 1915–1916 the spirit of the old London collapses; the city, in some way perished, perished from being a heart of the world, and became a vortex of broken passions . . . The integrity of London collapses, and the genuine debasement began . . .

For H.D. and Lawrence, London had become the "vortex" of their world, despite their being outsiders. Lawrence's prophecy in *Kangaroo* transferred itself to him and H.D.; London thereafter was never their true center. Neither ever found a substitute for that British world they had known, and each went into a permanent, rambling exile. H.D. touched base in London from time to time, like a seabird finding a spar, but she never felt the old central union of people and poetry that had been hers. Nor, for that matter, did Aldington, or Pound, or Ford . . .

this list is long. F. Scott Fitzgerald had his say in *Tender Is the Night:*
"All my beautiful safe world blew up . . ."

Aldington believed that H.D. and Lawrence were alike in their need
to idealize, to reach for perfection in the person and the moment. In her
it came from her Moravianism, the belief in an idealized community.
Lawrence, too, dreamed of founding a community of the same sort. He
called it "Rananim," a Hebrew word he translated as "Let us rejoice."
The members would be soul brothers, like the Murrys and Aldingtons,
invited by him to find security from the evils of society. One evil, money,
he wanted to be communally shared. The members were expected to be
decent and, unlike everyone else, very good to each other. Rananim's site
shifted from Florida to South America; its real location was in
Lawrence's mind.

It was the spiritual, mystical side of each that Aldington could not
share. They were powerful dreamers, and Lawrence was a prophet. After
H.D. had turned to astrology she believed that her perfectionism came
from her zodiac sign, Virgo, which was also Lawrence's sign.

Professionally, each was reserved in his opinion of the work of the
other. Lawrence found her longer poems rather boring; she did not like
Look We Have Come Through (not even its splendid title). She wrote to
him: "It won't do at all." He wrote Amy Lowell that "Hilda Aldington
says to me, why don't I write hymns of fire, why am I not in love with a
tree. But my fire is a pyre, and the tree is the tree of Knowledge." Hilda
greatly admired his early work *The Rainbow,* and she defended *Lady
Chatterley's Lover.*

Lawrence knew many American poets; he had studied them carefully
and sensitively. When he was in Cornwall in 1916 he wrote to Amy
Lowell:

> . . . how much older you are than us, how much further you and your art
> are really developed, outstripping us by far in decadence and non-emo-
> tional aestheticism, how much beyond us you are in the last stages of
> human apprehension of . . . things non human, not conceptual. We still
> see with concepts. But you, in the last stages of return, have gone beyond
> tragedy and emotion, even beyond irony, and have come to the pure me-
> chanical stage of physical apprehension, the *human* unit almost lost . . .
> that hard universe of Matter and Force where life is not yet known, come
> to pass again. It is strange and wonderful. I find it only in you and H.D.
> [Lawrence then quotes from Amy's poetry] You see it is uttering pure
> sensation *without concepts* . . . One step further and it passes into *mere
> noises* . . . But there is this to fulfil, this last and most primary state of
> our being, where we are shocked into form like crystals that take place
> from the fluid chaos. And it is this primary state of being which you carry
> into art . . .

Then he rationalized that Imagism comes from "the American psyche, which might were it not for the artistry of the three poets (Pound, also) have turned into as mindless a poetry as the Futurists produced."

This criticism shows Lawrence at his most perceptive. Lawrence was closer than he cared to admit to Imagism, because he was influenced by H.D.'s poetry—one hears echoes of her in his earlier poems. In exchange, H.D. caught the freedom of Lawrence's poetry; his passion is reflected in the intenseness of "Eurydice." This is a poem prophetic of her life; the poem also may have betrayed her inner knowledge that she could never possess Lawrence as she once possessed Aldington. His soul, that is, could never be owned by her. From "Eurydice":

VII

At least I have the flowers of myself
and my thoughts, no god
can take that;
I have the fervour of myself for a presence
and my own spirit for light;

and my spirit with its loss
knows this;
though small against the black,
small against the formless rocks,
hell must break before I am lost;

before I am lost,
hell must open like a red rose
for the dead to pass.

Each seeded poetry with flowers. Specifically, one thinks of H.D.'s favorite anemones, and hyacinths, of Lawrence's "Bavarian Gentians," and "Sicilian Cyclamens." H.D. never realized that Lawrence—when *The Ship of Death*, which includes the above poems, along with "Snake" and the title poem, was published posthumously in 1941—had become one of the great poets of their generation.

There is a parallel that runs between Katherine Mansfield's relationship with Lawrence and his relationship with H.D. There are likenesses shared by Katherine and H.D. too: neither was "English" in the way that would have disturbed Lawrence's sensitivity toward class and status. H.D. and Mansfield only met briefly, once when Katherine was with the painter Mark Gertler, and later when Amy Lowell drove the Aldingtons to Chesham where Katherine was staying, so it was not that they could possibly have copied one another's style; it was rather that they *shared* a style. They had quirky, artistic tastes in furnishing, in

dress. They kept statues of Buddha in their flats. They lit their rooms
with candles—Katherine stuck hers in skulls. These little customs are
shared by other "artistic" persons, but the ambiance in their rooms was
particularly guided by their own personalities, and it gave off a strong
aura. The rooms were decorated to illuminate the person who held court
within. In a sense, each woman was something of a courtesan, eager to
lure and captivate.

They had unique ways of dressing, not Pre-Raphaelite, not exactly as
Augustus John's Dorelia was to do—half itinerant gypsy, half earth
mother. They dressed a little like one imagines Gudrun and Ursula in
Women in Love. They were the women who astonished with those
brightly colored cotton stockings, the chic of the loosely belted dresses,
the hair sometimes cropped, sometimes braided, or bangs. They paid attention to the fabrics Lawrence lingered over in his descriptions of
clothes. And shawls—they liked to drape themselves. Each was theatrical,
and Katherine had been a professional actress. H.D. later would act in a
private, short-lived film company; for a while she had great hopes of a
career in films. Each knew how to dominate a room with her personality.
Katherine might sulk and then bring out a sardonic, clever remark. H.D.
would evoke Delphic oracles, or withdraw into a private, unseen Hellenic world. Each had lesbian loves. Cornwall and Hampstead, cottages
and flats were their locales, with escapes to France or Switzerland. Coincidentally, each had a Russian Jewish admirer. For Mansfield there was
S. S. ("Kot") Koteliansky; H.D. was the goddess of Cournos, or "Kor-
shune," as he signed his letters to her. Their Russian admirers called
them by Russian diminutives.

Coming from proper families, rather in the Victorian tradition, they
chose to represent the "new woman." Mary Kathleen Benét in her book
Writers in Love makes the point that Mansfield "was forced into the Bohemian world by the fact that she could not get what she needed in the
conventional world; but she was never again to feel really at home in either one."

H.D., who found herself in similar straits, spoke of her marriage to
Aldington when she wrote to Norman Holmes Pearson in the 1940s:
"And then the—the—I call it the Iron Curtain fell between me and my
somewhat well—not hot-house, but in a way very comfortable surroundings. I mean, I had in a way, a very petted and spoiled American life—
one girl with brothers . . . I was looking for a super-ego—that father—
lover."

So was Katherine, with her idealized "Pa" man. Each mistakenly
believed she had found it in her husband. Neither husband fitted into the
rigid class patterns—they were journalists, capable of enormous amounts

of work, "Dog eating dog sort of men." There was for each the lost brother in the war. These comparisons can be qualified, but they do add to the background and style of two extremely gifted young women of the period; similarities, and polarities, could be found among others, yet these two were to influence other earnest literary women.

Lawrence ended by distrusting them both. "Lies," he said. To Cournos, "Is Hilda still false?" "Only for poor Katherine and her lies I feel rather sorry. They are such self-responsible lies." Katherine and Lawrence did not meet after the autumn of 1918, and after H.D. left Mecklenburgh Square in 1918 for Cornwall and life with another man, she never saw Lawrence again. They corresponded once more in 1929 when, at the instigation of Aldington, she asked Lawrence to contribute to a late Imagist anthology. He sent her a poem, but he let her know then that all was over. His words were "There is nothing more to say."

The H.D.-Lawrence correspondence was lost when she left Mecklenburgh Square. Aldington claimed he burned it, but this would be way out of character for him. It is possible that the correspondence exists and may someday reveal more of the story of their breakup. Lawrence might well have been speaking for all his friends when he said, as he did to Aldington, "Our souls have had a long, hard day."

James Whitall's memoirs, *English Years*, give a rewarding glimpse of this period in H.D.'s life. He was a second cousin of Logan Pearsall Smith and Alys Pearsall Smith (Alys married Bertrand Russell). Reserved, cautious, frugal, he led a scholarly life translating from the Chinese. He is the same Whitall whom Virginia Woolf mentions in her diary of the early 1920s as being considered to replace Ralph Partridge at the Hogarth Press. She decided that "there is this American element in Whitall to be distrusted." He also had been a reader at Heinemann and had interested the house in the Hogarth Press. Mrs. Woolf obviously could not share H.D.'s delight in knowing Whitall. A Quaker from Philadelphia, he made H.D. feel as if she had come home.

The overheard literary arguments were at first too vehement for Whitall, but he was irresistibly drawn to the group. He reacted to H.D.'s beauty, and the social grace with which she made the person with whom she was talking feel absorbingly important. He soon was made to realize that her thoughts were not always of this world, but with the Greeks on their Aegean sands. It was her habit to engage in ordinary conversation and then suddenly to lapse into a silence of her own. Whitall endows her with all the graces of the Muses or those of a woman watching the ships of Agamemnon bound for Troy. He also noticed that she could quickly dominate the conversation and that her enthusiasm was elevating. He had a scholarly disdain for chitchat, and her lack of it was probably what attracted him to her. He was kind enough never to accuse her of posturing.

He describes Aldington at this time as having long hair and wearing a black cloak. "Dangerously charming," thought Whitall; nevertheless, "he seemed to have his feet on the ground." He also noted Aldington's energy.

Writers are ever fleeing the intrigues and sophistications of city life for rural seclusion. Dorothy Richardson declared that in order to write, one should have six months of absolute seclusion in a country cottage, with no friends or games. The impoverished Dorothy added that a charwoman would be needed. She said that she had found herself in this situation only once, and during that time she wrote the first volume of *Pilgrimage*. (She did have one friend on the landscape, John Beresford, who lent her his cottage and his confidence in her ability.)

Cornwall was a plucky center for many in prewar Britain. Richardson, Rebecca West, the Lawrences, the Leslie Stephenses, the Murrys. Devon with its mild climate, sea, and countryside was also considered a good place, and Devon was where the Aldingtons went, encouraged by Cournos, whose friends Carl and Flo Fallas lived there.

There were no apparent obstacles to leaving Hampstead. The Lawrences, always on the point of departure, would themselves soon be off. Only Aldington's call-up was hanging over them. He had decided not to enlist, but to await conscription. It turned out to be an extremely wise decision, given the massacres that were already taking place.

This would be, he informed everyone, his last serene moment in which to read and write before being assigned to camp. They moved into a cottage by a stream—primroses and marmalade-making. H.D. had so inhabited the air with her Greeks that when they bathed in the nude, Cournos saw her as a Greek statue come to life. H.D. privately held this conceit herself. There is her photograph album at the Beinecke Library that shows H.D.'s nude figure in the posture of a Greek nymph; her head has been substituted in photographs of several statues of the gods. The pictures initiate a private view of a charade on Olympus.

There were many picnics, much wine, and nude bathing—a celebration before the debacle. Aldington went about successfully seducing Flo Fallas. H.D. knew of the affair, and others, which were conducted in London, but she could not blame Richard, because she had developed an almost pathological fear of pregnancy and would not have sexual relations with him. Cournos was aware of the situation. H.D.'s poem "Amaranth" probably refers to Flo. It was Flo's "commonness," not her attractiveness, that bothered her—she feared it would "sully" Aldington's poetry.

Like "Eurydice," "Amaranth" is a poem with an angry grace:

> Am I quite lost,
> I towering above you and her glance
> walking with swifter pace,
> with clearer sight,
> with intensity
> beside which you two
> are as spent ash?

And the troubled H.D. asks again in "Eros," written at the same time:

> Is it bitter to give back
> love to your lover if he wish it
> for a new favourite,
> who can say,
> or is it sweet?

The situation relieved itself by Aldington's going off to war with Carl Fallas. The breezy cottage days were over. Cournos remained behind to pack Richard's books and to console H.D. A tense moment occurred between them when H.D. teased him by kissing him. At once each claimed they heard the spectral voice of Aldington call, "John!" Cournos was in love with her.

She wrote to him from Corfe Castle in Dorset, where she went to be near Richard's army camp.

> Last night I thought of you and those beautiful days we had together in Devon . . . I think of you with peace in my mind, but you seem to make me feel that there can be love and peace together. I love that Greek world . . . but sometimes the hard light, the cruel, bitter beauty tortures me too much. Then I turn to you as to some beautiful Florentine lover. You do not mar or interfere with my love of Richard, or my love of the Greek world. But you remain another phase, another world . . .

Cournos' dilemma is understandable after such a letter. Had his ego been less, he would certainly have suffered more than he did in his bewilderment. How many strands she wove to bind the people who cared for her! Perhaps the Circe role did belong to her. Perhaps Lawrence had shown more of the observer than the preacher when he told her to "kick over your tiresome house of life." H.D. had been told that she "tyrannized Richard's soul." She had denied it, saying that she wanted him to find his daemon, to become a great lover. Her constant cry to Cournos was "I only want to write! To write!" To construct a world in which she was free to write she would do anything, use anyone, all in the name of Art. She wrote to Cournos the truth when she said: "I have all faith in my work. What I want at times is to feel faith in my self, in my mere

physical presence in the world, in my personality. I feel my work is
beautiful, I have a deep faith in it, an absolute faith. But sometimes I
have no faith in myself." Her life's story is an attempt to get away from
this depersonalization, to appear to herself without the entrapment of
her art, justified as a real person in a real world without the adornment
of her work. She would never let go the consolation of her myths. They
in turn would hold the mythical mirror up to her face until her eyes
would be unable to see beyond it. Within this mirror lies the explanation
of her behavior: friends, lovers, all were seen within the mirror.

She found Corfe Castle, the little town dominated by its somber castle,
mellow and peaceful. "All the houses have beautiful grey tiles and turfs
of rock-moss between. We have plane trees and summer lilies in the garden and the same gulls inland from the sea."

The steep gray streets with their gray stone houses lead up to the castle ruins, which were a lodge in Saxon times. H.D. never mentions the
history of this town, which stands on one of the most famous ruins in England. Legend has it that the castle is haunted. Amid its ruins walk many
ghosts: there Edward the Martyr was murdered, and scenes from Shakespeare's *King John* take place, when he disposes of his nephew, Arthur of
Britanny. At Corfe Castle Edward II lived during the months before the
surrender of his crown. Under Oliver Cromwell it withstood attack;
treachery gave the castle away. The subsequent Lord Protector ordered
it blown up, but it refused to be demolished and its masonry resisted destruction. Today the town clusters around three centuries of ruins, which
can be seen for miles. All is gray stone, softened by Dorset flowers.

There, stimulated, and in what she would call an ecstatic state, H.D.
was writing constantly. Her inspiration did not come from Corfe Castle;
for H.D. there existed only the walls of Troy. She is like Amy Lowell
walking around her house, Sevenels, close to the mill towns of the Low-
ells, thinking of knights and golden baskets.

Her letter to Cournos reveals what she was like at that time:

> . . . you know I am living a curious imaginative life now. Everything
> burns me and everything seems to become significant . . . This is won-
> derful, this life for me—but I am torn and burnt out physically. Do not
> worry about me . . . I must stay here quietly for the present . . . In
> town I am almost too intense, too burning . . . And it helps me to think
> that you still sometimes put some of this restless spirit of mine into a
> "created legend" of your own . . .

Unfortunately Cournos did just that when in 1926 he published the
mock legend of *Miranda Masters,* ridiculing his former heroine.

She tells Cournos she is worried about her book *Sea Garden,* which had been published by Constable.[1] She notes, with a rival's pique, that Lawrence had sent his poems to be published about the same time and they are out for review. Next the Moravian voice is uppermost: "I would be lonely but for the intensity of my so-called 'inner life.' 'The Kingdom lies within you. Seek you first the Kingdom [of Heaven] and *all these things shall be added unto you.*'" (my italics) Then follows what Harriet Monroe called her pagan mysticism: "The Gods do not fight with us merely we fight with the Gods!" There is no conflict for H.D. in this perfect example of her religious belief or ordering. Heaven and Mount Olympus; the consolation of Jesus and the powers of the Hellenic world. At the same time she is saying that if we trust in God we shall be taken care of; if we turn against Him we are lost, not because of His anger, but by our lack of trust. How remarkably she now combines the classical Greek with the Judeo-Christian tradition.

Under these conditions of strain and impulse, H.D. was writing some of her finest early poems: "The Island," "Eurydice," "The God." She was, as she said, burning intensely, frighteningly; she believed that suffering was good for poetry, that one, indeed, should test the tightrope. Conversely, her poetry surprises us with its control and selectivity.

[1] A curious epilogue attaches itself to *Sea Garden*. Among Frances' effects there was found what must be H.D.'s copy. Inside the paper wrapper, and on the flyleaf, also over the title page, finally filling in the empty back pages, are poems Frances wrote in H.D.'s own Imagist style. She wrote of "Hermaphroditus," "H.D.'s Hands," "To H.D.," celebratory poems of the beauty and gifts of Hilda. In H.D.'s handwriting, strong and definite, there appear the words, written just above her title, *Sea Garden,* "H.D.'s book."

To H.D.

You were all loveliness to me:
    Sea-mist, the Spring
The blossoming of trees
The wind:
    giver of Dreams
    then
A wistful silence guarded you
    about,
As in the spring
Iris and anemone are guarded:
And like a flame
Your beauty burned and wrought me
Into a bell
Whose single note was echo of your silence
    Now
    you sing;
And I, muted,
Yet vibrate—throughout to that
    song's burden
"Spare us—spare us—spare us

      From loveliness."

If the poetry is in one key, it is a key that understands and controls its own vibrations. No one else writing in such a limited manner has so succeeded. H.D.'s poetry at this time is an archaic object, preserved and admired, allowed to exist within its own setting, preserved from the intrusions and alterations of a contemporary world. There is a kind of violence under a surface of exceptional calm. Amy Lowell's poetry has all the furbelows of a late Victorian parlor; Aldington's is a hair's breadth from the Georgians', self-indulgent and sentimental, especially in the celebrated "A Dream in the Luxembourg Gardens." Fletcher never really understood the rigors of Imagism; he simply allowed his limited imagination to find its cultivated way. Lawrence refused to be confined within the margin of an *ism*. It is a wonder Flint, with his rather narrow vision and clumsy line, ever became involved in the movement when he was so obviously attracted to the Symbolists. Pound promoted Imagism and then used it up and proceeded on his iconoclastic way.

The Aldingtons were preparing the Poets' Translation Series. Whitall was to be the translator of the poems of Leonidas of Tarentum. Anyte of Tegea's complete poems were translated by Aldington; choruses of *Iphigenia in Aulis* were translated by H.D. (She had been working on Euripides' *Ion* in Devon and later in Dorset, a translation she would complete in the 1930s.) It was a noble program. Whitall later signed a contract with Huebsch to translate Chinese poems and immediately fell into difficulties with the translation and consulted H.D. It must have been a ticklish situation for her to infringe on what had been acknowledged as Ezra's territory. With her help the final revisions read like a true Imagist poem.

T. S. Eliot wrote of H.D.'s translations: "These choruses from Euripedes by H.D. are, allowing for errors and even occasional omissions of difficult passages, much nearer to both Greek and English than that of Mr. Murray's." High praise, as Gilbert Murray was considered the authority on Greek translation at this time.

On the other hand, Douglas Bush, author of *Mythology and the Romantic Tradition in English Poetry*, has a harsh evaluation of H.D.'s translations from the Greek, and of her use of Hellenic subjects, claiming that her Greece is a never-never land and that her "self-conscious, even agonized, pursuit of elusive beauty is quite un-Greek." He argues that beneath the "hard bright shell" of her poetry resides the "Victorian Hellenists."

Today her translations are not reproduced. They represent, as do most translations, the period in which they were conceived. More important than the depth or exactitude of the translation is the fact that in *Ion* particularly H.D. succeeded in establishing her own voice in the choruses of Euripides, which turned them into excellent Imagist poetry.

In 1915 the poetry of Marianne Moore came from America; it was sent to *The Egoist*. H.D., in her position as Aldington's substitute on the magazine, immediately wrote to her, reminding Marianne that they had met at a Bryn Mawr fete; Marianne had been wearing a green dress. H.D. says she supposes that this is the same person who sent her poetry to *The Egoist*. She then impulsively invites Moore over to England, the inference being that if she can write so well under conditions from which H.D. had escaped, how much greater would her poetry be in a civilized country.

Later, in a review of a book of Marianne Moore's poems published by the Egoist Press, H.D. wrote enthusiastically: "Does it mean something?"; then she quotes from "Feed Me, Also, River God." She continues with: "I think that it does mean something. And if Miss Moore is laughing at us, it is laughter that catches us, that holds, fascinates and half paralyses us, as light flashed from a very fine steel blade . . . Miss Moore turns her perfect craft as the perfect craftsman must inevitably do, to some direct presentation of beauty, clear cut in flowing lines."

One is not altogether sure that Marianne Moore believed in this definition of "perfect craft," yet how quick H.D. was to recognize the value of this poetry that would later dazzle others. Her review ends with some generous flag-waving: "Miss Moore is an American. And I think in reading Miss Moore's poems we in England should be strengthened . . . And although there is a terrible war in England, in America Miss Moore is fighting a battle against squalor and commercialism. And we must strengthen each other in this one absolute bond—our devotion to the beautiful English language."

Writing to H.D. from camp, where he was enduring his own trials, and doing rather well despite his contempt for the machinations of war, Aldington suggested that H.D. return to America for the war's duration. Immediately she wrote Cournos inviting him to go with her, confiding to him her fear that Richard might die, or worse, something might die in him. "It is enough that I have seen the face of his God. Richard's spirit is cherished! If he dies, his God will take it. If he lives, he will have an awakening as you and I have had and he will see that 'heavens opening,' and in that knowledge we will be one—all of us! . . . We will see much of one another if we go to the U.S.A. Peace is coming to me—peace to do the will of God . . . Pray for me! Pray for me!"

There is no explanation of the "awakening" she and Cournos had experienced. Her letters swing from elation to despair. In all of them she either cries out to him for help or tells him how much she cares for him, and how grateful she is. She promises to send him a series of poems. And she tells him that with "two artists such as ourselves, there should be no reserve—especially none with our art . . ."

These letters do more than give us a picture of H.D. at this period of her life; they illustrate her dependency on yet another person to lend her stability. Just as she had depended on Pound the first years in England, so she turned to Cournos when the war separated her from Richard, whom she had turned to upon the "desertion" of Pound!

There is an element of Isadora Duncan in the style of her letters. One can see H.D. clad in a light Greek garment, waving her arms, crying out for her daemon to descend. When an embittered Cournos came to write *Miranda Masters,* he parodied their correspondence and speech. He asks Roy Christopher (John Gould Fletcher), "Do you believe in daemons?" Roy does. "You mean . . . in the sort of things the Greeks believed. A kind of invisible being who takes possession of one, an Alter-Ego, whose presence you feel, who urges you to do the things that are in you to do, though they may seem utterly mad to the person who does not understand!" Then Gombarov (Cournos) continues, "But what is the subconscious if not our ancient memory come to life, the ancient Greek daemon crying in us for fulfillment, for a more abundant life? Creation is life!"

If these were the prevalent mannerisms and speech, it would seem that Ezra Pound had let loose a Pandora's box when he introduced the Greeks into Imagist poetry. Given this as their dialogue, it is no wonder that H.D. and Cournos were dwelling on a level where nothing in nature or society was quite distinct. Cournos intentionally photographs H.D. at her most unflattering angles in *Miranda Masters;* it is wise to consult the poems she wrote then to resurrect their clarity and strength.

> Before an audience Miranda had this habit of speaking in passionate rhythms, soothing alike to herself and listeners. She projected her long body forward as she talked . . . One felt as she sat there restless, straining as at a leash, that she was possessed by some irrepressible thought which had to out. She half closed her excited grey eyes and like a soothsayer gazing into the remote distance, as regards space and time, resumed . . . It was as if some ancient demon possessed her, granted her ancient sight.

Somehow one can hear again the spectral tones of Aldington, "She was deuced attractive all the same." And he would write: ". . . the best poet of them all." This is the stuff of legends—like W. B. Yeats, who had his "visions," consulted his mediums, yet their scattered shadows never darken beauty.

The last scene in *Miranda Masters* carries us to the war's end. It shows a trembling and distraught Miranda showing up at Gombarov's flat in London and begging him to help her. "These war years have played havoc with me . . . I want to feel normal again. Now I feel like an outcast. It's hard facing things all alone."

She has come to him because she is pregnant.

He went over the whole history of Miranda in his mind. Here was one who had all and lost all, and in the end succeeded only in securing the one thing she did not want . . . The colossal irony of it, the sheer futility . . . What she did not want was the child she was carrying.

"What in heaven's name made you do it, Aspasia?" said he . . .

"You see," she explained, "after everything happened I began to think something was wrong with me. As a woman, I mean. The first child, you remember, was born dead. And I want this child to live. I need it to regain confidence in myself. I want to feel normal."

The Cournos-H.D. friendship concludes with this mocking book. They had confided in one another so much during those early suffering years, it was a pity that Cournos had felt so rejected and that H.D. should have been so self-indulgent in the romantic letters she sent him, in her teasing profferings of affection, in an allure he scented as love. In her defense, it should be said that she brought much inspiration and excitement into his life. She extended him the gift especially her own: a view of another dimension.

(The sulky Cournos wronged another author in the same way he believed H.D. had done to him. The lady was the detective story writer Dorothy L. Sayers, a favorite for her literary clues-manship. She fell deeply in love with Cournos, who fled from her, and she suffered greatly. Could one sixteenth or eighteenth of Lord Peter Wimsey be composed of John Cournos?)

There are so few immediate or final acts to relationships that it wasn't until the 1930s that the final curtain rang down on Cournos and H.D. Cournos at that time had appealed to H.D. to use her influence to obtain a sum of money for him from her friend Bryher. In 1938 H.D. wrote to Ezra Pound:

Don't let Cournos come to see me. He writes such letters . . . Please gather your wits and your remembrances, Dear Ezra and try to realize that Cournos means stirring up things for me . . . R. to be exact . . . And please remember that it is the heighth of irony that NOW I should see Cournos [she was divorcing Aldington], that now I should go back to a mire of memory . . . he wrote a most unseemly book about ME I think, some fool who as they always have it was a fool. Always in books, a fool and an incompetent and suppressed nymphomaniac . . .

After leaving Corfe Castle and visiting Richard at his army camp in Litchfield, H.D. returned in 1917 to London. They had rented a large room at 44 Mecklenburgh Square in Bloomsbury for use during brief visits to London while staying in the country.

In December 1917 Aldington was sent to France. His army career, despite his famous autobiographical novel, *Death of a Hero,* had not been all that disagreeable. It is only necessary to compare his book with Robert Graves' *Goodbye to All That* to realize that Aldington's experiences are not so desperate or tragic as he would have us believe. Although there is no doubt that he suffered severe emotional disturbances that would trouble him for years after, the truth seems to be that he never fired a shot. He had managed to be sent from camp to camp in England, rising in rank, until finally he had applied for a commission. He wrote to Cournos about his application, telling him that "the General was fearfully decent. I told him I was a minor poet and he said: 'Magnificent, magnificent, just what we want!'"

No doubt, he was temperamentally better able to adjust to war conditions than many other "heroes." His regret seems mainly to have been for the waste of time and the needless postponement of his real career. It is ironic that he should be known best for the book he wrote about that war and the hero who in actuality never died.

H.D. saw him off from Victoria Station. The troop trains drew in and out. While waiting for his train to leave, H.D. wrote a letter to Amy Lowell describing the atmosphere and reaching across the sea for her friendship and comfort. It conjures up an odd picture—H.D. scribbling somewhere on a station desk to the guardian of the Imagists, with the full approval of Aldington, who restlessly paced back and forth. They could at times be a most businesslike couple, and the grim scene before them added a necessary pathos to the letter.

CHAPTER NINE

Mecklenburgh Square

H.D. stayed on in Mecklenburgh Square after the departure of Aldington. There the cast would assemble for the drama H.D. unfolds in *Bid Me to Live*.

Today the square is distinguished by a plaque on the house where R. H. Tawney lived. The author of *Equality* and *The Acquisitive Society*, he is respected in America for his book *Religion and the Rise of Capitalism*, definitive of the Puritan society in which religion and acquisitiveness formed an amiable mixture. It was an unlikely square to welcome Tawney and his modest Fabians, with its prosperous nineteenth-century architecture, its echoes of European grandeur. The house at 44 Mecklenburgh Square survived the Blitz. H.D.'s flat, among others on the square, is now used, according to the William Goodenough Trust, to accommodate visiting Commonwealth postgraduate students.

The activities that took place there in H.D.'s time were more closely related to the circle of another economist, John Maynard Keynes: neighborhood Bloomsberries rigged out as Emperors of the East, graduates of the Chelsea Arts Club, or clever aesthetes would be more congenial to the inhabitants of Mecklenburgh Square.

The Lawrences, ejected from Cornwall by an angry wartime constabulary who accused them of pro-German sympathies, after appealing to H.D. were living in the Aldington flat. Cournos, who had lived in the attic, now departed for Russia. His legacy was Dorothy (called "Arabella") Yorke, a former love, whom H.D. had generously allowed to use her unoccupied room. Dorothy now rented Cournos' garret room. Very complicated. Unknown to H.D., when stopping at his London flat on one of his leaves, Richard had begun an affair with Dorothy. The atmosphere of intrigue that would gather now that H.D. had returned almost satisfied Lawrence, for whom such atmospheres were as necessary as fresh air. (Lawrence was at home in Mr. Tawney's neighborhood, as he had his own ideas, more apocalyptic than economic, about the roots of evil in society.)

There are glimpses of H.D. at this time, even more intense than usual, eyes widening while she listened to Lawrence, joining the plot he relentlessly spun for "cerebral burning women," as he called them, like Hilda Aldington. He always used the familiar "Hilda." Who could refuse the magnetism of Lawrence? Certainly not H.D., who by now believed he loved her. Inside the circle of her perpetual cigarette smoke, Frieda watched and made other plans. It was a drama made for telling. Frieda was not a "cerebral" woman (to Lawrence's delight). She understood that Lawrence ordered the "burning" to rise from his own flame.

A note from H.D. to Brigit Patmore: "Richard is back. Come today. We'll have a celebration. Hilda."

The Great War, accounted by those who lived through both as far worse than World War II, was made partly so by the closeness of London to the battlefields, the teasing separation of the civilians from their kin. Nurses and soldiers were crossing the Channel back and forth on leave; parties and theaters and marriages occurred, and then deaths within a week of those London celebrations. How many must have gone to their deaths shortly after relaxing with *Chu Chin Chow*, the season's musical hit, so far removed in era, costume, and plot from their lives!

H.D.'s book *Bid Me to Live* is a period piece. Like all of her prose it is based on what actually happened. She may have slanted her characters to suit her purposes; she may have portrayed herself as a person of more sensibility and kindness than the H.D. of that time, but *Bid Me to Live* must be read as a true story, as H.D. understood it. Also it should be realized that all actions within the story took place in another time scheme, during a war when emotions might erratically flare up or dim. It was just that climate of heightened intensity, where vulnerability was exposed, that suited H.D. and Lawrence. It was their natural element, crystal and fire.

The Aldington flat had apricot-colored walls and was lit by candles. Night blue curtains closed over the long french windows. On a table were fruit, wine, sausages. Gathered there were Lawrence and Frieda and H.D., whom Brigit described as then "a swaying, slim sapling almost destroyed by a forest fire. All blueness of flame gone into her large distracted eyes." There was a guest, Cecil Gray ("like a shaded candle, he held his intelligence watchfully behind spectacles"), come in from Cornwall, where he had known the Lawrences and perhaps had been a lover of Frieda: Arabella Yorke, "the only dark one amidst us, smouldering under her polished hair"—cross because Lorenzo (D. H. Lawrence) had compared her to a "lacquer box"; Richard, "fettered with the desperate gaiety of the soldier-on-leave and unresolved pain. He had the most robust body of us all." And beautiful, sensuous Brigit, the observer.

H.D. began *Bid Me to Live* in 1918, when she could clearly construct the events that had taken place at the Aldington flat. These events remained nearly as vivid to her while she rewrote the book during the 1930s and was finishing it in 1948. There was no simmering-down for H.D. It was not published until 1960.

Originally titled "Madrigal," her book can well be put into that form. Briefly, H.D. is fascinated by Lawrence; in her mind she replaces Aldington with him. Lawrence spins a magic web, but, and this is an important *but*, he does not spin the web around H.D., enclosing her. He does not take her to bed, although she would willingly go. Lawrence likes "cerebral women," but he wants them to remain on a "cerebral" level. When Aldington returns on his next leave, he becomes, with H.D.'s permission, the official lover of Arabella Yorke. To make this more clear to her readers, H.D. writes that she gives up her own bed to the lovers. Then she realizes that she has, despite her machinations, suffered two losses—Aldington and Lawrence. Now she places the blame on Richard, who has betrayed her with Arabella. She blames him for the adultery that would cause the breakdown of their marriage. Yet it is apparent that H.D. has already tired of Aldington for unrevealed reasons. When Cecil Gray, who is now in love with her, invites her to Cornwall, she goes to him, and in Cornwall she begins to write the tale of what happened in Mecklenburgh Square. The book in its last phase is a hymn to Lawrence, who would not be her lover, but whose genius she would worship.

In 1918 Lawrence wrote to Cecil Gray: "You want an emotional sensuous underworld, like Frieda and the Hebrideans: my 'women' want an ecstatic, subtle-intellectual underworld like the Greeks—Orphicism—like Magdalene at her feet washing—and there you are." Here Lawrence has given an intuitive description of the H.D. of *Bid Me to Live*. Instead of an intellectual attachment, she would have liked a brief caress from that underworld.

In *Women in Love*, Ursula says, "You go to your women—go to them they are your sort—you've always got a string of them trailing after you—and you always will. Go to your *spiritual* brides." (my italics)

Lawrence was able to use those Mecklenburgh days in his novel *Aaron's Rod*. In its early chapters his novel has a puzzling set of characters for whom there seems no purpose other than to create a setting for the main character, Aaron, after which they are allowed to disappear. In the book, Robert Cunningham is Richard Aldington: "A fresh, stoutish Englishman in khaki . . . he drank red wine in large throatfuls." Julia, Robert's wife, is H.D.: the "tall stag of a thing"; Cecil Gray is Cyril Scott: "a fair, pale, fattish young fellow in pince-nez and dark clothes"; Dorothy Yorke is Josephine Ford: "a cameo-like girl with neat black hair done tight and bright in the French mode. She had strangely drawn eyebrows, and her colour was brilliant." (Lawrence, perversely, seems to have approved of Dorothy more than the other women, and always remained fond of her.) Through Cecil Gray, Lawrence had met the composer Philip Heseltine, or Peter Warlock, as he called himself. Warlock appears in *Women in Love* as Halliday, who collected African sculpture, which was the latest craze of the avant-garde. H.D. must have been exposed early on to the primitive sculpture that influenced so much modern art.

For a very short period—that is, from the start of the Great War until H.D. left for Cornwall in the spring of 1918—Lawrence was a major figure in her life. She recognized his genius, and his magnetism had made her one of its victims. *Bid Me to Live* becomes a dialogue or duel between Lawrence and H.D., with all the added nuances and movements of the other persons who shared the flat in Mecklenburgh Square, like blurs of expressionist paint against which are slashed the heavy black outlines of two people—Lawrence and H.D. And these strokes of black describe the literary importance H.D. gives to herself and Lawrence; these are the heavy emphases that portray their genius, separate from the impasto in which the other characters are embedded.

Frieda later said to Aldington, who then repeated it to H.D., "Hilda is somebody." Lawrence would have agreed; too much so for comfort. He understood that H.D. would remain only a limited worshiper, in that her demands would be incompatible with the sacrifice of self he required of his disciples. While seeming exposed, he placed an invisible shield of protection around himself.[1]

Knowing she is going to Cornwall to be with Gray, Lawrence says to her, "I am not happy about this . . . You realise that . . . Don't you know what you're doing?" She answers, "So Rico, your puppets do not always dance to your pipe. Why, because there is another show."

Lawrence said farewell to H.D. in the early months of 1918. Neither he nor Frieda, who by then were living in Earl's Court Square, ever saw her again. In 1926 when he and Frieda were briefly in London, Bryher met Lawrence at a party to which H.D. had also been invited but had decided not to attend. Lawrence came up to Bryher and said, "Give my love to Hilda. Mind you, you are to give my love to Hilda."

H.D. left for Cornwall in April of 1918. By May the Lawrences were in assorted residences in Middleton by Wirksworth in the Midlands, near his family, where he would be placing his former companions within his new novel, *Aaron's Rod*. From there, according to an informed Paul Delany, the most recent biographer of Lawrence, he would write to Gray about his new interest in the historian Edward Gibbon. And money. Haunted by his need, he was trying to raise sums from the Royal Literary Fund. Lawrence was concentrating on himself and his problems: in

---

[1] It was an ability he shared with his onetime admirer Henry Miller. Miller, a believer, like H.D., in astrology, was contemptuous of Virgo traits. His dislike of what he called the overly critical Virgo mind was one of the conflicts that disrupted his planned book on Lawrence. This contempt did not prevent Miller from helping himself to Lawrence's intuitive, and more informed, critical mind.

respect to both, he was writing to the one woman whom he seems consistently to have adored and idealized, Lady Cynthia Asquith. Lady Cynthia was married to Herbert Asquith, a younger son of the former Prime Minister Lord Herbert Asquith. One of the Prime Minister's sons, Raymond, had been killed in the war; Herbert had been badly shellshocked and was suffering from a nervous breakdown. It is most probable that Lady Cynthia Asquith was the model for Lady Chatterley.

Paul Delany sums up the officially accepted reasons:

> . . . he used the Asquiths' marriage as a principal source for the Chatterleys in *Lady Chatterley's Lover*. In both cases they married when the bride was twenty-three, the groom twenty-nine; Connie, like Lady Cynthia, is of Scots ancestry; Clifford, like Herbert Asquith, has an older brother who is killed in 1916, is shattered by a war wound, and dabbles in literature. The novel is the culmination of Lawrence's perennial fantasies of carrying off an imagined English aristocrat rather than a real German one; having chosen the path of exogamy and exile, he nonetheless hankered after an ideal reconciliation with English womanhood and thus directly, with England itself.

Aldington must be made to appear the culpable male. He is an adulterer in his own house. (Lawrence is culpable also, but his was a seduction of the spirit. Hilda would have preferred it to be the other way around: she was certain of her spiritual hold over Aldington.) However culpable, Aldington is the stuff of which novels are made, especially when the novelist is his wife. *Palimpsest*, published in 1926, consists of three parts, each of which is a separate novella. The first is called "Hipparchia: War Rome (Circa 75 B.C.)" This is an earlier version, with a classical setting, of the later *Bid Me to Live*.

Hipparchia (H.D.) in Rome is kept by a Roman officer, Marius (Aldington). Their problem is sex: she wants intimacy without physical contact. "When one has slept perhaps on a rough estimate, one hundred and fifty times with one man, it is . . . somewhat of a shock . . . to find it has not been a man at all, merely a rather bulbous vegetable." The "vegetable" answers back: "I have just discovered that . . . I slept not with a woman but a phantom." They have another problem—he is a Roman and she is a Greek. Romans are cruder copies. (In *Bid Me to Live*, Aldington is said to look like a Roman.)

Nevertheless, Marius does appreciate his "exotic high-strung girl" even while he is turning to Olivia (Arabella), a voluptuous Sicilian who gives him sex without complications. From his various battle posts he continues to write of his need for the spirit of Hipparchia. (Here H.D. drew on Aldington's actual war letters from the Front. In a poem of 1919, "Simaetha," a name taken from Theocritus, H.D. had written that she wanted to be a Sicilian "witch-piece.") Marius' private conflict continues;

after having been with Olivia he feels "creeping like some insinuating wraith, or mist, the old glamour, the old insatiety, a disease, a mental unsteadiness, a thing that inexplicably lifts me out of my confining heavy members. I call it just Hipparchia." In truth, Aldington, despite his feeling for H.D., as his letters prove, went on to live with Arabella for some ten years.

Having none of the polish or professionalism of *Bid Me to Live,* the narcissistic characterizations still sweep "Hipparchia" along. It is so wistfully and romantically Graeco-Roman that it is the more endearing of the two. Hipparchia is so frustrated by her lovers. The conception she has of herself is as a devotee of Artemis, or priestess of Isis; the other characters are mere mortals. "Hipparchia" is a story of illusion necessary for the survival of a gifted woman.

H.D. even brings in Ezra Pound. Her account of him here shows how her mind had changed about Pound from the early days to the 1920s when she was writing this book. He is Philip, the intellectual tutor of the young Hipparchia. "'Work! Work! Work!' cried Philip. 'Better! Better! Better!'" In Rome, older and wiser, "She now saw Philip along with the rest of her family appurtenances as something outgrown, something she had stepped from like a moth from a split chrysalis." Later on she reconsiders and decides that "she would still see Philip as her highest idol." In *Bid Me to Live,* Pound is not evoked. The "idol" is Lawrence, a usurping "initiator."

In "Hipparchia," Cecil Gray is Quintus Verrus. He has a handsome villa at Capua (Cornwall). Their lovemaking is of a less rigorous nature: "There had been no striving. So Artemis must have felt, having been caught between long arms the form of the young Endymion. Snow caught and tangled in the wisps of her pollen-dusted hair . . . Snow permeating, penetrating . . . a new Danae with more frail-God-embodiment." The trouble with Verrus is that he is not serious, and Philip had taught her to despise such a person. Although at first she admires his "aristocratic languor," later she decides that he is simply intellectually immature.

Verrus is sensitive enough to notice that she appears to be only interested in the mind. He says to her, "You feel nothing, Person." Here H.D. is reducing a sentence from one of Gray's own letters to her, written before she had decided to go off to Cornwall with him. It is a love letter in which he addresses her in goddess language as "Dear grey-eyed One." In the letter he went on to say that he feared the cold, abstract, impersonal side of her. He worried that at any moment she might simply cease feeling for him, that he would no longer exist. In later letters to her, and in actual conversation, he would continue to call her "Person."

For a time Verrus is forgiven his faults, because his villa is "perfection." She repeats that word. It becomes the setting for the loveliness that Hipparchia, tired of the elegance of Verrus, now finds in herself. She has decided that Verrus could not love her as much as she loved herself: "She saw Hipparchia and she loved Hipparchia." She will leave Verrus.

The sequence of the villa in Capua must be taken as an explanation and description of the life H.D. had led with Gray in Cornwall. Biographically, it is of much interest. And there are sentences of delicacy and beauty; the setting particularly chills and charms at the same time. As literature the episode with Verrus is heavy going, remarkably heavy in contrast to H.D.'s carefully selective poetry. And yet—storm, cloud, sea-green, anemone, sea-birds, sand-stretch, polished stone—the familiar vocabulary reaches out like a cool arm from Hipparchia's "wine-red pillow."

Cecil Gray becomes Vanio in *Bid Me to Live*. The Lawrences had visited with him at his house, Bosigran Castle, in Cornwall, from their nearby house at Zennor. While staying with H.D. in London they invited Gray to visit them. He is not in the army because of a "heart tic," and thus available for invitations and eager to escape the loneliness of Bosigran.

The H.D. to whom he became attracted psychically resembles Hipparchia, the "exotic, high-strung girl" whom Marius loved. In the later version of the story, *Bid Me to Live*, Cecil Gray takes the distraught H.D. to a restaurant so that she might escape the intrigue that had settled into her apartment. She becomes faint, tired; it is apparent that she is in an anxious state. Vanio, or Cecil, was "a man who could always obtain taxis," wrote H.D., and so he drove away with the Camille-like H.D. to the theater. During the entire evening, memories overwhelm her. She is only with him in her physical state. Mentally she is elsewhere, amid her betrayed present. H.D. must have struck Gray as unlike anyone else he had known in his twenty-three years. She was nine years older. She was a distressed, excitable woman with a "mental unsteadiness" new to him. He found her marvelous. The affair probably began in London; shortly after he asked her to come with him to Bosigran, as he "loved and needed" her. In February she wrote to Cournos that she wanted to go to Cornwall: "Lawrence seems not to exist and R. seems far and far." Somehow an uneasy Pound from his Holland Place Chambers must have got wind of her preparations to leave Mecklenburgh Square. He sent her this message:

> Poor Dryad
> Buon Viaggio
> Ezra

Gray left for Cornwall in March 1918 to prepare the house for her arrival, although she had not given a definite promise to follow. He began pressuring her with letters, begging her to come to him. He wrote that he was suffering in her absence and brooding over what he must have confessed to her. What he had confessed were his hopes for the future in his career as a musicologist. H.D. always had invited, and always would invite, confession. She must have encouraged him in his dreams, and those dreams included an inspiring Muse.

There was strain from the beginning. Gray had planned for a long stay: he had asked her to bring blankets, volumes of Flaubert, her meat card, sheets and towels. He wanted his music and a companion to share it with. She must be beautiful. He believed that he had chosen well. He was making plans to remove them to nearby Tregerthen after his year's lease ran out in May, but that would be decided later. And Gray had told her that he loved her *very* much and respected her unwillingness to commit herself to him. H.D. was hesitant because, still angry at her rejection by Lawrence and Aldington, she was not ready to substitute Gray for them. She in all honesty misled him. He was, and the setting calls for the phrase, only a port in the storm.

What excited H.D., especially in the early spring with its wild flowers, was the mysterious beauty of the locale. She wrote to Cournos in early April that he must visit this "English Riviera." She called it "grave, Celtic-Druidic Cornwall." Bosigran was not truly a castle, it was a tinner's cottage set into the cliffside, near the ruins of the ancient castle. The walls were made of stone. There was a promised ghost whose knocking might be heard; Dorothy Richardson had lived nearby and in her house had heard the "ghost" knocking.[2]

On a table in the small sitting room Gray would try to work; mostly he shifted papers. She showed little interest in what he was doing, she was not proving to be his Muse. Hilda could not think of Gray as an artist, only as a wealthy young dilettante. Her model of an artist was Lawrence and herself.

Removed from wartime London and inspired by the graphic beauty of Cornwall, H.D. began to work well. She was translating the choruses from Euripides' *Hippolytus*. The Egoist Press had published her translations of *Iphigenia in Aulis* in 1916—ten years after that first performance of the senior class that had "awakened" her. Next she approached *Hippolytus*. This translation (or interpretation) would appear in 1919 in the Poets' Translation Series of the Egoist Press.

In *Bid Me to Live*, H.D. wrote about these translations she was then working on. "She was self-effacing in her attack on those Greek words,

2 In the houses of Cornwall there were frequent "knockers." The local explanation was that the knocks came from the ghosts of miners long ago trapped in the tin mines below. Miners had been called "knackers," partly from the noise of tapping and knocking when they went underground. The mines had been worked before the Saxons or Romans, who had built the roads, as long ago as the Bronze Age.

she was flamboyantly ambitious." She wanted the Greek to have the same shape and texture as the stones of Cornwall.

Anyone can translate the meaning of the word. She wanted the shape, the feel of it, the character of it, as if it had been freshly minted. She felt that the old manner of approach was toward hoarded treasure, but treasure that had passed through too many hands, had been too carefully assessed by the grammarians. She wanted to coin new words.

Cornwall—Greece—romance—a little upstairs chamber of her own in which she could encourage her own Muse. Idyllic? She wrote Cournos that never had she so lived in her imagination. She felt great distances between herself and reality. A few months later reality surprised her; she found herself pregnant.

Should she have the child? She had been called a "pagan mystic" by admirers of her Imagist poetry. Now she would behave as one. She decided that if a swallow flew into her room it would be a sign that she should give birth. The necessary bird accomplished its flight.

When Gray was told about the child isn't known. But about this time his movements become difficult to follow. He knew the lease was running out on Bosigran. He returned to London and contacted his friend, the composer Heseltine, asking him if he could rent his London flat. Gray must have inferred that H.D. would be with him, because there exists a brief note from Heseltine written at this time to Gray advising him that "2 persons, 1 room, 0 peace." In July 1918 H.D. was alone at Bosigran, but there is no reason to suppose Gray had deserted her. More than likely, she had not even told him about the child; recognizing their relationship was deteriorating in Bosigran, he had gone up to London to devise an alternate domestic plan.

Now that the child was on the way, H.D. realized she did not love Gray, nor did she under any circumstances want to continue living with him. The other person involved, Gray, is silent. We can only interpret his likely feelings from the autobiographical material he has left in his book *Musical Chairs,* published in 1948. At the time Gray knew H.D., he was young, with upper-class tastes and bohemian friendships. Afterward, he became a distinguished music critic, and the biographer of the composer Philip Heseltine (Peter Warlock). A contributor to the respected *Grove's Dictionary of Music and Musicians,* his own biography now appears there.

In another of his books, *Predicaments,* he states a philosophy that coincides with H.D.'s own concept of the structure of the novel:

Past, present and future, indeed, are in reality one and indissoluble, interpenetrating and impinging upon each other to such an extent that it is impossible to form a clear idea of the one without taking the others into consideration. As Spinoza says, the present is made up of a portion of the past, which is remembered, and a portion of the future which is anticipated.

Gray, for unknown reasons, only saw his daughter once, when she was visiting his friend Norman Douglas in Capri, where Gray also lived, renting the beautiful Villa Solario of Compton Mackenzie. That was in 1947 and Perdita was twenty-eight. Perdita said (to the author) that seeing him was like looking at herself. In 1951 the artist Laetitia Cerio (whose father was a reigning figure on Capri, where Laetitia had spent much of her childhood) one day took the recently widowed Cecil Gray aside, and with the curiosity of a young woman toward a glamorous older man, questioned him about his past. Gray then had confided unabashedly to her that he had a daughter. Signora Cerio, who later became a friend of this daughter, said (to the author) that it was obvious to her that Gray had been speaking of the daughter of H.D., as Perdita's resemblance to Gray was "startling."

Gray describes himself: "My naturally gloomy and sombre temperament . . . I am seldom, if ever, happy, in fact, except when transported by alcohol, love or art, by women, wine and song: and for me ever since I can remember *Italy* has always been the symbol and living source of this divine ecstasy, this liberation from myself . . ."

Originally he had gone to Cornwall to work on what H.D. had viewed as a "dilettante's" task, a musical interpretation of Gustave Flaubert's *Temptation of Saint Antoine*. This eventually became one of his more successful works. Having completed his cantata, Gray then declared he did not wish it to be performed, although the score had been read by other musicians. His reasons were that the musicians who would perform the music might intrude external sounds that would interfere with the purity of the composition. Bernard van Dieren had similar ideas about his work and refused to have his "Chinese" Symphony played, although musicians in London also knew this work. Gray's refusal to have his work tampered with or given any interpretation other than his own might give a clue to his diffidence in his personal relationships—a reluctance either to draw close himself, or permit another to share any personal intimacy.

He became for a time a reporter for several newspapers in a musical capacity, but always ran against the mode. For instance, Dame Ethel Smyth, an ardent self-promoter, complained that he didn't like her work and would give her unfair reviews. He was attached to the eccentric late-sixteenth-century composer Carlo Gesualdo; it was as the champion of Peter Warlock and Bernard van Dieren that he was mainly known around London. Born in Edinburgh in 1895, Gray died in 1951.

There are more dimensions to Cecil Gray than H.D. in her critical aloofness was aware of at the time. He appears as a character in *Casa-*

nova's Chinese Restaurant, one of the novels in Anthony Powell's *A Dance to the Music of Time.* In his autobiography, *Messengers of Day,* Powell has revealed that Gray was Constant Lambert's first link with Wyndham Lewis, via the Lawrence circle. The Gray of that period—early 1930s—comes most agreeably alive with the typical Powellian embellishments:

> A plump bespectacled rather unforthcoming Scot, Gray possessed considerable acuteness over and above musical matters. He was comfortably off, married (in the event, several times), with a small neat house in Bayswater facing the Park. His wife at this time (suicide of Heseltine) was Russian, daughter of a musician, her mother having later run away with a cavalry officer, then a Grand Duke (marrying him en troisièmes noces), who was at one brief moment during the Revolution declared the Tsar. That was a side of life in which Gray himself was totally uninterested, as he detested anything that threatened the imposition of conventional social life, even in so exotic a form. He had a capacity for putting away a great deal of whisky without visible effect.
>
> Gray (unfit for military service) had inhabited a Cornish cottage near the Lawrences during the first War. He was (as indicated by his marital career) a thorough-going heterosexual, indeed somewhat tolerant of inversion, but he was fond of telling the story of how, one afternoon in Cornwall, a knock had come on his cottage door. He opened it to find Lawrence standing there. "Gray," asked Lawrence, "how long have you been in love with me?"

Gray was, as H.D. earlier had not credited him, a man of considerable intelligence, with an ironic sense of humor and musical interests in advance of the public.

In 1932 H.D. went into a Chinese restaurant (not the invented Casanova's, but probably one in Soho) where: "A gent walked in stared, stared . . . It was a cross between Gray, Stephen Guest and Osbert Sitwell, this jostled me so that I stared back and cut him . . . I don't know who it was but *it knew me* . . . I finally decided it MIGHT have been Gray; that is the sort of place he might be found in."

It is likely, as H.D. indicates in "Asphodel," that Gray would have stood by her. Yet when she finally went to London to see him, her feelings had turned violently against him. From "Asphodel":

> She hated Cyril Vane intensely. If he felt anything he could say something, not this "the right thing touch—marry—lawyers—noblesse oblige—I am not going to stoop to you you wax angel." And that did it. "Vane said he would 'look after me' but I ran away. I couldn't sit night after night and see him not understanding well bred annunciation . . . We would have had a pretty house, everything I wanted and the romantic scandal but all patched up, poetical and his family so wealthy . . . I couldn't have stood it."

She, not Gray, made the choice.

In 1934 after having seen the vision of "Gray" in the Chinese restaurant, H.D. wrote to Gray:

> Would it be possible to see you? I did some work with Freud . . . In Vienna, some time ago—and lately, have felt so happy and rather triumphant toward fate and all that. I mean it would not only be laying old ghosts but it would be such fun now to talk about old Lorenzo—god rest his soul—and the others. I saw none of them, after! But, yes, Brigit and R.A. once more in Paris! But that was enough! I would like to give you tea or early sherry in my flat, if you could spare me an hour. Or if you prefer, I would meet you somewhere for tea or dinner.
>
> I don't suppose you would recognize me—save by my inches—I am fifty next September. Cornwall has always remained a dream, for which I deeply thank you! It linked up with a rare experience in a Greek island, circa 1920.
>
> I have read your Sibelius etc. with great interest.
>
> Yrs.
"Perzon"
>
> I am still: Mrs. H.D. Aldington

Had she been given the opportunity to read his autobiography, then unwritten, with his own revelations of his uncharitable attitudes toward mankind in general, and in particular to those who had caused him distress, she would never have expected him to answer this letter. Nor did he.

Aldington was conscripted in 1916. (It is difficult to follow his movements, except through his correspondence, as he does not give specific dates in his autobiography of his service in the army.) By then the regular army of professionals was reduced almost entirely by death or wounds. Aldington was able to postpone combat duty until January 1917, when he went over to France with the BEF (British Expeditionary Force) until April 1917. He was returned to Litchfield for training as a noncommissioned officer. By 1918 most of the conscripts had either been killed or wounded. From June to October 1918 he was again with the BEF in France, until he was demobilized in December of 1918, or January of 1919. In four years of combat each belligerent had largely run out of its original manpower. No conscript army had the strength or morale to fight more than four years. The Germans, who had earlier thrown in more manpower, were fought out. The British lasted longer, because they didn't get started until 1916. Aldington, however he maneuvered his actual combat duty, was one of the miraculous few to survive.

While H.D. was at Bosigran (the extant letters begin in early May of 1918), she had been writing to Aldington in France and receiving passionate letters from him. She also received checks from his army pay. It was H.D. whom he worshiped. She was his "Astraea," the daughter of Zeus and Themis, elevated to the heavens, where she became the star Virgo.

"I love you, but I desire l'autre," is a theme of his letters. This being so, he promised to give up Arabella; he was honest enough to confess he still cared for and desired her. Envious of "Grey" (*sic*), he told her she would be silly to believe their love could ever be destroyed by Gray. Aldington's dream of her was as his beloved in "a clean house surrounded by flowers and working at her Greek." Very nearly the words she would have chosen. He advised her not to stay in Cornwall too long, even if Gray "could give you sanity from that marmoreal calm of his."

He pities himself as one whose youth had been obliterated by war. His wounds were not from shrapnel; they were emotional. He would claim that he suffered from nightmares for years.

Aldington depended on the letters from H.D. to help keep alive the creative flame. She wrote him frequently from that elevated, creative world he so missed. He was a literary man who had been forced to abandon his species. Yet the war that separated them had given him a perspective on their conflicting natures. "There is a side of me which, as you know, goes hankering after unredeemed sensualism; and there is a part of you which is always seeking something finer and more spirited than me." He knew that she had a passionate sexual side; he had proof of it. He believed, however, that he had a moral obligation to Arabella, who if betrayed might become a "fallen woman." There is much conscientious dissecting of love and sex in these letters. H.D. must have made him feel very guilty for his quite natural passions. And he generously wrote her that "damn it, Dooley, I believe in women having all the lovers they want if they're in love with them." Boy or girl, he had added. Aldington understood better than anyone what Frances had meant to H.D. He would never taunt her with her lesbian loves.

The early faun reappears in several of the letters. Poets had always attached themselves to the faun, particularly in an era of Hellenic worship. Havelock Ellis liked to think of himself as a faun. And earlier, Nathaniel Hawthorne had written: ". . . the faun is a natural and delightful link between human and brute life, with something of a divine character intermingled." Now Aldington was writing that "he never never, NEVER forgets her. When the faun is free again she will love him as she used to . . . you see sometimes the faun kids himself he's dead and sometimes the Dryad kids herself she's dead," he ends wistfully. (In "Asphodel," her autobiographical story, which includes the period of Aldington's war letters, H.D. wrote: "People didn't call her Dryad. She had been Dryad in the old days.") Later he would write that he was not going to see Arabella again, that he would never have another mistress. Poor Aldington, he was always having to apologize for his sexual adventures. It was almost as if it were not quite the gentlemanly thing to do, to like sex. (Aldington would likewise be apologizing for the lowly social status of his mother. H.D. had been quite nasty in "Paint It Today" in pointing out the social distinction between Aldington and Gray.)

While the fauns and dryads were splashing in the Attic streams, while Aldington watched the heavens for the appearance of his Astraea, H.D., the real H.D. this time wrote from Bosigran in August that she was pregnant. Aldington accepted the news with surprising calm. He did not criticize or condemn her. At first he naturally believed that she would now continue to live with Gray. When he discovered this was not so, he reassured her by telling her he would accept and provide for the child. For a time, he became rather happy. He also offered practical advice. He told her to go to see a doctor to confirm her suspicions, as she had not yet been to one. He then changed his mind. He did not really want her to have the child. He had begun to worry if Gray would separate him from H.D., now that he had paternal rights. She must consult Brigit, an expert in these matters. He even suggested a method whereby she might abort herself.

Despite all the furor of the pregnancy, they continued to discuss their work and to make plans for the translations. He was concerned that he could never make up the time he had lost in the harness of war. While denying that there ever could be a future, he proved himself to be quite tough-minded and concerned about his literary career. In a letter to H.D. in July that reveals how dependent they were upon one another, he had written:

> Are you in a cul-de-sac? You have gathered your garland of sea-flowers, exquisite, unique; but another such garland, however exquisite will have lost something, the novelty which is a condition of beauty. You destroyed your work of a year; perhaps rightly, I don't know. You had some poems which were fine and vivid and inevitable, though bitter. But how are you going on now? Prose? No! You have so precise, so wonderful an instrument—why abandon it to fashion another perhaps less perfect? You have, I think, either to choose pure song or else drama or else Mallarméan subtlety. Which will you choose?

With her he is a judicious critic. Why indeed should she have left off writing poetry, she, the best of the Imagists? But he wanted her to push harder. Compared with her poetry her prose was formless and flighty at this time. Later she would find her form, and write in a stream-of-consciousness manner suited to her temperament. He was right, also, in suggesting the drama. It would be Greek drama, he supposed—translations.

He corrected her translation of *Hippolytus*. When she sent him the poem "Hymen" in December of that year, he told her that it was "delicate and fragile, with an air of much less maturity than your earlier work in *Sea Garden*. This is a most exquisite child-like quality in the earlier songs and the more sensual tone of the last three strikes me as a totally different impulse." (Later he would comprehend why his criticism was so apt, when he had met the real-life subject of "Hymen.") He wasn't interested, he told her, in the prose descriptions between the songs—a technique she would continue to use—but they should be left in when she sent the poem to Harriet Weaver for *The Egoist*, as Weaver would have to pay her more!

Aldington was not only useful to her writing, he was necessary. Throughout H.D.'s manuscripts and letters the reader does battle with her spelling and punctuation. Aldington adjured her *never* to submit her manuscript until he had been over it. He reminded her that she made careless errors in both spelling and syntax. With a blessing he adds: "H.D. cannot afford to be anything less than perfection."

"Sea Heroes" he believes to be the best of the poems she has sent him, although it needed a little working over. "Simaetha" is quite good! "Thetis" is a little weak in spots.

Thus far he was willing to go in her poetry—but what now about her life? Between August and December of 1918 Aldington begins to make his exit; he starts to equivocate. Having had such an intense and intimate correspondence with Aldington all the time she had been at Bosigran, H.D. had believed she understood his various moods. His first letter after the new year of 1919 surprised and unnerved her. He disavowed any plan to help her. He told her she must take care of herself and the child without relying upon him at all. He saw himself as helpless and poor. Worse, although he was being demobilized, he announced that he would not be able to visit her before she went to the hospital. She must plan her own life without depending on him. She had always known he was poor, that he had no money to take care of her and a child. What a blow! It was he who had sent her a blank check in case of his death in war. It had been he who had insisted she receive his army pay. She was his acknowledged wife. Now he planned to live, not die. For all he cared, *she* might become the ghost.

News travels faster in war than in peace. What had happened to bring about this change in the formerly sympathetic Aldington? Having been informed of a new presence on the scene, a powerful and wealthy one, Aldington must have decided to let H.D. pay her own way. H.D. now had her "l'autre." Aldington, having promised, perhaps whimsically, to forswear all women for H.D., may have believed it was his turn to be the abused one. At least that was the role he could make believable. In all fairness to him, the appearance and importance of "l'autre" can be offered as an explanation for his behavior.

PART TWO

We two remain:
yet by what miracle,
searching within the tangles of my brain,
I ask again,
have we two met within
this maze of daedal paths
in-wound mid grievous stone,
where once I stood alone?

"We Two" (*Heliodora
and Other Poems*)

"If she had friendship ever it would
be immediate, inevitable . . . Simply a
placing together of two lives."

Bryher, *Two Selves*

CHAPTER TEN

"I Met the Bryher Girl in Cornwall"

"L'autre," the other, who comes between us, was to be a young woman of twenty-four who called herself Bryher. She had adopted this name from one of her beloved Scilly Islands and later would take it by deed poll. She describes her meeting with H.D. in her autobiography, *The Heart to Artemis*. Having read Amy Lowell's *Tendencies in Modern American Poetry*, she was introduced to the Imagists, and she especially admired the poetry of H.D. She memorized all of *Sea Garden*. Determined to meet the poet, she asked Clement Shorter, who married her friend Doris Banfield and was the editor of *The Sphere*, a magazine owned by her father, if he could discover where H.D. lived. Shorter's friend May Sinclair supplied the address, explaining that "H.D." was a woman. Bryher immediately wrote H.D. asking if she might visit her. When H.D. read Bryher's letter she later told her that she thought it had been written by an elderly schoolmistress! Bryher was conveniently nearby, visiting her school friend Doris in Cornwall, so H.D. asked her over for tea. That was on July 17, 1918, and Cecil Gray was in London.

Bryher has written that she first recognized the house from the French edition books propped against the windowsill. The door opened and there stood the poet with her Grecian head. Bryher claimed that H.D.'s first words were to ask if she knew what a puffin was. Of course Bryher could describe a puffin as a sea parrot found in the Scillies. The scene of the beautiful woman asking about a seabird that only an expert on the Scillies like Bryher could describe sounds like a novelistic method of moving the dialogue to its purposeful conclusion.[1] Puffins or no puffin, Bryher had found the heroine for whom she had been searching; here, literally, stood the woman of her dreams. Bryher's first audacious move would be to ask if H.D. would go with her to the Scillies.

The proposed trip was an opening wedge for future and increasingly more intimate meetings. Bryher was unruffled by H.D.'s admission that she was expecting a child. In the minds of monarchs, such events would take care of themselves. More important was that Bryher be allowed to spin out her travelogues: first they would go to the Scillies, then Greece,

---

[1] In her youthful book *Two Selves* Bryher writes that H.D.'s first words were "I was waiting for you to come."

then America. This lonely young woman, if given her way, would make ambitious plans for a lifetime with H.D.

And H.D., what did she make of all this? "All this" could become a last-minute rescue. She soon realized Bryher was in love with her. "So madly, it is terrible," she confessed to Cournos. "No man has ever cared for me like that." Yet there was something repellent about this concentrated love that tended to make H.D. both cautious and fearful. In the unpublished "Asphodel" (1921–22), H.D. is at her most clairvoyant in writing of the young Bryher:

> . . . semitic little face, clear skin, wide brows, hair twisted in two enormous coils and that odd commanding look and that certainty and that lack of understanding and that utter understanding that goes with certain types of people . . . people who were simple and domineering never having known anything of scraping, of terror at the wrong thing, of the wrong people. Hard face, child face, how can you be so hard? The smile froze across the white large teeth and the white perfect teeth showed the lips as hard, coral red, clear, beautifully cut and yet the child was not beautiful. Each feature was marked with distinction, with some rare clarity . . .
> SHE WAS NOT TO BE LEFT DRIFT AND MERGE INTO THE FOREST . . . SMILE AND PLUNGE BACK HOME INTO YOUR LITTLE FOREST AND SAY I'LL NEVER SEE THAT HATEFUL HARD CHILD AGAIN HARD PEDANTIC AND SO DOMINEERING FOR YOU ARE DOOMED . . . [my emphasis]

H.D. in "Asphodel" gives her version of one of their early meetings. She writes of a letter Bryher supposedly sent her: "It meant so much to me to see you yesterday. I'll send the car over to fetch you . . . I never met anyone who knew the Greek Anthology . . . it meant everything to talk that day of Mallarmé . . . I am so very lonely."

H.D. goes to tea at Bryher's house. She is impressed. "The great world stretched before her" in the luxurious house, the car with its fur rug. This toasty, wealthy world was offered to her, yet H.D. is troubled not by it, but by Bryher's worship of the intellect. "She couldn't stand the perils of the intellect. She wanted to escape the mind and all it stood for. *She wanted to take from this girl not give to her.*" There H.D. would honestly state the dilemma that faced her all her life. The answer, needless to say, was that H.D. could never take without giving, try though she might. It was soon made clear to H.D. that like it or not she would have to give Bryher the strength to go on living. Bryher threatened suicide. It wasn't fair, as H.D. wrote, to talk of suicide when the baby was getting ready to be born.* She left Cornwall for a brief stay in Hampstead. Next she fled to an old friend in Bucks (Buckingham), Daphne Bax, where she and Aldington had first met the Lawrences and Murrys. A cottage next door was vacant. It was called Peace, and H.D. rented it.

*For H.D.'s attitude toward Bryher see "I Said" (1919), now published for the first time in *Collected Poems 1912–1944*, edited by Louis L. Martz, New Directions, New York, 1984.

By coincidence, Margaret Snively, now married and with a husband in the armed forces, was in England. H.D. asked her to share the house at Speen, along with Margaret's year-old daughter. H.D. kept the house until the beginning of 1919. It was at Peace she and Margaret learned the war had ended.

She had gone to Bucks to think things over. Then Bryher's letters began to show signs of helplessness. She had begun to mistrust the plans she and H.D. had made. H.D. herself scarcely believed in those plans. Bryher with all her gifts and her new love, her will and money, had begun to believe that she would always be a prisoner of her family. The household she had grown up in was Victorian in its demands on its daughter and an insistence on her dependence. Hadn't her father earned all that money for his "Dolly," as he reminded her? Bryher, despite her zest for the contemporary, her historical knowledge, and prescience of the future, for these family reasons and background, remained conventionally a Victorian. The bonds would be tougher than she had supposed.

Bryher best describes herself before the meeting with H.D. in *Two Selves*, published by Contact editions in 1923. "Two selves. The one complete enough, chaffed by every restriction, planning to reform the world, planning to know and experience everything there was to know and experience. But the other self . . . blown apart with every wind . . . it was painfully inadequate a covering."

Here is where H.D. shows her fortitude. It would happen again. She must be stronger and more willful than Bryher. Anxious and humiliated as she was, having believed for a hopeful moment that she had found another protector, discovering weakness where she had expected strength, still H.D. rushed in. She returned from the country to London. Without being conscious of the magnetic line, she now crossed it and threw in her lot with Bryher. She began to encourage her; to give her hope. H.D. was a strong rescuer. She would expect help when her turn came, yet now she managed to find courage in the last months of her pregnancy to prevent Bryher from going under. She asked Bryher to her shabby rooms in London. She wrote constantly to her reminding her of the world they would share. Work and travel! She began to revel in plans that formerly had belonged to Bryher.

What is characteristic of H.D. and remained so throughout her life is that her creativity actually accelerated during periods of trial. Again she was working on *Ion*. "I suppose Euripides is a good father image," she joked. She was encouraging Bryher to translate Callimachus. Aldington, scenting a possible patron, decided Bryher should be included in the Poets' Translation Series. H.D. showed Bryher back copies of *The Egoist* containing former translations and suggested she translate "Six Sea Poems" by Antipater of Sidon.

The poems H.D. had sent to Aldington—"Leda," "Lethe," "Song," the most passionate and erotic of her early poems—were written during the difficult period at Cornwall. "Simaetha," which followed in 1919 and was written in Bucks, came at another difficult time, either shortly before or after the birth of Perdita, when Aldington had decided to free himself of her troubles. In this poem (based on a poem by Theocritus) she pictures Simaetha betrayed by her lover, crouching by the fire of laurel leaves. The girl chants, "Laurel leaf, O fruited / branch of bay, / burn, burn away / thought memory and hurt!" Simaetha or H.D., may have been deserted, but the poet has her laurel leaves to chase away the human hurt! (That Christmas of 1918 in Bucks they had a laurel tree.)

All throughout 1918–19 she had been writing her long poem "Hymen," which may be a "wedding song" for Bryher, child bride of the band of Artemis, reluctant at the marriage rites. Finally her book called *Hymen*, containing "Leda," "Song," and "Simaetha" along with the title poem, was published in 1921 by the Egoist Press and subsidized by Bryher, as were the Poets' Translation Series. The powerful "Eurydice" was published earlier, as were "The God" and "Lethe." These poems would be contained in her first *Collected Poems*, published by Boni & Liveright in 1925.

After her first book, *Sea Garden* (1916), early springlike, the poems that followed are more passionate, privately erotic. They are less "perfect" in the Imagist sense. They remain still, but they are not icy. She is selective, but not so inhibited.

There was another side to her character. H.D. was not all Parnassus and Delphi. In November 1919, after the birth of the child, H.D. wrote a letter to Cournos that shows she may have felt guilty at the time she began a fresh relationship on the ruins of the old. She may have wished to excuse that element of opportunism she had already showed in rushing off with Gray. She sent her old admirer views of herself as a self-sacrificing woman who had thrown in her lot with Bryher because Bryher had threatened suicide. She then explained to Cournos that Bryher was a tragic personality who needed H.D. In case he had thought otherwise, living with "l'autre" could be hell.

> I have again and again told her that I cannot stand the strain of living with her and yet I cannot leave her. She helps in many ways but I want freedom and if this tie becomes too much, I must leave her . . . But I am not a philanthropist. I must have my freedom first and if the strain becomes too great, I shall just chuck her and the maddening problem of her life. There may be a doom over her and I may be only hurting myself in trying to help her . . . She seems possessed at times with a daemon of spirit outside herself. One side of her is so childlike that I am moved I must be tender, then this other thing comes.

Earlier, in September 1918, in one of her more careful letters to Amy Lowell, H.D. had answered Amy's question as to who was the person who had embarrassingly written so laudatory an appreciation of her poetry:

I met the Bryher girl in Cornwall. She is about twenty-four. I think, too shows great promise. She simply worships your work. I go to see her this afternoon and will write you further of her. She comes from wealthy people. Do not tell her I told you as she is very queer about it. But her wealth could make no difference to *you,* nor to any real friend. She imagines any kindness and interest comes *only* because her father is reputed "the richest man in England." Of course one can understand, but if she is good at all, her father's position will not hurt her. (Her name is not Bryher.) Of course I did not know this when I met her, and my interest was genuine. She wants to meet people who write . . .

Amy Lowell's answer is quintessentially Boston:

To me came your good letter of what date I cannot say, since you never date them, but the one in which you tell me that Winifred Bryher is not Winifred Bryher. My dear what a bomb shell! Who on earth is she? My mind does not run easily in the purlieus of "richest men." I have not the ghost of an idea who is rich in England and who is poor. I had an idea that the Duke of Westminster was the richest man in England, but from what you say I can hardly suppose that Winifred is a young peeress. The only things that I can think of are a cosmopolitan banker and a large, native, good-natured brewer.

But in either case, I cannot see what that has to do with Winifred, and I regard her self-consciousness on the subject as extremely foolish, and I would write and tell her so, only you tell me that I must not mention it to her.

It is a handicap to be even well off. My father was not the "richest" anywhere, and yet I have had enough trouble in getting people to realize that I may be a decent poet even if I am not starving in a garret.[2]

Amy Lowell then promised to be as kind to Bryher as possible when she visited America. And Amy did keep her promise, although she never succeeded in liking Bryher. Shortly after her correspondence with H.D., along came a letter to Amy in December 1918 from D. H. Lawrence that must have confused her. He wrote that when he was in London he had seen Aldington on leave looking fit and learned that H.D. was expecting another child. "I hope she will be all right. Perhaps she can get more settled, for her nerves are very shaken and perhaps the child will soothe her and steady her. I hope it will."

H.D. had not said anything to Amy about the expected child, or her separation from Aldington, so naturally Amy would have assumed from

[2] Winifred Bryher, *Amy Lowell: A Critical Appreciation* (see bibliography).

Lawrence's letter that the child was Aldington's—evidence of a more proper relationship than that questionable one of H.D.'s with the little heiress.

July 17, 1918, was the date on which Bryher and H.D. had first met. Each time it came round they would celebrate it as an anniversary. If separated they would make certain that a special letter arrived. H.D.'s nearly always included the phrase "Every year I thank you for saving me and Pup [her child] . . ."

H.D. had been living in a pension in Ealing (recommended by Margaret Snively Pratt) to be near the nursing home (in England a nursing home is a small private hospital) she planned to enter later for the birth of her child. One day Bryher arrived and found her ill. It was pneumonia. H.D. was a near casualty of that epidemic of 1919 that claimed nearly as many victims as had the war. There was a frantic overworked doctor and no nurse. Bryher, unprepared for an emergency, at first did not recognize the danger. She talked with H.D., gave her flowers, and then left for her home. The next day, and Bryher said that she would never forgive herself for not having acted sooner, she found H.D. much worse. The landlady accosted her outside the room and asked her who would pay for the funeral. Bryher went into action. With the aid of the faithful Brigit, she had H.D. moved to St. Faith's nursing home. She hired a private nurse. H.D. rallied.

"If I could walk to Delphi," H.D. had whispered to Bryher in her account of this episode in "Asphodel," "I should be healed."

"I will take you to Greece as soon as you are well," promised Bryher.

The child was born March 31, 1919. She was named Frances (after Frances Gregg) Perdita, to be known as Perdita. With her mane of heavy black hair and her slightly upward-tilted eyes she resembled her father, Cecil Gray. She was not "Grecian," like H.D. More like a "Japanese Empress," they would say.

Perdita was the "lost" daughter of Hermione the Queen in *The Winter's Tale*. How H.D. tread upon her traces! Shakespeare's Perdita, as hostess for her foster father at a sheep-shearing festival, welcomes her guests with flowers. She apologizes for not giving them the flowers of spring such as

> . . . daffodils,
> That come before the swallow dares, and take
> The Winds of March with Beauty.

(It was a swallow that had flown into H.D.'s room in Cornwall to decide the fate of the embryo.) Perdita then tells her guests the sad story of Persephone, kidnapped by Pluto while picking lilies and taken captive to the underworld ("Eurydice").

The name "Perdita" might also be that which is "lost"—the former stillborn child—and found again. It is a lovely name with its overcast of sadness lightened by hope.

The wayward "relative," Ezra Pound, showed up at the nursing home and announced that he wished the child were his. Dorothy Pound gave the baby a coral chain.

Lawrence wrote to Koteliansky: "Hilda's child born last week. A girl. Gray behaving wretchedly. Aldington marvelous." (Harry T. Moore, who edited the Lawrence letters, noted innocently that the child's name was Gray.)

If H.D.'s account (in "Asphodel") of the behavior of Aldington is at all accurate, he did act like the "cad" whom Frances Gregg had so disliked, although his actions do not in any way parallel his respect for H.D. The situation in which she found herself could delicately be called "distressed." Aldington would reason that her behavior had not been predictable. She had been thoughtless and careless and it was up to her to face the music. He certainly was aware that H.D. was not helpless, that Bryher and Brigit would take care of her. In particular, and this would always be a concern of Aldington's, he knew that "the bloated billionaire" would provide funds for H.D. The least that can be said is that he showed no noblesse oblige. Let her take the consequences.

Here it is necessary to rely on H.D.'s version in "Asphodel." She wrote that he turned up at the nursing home. He led her to believe that he was prepared to assume responsibility. "'Astraea, come with me,' he beckoned with his cane." Off she went with him to the Hotel Littoral in Soho. When there, he demanded that she register the baby, but not under his name. He threatened to sue her for divorce as an adulteress. There they are in that shabby hotel in Soho. The adamant Aldington putting forth his arguments, and the still weak H.D. hearing him out in horror. He told her that he cared for Dorothy Yorke. She countered with the threat of suing him first for adultery. But why had she gone with him? He must have exercised some persuasiveness over her. He must have held out some hope. As the battle raged she accused him of permitting her rich friends to pay for the expenses of the nursing home; then he had lured her to the hotel, taking her away from her friends.

The probability was that she desperately needed a father's name for the child. Not only a father's name, it should correspond to that of her husband. She wanted no shred of illegitimacy to adhere to her child. This must have been her gamble. And Aldington, of course, knew this. He was also angry. The real question remains: Did she want him back? Anyway, she outdid him. She registered the child, as she legally could, under the name of "Aldington." Richard then telephoned Bryher from the hotel and told her (or so H.D. wrote to Cournos) that "Hilda must get out of here at once."

From this time dates the name "Cuthbert," which she and Bryher would privately call Aldington. In the Great War one of the meanings of "Cuthbert" was a "white rabbit" dressed in the bright blue uniform of wounded soldiers with white shirt and tie. Cuthberts were cowards, malingerers. H.D. succeeded in degrading Aldington; the figure of the Roman soldier would no longer dominate.

After first seeking refuge in Pound's old flat at Holland Place Chambers, H.D. returned to Bryher. "Asphodel" concludes with a conversation in which H.D. tells Bryher that she will make a bargain with her. Bryher's share of the bargain is never again to threaten suicide. H.D. will then give her something. Here H.D. confesses that Aldington is not really the father of the child. This information Bryher receives joyfully. She tells H.D. she hates Aldington. Then H.D. announces her share of the bargain, which is to offer Bryher a chance to bring up the child.

"I want you to promise me to grow up and take care of the little girl."

"Do you mean—do you mean . . . for my own . . . exactly like a puppy?"

"*Exactly* . . . like a puppy."

Bryher, or Annie Winifred Ellerman, or "Dolly," as her father called her (if ever there were a misnomer), was the daughter of Sir John Ellerman (1862–1933), one of England's great shipping magnates. A poor boy, probably of Jewish origins (as Bryher reported to Robert McAlmon), Ellerman was born in Hull, a center for Jewish immigration from the Continent, and given his start by Sir Frederick Leyland, the prosperous Liverpool shipowner and patron of Whistler.[3] By 1892 Ellerman had joined the board of Leyland, and shortly thereafter he became chairman. By 1900 he had acquired for himself the Mediterranean services of Leyland's after bringing off a complicated deal with John Pierpont Morgan. In 1901 he founded the Ellerman Lines, and quickly absorbed many other lines, including Wilson's of Hull in 1916. By this time he had

[3] This was the same Leyland who had commissioned Whistler to decorate the dining room in his mansion under construction at Prince's Gate, Hyde Park. Leyland, at much expense, had purchased aged Cordoba Spanish leather brought to England by Catherine of Aragon. Whistler treated this mellow leather capriciously as a canvas for what became a peacock's paradise. An enraged Leyland discovered peacocks with tails spread covering the entire walls, except for one wall on which Whistler had hung one of his "harmonies." In blue and gold, it is a portrait Whistler called "La Princesse du Pays Porcelaine." She faces the opposite wall on which is placed Leyland's exquisite collection of blue and white china, which set a mode for the era. This room has been transported intact by the late Charles Freer to the Freer Gallery of Art in Washington, D.C., where it delights all admirers of Whistler.

For the interest of researchers into the Stephen-Duckworth family, their relative Thoby Prinsep, Leyland's grandson, appears in Ellerman's will, and took over the management of Ellerman Lines after Sir John's death.

enlarged his fortune by joining Lord Northcliffe as a major shareholder in *The Times* of London and in Associated Newspapers. Later he took over the bulk of the shares of a number of London magazines, including *The Illustrated London News, The Sphere, The Tatler,* and *The Sketch.*

While steadily moving up in the shipping world, Ellerman had met (and as far as the world was concerned, married) Hannah Glover, a woman from the lower classes, unmannered, and without aggressive pretensions. Bryher was born in 1894, but the Ellermans did not in fact legally marry until the birth of their son John in 1909. After young John was born, Sir John offered to legitimize Bryher, but rather staunchly, albeit unreasonably, she declined. She already knew her worth to her family, but she would have received more of her share of the wealth had she been legitimized. She was fanatically devoted to her father and very much loved her rather silly and kindly deaf mother. The Ellermans had delayed marrying, at a guess, because of a recalcitrant former husband in the background. Perhaps Sir John bought him off, although Victoria McAlmon, Bryher's sister-in-law, declared that the marriage took place upon the convenient death of Mr. Glover.

The Ellermans lived in an enormous house at 1 South Audley Street in Mayfair. They summered at respectable Eastbourne. That seaside town may have had some of its aura diminished by harboring Karl Marx and Friedrich Engels, but Sir John was unaware of this, his ideas of capital being the dispersal of the largest shipping fleet in England over the sea-lanes of the world. The house at 1 South Audley Street was equipped with footmen and maids, and Sir John's rather banal collection of European paintings. Although regal, it was a sadly empty house. The Ellermans appear to have had no friends other than business acquaintances, and Hannah, with few social graces, enjoyed afternoon matinees—to the subsequent pleasure of Perdita, who would later accompany her to see and hear such glamorous figures as Ivor Novello. The usual poor relatives were also missing.

Bryher grew up intelligent, rebellious, and furious that she was not a boy. She wanted to inherit and direct her father's business. She knew she could run it and she was probably correct in this assumption, as later she would subscribe to five financial papers and move the money pawns as wisely as any broker. Her father would have liked his Dolly to run the business, but he explained to her that women weren't permitted by men into their clubs or allowed to sit in on their business transactions. "Outsiders" such as women would be forced to play a losing game. They were a close pair and Bryher admired her father not only for his business acumen and his kindness to her, but his rating as a noted Alpinist. Although she spent much of her life in Switzerland (at the suggestion of her father, obviously for tax purposes) she never followed him on the Alpine slopes.

The family was thus self-centered, overly protective of the son, and proud of their prodigious daughter. During the Great War Sir John had been given an important position in the government, probably in supplies, as his ships could be deployed all over the world. He frequently discussed the war with his daughter. He emphasized that she must never forget "it had been a very near thing." His opposite number in Germany had committed suicide. Her father's post impressed Bryher. Indirectly, it led to her own interest in wars of the past and the probable future. Although young during the Great War, she was haunted by its disaster, as was H.D. Concern over that war led to her forecast of World War II.

She and H.D. were equally admiring of their fathers' accomplishments. H.D. would repeat, "My father, the Astronomer." To which Bryher might reply, "My father, the Alpinist." She would have thought it unnecessary to add "the millionaire."

As Bryher grew older she found much pleasure in discussing business with her accountants, legal maneuvers with her lawyers, money with her bankers, and manipulating her stock on the market. Like many of the exceptionally rich, she was a scrupulous counter of pennies. How shocked she would be on a visit to New York to find the Waldorf had charged her ten dollars a day! Her personal tastes were simple. Although at South Audley Street she was forced to undergo the rigors of a French bedroom with its draperies, chaise, and satins, when she had her own house she occupied a tiny room like a third-class ship's cabin, hung her clothes on an old-fashioned wooden coat hanger that stood in the center of the room, and slept on a very narrow bed. She preferred nursery food, beef, and cookies. She went to tea shops and never drank alcohol. Yet her husbands would be extravagant, one of them a gourmet, and both alcoholic.

Her extravagance would be in centering her life around H.D. Next would be literature and travel. She had been sent to a girls' school about which she had written a remarkable novel. Despite her articulate criticism of the school, she managed to enjoy it and make several lifelong friendships. One of them was Dorothy Pilley, who became a noted mountaineer and married I. A. Richards. Once a decision had been made by Bryher it was usually for life. She had no interest at all in being or pretending to be a girl. She never learned, for instance, to cook. One of her unconsciously amusing descriptions in a letter to H.D. is about the use of an icebox, a discovery she made in her early forties. Her private dream of herself was that of a cabin boy on one of her father's ships. Dream, indeed. Bryher, to her disgust, was a poor sailor!

In return H.D. gave Bryher the gift of her genius, of her creativity, her temperament, her instability, her sorcery. If she found it necessary to escape from the domination of Bryher, she would always return. She relied on Bryher during her numerous breakdowns. Most of all H.D. helped establish for Bryher the atmosphere she so yearned for, that of the creative life. She wrapped Bryher in an aura of "sharing" the most important—to them—act in the world, far more than the sexual one, the creation of literature. Bryher was pupil, H.D. was teacher. Bryher thought always of H.D. as a *star* shining in an intellectual firmament far removed from her. In truth, Bryher had her own star; her intellect was the stronger of the two. She also had—regardless of the manipulations, the tantrums, the schemes, the need to program everyone's life, and despite her eternal childhood—the good fairy's gift of common sense. The bad fairy had made her a permanent child. Sadly, her capabilities could not prevent her from remaining forever a child in a world of adults.

To compensate she wrote splendid adventure stories. They were historical novels with settings in which a lone boy, faced by danger, would conquer all. There was always a battle and there was always a boy. Bryher's novels are excellent examples of historical fiction upon which children can build their early concepts of history. The pathos was that she believed they were adult books. She could never understand why editors would tell her to put sex in her books so that they would sell. She knew sex existed, but she could not find its place in her novels. There Bryher was wiser than her editors. Her brother's boy adventure stories, which she so loved to read, never had sex in them. Why bother? It was the action that mattered.

What did exist within her was that quality so missing on earth, loyalty. And this in spite of her gift of seeing through people. She was no paragon; from time to time she relished her little excitements, mostly with those women who shared H.D.'s star quality. Amusingly, in her private life she shared a masculine appreciation for pornography.

As long as H.D. lived she was idealized by Bryher as her heroine—which didn't prevent Bryher, as Thornton Wilder observed, "from looking like Napoleon and acting like Napoleon."

Who knows what might have happened if H.D.'s "daemon" had not waved a helpful hand in the direction of Miss Ellerman. Gray might have stepped forward, although one cannot envisage H.D. and Gray together for long. Aldington might have presented more solid terms, but their marriage was doomed. From what is known of H.D.'s life, it is certain that *someone* would have been there to support and protect her. A bright messenger was bound to appear. How extraordinary that it would be the Ellerman girl, Bryher, waved thither by H.D.'s Imagist poems. Bryher had memorized the poem of H.D. that led her to Cornwall.

> I saw the first pear
> as it fell—
> the honey-seeking, golden-banded
> the yellow swarm
> was not more fleet than I
> (spare us from loveliness)

CHAPTER ELEVEN

The Psyche Unraveling

The carefully brought-up daughter of a professor, the admired Aspasia of an elite group of poets, had taken a perilous step when she had left the apparent security of marriage for a lover. She had carried her child under difficult circumstances, and finally she had been rescued from illness and near death by a woman whom she could not officially reward by marriage.

As a survivor she showed little interest in the social and economic plight of women in general. She would always be sympathetic and helpful to a particular woman, but toward a "movement," such as the suffragist cause, there is no evidence of her support. There is one story of hers with a suffragist theme, and that may have been written to please an ardent supporter of the cause, May Sinclair. Specifics, not generalities, were her specialty. She once mentions casually in a letter to Bryher that she had passed a parade of hundreds of protesting "Miriams." She did not include herself. There were in her life no evening gatherings with angry suffragettes, no Emmeline Pankhurst histrionics, parades, or jails. To take it further, H.D. avoided politics of any kind.

H.D. had behaved the same way toward Imagism. She had left its politics and propaganda to Ezra Pound, and after him to Amy Lowell. The banner she waved was her own poetry, and after that the creative efforts of those dear to her. For those whom she loved she would do anything; toward the advancement of womankind she would spare herself.

Bryher, whom one would expect to be ardently suffragist, showed an equal disinterest in the movement. Her reasons were different. She firmly believed that only through education could the lot of women be improved. Laws and votes were not sufficient, until women had been educated through vocational programs and training to find jobs that would provide them an adequate living. She admired women who operated on their own, like Adrienne Monnier and Sylvia Beach, who had opened bookstores in Paris. She preferred the anonymous women who ran tea shops on a survival basis. Later she would establish funds for the support of these courageous women. It was the Miriams of the world, the ill-paid women like the Miriam of Dorothy Richardson's *Pilgrimage*, typists and dental assistants, occupying bed-sitters and eating in bun shops, who were the heroines of this wealthy woman. Bryher was the pragmatist, H.D. the dreamer. Neither joined the suffragist movement.

The immediacy of Bryher's problem with her parents, and consequently her own plight, troubled H.D. in the spring of 1919. Between them Bryher and H.D. decided that H.D. would present herself to the Ellermans as a chaperone, an older woman who could safely lead Bryher out into the world. They counted on Lady Ellerman's ignorance of any more tangible relationship. Lady Ellerman was not sophisticated, but she had survived her share of the tussles of the world and they had left her not precisely an innocent. There would be little empathy between Lady E. and H.D. On the contrary, Bryher's mother made H.D. extremely apprehensive. Her social fears trebled when she entered South Audley Street. She worried about her clothes, her conversation. Why poor Hannah Glover should cause so much embarrassment to the proud, socially more adept H.D. was a mystery. It would always be so, this awkwardness in front of a woman who may now have been wearing the riches of the world, but who had originated in surroundings far humbler than a Pennsylvania professor's house. H.D. usually took a tranquilizer before appearing at the Ellerman house. Her apprehensions may have sprung from guilt. She admitted to Bryher that she was always acting when she was with the Ellermans; her role was a respectable matron, and she hated the pretense and could only maintain it for a short while.

Lady Ellerman liked the little girl. Perdita's childhood was a series of visits to the household. She even became an attendant to the woman, a sort of page setting out in the Daimler to view London with her. Bryher's mother may have been conscious of obscure currents beneath the facade; deaf as she was, it was she who ran the show. For all the modesty of her own upbringing, she bore her riches well. She was tolerant, because she loved her daughter and wished her well on her adventures. Surprisingly, she would give her moral and financial support in the more complex spheres of literature and music.

Sir John was so taken up with the numerous concerns of his empire, with his chats with his little girl when he relayed information to her about finance and its games, that to him H.D. was no encumbrance. Like most tycoons, a remoteness had descended upon him into which only Bryher in the guise of an associate might intrude. Her plea for independence seems not to have penetrated; he liked having her around. Sir John—and this trait Bryher inherited—was innocent of vistas beyond his own complications.

Bryher's tantrums or H.D.'s forced charms may have done it, but somehow permission was granted for them to go off to the Scillies. Next it was up to H.D. to adjust to separation from Perdita. Any qualms she may have expressed—and she did—were hushed by Bryher, who insisted that for H.D. to devote herself to a child would be a loss to literature.

Cot and babe indeed! What about her Greeks? There was a pathetic appeal, a brief one, from H.D., who murmured that Perdita was becoming such a dear little baby. Then off went the child to board at the Norland Nursery in South Kensington with peerless Brigit promising to look in on her. The women then set off to the Scillies. This may not have been the primal break from the Ellermans, yet it was a fissure that would be widened.

To the uninitiated the Scillies offer nothing spectacular. It is always a surprise to learn that for some the short voyage from Cornwall to the Scillies conveys the same thrill as that of an approach to an exotic island. Domestic gardens raising flowers for the early London market mount guard over the wildness of the sea—rain and gales, shipwrecks and sturdy islanders. Is it the first glorious separation from the mainland? Different rules, skies, sea, a taste of freedom? Bryher first had visited the Scillies with Doris Banfield, her schoolgirl friend who came from Cornwall. They were Bryher's own discovery and they separated her from a family who had taken her off to Greece or Egypt. The Scillies were her youthful Arcadia, from whence came the name that initiated her entrance into a world of her making; naturally she wanted to share the islands with H.D.

On this first jaunt together they began to assort their patterns, establish work habits. Here was an admirer, a worshiper, who insisted on the importance of the poet being separated from any intrusion from herself or the outside world. Bryher proved then that she would not compete, but content herself with encouragement. She would nourish H.D.'s creativity and fend off invaders. A guardian, yet not a housekeeper; Bryher would never content herself with a merely passive role. H.D. would thus avoid the subtle offensive of the passive protestor. What more could an artist ask? H.D. had announced that although she had an unquestioning belief in her own work, the mechanisms of the outside world terrified her. Bryher determined to protect her in every practical way: the publican would be kept at bay; the artist would perform. There is, however, always ice to be crossed in such commitments. Here the ice was Bryher's irritating emphasis on performance.

Once only did Bryher err. She interrupted H.D. while she was writing. H.D. put her hand on the sheet of paper and glared at Bryher. Then she tore the paper into pieces and coldly told Bryher that never must she interrupt her while she was at work. Bryher respected such discipline. She never forgot the scene, nor its admonition. She recalled it in an interview at her home in Switzerland in 1978.

What H.D. really felt about the Scillies isn't known. She never returned. She saw scores of puffins, a matter-of-fact bird that lays just one single white egg and has white puffed cheeks. It was in the Scillies, divided by mist and sunlight, that H.D. experienced what she described to Freud as the "sense of being in a bell jar."

> We were in the little room that Bryher had taken for our study when I felt this impulse to "let go" into a sort of balloon, or diving bell . . . that seemed to hover over me . . . When I tried to explain this to Bryher and told her it might be something sinister or dangerous, she said, "No, no, it is the most wonderful thing I ever heard of. Let it come . . ." I felt I was safe but seeing things as through water. I felt the double-globe come and go and I could have dismissed it at once and probably would have, if I had been alone. But it would not have happened, I imagine, if I had been alone.

She was covered from head to waist by the top of the jar, where she floated; the bottom of the jar covered the rest of her. Thus she was disembodied, floating in a protected space. This scene never left her. After hearing her out, Freud asked her, "Are you lonely?" She quickly denied it.

These two women living together for the first time, testing themselves, experimenting, receiving and giving love were passing through a tense period of trial. Each enveloped the other. Bryher was one part of the bell jar, and H.D. the other. They had isolated their relationship until it had become a lid that covered them. H.D. later described her peculiar mental state at that time in the Scillies as like being under a cap, under enormous tension and strain.

H.D. had passed through so much trial before and after the birth of Perdita that she could scarcely have recovered from that experience. Also, she now recognized that she had broken with her past. She was, indeed, "floating." She must have been for many weeks in a state of hyperconsciousness, and thus extremely vulnerable to any threat to normal life. It must be admitted, though, that this state would be a more usual one to her than to others.

H.D. and Bryher created around themselves such an intenseness it was difficult for others to break in. Bryher, in particular, never seems to have reveled in what Roland Barthes has called the right "d'être bête." She liked the music pitched high. H.D. liked extremes also, but she had the counterbalance, most fortunate for her, of a more commonplace childhood. Bryher, on the contrary, had always lived in her brain; she was continually preoccupied with ideas. H.D. would accuse her of having a brain where her heart should have been. There is an air of the willful superbeing about Bryher. Naturally she would urge H.D. to plunge into her "floating." Bryher with her scientific objectivity could only experience such states vicariously. Bryher, preanalysis, was unable to recognize that the bell-jar episode was not a pleasurable poetic account, but a symptom of a mind under stress—and most likely a symptom of depression.

H.D. was writing what she called "Notes on Thought and Vision." It is unlike anything she ever wrote. Some of the "Notes"[1] read alarmingly like D. H. Lawrence at his philosophic worst. The word "super" overwhelms us. She speaks of "the super-feelers of the super mind." She continued to argue that "there is no great art period, without great lovers. We must be 'in love' before we can understand the mysteries of vision . . . A lover must choose the same type of mind as himself, a musician a musician," etc. Then, less agreeably, she adds: "Two or three people with healthy bodies and the right sort of receiving brains, could turn the whole tide of human thought, could direct lightning flashes of electric power to slash across and destroy the world of dead, murky thought." Now hovering over and beyond this superworld is the idea of Christ. "Christ was the grapes that hung against the sunlit walls of that mountain garden, Nazareth. He was the hyacinth of Sparta and the narcissus of the islands . . . He was the body of nature, the vine, the Dionysius, as he was the soul of nature."

There are some thirty-two pages of this. In it appear the selective writer-lover, Bryher; Lawrence's dream of a superworld; Havelock Ellis' plea for the acceptance of sexual relations; her combined ideas of the Greeks and Moravians in the body of Christ. These are heady ("under a cap") notes and visions. Ellis, when she was later able to show it to him, was unimpressed by this Scillian tract, in fact he didn't like it at all, and for this she never forgave him.

When they returned to London in late 1919, H.D. took a flat in Bullingham Mansions, in her now familiar borough of Kensington. She was in a peculiar mental state. She was still "under the cap," the tension had not gone away. She needed help of a different kind than Bryher could supply. Now it would be said that she needed a psychiatrist. She had been introduced to Havelock Ellis by Daphne Bax, who once more proved a reliable friend. "The Prophet of Brixton" lived not too far away from Daphne, and H.D. knew that he would be kind enough to receive her. She may well have had a sexual problem at this time and who better able to counsel her than Ellis?

It is more than likely that H.D. was never physically attracted to Bryher. H.D. would use her sexuality, strengthened by Bryher's fixation on her, to retain her hold over Bryher. It is certain that she never felt the physical passion she had experienced toward Frances Gregg. She may never have felt so strongly for another woman in her life. When she did have a woman lover she tended to confuse that person with Frances. Now she hoped that Havelock Ellis would console her and help repair her physical and mental state. Ellis had written: "When the Soul has lost its wings the body too grows weary."

[1] Published in 1982 (see bibliography).

The title of Havelock Ellis' autobiography is *The Fountain of Life*. He has written his story in diary form. In the spring of 1921 (although Ellis' biographer notes that the year actually was 1919) his diary records that a "Person" would from time to time drift into his room "like a large white bird . . . a shy sinuous figure, so slender and so tall that she seemed frail, yet lithe, one divined, of firm and solid texture." He finds her beyond the distinctions of sex, virginal, yet a mother, a woman, yet a youth. She was different from any woman he had ever known. She would let loose garments "glide from her." Her body was "itself too full of meaning, and itself too full of mystery to need garments or to bear being garmented. I dimly divined this as I caught careless entrancing glimpses of this body."

He describes her body in no careless terms. It is at once Egyptian and Grecian.

> Even as in her form the virginal and the maternal were marvelously united into a harmony of adolescent youth, so it was in her spirit. The strange discrepancies of her soul lay peacefully side by side, the lion by the lamb. The thin austere lines upon her intellectual brows were the outward sign of a subtle brain that played among the glistening points of glacier heights, pursuing there delicate fancies of imagination that almost seemed to elude perception . . . Yet without any violence of transition, she would linger maliciously over the stories of human weakness and brood deliciously over licentious images, until lascivious pearls of sweat gathered together in the sheltered recesses of the prostrate form lying passive . . .

Ellis published his book in 1924, and for all these years—until the revelations based on his unpublished letters were made known by Phyllis Grosskurth, in her remarkable *Havelock Ellis. A Biography* (1980)—no one has known that the above passages are a descriptiom of H.D. at the time of her visit to Havelock Ellis.

Returning to the *Fountain of Life*, we learn that H.D. is willing to comply with the sexual demands of Ellis, which is to have a woman urinate on him. His ornate language had previously concealed the simplicity of the physical act. It is H.D. whose "tall form languidly rose and stood erect, taut and massive it seemed now with the length of those straight adolescent legs still more ravishing in their unyielding pride, and the form before me seemed to be some adorable Olympian vase, and a large stream gushed afar in the glistering liquid arch, endlessly, it seemed to my wondering eyes, as I contemplated with enthralled gaze this prototypal statue of the Fountain of life . . ."

We are further indebted to the researches of Dr. Grosskurth, who tells us that when Ellis wished to use this episode in his book, he wrote to H.D. for permission. She asked him to delete it. His reaction then was, "She wants me to leave out the impression of the whole account of the rainbow stream . . . the cheek of that Hilda!" H.D. did capitulate when he convinced her that no one would know the identity of "Person." In her letter permitting him to use the passage she wrote: "It is certainly quite, quite too beautiful for the 'person.' I must believe it was meant for someone else and so admire it (or try to) impersonally."

This episode also echoes the spirited early Hilda, racing over the Pennsylvania countryside, her skirts held high. "Not too careful," as William Carlos Williams had observed.

At this time H.D. both loved and respected the unique "Prophet of Brixton." His courage and humanness, his instinctual regard for mankind, regardless of its aberrations (of which he had his share), sent a saving wave over the muddied tides of the nineteenth century. Ellis was a prophet of the twentieth century. H.D. quotes the usually skeptical Norman Douglas, who said of Ellis, "He is a man with one eye in the country of the blind."

When she consulted him at this time, Ellis had affectionately seen her as an "image of creative arrogance." He had brought back to her the sexual passions that for so long had been dormant. Whatever the aberrant nature of the sexual proceedings with Ellis, he possessed an uncommon ability to renew, or restore, a sensual physical life, which driven underground, as it had been with H.D., could cause serious wounds to the psyche. He did not cure those wounds. He only brought them into the open, and repaired them. Part of his method of repair with her, as with other women who entered into his life, was to renew her image of herself as a physical being, to give her confidence in herself as a woman.

There was so much informality in those early days with Ellis that H.D. could easily introduce him to Bryher, and he would enter their lives to be called "Chiron," the teacher of Achilles—after their Achilles' heel? If so, Bryher brought only one heel, and that was her family. She needed Ellis to give her the strength to recognize her own status, that of a person, separate from her family. He was there to give her comfort and assurance. She did not need a father, but a wise uncle with his long beard, and his avuncular knowledge that gave without demands. Her father had cautioned her to be careful of takers who did not give.

Bryher did not think of herself as having a "lesbian problem." She was a boy to herself. Her instinctual desire to approach women, not men, was never a problem for her. She cautioned H.D., as Gertrude Stein had her friend Alice Toklas, never to refer to her as a "she." That would be a pronoun of opprobrium, and would cast an illicit shadow on their relationship.

Ellis urged Bryher not to shock her parents with her extravagant speech; at the same time she must maintain her independence. It was Ellis who gave her the first paper by Freud she had ever read, and it would be Ellis who would give her the introduction to Freud in 1927.

They decided to ask "Chiron" to come with them to Greece, and he accepted. Yet it was he who later tried to dissuade Bryher from going to America, telling her, "Birds have an unfortunate habit of coming to grief on their first flight."

It remains to be decided if his prophecy was accurate. But stop Bryher! Never. Had not H.D. written to her when their voyage to Greece had appeared hopeless:

> Don't let us slide back into our old despair. We *can* do what we want. We *can* do it, once we have a clear and final sense of direction. We have wasted a lot of energy, at least I have, trying to comprehend—trying to compromise is what it amounts to. I admire and really have a great tenderness for Brigit, but it is lies, lies, lies the life she leads and *enjoys*. She really *likes* the dances and the mob at races and theatres. And I am proud of her and grow weak and think I am personally repellent to people—which I apparently am, though in a bigger sense. But at times I am afraid of them . . . I will go to the East with you, if you want. I should like Dr. Ellis along . . . I should like to lie in the sand and sleep under giant stars —there were giant stars in America. I can leave Perdita once I have made a few worldly friends for her—just to protect her till we come back. You will help me to arrange for her and get some money in any way we can. And I will come with you. I dream of a great house and the sun, the sun!

The Hellenic overture began when they embarked on one of Ellerman's ships, the *Borodino*. Chiron (Ellis) accompanied them. Ellis' early letters from Gibraltar and Malta are "rapturous." After their arrival in Athens, February 27, 1920, Ellis remarked rather enviously that the two women were "comfortably ensconced in the most luxurious hotel in the city." (The hotel was the Grand Bretagne, and H.D. entered into the expense ledger twenty pounds a week.) Ellis was housed in a more modest pension. He was beginning to be displeased with an uncertain atmosphere between himself and his companions that his antennae told him might become unpleasant. He climbed Mount Lycabettus and decided to remain there reading while the two women toured the ruins. Formerly he had seen Bryher and H.D. separately. Now he was finding the two together a formidable combination.

In a letter home he wrote: "They are both very peculiar," especially was this so of Hilda, who in spite of some good points was "selfish, weak and excitable." The trio abruptly broke up when Ellis decided to return home. His excuse was that Cyprus, which he had particularly wanted to see, was inaccessible due to postwar troubles. Ellis was reading an early handwriting on the wall; he had decided to depart before temperaments could explode. Professionally he foresaw difficulties that were beyond his stratagems.

H.D.'s letters to her friend in America, Viola Jordan, are filled with flowers, colors, rocks. She was making a trip of homage, rather than an archaeological one, and her enthusiasms are entirely personal, without any scientific or historical detail.

Bryher's behavior was dutifully appreciative. Their major disappointment was that as two unaccompanied ladies they were not permitted to go to Delphi. From her hospital bed, H.D. had willed herself to walk the Sacred Way. Now the Greek authorities prevented her.

What is troubling in her letters and notes of that trip is a feeling of estrangement that runs through them. There is no spontaneous reaction to the setting of her poetic inspiration. The major reason was that she was anxious and on the verge of a breakdown. Her reactions were dulled by inner pain clouding the psyche. In the unpublished "Majic Ring" she has written an account of this trip, and a paragraph from it helps explain the confused and guilty state in which she found herself:

> I was Sir Miles' [Sir John] guest, this was his daughter. I was filled with a sense of responsibility, or had been. But this moment, seeing her in the glass with her wide eyes and her head now lifted on her forward-hunched shoulders, it seemed that I had failed her. I have not *given* her enough, I had not given her anything. I had, it is true, given her an incentive, those last plague-stricken months in London, to hold on, as she had given me. We had made a pact; if I got well, she would take me to Greece. I got well. But something was lacking. Something had gone. I was convalescent, you might say, psychically, I had indeed taken up my bed and walked. But where had I walked?

On the boat to Greece she had met a man whom she refers to in her stories as Peter van Eck. His real name was Peter Rodeck and he lived in London. There must have been a mild flirtation, and he asked her to continue her trip with him, leaving her companions. This she refused to do, because of her obligation to the Ellermans and to Bryher. She liked him. She developed one of her crushes on him, and later saw him in London. (He must have understood her esoteric tastes, because he sent her a crystal ball.) This meeting appears in several guises in her writing; once she intimates that he had been a hallucination. But he was real, and had circumstances been different, it is possible she might have gone off with him. Once again she was tempted to flee. And that flight forfeited could lead to trouble.

The Rodeck episode, a shipboard acquaintance, a meeting on the Acropolis, an invitation to continue the voyage in his company—an ordinary story. H.D. used this material over and over in her own stories, and she would recount this little history to Freud. There was no incident in her life that did not gain in proportions. Peter Rodeck would be a continuing theme for many years, and a puzzle as to his reality when she changed him into a hallucination in her fiction.

One way or another these two women were headed for the explosion

Ellis had foreseen. They reached Corfu, that most Venetian of all the Greek isles, with its arcades, shops, and European-style houses. "A very small tittle-tattle place," had sniffed Edward Lear. It is an island created for pleasure and gentle dalliance; a more archaic choice would have been expected of Bryher.

They settled into the Hotel Belle Venise, the best hotel in Corfu, offering a Venetian-Victorian decor. As a stage set for H.D. to experience a major hallucination, it was not promising.

H.D. was reclining on one of those Victorian sofas like a figure from Euripides. "On her sacred tripod sits the Delphian priestess, chanting to the Greeks the Oracles charged to her by Apollo." At first she saw on the wall a tripod. The helmeted faces nearby might be airmen, or her dead brother, or Nike, the Goddess of Victory. Then came "a sort of pictorial buzzing—I mean about the base of the tripod there are small creatures, but these are in black; they move about, in and around the base of the tripod, but they are very small . . . they are tiny people all in black or outlined as in, or with shadows . . ."

> They are not important but it would be a calamity if one of them got stuck on one's eye. There was that sort of feeling people, people—why did they annoy me so? Would they eventually cloud my vision, or worse still, would one of them get "stuck in my eye"? . . . I did not hate people, I did not especially resent any one person. I had known such extraordinarily gifted and charming people. They had made much of me or they had slighted me and yet neither praise nor neglect mattered in the face of the gravest issues—life, death. (I had my child, I was alive.) And yet, oddly, I knew that this experience, this writing-on-the-wall before me, could not be shared with them—could not be shared with anyone except the girl who stood so bravely beside me. This girl said without hesitation, "Go on." It was she really who had the detachment and the integrity of the Pythoness of Delphi. But it was I, battered and disassociated from my American family and my English friends, who was seeing the pictures, who was reading the writing or who was granted the inner vision.

The scene is described in detail by H.D. in *Tribute to Freud*. Here it has been shortened and synopsized. The tripod, the Goddess of Victory, Nike, are evoked again. There is more detail about the meaning of these black dots and dashes. The importance here is the association H.D. makes between this hallucinatory scene and the events of her own life. She was sensitive to an abnormal degree to the judgments people made about her.

Frightening as it may have been at the time, in later life H.D. took pride in having experienced these visions. Today there would be the suspicion of their having been drug-induced. When she related the scene to Freud she was unavoidably proud when he shook his head, drew on his cigar, and told her that she had related "the only dangerous symptom." She does not define what he meant. She may not have known. He could have suggested that there was evidence of borderline instability. He could have thought that here she had "crossed the line," a phrase she was fond of using about others. Finally Freud interpreted the "writing-on-the-wall" (the original title of *Tribute to Freud*) as a desire for union with her mother. "Union with her mother"—it sounds as if that were a more solemn rendering of "homesickness." A need to nest under the home feathers, an exile's lament. In psychiatric terms, to carry it further, disassociation, even to the point of depersonalization.

Bryher had been enjoying herself. This scene was better than the curtain-raising bell-jar episode in the Scillies. She would urge H.D. to continue. She always wanted to poke behind screens, to allow someone else's unconscious to flow. When H.D. grew exhausted from interpreting the "writing-on-the-wall," Bryher took up where she left off. Bryher herself "read" the wall. Neither questioned the validity of Bryher's "visions." But Bryher did not discuss them later. The moment belonged to H.D. and the Corfu wall scenes would enter her history. It was as if, indeed, she had gone to Delphi, and had sat on the sacred tripod.

When it was over, Bryher became sad; like an excited child she demanded more. H.D., and where her energy came from is anyone's guess, obliged. "I began to act out what I called Indian dance-pictures. There was a girl in the mountains, there was a medicine man seeking for plants in the woods, there was . . . our old friend Minnehaha, etc." H.D. suggested to Freud that "this might be some form of possession." Freud, sensibly, brought her back to earth, telling her that it was "drama, half motivated by desire to comfort Bryher and neither 'delirium' nor 'magic.'"

There would be other times when Bryher would demand to be amused, and also shaken out of her melancholy. She respected writers and poets, because she believed they had this special gift of evocation. H.D. and Frances had often discussed "possession" and "magic."

Entertaining Bryher, as in the Indian games, in order to whisk away her melancholy, must have placed an additional strain on H.D. And yet, there would in later life be crystal balls, table tipping, tarot cards, numerology, astrology. These were not amusements, although she would hastily pretend they were when Bryher accused her of senseless dabbling. They were expressions of a metaphysical need to reach beyond apparent phenomena.

H.D. and Bryher are silent about what happened afterward and their subsequent departure from Corfu. If we choose, we can believe Havelock Ellis, who wrote that "Hilda went 'right out of her mind' and Bryher had to bring her back *overland.*"

When they returned to England, Bryher took an exhausted H.D. to a pension high on a cliff at Mullion Cove in Cornwall. While Bryher visited with Doris Banfield, H.D., although near a breakdown, forced herself to correspond with Amy Lowell. Not only was Amy by way of becoming a father confessor, but she was a demanding correspondent.

She wrote Amy that she found England altogether depressing and that she and "little Bryher" were planning to come to America. She was curious about Amy's opinion of the Anderson-Heap *Little Review,* then flourishing. The magazine started by Margaret Anderson in Chicago would move to New York and thence to Paris. During the time of its existence, for what its editor called *My Thirty Years' War,* until its demise in 1929, it was the center for the avant-garde. Many of its most talented writers were brought to it by the European editor, Ezra Pound.

H.D. really wanted to learn more about the literary climate of America. This was during the tong war between Amy Lowell and Pound over who owned the Orient. The gunpowder was being fired within *The Little Review,* where Pound's introduction to Ernest Fenollosa had finally appeared, and *Poetry,* where Amy's foolhardy Chinese interpretations were printed.

H.D. may not have been aware of all this. She wanted to encourage Amy to place her poems in magazines in America. Probably Amy knew that her archenemy, who called her the "hippopoetess," Ezra Pound, had cautioned Anderson to be "more careful than ever NOT to have in too much Amy, and suburbs." He had gone on to explain that provincial Amy wasn't up to the "mondaine London clientele." Amy now countered by explaining to H.D. that she didn't much care for Anderson and her crowd.

Fortunately H.D. did not know that Pound, the year before, in 1919, had written to Anderson:

[Re H.D., Aldington and Williams] . . . I don't think any of these people have gone on; have invented much since the first "Des Imagistes" anthology. H.D. has done work as good. She has also (under I suppose the flow-contamination of Amy and Fletcher) let loose dilutations and repetitions, so that she has spoiled the "few but perfect" position which she might have held on to.

H.D. sent Amy the manuscript of poems that Boni & Liveright had asked to publish, querying if Amy believed them to be the right publishers. Most of this poetry had already appeared in magazines. Claiming that she was out of touch with the present generation, she looked to Amy to guide her; in what would become a typical H.D. tactic she entrusted *all* to Amy's judgment. She then confided that Bryher's meeting with Pound had been a fiasco, although not so great a one as Bryher had pretended. He had treated her like a child, patted her on the head, and asked for some chocolates. It was his way of punishing H.D. for transferring her interest from him. (Possibly another way had been that letter to Margaret Anderson.) He must have been surprised that anyone so young as Bryher was willing to become involved in the hectic affairs of H.D.

At least fourteen of H.D.'s poems had appeared in America throughout 1919 and 1920, refuting H.D.'s lament that she was not in the current movement. She was printed in every major literary magazine, and so frequently in *Poetry* as to belie Harriet Monroe's notion that H.D. was hiding from real life under a chiton.

CHAPTER TWELVE

"I Am the Goddess of Liberty"

Their visit to Cornwall, short as it was, had a calming effect on H.D. She recovered sufficiently from the threatened breakdown to return to London with Bryher and make plans for a trip to America.

Bryher was now recognized as a published author. In 1920 *Development*, the story of her school days at Queenwood, published by Constable, had been an unexpected success and had gone into a second printing. Bryher was modest about this book, yet she must have been pleased that she could now address herself as a professional writer. Toward H.D. her attitude would still remain that of a neophyte at the shrine of the genius. Throughout the American trip she kept what she believed to be unsatisfactory notes on her American impressions: although uniquely Bryher, they are suitable company for Mrs. Trollope. The United States, immodest as it was, lent itself to the acid comments of its foreign visitors. It was fortunate for Bryher's writing that this first trip made such an impression. Later, more favorable visits weakened her criticisms.

H.D. suggested that Bryher cut her long hair. Her own had been cut some time before. Now each wore the bob of the period. It was a hairstyle that initiated a dramatic change—the twenties had officially begun, although skirts had yet to be lifted. Cutting one's hair symbolically cut one off from the family ties and mores, just as formerly "putting up her hair" had indicated that the girl had become old enough to be "put" into the marriage market. The bob introduced a new rite of passage, the break with the nineteenth century. Bryher had beautiful, strong hair, and short hair became her. She would never let it grow long again. As the years passed, her hair was routinely clipped until it became shorter and more mannish in style. (In her letters Bryher notes, as frequently as a male diarist, her trips to the barber.)

On September 10, 1920, H.D.'s thirty-fourth birthday, she and Bryher, accompanied by Perdita and her nurse, landed in New York. Once arrived, they were met by Amy Lowell and her companion, Mrs. Ada Russell, always to be addressed as Mrs. Russell. Amy took them to her favorite hotel, the Belmont, then rather grand with a spacious entrance hall, marble walls and floors. H.D. once more wrote into the notebook kept for expenditures that the room cost ten dollars for the night, and that food was not included. She kept these wretched notebooks with expenses carefully jotted down whenever and wherever she traveled. This exercise does not seem at all characteristic of H.D., who rarely dated letters. And yet she was in many ways quite methodical. Her diary was kept up to date. Her bank account was in order. In fact, she was hounded by a fear of imminent poverty that made her dislike to spend any money at all. Like all Puritans, she was industrious and thrifty. She was continually nagged by the notion of spending small sums of money, such as those for tips in the hotels she would patronize all her life. Yet she demanded flowers in her room and delighted in expensive materials for dresses. These extravagances, it should be added, were not paid for by H.D., who could well afford them. The small details she could handle, it was the major details that inhibited her—publishers, contracts, leases, rentals, anything that had to do with the transfer of money, passports, travel plans, etc. These duties she quickly shifted onto others.

After they had partially recovered from the shock of the luxury of the Belmont, they began to look about them. Reality rarely parallels the imagination, and Bryher found the New World most puzzling. She was surprised at the old-fashioned speech and ideas. She may have expected noble savages to come forth mouthing the latest technological terms. She certainly wasn't prepared to hear about the evils of drink, an issue that would result in the disasters of prohibition.

It was fortunate Amy Lowell was there to guide them; merchant princess that she was, she still represented a Boston culture that eased Bryher's disquiet.

Bryher decided New York was "barbaric and arrogant." The fertile native dissonances American writers in search of subject matter hearkened to she found alarming. How could the "Viking," as she liked to consider herself, have anticipated such a society? This was not the America she had been introduced to through Amy Lowell and Ezra Pound with their cavaliers, Chinese emperors, medievalists, and other masks. Was it from here the Imagists had made their escape in a broken line of verse? Here was the country of H.D.'s "Pear Tree"; her "Islands," offshore from Maine. Here was the "Orchard" of Hellenism. Was it? When she asked why the poets she preferred had escaped from America, she found her answer in the profile of a shrill, unyouthful country.

American writers who had not retreated were willing to exploit the isolation and the hog-butcher towns that Sandburg and others wrote about. Edwin Arlington Robinson, who then took refuge in Greenwich Village, was writing about the disassociation felt by people in American towns who, like "Miniver Cheevy," gave the appearance of adjusting themselves to society while they concealed their real feelings, which could lead to a bullet hole in the head.

William Carlos Williams was inspired, he believed, by the life of a doctor in a rural community where poverty and primitivism concealed, but did not spoil, the asphodels of the field. John Reed and Max Eastman thought they had found their bolt-hole in Russia. Vachel Lindsay, most popular of poets, was banging drums and thundering about black savages, an early Rousseauesque vision of a real storm.

Marianne Moore had written:

> Is it Nineveh
>   and are you Jonah
>   in the sweltering east wind of your wishes?
>   I myself, have stood
>   there by the aquariums, looking
>   at the Statue of Liberty.

What had Bryher expected? The NEW. Hadn't Pound preached its value? She anticipated a sociological fairyland. With such hopes, it was fated she would be unhappy and truly disappointed. Bryher remained very British despite her theories. When she first met Marianne Moore she begged her to come to Europe, no doubt hoping to save Miss Moore's life. Miss Moore refused. She knew where her material lay. If it was to be aquariums and zoos, or the human species, let it be American.

Bryher could be her own shrewdest sociologist and historian. *West*, the book she wrote while she traveled in America, proved it.

> For an American to survive as an individual and not as a unit in a community, one must possess an extreme sensitiveness, an extreme strength . . . And everything is public. Personality, it seems, is a crime. Privacy is to be purchased only with dollars . . . It is degrading to live in a country where to be happy one must center one's mind upon adding to one's income. My friends were all Americans. I wanted to know the country that they came from. Now I understand their sympathy, the flower-like quality that they have about them.
>
> I doubt if the books which brought me over could have been written if their authors had not escaped to Europe from the environment of their adolescence. There's a passion of beauty in them. A whole new world created. I thought that they were writing of what was about them. They were getting away from it. It's a great joke.

H.D. had no such eye. There is a possibility at this time that had there been no dissenting Bryher with her, H.D. would have remained in America. This was her first return after marriage, war, motherhood. She was enjoying its creature comforts. The sky was so blue and high; she embraced the fresh air and flowers after the fog and coal-dusted air of England. Best of all, she was no longer brooding on the past war and its attendant personal disasters. She wrote to Amy Lowell that there was in America "plenty of good food." She was feeling deprived; she had suffered starvation of sorts. She may even have felt young again, particularly when with poets her own age.

There was a simplicity and a camaraderie that she may have missed in the now war-grimed and more cynical England. Over and over she would remind Bryher that she had possessed a life in America before she had met her. "I am the Goddess of Liberty," one can almost hear her scream at Bryher. "I set you free. Free. Free." She still used Americanisms in her speech and correspondence, although her accent had become transatlantic; she never thought of herself as English, yet she was pleased when someone took her for an English lady.

She was much admired by other American poets. Louis Untermeyer and William Rose Benét praised her, as did Marianne Moore and Amy Lowell. And of course she was respected by the editors of the leading magazines: Harriet Monroe, Margaret Anderson, and Jane Heap. American little magazines were in the midst of a renaissance. How many there were! *The Dial, Poetry, The Little Review, The Masses, Pagany, Contact, The Nation.* To them H.D. was an important poet. In England she had a select, tasteful audience, but not, as here, a widely developed one, due in part to the labors of Amy Lowell.

She had written in advance to William Carlos Williams that she and Bryher would be in New York. Williams came to see them at their hotel, bringing with him a young man from the Middle West, Robert McAlmon. In his *Autobiography* Williams writes that he had said to McAlmon:

> "Wanna see the old gal?" I asked Bob. "Sure. Why not?" So one afternoon we decided to take in the show. Same old Hilda, all over the place looking as tall and skinny as usual. But she had with her a small, dark English girl with piercing, intense eyes, whom I noticed and that was about all. "Well how did you like her?" I asked Bob when we came away. "Oh, she's all right, I guess," said Bob. "But that other one, Bryher, as she was introduced to us—she's something."

When she met McAlmon, Bryher, without realizing it at the time, had discovered a writer who, as much as any other, including Sinclair Lewis and Theodore Dreiser, was representative of the grass roots of America. Ezra Pound said that McAlmon was too American for the Americans to like him. True. He was never taken up by an American publisher until New Directions, at the recommendation of William Carlos Williams, published his poems *Not Alone Lost* in 1937. Bryher, like a fortunate explorer, had tapped a source in McAlmon. Without leaving New York, Bryher had arrived at the source. No better judge than Ford Madox Ford in his *Transatlantic Review* would write that "McAlmon represents— though geography is not our strongest point—that West-Middle-West-by-West of which we have been taught to do and expect so much." The poet Basil Bunting, English acolyte of Pound, immediately recognized that

McAlmon didn't seem to have any literary background at all. Like Topsy, McAlmon, the prairie dog, could say, "I 'spect I growed."

Coming from a family of eight children, son of an impoverished Presbyterian minister, he had a difficult boyhood in a small town near the Minnesota border. The scene, as he would describe it, was always a small town, always drear, dusty, and in winter snow-covered. It was provincialism, complete. McAlmon left home. He enrolled at the University of Southern California for a semester. From California he wandered to New York. He was in search of literary talk and companionship (much as Bryher in her different circumstances had reached out). Finally he found what he was searching for in Greenwich Village and in his friendship with William Carlos Williams. He was the sort of person Williams would appreciate. Self-instructed, forced to be self-reliant, he was rough, but tender, wary, yet sympathetic. When he met Bryher and H.D. in New York, he had been earning a dollar an hour as a male model in art classes at Cooper Union.

Then there was the meeting with Marianne Moore. She and her mother shared an apartment and Miss Moore was assistant librarian at the Hudson Branch (in Greenwich Village) of the New York Public Library, an unusually handsome, vintage brick building. It was a reunion for the Bryn Mawr poets who equally admired one another's work. H.D. was usually wary of revealing her attitude toward the work of her friends, but in Miss Moore she had immediately recognized an original talent and had praised her in *The Egoist*. Privately, she considered herself and Moore far superior to other women poets such as Elinor Wylie, Edna St. Vincent Millay, or Sara Teasdale.

Bryher's immediate reaction to Miss Moore when she saw her with her massive golden hair like a headdress was: "It's a pterodactyl!" And "Dactyl" she became forever in their private conversation, just as H.D. was "Cat" and Bryher was "Fido," names they would always use to sign their letters to one another. Marianne Moore became a lifelong friend. She was the first recipient of the Bryher Foundation Fund, which Bryher was later to set up to help artists and deserving people who were short of funds. McAlmon, who would have been in a position to know, swore that Marianne Moore sent Bryher a lock of that shining hair!

It wasn't only the literary life that occupied H.D., it was her family as well. She was reunited with her mother. She could put Perdita into her mother's arms and feel at last that she had established a family. She wanted to share her new, expanding life with her mother, and in turn she would rely upon Mrs. Doolittle to give stability to this ménage of two women and a child.

Then there was Viola Jordan, a member of the original group around Pound. Viola was now married, had babies, and was living in New Jersey. Sentiment may initially have led H.D. to seek her out; she needed to

reestablish her own roots. This meeting with Viola led to a long correspondence carried on over the years wherein H.D. confided personal
thoughts and whimsies she would hide from Bryher. She revealed to
Viola her feminine side, the one of "perms" and worries about age, and
what to do with one's looks. She also wrote of some of her secret occult
research. Viola reacted much as Bryher did to this confidence, and was
scandalized. The voice of H.D. to Viola is that of the girl from Upper
Darby, and one hears in it their letters over the years. Secretive by nature, H.D. seldom told the exact truth, content to veil it by allusions, pre-
ferring the other person confide in her. She practiced what Emily Dickinson had said was "truth told, but told aslant." Viola was close to H.D.
in a way hidden from others, oddly assorted as the two may have appeared. The suburban wife with her discontents and marital troubles, her
children, and her unchanging fidelity to Ezra Pound (this fidelity included H.D.) proved the attraction of opposites. It must have been a relief to confide in the faithful, if on this occasion unreceptive, Viola in
contrast to the clever people H.D. would meet.

After New York came California. H.D. had never been there and
Bryher was eager to go, because she evidently had imagined California
to be one vast Mediterranean sunlit island afloat in America. The native
H.D. would combine health with culture. H.D. was happy to be traveling with her mother and Perdita to visit Wolle cousins in Southern California.[1] She needed the touch, light though it might be, of a family.

After a brief stopover in Los Angeles (long enough for H.D. to make
note that they spent twenty dollars for room and bath), they arrived at
the Clifford Howards' in Monrovia, California. In her autobiography,
Bryher speaks of visiting "cousins" in Monrovia. In an obvious effort to
shield what their actual relationship was, she would insist that she and
H.D. were distant relatives. When interviewed in Switzerland in 1978,
she spoke of "my cousin, H.D."

Monrovia in 1920 was a village surrounded by orange groves. Most of
the houses were small, frame bungalows situated within the groves. Cali-
fornians can remember the smell and smoke of the burning smudge pots
that were set in the groves to keep off the winter chill from the oranges.
There were tuberculosis sanatoriums in the hills nearby, as the air was
fresh and considered healthy. But where was the culture? After Thanks-
giving and Christmas with the Howards early in January 1921 the party
proceeded up the coast toward the recommended Carmel highlands.

In Santa Barbara they briefly stayed at the El Encanto Hotel; from its
hillside they could see one of the churches founded by Fra Junípero

---

[1] Bryher told Norman Holmes Pearson that "the Beaver" (the name H.D. and
Bryher had given Mrs. Doolittle) never knew the real truth of Perdita's parentage.
She took for granted that the child's father was Aldington.

Serra, and past that the sea. It is a glorious view over the tiled rooftops of the pseudo-Spanish houses of the town, but it wasn't authentic! In the notes Bryher would include in her book *West*, she wrote:

It was the smell of the place. Nothing you could lay your hands on, catalogue artificial. Costing money. Giving nothing. Meaning nothing. You paid for Egypt but you got the Pyramids. Greece was cheap and you had Hymettus. New York was New York, arrogant and barbaric. But here you weigh out gold and silver for suburbia, gone reckless, for the grind of wheels and an indefinable sense of restraint . . . They had forgotten adventure. Forgotten the sea. The sense, the sound of life.

When they arrived in the Carmel highlands, Bryher scarcely recognized that California was offering her literary past: it was in the highlands that Jack London and Robert Louis Stevenson had lived. Carmel and adjoining Monterey were a kind of Valhalla in contrast to the literary emptiness elsewhere. The intelligentsia of San Francisco gathered there. Bryher remained appalled.

A film company was filming Mary Pickford next to their hotel. H.D. was fascinated. Bryher hid. It was too soon for the cinema to attract her. (H.D. must have needed the consolation and shelter of her mother in order to put up with such bratlike behavior.) H.D. was writing her Greek essays. High on a cliff above the sea, she might well be in her beloved Greece, and she had the additional diversion of watching Mary Pickford, America's Sweetheart.

This continued disappointment in her travels forced Bryher to work on a book in which she could confide her real feelings about America. The book is a medley of comments on the American West together with Bryher's ideas on education; its heroine is Marianne Moore! *West* is a marvelous little book, although Bryher was later embarrassed by it. There she was wrong. Her own arrogance led her to observations others more conventionally minded would not have made. *West* was published in 1925 by Jonathan Cape after Bryher had established herself in her own, more agreeable sanctuary in Switzerland.

In *West*, Marianne Moore is called Anne:

. . . she seems curiously tied up, mentally. It is all very well to be opposed to indiscriminate publication, but why is she so averse to life, any sort of life? . . . Anne is really a young Byzantine scribe, all strange colours and angles. Her mind was a bright mosaic . . . Mosaic is not marble.

I should like to cut her hair short, her wonderful hair. Break her from everything to which she is accustomed and plunge her into a new world.

You see, says Anne, I feel if I am to create anything I shall do it when I am, say, forty-five.

Later, Here we have no neighbors but a few friends, says Anne. And the cinema posters. Occasionally we visit a play and in themselves the

streets are romantic films. The shot of bright silks in the windows. The fur
one sees. Soft grey and black shapes like a tent. The museum. Sometimes
a circus . . . There is at the zoo a spotted lynx in a cage with markings
on its fur as delicate as those the forest traces . . .

Cut the masochism out and come with us to England.

Why did Anne carry it on, this Victorian tradition? Was it because
America was in the throes of a somewhat similar period that she preferred
a spirit already stamped with history . . . Her shrinking from life was a
masculine rather than a feminine gesture. It was a boy's denial of himself
for some misunderstood ideal . . . Duty had served her for emotional outlet.

I want Anne to come to Europe.

It might affect her work to be broken from her environment.

Mrs. Trollope [Anne's mother] smiled. It is the thing that galls us most
that is best for us. Discipline is good for the spirit. It is by accomplishing
our little irksome tasks that we achieve.

Meanwhile McAlmon and Bryher had been corresponding. He had
read a review of *Development* in the *New Republic*. He agreed with her
about school. He hated it—along with civilization. He thought Marianne
Moore was a "closeted intellect." She represented all those things against
which he rebelled: carefulness, judiciousness, "timid stepping." He
believed in intense feeling, even if it included violence. H.D., he is careful to say, is the best of the Imagists. However, he doesn't really like
Imagism. He thinks it is some sort of escape, only an abstraction. Finally
he says that he would like "to be able to sing with my own voice, dance
on my own legs and blaspheme and fight—express impulses rather than
trying to squeeze them into writing." He would succeed better than he
expected in this program.

Bryher had told McAlmon her old desire of wanting to be a boy. He
called it nonsense, describing how difficult a boy's life actually was.
Bumming around, bedbugs, and unclean food. (And Bryher was com-
plaining about the Carmel highlands!) He praised jazz and damned in-
tellectuality. He told her Shakespeare knew as much as any analyst. He
gave her his blessing, telling her she was better than Imagism. Finally
these are the poets he approved of: Bill Williams, H.D., Marianne
Moore, T. S. Eliot, and Wallace Stevens.

McAlmon did not hesitate to criticize H.D. He told Bryher that H.D.
"intellectualizes" or "freezes" her emotions. He said that she managed to
be cold and withdrawn and passionately beautiful—but—alas, says McAlmon, "passion withheld."

This is a remarkable summing up by McAlmon after such a short personal encounter with the two women. He must have been reading H.D.'s
work, and possibly discussing her with Williams. He was genuinely interested in Bryher. It is there in his letters, proof that he approved of her

and wanted to encourage her work and personality. These letters reveal the essential McAlmon, whom nothing would change. His views would not alter, no matter in what society he moved, however rich or poor he might be. He did not write love letters. Nor did he receive them! He wrote on the same latitude as Bryher must have written to him. Conscientious discussions, passionate affirmations, not of love, but ideas. His letters to her are attempts to arrive at the solvable Bryher; he held out his hand to her. It is no wonder that having read his letters, she would react to them so strongly. She needed someone to remind her that she must have "fortitude or humour, or whim, anything but this deadly, heavy thought-torturing anguish. See the lightness of wit and clarity of perception of your Greeks—and Elizabethan comedians."

H.D. might similarly have benefited from the advice of this self-educated man. She also had been corresponding with McAlmon. It was she who confided Bryher's personal difficulties and encouraged him to help Bryher to believe in her own strength. H.D. had already begun to lend herself to the conspiracy of a Bryher-McAlmon marriage.

As soon as Bryher returned to New York she met with McAlmon. He had been about to rush off to Europe on a freighter and she told him to wait for her arrival. She had taken his advice, which was to do anything she wanted, to believe that everything was possible. Why shouldn't she and McAlmon marry? She made it clear that it would be a marriage in name only. For her it would be a marriage that would free her legally from her parents. If McAlmon accepted her proposal, she would assume all financial burdens. The expenses of the marriage and of the household would be paid by her. They would live in Europe, and he would be free to travel.

McAlmon had said that he believed in chance, rather than caution. Here was his opportunity to act upon it. He accepted her terms. It was not exactly a callous choice he made. He liked, he respected Bryher. It would be a pity he could not be her lover, but he was willing to accept her terms.

H.D. supported this alliance. She knew well that she had only to threaten Bryher with her disapproval, and such was Bryher's love and dependency that she would have given up marriage with McAlmon. The two women must have held many consultations. Bryher's disproportionate fear that she might be trapped by her parents when she returned to England, despite the protection of an older woman, made both women determined to work out the plan with McAlmon. H.D. also may have been exhausted handling the moods and tantrums of Bryher. Secretly she must have longed to shift the burden. Confident of Bryher's loyalty, she decided to go along with the decision to marry McAlmon.

Bryher and McAlmon were married at the City Hall in New York City on February 14, 1921, St. Valentine's Day. The tabloids shrieked: "Heir-

ess Weds Unknown!" Gossips were busy, and not only in the literary
community. When it was revealed that "Bryher" was the daughter of Sir
John Ellerman, the shipping magnate, *Burke's Peerage* was consulted. It
was discovered that Bryher, oddly, was not listed under "Ellerman," only
a son. Of course this was because Bryher was illegitimate—an irrele-
vancy when it was settled in the minds of all that this little Bryher had a
considerable fortune, and that McAlmon had gotten hold of it. How ignorant was McAlmon of the amount of money Bryher possessed? She
had not pretended to be poor. He had known he was marrying money.
Neither he, nor the press, was clear as to how *much* money she had.

A wedding party was organized at the Hotel Brevoort. This hotel once
reigned at the corner of Fifth Avenue and Eighth Street, a short block
from Washington Square. It figures in many idylls of the past, along with
the nearby Hotel Lafayette. It was one of the few refuges in which
American and European travelers might find a Continental welcome. It
was very unlike the sumptuously American Belmont selected by Amy
Lowell. The Brevoort more nearly resembled a Left Bank hotel, one of
the more expensive ones, of course. It was consequently adored by the
Paris–New York axis. The waiters were dressed like French waiters,
and the food was nearly as good as that of its neighbor, the Lafayette.
The Brevoort with its cosmopolitan crowd was definitely not one of those
hotels found out West. Bryher, though penurious, when in town was accustomed to a civilized roof.

The wedding party had been quickly assembled by H.D. and consultants, one of whom would have been Marianne Moore. A list can be
found on an envelope on which H.D. has written the names: Lola Ridge,
Rolfe Humphrey, Evelyn Scott, Marsden Hartley, William Carlos Williams and his wife, McAlmon, his sister, Grace (a nurse who was attending a patient in New York), Gwen Richards, Marianne Moore and
Mrs. Moore, and Scofield Thayer, who subsidized *The Dial*.[2]

When Williams returned from the party, he found a mystery postcard
illustrating a scene from a current play in which the actors are shown
with their hands in a pot of money. It was signed in bold letters "D.H."

[2] Scofield Thayer died on July 9, 1982, at the age of ninety-two. Sixty-two years
previously he had been a patient of Freud. Upon his death his private art collection,
worth many millions, passed to the Metropolitan Museum of Art. According to the
New York *Times* it included paintings by Braque, Picasso, Munch, Demuth, and
Matisse. He assembled this extraordinary collection of 450 works of art between 1919
and 1924 while editor in chief of *The Dial*, and it is known as "The Dial Collection."
In advance of its time, the collection was first shown in 1925 at his hometown museum
in Worcester, Massachusetts, where it was viewed with contempt. As a result, Thayer
changed his will in favor of the Metropolitan Museum in New York. The New York
Times quotes him as "expressing his dislike of provincialism in a letter to James Joyce.
Apologizing for not publishing parts of 'Ulysses' in *The Dial*, Thayer wrote: 'We in
America live and move and have our being in the sinister shadow of an appalling
Presbyterian post office.' "

Williams accused H.D. of having sent it. This she vehemently denied. Williams never believed her. He should have. The gesture was entirely out of character. According to McAlmon, the postcard had been sent by Scofield Thayer for reasons best known to himself. Williams repeated this incident in his *Autobiography,* still accusing H.D.

Williams is more mysterious than the postcard. Why did he show such rancor toward H.D. at this time, and later in his *Autobiography?* Had he, indeed, been hurt when, as a girl, she had turned so abruptly from him to Pound? Was his uneasy pride injured? Williams was such a complex man that it would be difficult to sort out his reactions. How could one guess the nature of his original feelings for H.D.? They do not show themselves in his letters. Or was the true rivalry between him and Pound on a professional level, and H.D. represented one more star in Pound's meteoric rise, while Doc Williams remained at home to deliver babies? H.D., also, had a considerable reputation at this time. Was Williams, who was no indiscriminate admirer of her poetry, jealous of what to him would have been an undeserved acclaim? Was Williams angry with Hilda that once more, as with Pound, she had laid claim to one of his friendships, this time with McAlmon?

In turn, H.D. never showed any interest in Williams' work. In fact, she rather disliked it. As a woman, she did not behave in the way Williams would have perferred her to behave: with her power reserved for the hearth. He had smirked at Hilda spiritedly jumping over stiles—was this disapproval? In the world where men competed with men, Williams would not be the most outspoken advocate of woman's equality. He had witnessed their strength in the sickroom, and in childbirth. His own mother had been the equal of any man. And yet in that outer competitive world where armies clashed by night? . . . All questions. At the same time as he remarked on H.D.'s awkwardness, on her height, on her way of "throwing herself around," when he was in Paris he selected her, along with Nancy Cunard and Iris Tree, as the most interesting types in Paris. He had a good eye. But H.D. refused to take Williams seriously as a man, or as a poet. There was a shared lack of sympathy. Williams should have known H.D. better than to have accused her of the gaucherie of sending that postcard. Could it have been that at the wedding reception H.D. may have been displaying her charms in other directions, ignoring Williams, the once "Dear Billy" of her girlish letters?

The McAlmons, H.D., and Perdita sailed shortly after the wedding. Mrs. Doolittle had decided to remain in America for a time before accepting Bryher's invitation to join them in Europe. During the crossing, McAlmon sang, "Our menagerie of three is the best menagerie."

The three writers, when not taking turns watching the child, busily took up pen. H.D. was continuing with a correspondence she had begun with Marianne Moore while they had been on the Coast. Because she respected her so, H.D. would always be warmer and more sincere in her letters to Miss Moore than with others. The letters to Marianne, unlike many of her casual and charming ones to friends, reveal her as an artist, writing to someone she considered her equal. From Monrovia early in 1921 she had written that she wanted to "build big rock structures and invoke images—live men and women." She then admitted that although she has "faith to remove mountains," she seems to lack "the power of quarrying out the rocks necessary for my framework."

Then, ceasing to write about her poetry, she had spoken from the heart about herself. *"I am beginning to feel as if the world approved of me—and I can't write unless I am an outcast. I have tried everything. I have been respectable and I have not been respectable. And now I am mediocre."* (my italics)

The acceptance of the world threatened her privacy. H.D. liked to hide her ambitions. She wanted the world to notice her achievements, but she did not wish to seek out the world. She would have remained more obscure as a writer had her affairs been left to herself, and not, as previously indicated, rested in the hands of powerful friends. She, personified, remains a figure of concealment beneath selected veils. The truths she chooses to reveal are dragged from her. They often consist of one or two lines. Yet sparseness does not obscure passion.

As the voyage continued she wrote to Marianne: "We have been happy in our surly way . . . Bryher has been an absolute slave to Perdita so she (Bryher) has every right to her sulks. I have sulked or rather thoroughly enjoyed myself lying in bed—and Robert has sulked for various reasons."

She reminds her that "they all miss the Dactyl." She also described McAlmon as being kind to Perdita and congratulates Bryher on knowing what she wants, how much, and how little!

Marianne Moore responded charmingly to the oceanic-party "sulks" by saying that she "hadn't thought of anything so rational and domestically poetic as a little sulking." (How like Dorothy Wordsworth she sounds, replying to a honeymoon letter from Mary Hutchinson.) Then Marianne Moore, as would be her way, spoke frankly. She revealed that she had been shocked by the McAlmon marriage. Her attitude was that McAlmon, adventurer that he was (privately called "piggy" between her and her mother), had done this for a lark; he had wittingly taken advantage of Bryher for his own reprehensible reasons. There then follows a wistful, thoughtful paragraph:

It may be that there is no such thing as a love affair in the case of people under forty and that an improvised duet doesn't signify but my intuition doesn't corroborate my wish in this matter. I think Chesterton is right as I said to you the night after the party—at the Brevoort. (There is no such thing as a prudent marriage) marriage is a Crusade, there is always tragedy in it; in the case of one so finely adjusted as Bryher, one's spiritual motive power is sure to receive a backset, and I can smile only very ironically at Robert's harmonizing so nicely with the family, in his adaptability to Perdita.

In G. K. Chesterton's *Autobiography,* in particular the chapter about his family and their origins, "Hearsay Evidence," with its praise of the worthiness of the middle-class Victorians, the affinity between Chesterton and Marianne Moore can be detected especially in regard to her mother and her brother.

Chesterton obliquely inserted his views on marriage into his essays, whether on religion, personalities, or social and political comment. For instance, in *Orthodoxy* he wrote: "Christian marriage is the great example of a real and irrevocable result; and that is why it is the chief subject and centre of all our romantic writing." He wished, above all, for marriage to be taken seriously. Laurence Stapleton, in her perceptive book on Marianne Moore, has ventured to guess that Miss Moore's poem "Marriage," a poem unique in that it proceeds with a separate first line, not taken from the title ("This institution [marriage] . . ."), is a roman à clef. She suggests that Moore's notebooks show a preoccupation with this subject in the early New York years and, further, that "in the background of the poem was the widespread discussion of Bryher's marriage to Robert McAlmon." After the newspaper stories had broken with the headlines of heiress and village poet wed, "Marianne refused to see anything humorous in the newspaper story, and said that she found the marriage anything but romantic."

Bryher was twenty-six. She looked eighteen, and Marianne Moore was unexpectedly protective toward her. She and her mother had been impressed both by her mind and manner. McAlmon, born in 1896, was only twenty-five, although no one seems to have taken his youth into account, assuming that he had been fending for himself for so long. Marianne had written to McAlmon that "Bryher is not like anyone—talented or untalented—that I have ever seen." The Moores had not been in the least influenced in their opinion by Bryher's having given Marianne three hundred dollars on which to take a holiday. There was a shared feeling of gentle respect between Bryher and the Moores. Neither "Rat," as Marianne was called within the family, nor "Mole," her mother, could possibly have guessed that the missing romance they attributed to McAlmon had originated with Bryher; that it had been she who had insisted on the rapid marriage.

Marianne's attitude toward the marriage must have been explained to McAlmon, because once in London he wrote her reminding her that there is also "a little impulse" in the world, as well as "romance." He represented himself as one who had been chosen to help Bryher escape the family yoke. "Wildness" was necessary to a British family with its somber appearance.

A good many people considered the marriage unusual. It had been the topic of letters exchanged between Marianne Moore and Amy Lowell. Finally, in March 1923, Amy's curiosity led her to write to H.D. saying that she had learned the McAlmons were settling into marriage. "I cannot make out how. Marianne Moore seemed to think it was a marriage of convenience and that they were not living together as man and wife. Personally from Winifred's letters [she refused to call her Bryher] I should doubt this. I should doubt it still more from her poems, and I do not know whether Marianne Moore knows any more about it than I do . . ." Then Amy went on to discuss the reception in England of the anthology Conrad Aiken had edited, *Modern American Poets,* in which H.D.'s poems from *Sea Garden* and *Hymen* had appeared. Amy's attitude was that "the animosity of the British press toward American poetry is one of the things that prove how extremely vital and interesting American poetry is . . ." Then she went on to ask H.D. to give her exact information about the McAlmon marriage.

H.D.'s answer to Amy is an admirable example of a discreet letter. It took her over a year to compose.

> About the McAlmons. It is difficult to say. They are together a good bit of the time off and on. . . . I myself feel that both she and Robert have done very well for themselves! The marriage certainly is most unconventional but they are together a good deal and viewed from the ultra-modern or even modern standpoint their attitude is normal enough. Bryher, of course, is *very* uneven. She takes colour from the company she is in or from the person she happens to be attached to, and then volte-face, she utterly changes, becomes another person, almost a disassociation stunt. Well—perhaps this is not answering your question. But it is a difficult question—Bryher's whole problem is unusual. Also it is hard for me to know just how much to tell (even to you in confidence) as *both* the McAlmons have poured into my sympathetic ear their entire physical, psychological and metaphysical histories. I want them to be happy though they do the most awful things. But I love them both and do want them to be happy. And I feel more and more, that their marriages (or marriage) is in its funny way, a success.

Two interesting things emerge from this letter. The first is the point that H.D. makes about Bryher being influenced by the person nearest to her. That temptation of Bryher's, not unusual in anyone her age, to do a "volte-face" caused H.D. much unnecessary worry. She feared at this time that Bryher might become involved in other situations that would influence her and a resulting rift might be made between herself and Bryher. The other involves the perhaps Freudian slip when H.D. pluralizes "marriages" in the last sentence. She may have let slip that Bryher and McAlmon had a his-and-her marriage. Each viewed the marriage from a separate angle and behaved accordingly, so that by no possible means could one refer to their legal situation as a "marriage of true minds"; rather it was a case of two wills taking their separate courses. Amy Lowell, had she chosen, could have read between the lines.

CHAPTER THIRTEEN

The Oberland Express

Sir John had wired the McAlmons to come to Mayfair when they arrived in London, as they would be welcomed at South Audley Street. H.D. was then installed at St. James Court, Buckingham Gate, not too far from the Ellerman mansion. Perdita, aged two, went again to the now familiar Norland Nursery to board and be visited there by her mother.

H.D. was waiting for *Hymen* to appear. When it did shortly after her arrival, it was reviewed by May Sinclair, who again proved herself on the side of the Imagists by unabashedly stating that "there is nothing in contemporary literature that surpasses these poems." The *Times Literary Supplement* found *Hymen* "deadening and monotonous." Previously, Gilbert Murray, an authority on Greek translation, had praised H.D.'s translations, so this must have come as a surprise. She doesn't seem to have been much moved by her reviews, although naturally she was grateful to May Sinclair for her continued devotion. Marianne Moore's praise was also welcome. Marianne would have liked these early poems of H.D.'s. Yet the question is up in the air as to what her opinion must have been of the later H.D. Miss Moore once had made the statement that "I have a mania for straight writing—however circuitous I may be in what I myself say of plants, animals, or places . . . I mean, in part writing that is not mannered, over conscious or at war with common sense." The final clause could never be applied to H.D.'s poetry, particularly in its later phase.

Once more H.D. took up the concerns of the McAlmons. Robert was living grandly and disliking it. The Ellermans were evidently kind to him,[1] and he found he liked Sir John and could tolerate his wife. Like everyone else, he considered Bryher's brother, John, pathetic. This twelve-year-old boy was never permitted to go out unattended. He knew nothing of the value of money as, like royalty, he was never permitted to carry any. He had to wear a bowler hat wherever he went. He had been sent away to a school he detested. At fifteen he wrote a book about his school, Malvern, called *Why Do They Like It?* and Bryher published it. John used the pseudonym E. L. Black, and the foreword was con-

---

[1] According to Grace McAlmon Marissael, in a letter to the author, Lady Ellerman frequently corresponded with the McAlmon family in America. She always remembered them with gifts at Christmas and on birthdays.

H.D. and Bryher, 1920. *(The Rosen-bach Museum and Library)*

Havelock Ellis. *(Beinecke)*

H.D. in Egypt, 1923. *(Beinecke)*

D. H. Lawrence—Pen and ink draw
ing by Knud Merrild, author of *A P*
and Two Painters: A Memoir of D.
Lawrence. (Courtesy of Barba
Guest)

"Study for The Vorticists
at the Restaurant de la
Tour Eiffel London
Spring 1915" by William
Roberts. Ezra Pound is
seated at the extreme
left, Wyndham Lewis in
the Center. *(Photo-*
graph: Anthony d'Offay
Gallery, London)

H.D. in the 1920s. *(Beinecke)*

Robert McAlmon, ca. 1928. *(Courtesy of Grace McAlmon Marissael)*

CONTACT COLLECTION OF
CONTEMPORARY WRITERS

Djuna Barnes
Bryher
Mary Butts
Norman Douglas
Havelock Ellis
F. M. Ford
Wallace Gould
Ernest Hemingway
Marsden Hartley
H. D.
John Herrman
James Joyce
Mina Loy
Robert McAlmon
Ezra Pound
Dorothy Richardson
May Sinclair
Edith Sitwell
Gertrude Stein
W. C. Williams

to Sylvia Beach from
Bob McAlmon June 5 192
Ernest Hemingway

Marsden Hartley

H. D.

Bryher

Ford Madox Ford

May Sinclair

Signatures of authors in Sylvia Beach's copy of *Contact Collection of Contemporary Writers,* 1925. *(Princeton University Library)*

Kenwin. *(Beinecke)*

Paul and Eslanda Robeson in *Borderline*, 1930. *(Beinecke)*

H.D. in *Borderline*, 1930. *(Beinecke)*

Robert Herring, Kenneth Macpherson, and Bryher at Spitzbergen in 1929. *(Beinecke)*

tributed by a dutiful Dorothy Richardson. It is an odd little book, a rougher version of Bryher's own *Development*.

McAlmon summed up the Ellerman household at the time he lived in it: "Wealth, the war, the phobias, manias, dementias, prejudices, and terrors that come from both were the dominant factors." Flamboyant as the statement may seem, assuming there is an element of truth in it, Bryher seems to have made a remarkable, if flawed, escape. The McAlmons soon moved out of South Audley Street and into H.D.'s flat, whose furnishings horrified Bob with their "dim and stuffy Anglo-respectables."

The Egoist Press, again with the financial support of Bryher, published McAlmon's book of poems, *Explorations*, which went deservedly unnoticed. In 1925 he wrote a long poem, "Portrait of a Generation," in which Sir John describes his shipping operations and Lady Ellerman discusses her deafness and clever people whom she liked, although she realized she wasn't clever herself.

With his flair for seeking out people, McAlmon soon found his way around literary London. He met Wyndham Lewis and made an unsuccessful attempt to get Sir John to buy a painting from him. He had tea with T. S. Eliot, who seemed kind, but "tired out." Eliot's respectable appearance dismayed McAlmon as much as had the erudition of his poetry. Altogether McAlmon complained about the fustiness and primness of London, almost as much as Bryher had complained about the barbarism of America. Clearly, he did not fit into British society and never would, despite the proffered good will of those around him.

McAlmon's father-in-law, who was as disconcerted as McAlmon, but for obviously different reasons, was looking around for a position for his difficult son-in-law on one of the publications—*The Tatler, The Sketch, The Sphere*, all of which he at the time controlled. McAlmon immediately decided the editor of *The Sphere*, Clement Shorter, gave him "the willies." (H.D. had her own reservations about Shorter.) Little did these helpful people suspect that the maverick in their midst was hatching ideas for publishing far removed from their genteel operations. It was the Establishment represented by Ellerman's magazines that revolted McAlmon.

McAlmon has left a shrewd sketch of his father-in-law that leaves no question as to the reasons for Bob's ultimate decision to remove himself from the Ellerman scene.

> Sir John was by no means the first rich man with whom I had been in contact, and I had some time ago decided that moneymakers on the grand scale are monomaniacs and fanatics and self-willed. As regards finance, Sir John had that thing which need not be looked upon with awe, genius, but in many other respects he was a perfect case of arrested development, suffering innumerable childish fears.

The description might well fit Mrs. Bryher McAlmon.

By 1922 the "menagerie of three," which now included Mrs. Doolittle, who had joined them in Europe, would have established a pattern of travel they would follow for the next four years. It would be London-Eastbourne (for the McAlmons)—Paris—Switzerland, where they rented rooms in a pension called the Riant Château at Territet, a suburb of Montreux.

The Swiss establishment was chosen to avoid taxes, as Bryher could begin to establish a residency outside of England. The Riant Château would be a nesting place until 1930, when Bryher would build her own home in nearby Vevey. Meanwhile it was an immigrant's outpost for their friends to visit, a temporary Coppet.[2] There H.D. could offer a home to her mother, and later a visiting Aunt Laura, and at last Perdita could live en famille, rather than in the Norland Nursery. It was a serious household, unlike their other outposts, with cook, nurse, and later a French governess for the child. When Bryher was in residence, there was the daily schedule of writing, then Bryher's tap at H.D.'s door, "Ready? Fido's waiting." They would walk down to the lake before stopping at a tea shop where H.D. would be permitted a vermouth.

H.D. may have lamented the seclusion, and she did, but she was given time and space in which to write. She was working on the stories of her youth, friendship with Frances, and marriage. "Paint It Today" and "Asphodel" are so reliably autobiographical that they have been drawn on many times to clarify and explain the events in H.D.'s life. She was also writing the poems that would be in her next projected book, Heliodora.

Idyllic as these conditions appear in retrospect, H.D. chafed at the isolation, and the restrictive presence of her relatives. H.D.'s attitude toward her mother was as ambivalent as it was toward anyone else. Whereas she was relieved of much responsibility when her mother was around, especially where Perdita was concerned, her mother's provincialisms maddened her. For instance, according to H.D., her mother expected her constantly to praise the States, to remember her birthplace, her old friends. What Mrs. Doolittle really wished was for H.D. to admit that she would prefer to live in the United States in a safe place like Philadelphia, rather than running around like a permanent exile, or expatriate, which she had become. When Ford Madox Ford had written in transition about the narrowed horizon of New Jersey and the probability of its effect on Williams, she had agreed. She told Bryher, "Ford is right. They are the Prussians of today." When her mother would recount an anecdote from H.D.'s supposed privileged and idealized youth, H.D., according to McAlmon, who had witnessed such a scene, would roll on the

---

[2] Bryher, in her Swiss exile, as will later be noted, frequently puts one in mind of her former neighbor at Coppet, Madame de Staël. The same energy, respect for ideas, and literary production; the unusual assortment of friends, and the general air of dishabille created by the coming and going of retainer-friends.

floor screaming, "How wrong you are!" She would then remind her mother the kids had called her "string bean," and because she was so tall asked her, "How is it up there?" Not excessive behavior for children, yet H.D. would never forget a slight or insult. She blamed a good deal of her suffering on the Quaker State. She would tell Bryher that of course she was interested in the United States, but in her own way. "Can you see," she would ask Bryher, "how London at least left me free? Will you ever realize what it means? Thank God, I say sometimes, even for Araminta [Dorothy ("Arabella") Yorke]. She was bound up anyhow with my escape." Did she mean by this that had Aldington not gone off with Dorothy she might have, like a good soldier's wife, gone back to live with her parents and not entrusted herself to Cecil Gray? And after him, Bryher?

If Freud was correct and H.D. did seek her mother throughout her life (or wanted a mother's attention, because it had not been bestowed upon her as a girl), it is curious that when she did have her mother to herself, a feeling of claustrophobia would come over her. Territet with her mother meant being cut off from the real world. Rebelling, she would dash off to London, where she spent weekends weeping in her hotel room. H.D. would see herself as homeless, even when surrounded by the comforting presence of her real mother. Or was her real mother not the prosaic "Beaver," but that unattainable Helen of Troy whom she would so often evoke, whose daughter was Hermione?

When in London, in the early 1920s, H.D. had taken a room at the respectable Hotel Washington on Curzon Street. Then began a bleak period. She felt nearly as separated from the world in the midst of London as she had among the foothills of the Alps. She was fearful, anxious. Besides, she was lonely for Bryher. She forced herself to take walks; she went to matinees, which would always remain a useful escape for her. Sad days and letters. She sent Bryher the most explicit love letters she had yet written: she will not desert her pedestal for the common pursuit, but she doesn't hesitate to remind Bryher that emotionally she is fragile; spiritually she is constant. Reading the letters would lead to an overwhelming supposition, not entirely true, of H.D.'s dependency on the younger woman.

At the same time as she was sending her weepy, courting letters to Bryher, H.D. had begun a correspondence, unfortunately lost in the Blitz, that would eventually run into an estimated five hundred letters and postcards over the years of her friendship with a then very young man, whose name was Harold P. Collins.

Collins, just up from Cambridge, had first set foot onto the literary scene with a job on the civil service monthly, *Red Tape*. In 1921 he had noticed that *Hymen* had been given a slighting review in the *Times Literary Supplement*. (Later they produced an unsigned two-column essay on Imagism and vers libre with a laudatory emphasis on H.D. Could this afterthought have been prompted by the jostling of Sir John's huge shares in *The Times*?) Collins in his minor way remedied the *Times* review by a laudatory review of his own in *Red Tape*. By now he had become interested in The Poetry Bookshop, T. S. Eliot, and other new poets. He decided next to try his hand at literary criticism by writing a book on the new poets.[3] He was encouraged in his effort by John Middleton Murry, who became his mentor and his future editor at *Adelphi* magazine, where Collins eventually became literary editor. Needing permission to quote from H.D.'s poetry he would feature in his book, Collins wrote to her in 1923 when she was at Territet. She answered by inviting him to the Hotel Washington when she would be in London in September of that year.

Bryher was absent. Perdita, as usual, was tucked away at the Riant Château. H.D. for the benefit of Collins became her prewar Egeria self. Wearing what the unsophisticated Collins thought could only be a Parisian dress, her figure slender, tall, and elegant, she was the essence of his stifled middle-class dreams. She was surprisingly confiding with Collins, even at this first meeting. She told him she detested Victorianism, especially Mrs. Browning (who, privately, Collins believed she had never read). She caught him up when he disparaged Swinburne and Poe, reminding him that Poe had written the immortal "To Helen." One can easily place the scene. H.D. at her loveliest, and her most poetic, beside her the humble, sensible, struggling Collins. She needed a squire. She would always need one, in particular a young squire. Here was the ideal person of nearly twenty-three to her youthful thirty-seven years. Before he left that day she handed him a typed copy of the manuscript of *Heliodora*, asking him for his criticism. Collins returned to his humble digs, believing he had been with Sappho. And he was at once useful. He made her "omit a very bad paraphrase of Homer in sketchy free verse." He never thought much of her knowledge of the classics. In fact, he was convinced of her ignorance.

Then it was time to introduce him to Bryher at a birthday party—they were all three Virgos—and the friendship was off the ground. In return for the intensity and excitement of her presence and her introductions to her friends, he helped edit her poetry and helped to find reviewers for her. He also gave her reviews to write when he went on to the *Adelphi*.

[3] H. P. Collins, *Modern Poetry* (London: Jonathan Cape, 1925). Collins devotes a chapter on H.D. of nearly fifty pages in which he examines her translations and poetry. This chapter contains the most appreciative, scholarly, and sensible examination of her work up to 1925 that has yet been written. His praise is restrained, yet it is apparent that he considers her a writer of a "technical uniqueness" who shares a quality of classicism, and yet is modern, and he is not often reluctant to use the word "genius," with thoughtful moderation.

Oddly, she was in the old Mansfield-Murry world again. Collins' intimate memoirs of her, written at the request of Norman Holmes Pearson, when Collins was a much older man, show H.D. not as she pictured herself to Bryher in the 1920s—an aging, dowdy, unfulfilled, and ignored woman— but as she appeared to the world of Collins and his friends, associates, and family. In a word, glamorous. She smoked only Egyptian cigarettes, which she shared with the then impoverished Collins. She drank occasionally, only the most expensive whiskey, provided by Bryher. Her small apartment on Sloane Street was filled with flowers. Bryher in 1929 gave her a dress costing one hundred pounds, which then would have been the equivalent of nearly five hundred dollars and today five thousand dollars. Collins assumed that all her cloudy, exquisitely made, amusing, and sometimes outlandish dresses were made in Paris. She even wore such clothes to the tennis matches at suburban Pedham. The innocent Collins believed she did not know what a tennis match was, living on such a superior level of the intellect and disliking the suburbs, as she told him, so much. Of course, Hilda knew about such matches from her Philadelphia days, but she had set out to form an image of herself for Collins and she did not wish to interfere with that image. Here she is revealed as Wilkinson in *The Buffoon* parodied her.

To Collins, H.D. represented an aristocracy of the mind. As an American she did not fit into the rigid British social structure and thus was free to behave as she pleased, in what he considered to be the delightful casual American manner. He found her conservative politically. She never read any of the "penny dreadful" newspapers. She was shocked by the general strike. She kept to a world beyond cockneys and political strife. He watched a highly nervous H.D., at a dinner she gave for May Sinclair in 1924, completely bewitch the older woman. H.D. concealed her social timidity with laughter and wizardry, and that touch of the rebellious, gifted poet that May Sinclair, with her sedate modesty, could not resist.

Collins wrote that he did not believe H.D. could have existed financially or emotionally without the support of Bryher, she was too intense and overwrought. Later, in answering a request from her (she was a great commissioner), he responded, "Glad to be of some use." H.D. gasped. "That is what Richard said when asking me to marry him and I thanked him for his lovely name. 'Glad to be of some use.'"

She carried Collins about with her everywhere and introduced him to Brigit Patmore, hoping he would find Brigit a publisher. Collins was shocked at the "homosexual" dedication of Brigit's novel, addressing H.D. as "Beloved." He met Wilkinson and respected him, although he was suspicious of Frances Gregg. H.D. always came to Frances' defense, which was *not* the case with her own family. She declared she didn't like them, particularly Melvin, who at that time was with the Ford Agency nearby. She defended McAlmon, but she pretended not to like what Contact Editions published. True, or untrue. She never much cared for the work of others. Among the Americans at that time, Henry James was a safe and snobbish choice.

In Collins' "Memoirs" he writes that H.D. only told him of the circumstances of Perdita's birth after they had known one another for five years. Collins, it seems, scarcely knew Perdita, and Perdita, when questioned, does not remember him. He did see Bryher frequently, and it was Bryher who commissioned Collins' "Memoirs" for Pearson. And yet Collins in his role as H.D.'s squire and useful critic, reviewer and literary man, continues to mystify.

Finally, perhaps after his marriage, H.D. may have tired of him as she progressed to others. He mentions that the war separated them and he knew of her breakdown. There is no mention of a love affair. He seems to have furnished her with the adulation she found so necessary. He filled in the periods between the absences of Bryher. Yet from 1923 to the Second World War is a long time. The end of the story here is that once more H.D.'s instincts had led her to a worthy, conscientious, and useful man in a time of psychic and physical disorder. A gallant man who rallied to her side, rewarded by the intense meaning she added to chosen things, the flair for excitement she added to life, and grateful that as a man of letters he could be of help to her.

From Territet she wrote to Bryher: "You are a great benefactor to the town and such a pet and lamb and Fido darling to a lonely Cheval. Come soon . . . and be kissed and adored." From the Hotel Washington she wrote to Bryher in Eastbourne: "This is just to say I love and love and love you. I missed not hearing this morning horribly, not a note came last night no doubt one will arrive ce soir. Dear Heart, 1001 kisses." Fortunate correspondents to be able to rely on the many mail deliveries of a kinder era is the often repeated thought as the Bryher-H.D. letters pour forth at all hours of the day and evening.

The pattern of their daily letter writing was now established. H.D.'s letters are gossipy, tinselly, nervous, apprehensive, distinctly not "clever." Bryher's are full of sound advice (sometimes ad nauseum) about possessions, Perdita, dogs, magazines, countless plans for housing, travel, and also gossip, in which they both delighted. H.D. reveals her phobias, the claustrophobia she felt in crowds, and, oddly enough, her fear of travel. She would always be frightened of taxis, certain that one would strike her down. She never ate chicken because she feared it might be cat! There is no discussion of their writing. These early letters are the love letters. Later there is a gradual diminution of the expressions of love, substituted by affection, as in the natural course of a marriage. Only in these early years is there any mention of physical passion. Like all addicted letter writers, H.D. and Bryher composed a fairly luminous portrait of themselves. What is most noticeable is that there is no real quarrel in these letters, no hint of a definite marital separation. Their geographical separations were largely unnecessary, but were needed by H.D. to assert her claims to freedom from the insistent watchdoggery of Bryher. These separations gave them space in which to confirm their real selves. H.D. is very cautious with Bryher. She is much more discreet in her letters, with these few early exceptions, than she probably was in person.

Colette comes to mind. After her separation from Willy, Colette tells us that she came to rest under the wing of "Missy," who was the youngest daughter of the Duc de Morny. Married briefly to the Marquis de Belbeuf, the experience had so shocked her that she had turned to women. The Marquise in some ways resembles Bryher. Colette writes of the Marquise that ". . . the salacious expectations of women shocked her very natural platonic tendencies, which resembled more the suppressed excitement, the diffuse emotion of an adolescent, than a woman's explicit need. 'I do not know anything about the completeness in love,' she said, 'except the *idea* I have of it.'"

Bryher, unlike Missy with her totally male attire, wore a severely cut jacket and skirt, still seeking the coloration of the male as she assumed his protective role. As we read between the lines of *The Pure and the Impure*, we discover, as Colette did, that what these women so often needed was a person upon whom they might bestow their unrecognized maternal or paternal affection. Sex played a much less important role. Tenderness expressed by close friendship was essential. Since many of the women Colette describes were of the upper classes, if not the aristocracy (as was "Missy"), they had been deprived from childhood of the warmth of a family. They sought to replace this with their *petites amies*. Like Bryher, they were protected by their wealth and sought the freedom to establish their own ties. Bryher was more fortunate than most, as she was able to maintain a lifelong relationship she was careful not to destroy, no matter how precarious the balance might become, and test it though she might. This is also true of H.D. They would sometimes find themselves on too difficult a plane—one that imposed itself between the idealization of H.D. by Bryher, and the gratitude of H.D. for the care and thoughtfulness of Bryher—and then their personal edifice might tremble, but not for long or forever.

In August of 1923 H.D. was writing from the Hotel Washington:

> Just to prove to my darling that I think of "HE" all the time. I bought some pink roses to put before the sweet Man Ray portrait [a photograph of Bryher taken by Man Ray while Bryher had been in Paris with McAlmon]—my little altar—just you and Baby and the little . . . Greek Boy [the photograph of the hermaphrodite sculpture H.D. had discovered on her first visit to Rome].

In contrast to the affection of the letters, there was still the behavior of Bryher and H.D. when together that turned them, according to McAlmon, into two quarrelsome, bickering females. This would be true particularly, he said, in the railway carriages that took them back and forth from Switzerland to Paris and on to England.

McAlmon finally decided that both H.D. and himself were victims of Bryher's excessive urge, inherited from her father, to plan every moment of the other person's day; he believed that her idea of a loving relationship was also the same as her father's. "The beloved was to be reduced to a state of shrieking trembling hysteria, and then she would be conciliatory and say, 'There, there, calm, calm. It's a nice kitten.' " McAlmon in order to escape these tactics would retreat to a bar. "Then Bryher would call on H.D. . . . realizing that the solid Lump [Perdita] was too much her own emotional age to be made hysterical, she tackled Hilda, and always produced results.[4] By merely mentioning experiences of the war years or an unhappy episode in Hilda's past, and dwelling upon it long enough, she soon had the high-strung Hilda acting much like a candidate for the strait jacket. She did it, she said, because of her own thwarted childhood." Bryher's behavior, it could be added, resembles that of a neurotically jealous male who agonizes over his mistress's past affairs.

Brigit Patmore in *No Tomorrow* (1929) has rewarded the Bryher-H.D. alliance with a careful scrutiny:

> The child [Bryher] had generous ideas, but when it came to action she was cramped and ugly, and had a strange bargaining sense—for so much money or its equivalent she expected so much in return, principally in submission, for she loved power and needed it for her lack of attraction and genius. She pressed Helga's [H.D.'s] freedom away with little importunities and wistfulness and protection and gifts . . . the effect was depressing and annoying, and inclined to encourage Helga's retreat from people.

There are several things that come to mind in reading Brigit's analysis. The first is that Brigit was never friendly with Bryher; they each may have actively disliked the other. Brigit was "in love" with H.D. When she visited the Patmore house in 1914, Brigit's son Derek adoringly called H.D. "the Crocus lady."[5] Secondly, Brigit is speaking of the early Bryher before time had dusted her with a little temperance and the world, which then appeared to her as either pro-Bryher or anti-Bryher, had proved to have more protective hues of gray. Thirdly, an outsider is never fully ac-

---

[4] "Lump" was McAlmon's name for Perdita.

[5] Brigit's 1926 novel, *This Impassioned Onlooker*, also about H.D., had such an "embarrassingly homosexual dedication to H.D.," Harold Collins told Pearson, that without H.D.'s ever having seen it, Collins forced Brigit to change it.

quainted with the intricacies of another's relationship. And finally, what Brigit has described undoubtedly took place. It is to be supposed that Bryher's behavior—and H.D.'s—did not remain as static as Brigit's printed page.

McAlmon, who usually proves to be honest in his accounts, was still another biased observer. William Carlos Williams, who had met Bryher only in 1920 in New York and in 1924 in Paris, had been impressed, as so many people were, by Bryher's seeming steadiness, as opposed to H.D.'s more hysterical behavior. In a letter to Norman Holmes Pearson in 1953, McAlmon disputed the account of H.D. and Bryher in Williams' *Autobiography*, which was presumably based on information supplied by McAlmon. Williams had written that the McAlmon marriage breakup was due to H.D.'s interference. McAlmon wrote to Pearson: "Plainly he [Williams] did not gather that I thought H.D. a victim, and Bryher gloating over her then economic dependence. Bryher always seemed to Bill and most people so balanced and calm, clearly analysing and stating cause and effect. Jesus, to write her up as she was and with H.D. in the picture, would make Djuna's *Night Wood* [*sic*] a limpid and innocent parable."

McAlmon finally decided that the women may have *enjoyed* their teasings and neurotic battles, that it was he who was such an outsider and could not comprehend the inner triumphs that rewarded the outer defeats.

From "Halcyon":

VI

You're impatient, unkind,
lovers aren't that,
so it can't be love;
you're invariably blind,

bitter and crude to me,
cruel, whimsical;
since you don't find
this colour agrees with you

(You say my dress
makes you sick)
go find some one else
there are plenty about;

yes, I will shout,
don't say my voice displeases you,
nor my ways;
O the days, the days

> without these quarrels,
> what were they?
> something like a desert apart
> without hope of oasis
>
> or a grot lacking water
> or a bird with a broken wing . . .

When Fido (Bryher) arrived at the Hotel Washington smoking her cigars, bringing flowers, books, sweets, then it would be "How sweet to see, to smell, to touch, to taste Fido again. And how good of him to rush in wagging his beautiful tail."

Yet Bryher was away frequently in Eastbourne or Paris. It was that time in Paris when McAlmon declared, "Everyone wanted to look like the music hall star Elsie Janis as a cowboy with hat and handkerchief." In one day Bryher had visited Brancusi, a Tuileries exhibition, and Gertrude Stein. Gertrude Stein had spotted Bryher and McAlmon on the street and noted that McAlmon had with him a "pure ethnic type of Jewess." When they reached Stein's, she was rushing on to Ezra Pound's, where Mrs. Joyce had just arrived. Afterward they went off to Jean Cocteau's newly opened Le Boeuf sur le Toit, a cabaret that catered to an international set for more than a decade. Robert tried to fix her up with one of the girls—usually lesbians, slangily called "pumas." (Lawrence had called a girl friend of the composer Halliday a "puma" in *Aaron's Rod*.) Then Bryher saw "dissipated" Cocteau and had dinner with Man Ray and his model, Kiki of Montparnasse, whom she preferred to almost everyone, because Kiki was so intelligent with or without her clothes. McAlmon had done Joyce a great service in introducing him to Bryher. In his *Letters* Joyce writes that he was hoping to obtain money from Lady Cunard, but that if that plan fell through, he had a fallback in "Lady E." Lady Ellerman did succeed Lady Cunard in Joyce's plans, and her money helped the Joyce family over a difficult period; not that there were any smooth periods for this both impecunious and extravagant family.

Bryher's excited letters from Paris made H.D. even more depressed. Again she was consumed with that old feeling of being left out. She wrote to Amy Lowell: "I as a matter of fact, seem, save for yourself, not to have even a speaking acquaintance with a single surviving Imagist. However, the little royalties come in as a reminder of the good old days!" The royalties were not sufficient for H.D. to declare a financial independence from Bryher. This may have been what prompted her to ask Brigit Patmore to intervene between herself and Cecil Gray with a request for support for Perdita. She had never asked for anything from him. Brigit did approach Gray, as her letter of September 13, 1922, proves. She

found Gray taking hashish and involved in a crowd, including Mary
Butts and Heseltine, around the notorious Aleister Crowley, who was accused of celebrating black masses, and various eviltries. It was a bad
time to ask Gray for anything. He was spending all of his allowance on
the composer van Dieren, and he had just paid the sculptor Epstein one
hundred pounds for a bust of van Dieren. Confusion, sloth, and a hopeless sort of paralysis had overtaken him during this unfortunate period.
He made no payment to H.D. Gray's refusal to recognize his obligation
may have been prompted by his remembering Heseltine's advice. At the
height of the Gray-H.D. affair in 1918, Heseltine, who detested H.D.,
had sent this poem to Gray:

Heseltine: 5 August 1918

> *Then* you will know whom you must choke
> Before they get beyond a joke . . .
> To love a flower, a bird, a beast
> Is to enjoy a spiritual feast,
> But do not keep a vampire bat,
> For love of Nature in your hat,
> Nor take the accompanying sensation
> Of loss of blood for inspiration . . .

The reason H.D. may have been disposed to ask Gray for money in the
fall of 1922 was that it was a period when Bryher had been especially
unkind about her relations with Gray. After Bryher had adopted Perdita,
she chose to take the stance that inasmuch as Gray was Perdita's father,
he was to be treated with a reasonable degree of respect. She may have
been influenced then by her friend, the champion of Gray, the writer and
historian of Capri, Norman Douglas.

It was about this time that Bryher received a letter from H.D., moping
in Territet:

> I feel so grateful to you for your sweetness but always remember that a
> very wild horse has been trimmed down and kept pretty close in its pad-
> dock. Not that it wanted to kick up its heels and have twenty stallions at
> it, but after all, it needs a certain amount of free roaming and these old
> Flanders mares and this very fat COLT sometimes make it feel it has lost
> itself in a strange field. I don't want to run amuck but if the gates clang
> too too tight I shall one day, in spite of myself, simply jump the fence and
> perhaps never come back.

Bryher decided to resort to her usual strategy of solving problems by
taking a trip. She invited H.D. and her mother on a handsome excursion
that would commence in Florence and end in Egypt.

Italy, Greece, Constantinople, Egypt were to be the itinerary of
1922–23. First, there was Norman Douglas to be encountered in

Florence. Norman Douglas—the author of the classic *South Wind*, the book that would fascinate a generation with its description of a magic and diabolic island that was in real geography Capri—was known to Bryher through his book *They Went*. She had written him a letter complimenting him on this earlier, and now little-read, book. The exemplary biographer of Douglas, Mark Holloway, explains that "it was this fascination with the living actuality of history and the attempt to present it in terms of art which made her feel that *They Went* might have been written for her."

From Holloway we also learn that in 1923 Bryher helped Douglas acquire a flat in Florence. The charm Douglas possessed to an extraordinary degree, and which he usually chose to hide from the ordinary world, could work wonders when he so wished. A portrait of Douglas at this time is sketched by D. H. Lawrence in *Aaron's Rod*, where Douglas appears as the sybaritic Argyle. Bryher and Douglas became great friends, considering Bryher's dislike of alcohol of any kind, and Douglas' inability to understand how anyone could reside in Montreux. He told her he wouldn't allow his worst enemy's cat to be buried there. (Poor Douglas, the Second World War forced him into a hotel near Montreux.) Holloway comments that "Douglas was one of the many of Bryher's 'Drunks.'"

H.D. and Bryher began their trip in the most magical way possible, which is to sail from Venice in the evening when the ship glides by the palaces and churches, and the moonlight falls on the soft waters. The traveler then knows he is following the ancient Venetian path of the Adriatic to the queen of cities, Constantinople, and the world of the Hellenes. This second trip to Greece found a more rested and observant H.D. This time she is a more careful traveler, making notes of flowers and less hysterically observant. It is Constantinople that causes the most enthusiasm, and a short trip to Corfu seems to bring back no unpleasant memories.

Between 1922 and 1923 there are so many trips, the landscape flicks by, Chistmases in Florence, then a short visit with Douglas on Capri; finally in March 1923, leaving Perdita at Riant Château, off they go, this time to Egypt, accompanied by Mrs. Doolittle. The biographer becomes lost among the shifting cities and countrysides. There is a frantic search dictating all this traveling, beyond the fact that travel then for those with adequate funds was less costly. The various nationalities during the twenties were constantly running from country to country, urged on by a need to grasp the mirage before it disappeared in another war.

"Karnak and Luxor and Valley of Tombs day, the latter I consider in retrospect the fullest most perfect day of my life." So wrote H.D. to Bryher. She dedicated her book *Palimpsest* to Bryher, the book in which the last section is a fictitious record of their trip to Egypt. The

poem that is the dedication contains the movements of the stars and the
sight of ships, which were so much a part of their life in the early 1920s,
the years of travel; work, as her book proves, also kept its pace.

> To Bryher
>
> •   •   •
>
> yet disenchanted, cold, imperious face,
> when all the others, blighted, reel and fall,
> your star, steel-set, keeps lone and frigid trist
> to freighted ships baffled in wind and blast.

It's all there in the poem. Bryher, who had such tremulous childhood
memories of Egypt, which she had visited with her parents, was now disinterested, or disenchanted. Let Bryher keep her "lone and frigid" trysts.
This was going to be H.D.'s show. No more putting herself out to entertain Bryher, or bothering so much with her whims. Egypt had been a
gift, and H.D. made the most of it.

They had arrived at the opening of King Tut's tomb, and H.D. does
not hesitate to exploit the mystery that hovered about the tomb and its
excited visitors. "Secret Name; Excavator's Egypt" in *Palimpsest* is a record of H.D.'s Egypt. The story is another variation on "Blue Nile" men,
an Aldington type, an H.D. It has a Henry Jamesian touch with a dove-
like Milly Theale young woman, and another Kate Croy, one of those
sublimely knowing women James was so adept in dealing with. What
H.D. wants to convey is mystery and moonlight and questionable relationships. It is in arranging atmospheric effects that H.D. excels. There is
the electric light in the tomb, the hotel, dust, bright dresses, the softness
of a glove, an evening wrap absorbed in night air, a sparkle of bead here
and there. When Mrs. Fairwood, who is H.D., has morning coffee, it is as
important a part of the day as her fantasies about the Aldington-male.
Secretly, she is luxury-loving, dreaming; openly, she upholds an intellectual front.

One sentence stands out. *"The Greeks came to Egypt to learn."* (my
italics) From now on Greece and Egypt will form an axis, joining in her
last book, *Helen in Egypt*. This Egyptian trip taught her a respect and
admiration for the Egyptian world; the Greeks would remain a constant
source with their myths and heroes, yet they would have to compete
with Egyptian dynasties, with Isis holding her peace: "Never a word did
she speak for she knew that Ra had told her the names that all men
know; his true Name, his Secret Name, was still hidden in his breast."
This quotation from the Twentieth Dynasty would mysteriously lay its
hold on H.D. The complicated, mathematical structure of Egyptian
thought would begin to supplant the Greeks, whose minds were no
longer so instructive, whose modern land had somehow failed to en-

chant. The Greeks were less complex, purer. What she had sought and pretended to find in the Delphic rites was what the Greeks refused to believe in—mysticism. As H.D. began to turn toward the mystical, in its various forms—the Cabala, spiritualism, Moravianism—whatever would lead her thought into the unknown, a "higher thought," toward the Sacred Name, it would be the ritualistic Egyptians with their Isis and Ra, their sacred Cat, who would more and more attract her.

From "Egypt"

> We pray you Egypt,
> by what perverse fate,
> has poison brought with knowledge,
> given us this—
> not days of trance,
> shadow, fore-doom of death,
> but passionate grave thought,
> belief enhanced,
> ritual returned and magic . . .

She brought back the poem "Egypt" with her to be included in *Heliodora*, which would be published in 1924, the following year.

CHAPTER FOURTEEN

The Bunch

H.D. was scarcely back from Egypt and settled at the Riant Château, where she planned to write her story with its Egyptian setting and gather together her poems for the collection Jonathan Cape was about to publish, when in the spring of 1924 Bryher wrote her to come to Paris. Bryher this time suggested bringing the "Pudding." Perdita's plump little self with its round face, unlike the planed features of her mother, lent itself to an affectionate, nursery name. Bryher continued: "I can just see it in Paris. Very stately and very spoilt. More almost than you because you look scared and that makes me nervous whereas the woof swoops in as if she owned the city."

II.D. was not in the mood for pretty clothes. Paris, visited by her older self, frightened her. She did not feel like Bryher's projection of "a young pretty Baby Unicorn." Contemporary Paris with its new expatriates, busy cafés, and nightlife puzzled her and made her uneasy. She thought of herself as shabby and awkward, even old among the younger shining bobbed heads. Her Paris had existed in the past before her marriage; it was the Paris of a prewar generation, or so she tortured herself. It was really the old fear of being "démodé among elegant people." Further lines from "Halcyon" poignantly convey her feeling about herself:

> I'm too staid
>
> for grape-colour
> for fringe and belt and straps
> and ear-rings perhaps
> and head-band of hammered silver;
>
> I'm ill; I want to go away
> where no one can come;
> O little elf, leave me alone,
> don't make me suffer again,
>
> don't ask me to be slim and tall,
> radiant and lovely
> (that's over)
> and beautiful.

Then H.D. would brighten and promise to "buy some green corsets and lie on the bed done up in magenta scarves. I will perhaps have my hair carroted as a nice little surprise. Now kiss its own horse and don't be hurt." Yet she had decided in advance that Paris would offer no real solution to her unhappiness, which was isolation, and a sense of exile from place and people. William Carlos Williams and his wife were now in Paris and it would be good to see someone from home. McAlmon was there. He understood her terrors of being cooped up in Territet, of being alone in a hotel. He had written to Bryher: *Too bad to make a bird in a gilded cage out of a person who's such a mixture of butterfly, hummingbird, giraffe, workhorse.*" (my italics)

In Paris she went to the Left Bank hotel the Foyot, near the Odéon, where Sylvia Beach had reserved rooms so that H.D. and Bryher could be near her bookstore. H.D. was welcomed by McAlmon's celebrated war cry, evocative of the American small towns he would grimly celebrate: "Rats!"

McAlmon was everywhere—even at the Dôme having drinks with Marsden Hartley, the painter, and Djuna Barnes, the American mistress of the gothic tale, whose *Nightwood* would soon make her famous if her modish clothes and assorted entourage of males and females did not. Djuna was McAlmon's wicked, wonderful lady, artful and brilliant, an opponent whose rapiers must be avoided. H.D., although fascinated by her as much as anyone else, makes no intimate notes of conversation or meetings with Djuna Barnes. McAlmon could be found at Le Boeuf sur le Toit with Nancy Cunard, Nina Hamnett, the gifted English painter, and, just over from London, Iris Tree, whom Lady Diana Cooper, her close friend, called "that perpetual renewer of spirits." McAlmon chose his ladies well, in particular the stunning, sympathetic Kay Boyle. In the early hours of the morning he would progress from bar to bar, collecting subscriptions for Sylvia Beach's publication of *Ulysses*. At a more respectable hour he had been at Miss Beach's bookstore, Shakespeare & Co. Miss Beach had been a native of Princeton, New Jersey, until she left home for Paris to open a bookstore on the rue de l'Odéon for the British, Americans, and Anglophile French; across the street from Shakespeare & Co. was her friend Adrienne Monnier's select French bookstore. Then he was escorting Williams and Flossie, or Man Ray (established as a photographer and filmmaker in Paris), around the city and introducing them to the regulars. He was the instigator of many of the legendary high jinks of Americans in Paris.

Yet there was a very serious side to McAlmon. With Bryher's funds he had set up his own press, one of the early small presses in Paris, Contact Publishing Company. William Bird, who was one of the very first to publish small collections with his Three Mountains Press, would help in the distribution of Contact publications.

From his hotel, McAlmon had announced that anyone who had fresh work might send it to him. The news had gone around that he had been given a handsome sum by his rich father-in-law, which would underwrite the publishing experiment. As can be guessed, he was inundated with manuscripts. Privately, McAlmon had decided to publish his own selection of the expatriate writing. Not enough credit has been given to McAlmon for his incredible list of first titles. Between 1922 and 1930 he published Ernest Hemingway, Gertrude Stein, Ezra Pound, Nathanael West, William Carlos Williams, H.D., Djuna Barnes, Bryher, Mina Loy, and his own books—incredible in that the writers were unknown at the time to the general public, with the exception of H.D. and Ezra Pound! McAlmon's Contact Press represented the avant-garde of the expatriates of the 1920s—"the Bunch," as he called them.

These were McAlmon's golden days before he wandered into the American desert in the late 1940s and faded away. To his credit, he was conscious that he was in the foreground of an important literary and artistic landscape. He tried to share his brief interlude with H.D. and Bryher. Everywhere he was picking up the tab, in all the bars, and that meant he heard everything of importance; he was supporting the James Joyces on Bryher's contribution, which was a not negligible one hundred and fifty dollars a month. He had arranged that George Antheil should be supported by Lady Ellerman during the time he was working on his *Ballet mécanique,* the outrageous music that would parallel the Dadaist poems and experimental films.

From all this excitement generated by McAlmon and his friends, H.D. held back. The poem she wrote to Bryher, "Halcyon," in part explains her shyness. (Yet she was more beautiful than ever; the Man Ray photograph of 1929 would prove it.)

H.D. herself shared the Bunch's awe for Nancy Cunard. Nancy was first presented as the scandalous daughter of the American Lady Cunard, one of the ambitious hostesses of London, whose public warfare with her daughter was notorious. Nancy Cunard would make a name for herself as a publisher of the Hours Press. She was as serious as she was stunning-looking; she was Iris March of Michael Arlen's best-seller *The Green Hat.* The contrast between Nancy Cunard, daughter of Sir Bache Cunard, a shipping magnate, and Bryher, likewise the daughter of a baronet shipping magnate, could not have been more complete. Nancy would be uninhibited, alcoholic, a belle of the Bunch. What she and Bryher shared was a generous attitude toward writers. Bryher backed the Contact Press, just as Nancy was the publisher of the Hours Press. Bryher, as she continued to publish, would use the great printer Darantière from Dijon, the printer of James Joyce's *Ulysses.* Nancy would have her own hand press and would set up the print with it herself.

To H.D., Nancy Cunard represented an earned freedom from repression. Nancy must have been an idealized Brigit Patmore, more literary, explosive, and now more representative of the current generation. Nancy

Cunard was also generous. She was kind to H.D., recognizing the shyness, for she had experienced fear in that form. They were never close friends, yet Nancy's exuberance helped H.D. escape into the life of the French Quarter for a few brief days.

For the most part the Paris carnival did not interest H.D. She tired of the Dôme and the drinking parties. Hemingway gossiped (falsely) to Gertrude Stein that McAlmon was teaching Bryher to drink. "Is that in the Greek Tradition?" he asked. H.D. wanted to see her oldest friends, Pound and Williams. Again we return to the Williams *Autobiography*. Williams wrote that he and his wife had "met Bob and Bryher at the Dome, H.D. having finally been shaken." He considered her responsible for the rifts in the McAlmon marriage. He stated that if she had not been continually a part of the ménage, the marriage might have had a much better chance. He based his opinions on Bob McAlmon's complaints to him. In 1951 McAlmon wrote to H.D. about this subject that had troubled both of them over the years:

> Never once did I say or in any way imply that you were the cause of my unrest in my relationship to Bryher . . . Williams misquotes and misrepresents everyone he mentions . . . But utterly apart from his many errors I think the book cheap, exposing that Bill, far from being a better human than a writer, is a petty individual trying to give importance to himself by scandal about people he knew not too well in most cases . . . Not in the book or ever in life have I heard Bill express an appreciation of other's works . . . I want you and Bryher to know that the book angered and disgusted me and that whatever he has said by implication of my feeling about either of you was entirely presumption on his part. I knew who the card marked DH was from. It was from Scofield Thayer, who wrote a poisonous bit about Bryher and myself in the Dial. Williams knew I knew that . . . Neither Iris Tree nor Djuna Barnes liked him, Djuna thought him a weakling mess.

It should here be pointed out that H.D., with the exception of Marianne Moore, and a few graceful compliments to Edith Sitwell, rarely expressed herself on the subject of other poets. For instance, H.D. was not friendly with Mina Loy, who was in Paris at that time, a vivid personage with her beautiful children, bravely attempting to earn her living making lampshades. McAlmon and Loy were frequent companions. Laura Riding, one of the most exciting poets of that generation, had no use for H.D. and excluded her from her anthology of contemporary poets. H.D., so far as can be traced, never spoke of Laura Riding, although each wrote of the classical world.

Of her reunion with Williams in 1924, H.D. wrote to Viola Jordan, their mutual friend from their youth:

> By the way, I thought Williams most banal. Don't tell him so, and Florence we all thought was too silly. She tried to carry on like a movie

vamp and it didn't become her and it was so futile with a husband in the background. They both wanted "relationships" we all thought. But no one was having any from either of them. I thought Williams commonplace and banal. Don't say so to anyone. I can't afford to make enemies. But really, really there are limits.

Did Viola, after all, confide the contents of H.D.'s letter to Williams? Would this have caused the rancor in his autobiography? Again the path traces itself back to questions. It is not difficult to guess that H.D. might have presented herself as a sophisticated European at their meeting, as compared to Williams' hometown Yankeeism. She was not above such a pretense. She had never forgotten her gawky youth, and now the formerly "sophisticated" Williams, the elder writer, might be a tempting subject to snub. He would remember those early letters when she, the poet of international repute, had wanted to learn about literature from *him*. More simply, they unquestionably got on each other's nerves.

McAlmon must secretly have admired H.D., much in the guise of a knight-at-arms. She would have that effect on people. In all his letters, and in particular in the long, unpublished story he wrote about her, with its typically McAlmon title, "Some Take Their Moments," written in 1929, he remained, as he would be during this visit to Paris, her bantam champion. He defends her in her encounters with other people. He never views H.D. as responsible for her misadventures. He once had written to her that he had always detested Cecil Gray. In his unpublished story, however, he portrays Gray as offering to take the child and marry her if she divorces her husband. He also comments in this same story that "she was happier with him [Gray] than she had ever been with Andrew [Aldington], because he was gentle and less passionate." She refuses to accept Gray's offer of marriage, and so he wanders off to London and the Café Royal friends with whom he drinks and takes drugs. It is fairly obvious that H.D. had briefed McAlmon on Brigit's visit to Gray when she had been asking for money for H.D. for the support of Perdita. "Some Take Their Moments," in its contrast of Gray and Aldington, must have leaned heavily on H.D.'s *Palimpsest* account of her life with the two men: McAlmon had published her book in 1926.

In McAlmon's story there is a marvelous vignette of Garrick [Bryher] coming to Gail [H.D.] "wanting to know how one was to tell when water was boiling. The next morning she scalded her hand trying to pour herself tea." Then McAlmon brings the Lawrence-H.D. theme into his story. He describes Gail as being seriously distressed when she receives a letter. It was from a novelist she knew

> . . . who wrote books groping through the darkness of subconscious being . . . She had thought her friendship with him nicely detached and companionable, but his letter disclaimed further acquaintanceship with

her now. Of course his letter was mad, a confession of something pathological in himself. Having heard that she had a child he rejected her
venomously. She, he had thought, was one woman who would not go the
way of all females. He had visualized her as an artist, consecrating herself
to higher causes than the usual human muck. Now she had been caught
he never wanted to see her again . . .

There were several luminaries in Paris that spring of 1924 to be welcomed who were not within the McAlmon circle. Margaret Anderson
and Jane Heap had left New York in 1923 in order to settle in Paris and
from there print *The Little Review*.[1] For the first time they had met their
European correspondent, Ezra Pound. "It will be more interesting to
know him when he has grown up," acidly commented the youthful Anderson about the thirty-eight-year-old Pound. She and H.D. were born in
the same year and became friendly while in Paris, thus cementing a
literary connection begun when H.D. had questioned Amy Lowell
about the magazine. Margaret Anderson, after the departure of Jane
Heap from Paris, would for many years maintain a lesbian relationship
with the beautiful Georgette LeBlanc. When she had terminated her editorship and, incidentally the magazine, Anderson became an enthusiastic
disciple of Georges Gurdjieff. Her beauty, which was notable, remained
undiminished, and her strength of character, which she had used so for-
midably to publish one of the finest literary magazines, carried her
through any personal or economic crisis. She and H.D. retained a distance, yet continued to be friends.

Harry Crosby, the poet and editor of the Black Sun Press, was
also in Paris at that time. He was a madder, more avant-garde Fitzgerald prototype. Dedicated to sun-worship in people as well as nature,
Crosby could always detect sunspots. More sophisticated, of inherited
wealth, Crosby was a goldfinch to McAlmon's dusty pigeon. Like McAlmon, Crosby was fascinated by H.D. He found her "Very crisp, very
chiseled." In his diaries, *Shadows of the Sun*, he quoted Amy Lowell as
saying, "H.D.'s life is that of a true artist. It is one of internal mental and
emotional experiences not of external events." Crosby held up the example of H.D. as a model for himself in his attempts to break away from
the Montparnasse scene and its distractions.

Like Mary Poppins arriving by umbrella from another world, the
maiden lady from London, Harriet Weaver, appeared. Bryher had urged
her to come over to Paris, where she would be welcomed by her loyal
and grateful admirers. Timidly she ventured to a dinner party where
there awaited her the McAlmons, H.D., Djuna Barnes, and the William

[1] This plan did not work out. Jane Heap returned that year to New York, where
she edited *The Little Review* sporadically until 1927. In 1929, together they published
the final issue from Paris.

Birds. The group urged this daring woman who had fearlessly struck out against the obscenity laws in order to publish Joyce's work to sip a small glass of wine. Gathering her courage, Miss Weaver finally decided to taste the exotic drink. As she was carefully sipping the wine, Pound entered the restaurant, and upon observing her glass made some sort of idiotic remark, such as "Drunk again, Miss Weaver?" The abstemious Miss Weaver really believed that a few drops of wine caused one to be drunk. She looked thoroughly frightened. The others were equally appalled at Ezra's effrontery. The sacred pedestal on which Miss Weaver stood had been rudely shaken. It was suggested that Miss Weaver might like to go home. H.D. escorted her to her hotel.

When H.D. returned, she told the others that Miss Weaver had considered her quite brave to walk alone back to the restaurant. It had been H.D.'s duty to persuade Miss Weaver that Ezra had been joking. Her loyalty to Ezra was such that she did a good job of it, and Ezra, who had played so active a role in the early *Egoist* days, was permitted to remain a friend of Miss Weaver.

Before leaving Paris, H.D. met the editor of *transition*, Eugene Jolas, who would establish in 1927 by far the most provocative international magazine to be published during this era. A publication in *transition* was a necessary debut in the life of any literary aspirant. A list of contributors is a veritable sociology of the literary life of the period. Jolas himself was devoted to James Joyce, as was his wife, the redoubtable Maria Jolas, originally from Louisville, Kentucky, who to this day retains a southern accent in her French speech. Although primarily concerned with Joyce, they were the center of the most serious literary activity among the international literary community in Paris.

Each little magazine of that period offered a variant literary policy dependent upon the relative genius of its editor. There had been Ford Madox Ford with his *Transatlantic Review*, then Margaret Anderson's *Little Review*, and, crowning the trio, *transition*, which was to remain active for years. H.D. appeared in all three magazines. Thus her name, despite her efforts at shyness, appeared on the covers of these magazines. She could scarcely be called "retired" from the public eye, although, among so many of the bright lights of Paris, she considered herself to be but a fading reflection.

Evidence that she was not neglected, that H.D. and the Bunch were being regarded from across the Atlantic, is found in an essay by Edmund Wilson, "The All-Star Literary Vaudeville," which was published in 1926 in a book with the same title. Wilson reviews the poetry of the new movement of "twelve years ago" and questions its "heroes." Carl Sandburg, Vachel Lindsay, Edgar Lee Masters, Amy Lowell (her work like a "great empty cloisonné jar") were among those disparaged. He found Conrad Aiken merely "curious," Frost "dull." Pound he praises for the majesty of his attempts, but faults because his poetry is fragmentary. Among the poets of "the literary left," a clever Wilsonian distinction, Marianne Moore is "a fine observator"; H.D., he decides, "writes well, but there is not much in her." Wallace Stevens is a "fine decorative artist." William Carlos Williams he simply could not believe in.

Edmund Wilson was a shrewd critic of frailties among those who were not of his persuasion. As the lover of Edna St. Vincent Millay, at one time he believed her to be "the finest woman poet." He praised Lizette Woodworth Reese and Sara Teasdale. Elinor Wylie turned his head.

America's most sophisticated critic considered a stay of a year or so in Europe desirable, but not permanent exile, as in the case of Pound and H.D. The shorter exposure to Europe was beneficial only if its civilizing aspects were returned to America. It was the artist's *duty*, like that of a latter-day Jefferson, to import the benefits of an older civilization to shores that, as he saw them, glistened with opportunity, if not culture. He did not *approve* of writers, as he wrote of Turgenev, who turned their backs on their native land. Both Russia and America with their unredeemed resources needed the experience wrought from a wearied, yet cultivated, Europe.

In those years between 1912 and 1926, the years in which H.D. came under his consideration, Wilson liked literary women to be charming, witty, with a touch of *tristesse* to their gaiety. Their looks, as proved in his attraction to Millay, might be *belle laide*, lit up by fires within. He enjoyed a woman poet's pretense of helplessness. He could be very soft on women poets if he liked them. Poor Amy Lowell, he may have disliked her poetry for its Cathays and overtures toward the Symbolists (about whom he was much more of an authority), but more for her personality. Most important, his heroines should remain American. H.D., although passing on several counts, failed on others. Ironically, both Millay and Mary McCarthy, a later heroine, prided themselves on being Latinists, and Wilson admired this sort of learning. H.D. (again like Pound), although relying on Latin translations, never affected a Latinate sound, either in poetry or prose. Had this been so, Wilson undoubtedly would have respected her more. Ultimately, Wilson, who, unlike his provincial colleagues, had read everything, as witness his landmark *Axel's Castle*, was then more at ease with prose than poetry. (The major exception was the poetry of T. S. Eliot; another exception would be his later admiration for Pound at the same time his approval of Millay had passed. Wilson preferred "the heavies.") For H.D. the espousal of her poetry by a critic of the stature of Wilson would have been both interesting and provident. Yet she never showed she missed it.

CHAPTER FIFTEEN

Work Horse

Bryher, holed up in Eastbourne, received from H.D. on her "Fido Birthday" (September 2, 1924) a gift of poems. With them was a note from H.D. saying that here were "seven chiseled, polished gems I so laboriously wrought . . . You might think they cost me no sweating so perfect is the slight crystalline finish you might have thought I blithely turned them out one half hour before tea." The poems included those she had sent to Louis Untermeyer for the anthology he was compiling of his edition of *Modern American Poetry*. "Lais" and "Helen" had been written during visits to Vaud and London.

In his biographical sketches of his relatives, Francis Wolle reports a scene at Territet in 1925, before Mrs. Doolittle left for America. When the Untermeyer anthology arrived, it included a photograph of H.D. taken when she had last been in Greece. She is leaning against one of the columns of the Parthenon. Unfortunately, the photograph shows an unflattering picture of a rather tired and aging woman. When H.D. saw this photograph, Mrs. Doolittle told Wolle that H.D. had cried out, "My life's work is all ruined!" Her mother reminded her that it was she who was responsible for having sent a picture that did not show her real beauty. H.D. then screamed that it was not the portrait of herself that disturbed her, it was "any picture! The initials H.D. had no identity attached; they could have been pure spirit! But with this I am embodied! Oh, it is too much!" She wept and left the room. She refused dinner, then breakfast the following day. When her mother called her for lunch, she was told to go away and not disturb her. Mrs. Doolittle then informed H.D. she would stand at the door and knock on it until she answered. "Then a pleasant voice called, 'O mother, are you there? Just a jiffy until I slip into a dress.'" And in a few moments, "the usual charming Hilda smilingly emerged saying, 'So sorry I kept you waiting. Shall we go down to lunch?'"

This story may or may not be true, as Wolle previously reported a scene with H.D. on Lesbos, where she, tremendously excited, was supposed to have paced the island and then demanded that, instead of staying for the night as their trip called for, they immediately leave. She could bear the intensity of being near Sappho no more. There is no evidence that H.D. was on Lesbos with her mother then, or ever. However, the last trip to Greece had been with her mother and they had spent three weeks in Greece—quite long enough to have taken a boat to Lesbos, although H.D.'s later, and usually accurate, chronological account written for Norman Holmes Pearson does not include a trip to Lesbos.[1]

Heliodora and Other Poems was published in 1924 by Jonathan Cape. It was advertised as "Poems by H.D. Her work blends European suavity with a kind of red-Indian terseness, nerve and barbarity of phrase." A more deliberately inaccurate description of one of her most selective books could scarcely have been written.

From St. Luke's Place in New York, Marianne Moore wrote thanking H.D. for a lavender sachet she had sent to her mother and saying: "What an epitome of England in its flowered pongee bag!" She regretted for Bryher's sake that she had no place to review *Two Selves*. She had also read with "equal pleasure and regret, trite praise of your *Heliodora*." The book had been published in the United States by Houghton Mifflin simultaneously with its British edition.

For a biographer, *Heliodora* is a honey hive. The poems were written over a number of years, many of them dating from the early days with Aldington. "Heliodora" contains the lines "the rose, the lover's gift / is loved of love." The last three words would be used in a book plate designed for H.D. by a friend (once again from Philadelphia), George Plank, who would later become part of the Bryher-H.D. set in London. "At Baia," one of her loveliest poems, had been sent to Aldington when he was in the army. He had objected to the rhyme scheme, especially in the last stanza, where H.D. rhymes "this" with "kiss." Despite Aldington's objection the poem is successful with its flickering gold and silver blue. It is reminiscent of the story of the Italian writer Giuseppe di Lampedusa, who would years later write "The Professor and the Mermaid," his magical story of a mermaid with her seductive powers. H.D.'s poem is all hovering, distressful beauty. In "Flute Song" she must have been writing about the very young Perdita, who is bothering her mother while she is at her desk and is reprimanded: "Little scavenger away, / touch not the door . . ." In "Fragment Forty" a brief line of Sappho, translated as "love . . . bitter sweet," is directed by H.D. to the Aldington of the Corfe-London days, a husband who would sneak off to his mistresses: "Is it better to give back / love to your lover / if he crave it? / Is it better to give back love to your lover if he wish it / for a new favourite? / . . . What can we do / for curious lies / have filled your heart . . ." In another poem the warrior, Aldington, is told "I envy you your chance of death."

---

[1] These episodes, the first of which may be true, are reported here because they unveil aspects of H.D. that correspond to what we know of her fondness for the dramatic scene, together with a persuasive outburst. (They also prove that H.D. was not always a heroine, and possibly an occasional irritant to her family!)

"Toward the Piraeus" is directed forbiddingly at Pound with its beginning line "You would have broken my wings," then:

> It was not chastity that made me wild, but fear
> that my own weapon, tempered in different heat,
> was over-matched by yours, and your hand
> skilled to yield death-blows, might break
>
> With the slightest turn—no ill will meant—
> my own lesser, yet still somewhat fine-wrought,
> fiery-tempered, delicate, over-passionate steel.

There are other poems in the collection influenced by the Elizabethans, particularly by Robert Herrick and the later Metaphysical poets. They anticipate the titles of her autobiographical story, first called "Madrigal," and later, *Bid Me to Live* (from the first line of Herrick's famous "To Anthea").

Now she was finishing the section in *Palimpsest* based on her trip to Egypt. There would also be "Murex," a story that concerned her relations with Brigit Patmore. Then would follow "Hedylus" and "Hippolytus Temporizes." Of course, she had been working on the translations over a period of years, but "Hippolytus Temporizes" is her own interpretation of the play. The last sections of *Palimpsest* would not be completed until 1926. And yet, how much work she accomplished! There would also be material to be gathered for her *Collected Poems*. Territet was a setting created for her, moan, complain as she would, and wish to leave. There all the compulsiveness that led to her writing could have free rein. There would be a price to pay, naturally. She would be stricken with nerves, constantly on the edge of breaking down, totally self-involved—with its attendant "selfishness," and yet work was what saved her, and work she did. Later there would come a critical attitude toward her own stories, which would include those in *Palimpsest* and unpublished ones, the momentary qualms and sadness of a writer who had put too much of herself into her writing. In reviewing her prose writing, she would be too harsh.

> I didn't think my own personal patterns of husband-friend-self or of mother-father-child and the various elongated or squat shapes of the eternal triangle was ever as important as my mind seemed to make it or as my mind seemed to want to make it. That is why the various stories or the novels has [to herself] proved unsatisfactory, had been a lot of useless stuff . . .

Hedylus, which followed *Heliodora*, marks the beginning of H.D.'s concentration on her own initials for titles. *Hedylus* is one of her least successful experiments. It has a clumsiness, possibly because she is attempting to deal with a Greek environment on a social, daily level, never present in her poetry. Edith Sitwell commented that the writing of *Hedylus* was "hallucinated." H.D. may have willed herself into that state when she attempted to evoke the spirit of the woman poet Hedeyle, gifted and dissatisfied. H.D. later admitted that *Hedylus* is a retelling of her own story in a classical setting.

Ezra wrote, as H.D. would say, "brutally" about a section of *Hedylus* that had appeared in McAlmon's *Contact Collection of Contemporary Writers*. Pound was no longer interested in, nor did he approve of, H.D.'s dependence on Greek subject matter. He warned Circe to "get out of her pig-sty."

When asked about *Hippolytus Temporizes* (exquisitely printed by Houghton Mifflin, with a cover bound in vanishing shades of pink to gray to gold), H.D. made this statement: "I was realizing a self, a super-ego, if you will, that was an octave above my ordinary self and fighting to realize it. Once the poem was created, this world was created. I had to come back, to return to the ordinary things. I am tremendously touched by the play and admire it, technique and subject matter. But how did I write it?"

In this book she stresses that Hippolytus, who loved only the chaste goddess Artemis, could not be dissuaded from the pure—i.e., the selectivity of the poet who wrote in careful images. He was in love with an image.

H.D. must have strongly identified with this play of Euripides. She had already translated portions of it. Four lyrics in her *Collected Poems* are associated with *Hippolytus:* "Hippolytus Temporizes," "Phaedra," "She Contrasts Herself with Hippolyta," and "She Rebukes Hippolyta."

In "She Rebukes Hippolyta," the question is repeated: "Was she so chaste?" The mother of Hippolytus, who was a worshiper of the virgin goddess Artemis, would have left a heritage to her son of coolness, discrimination, nonsexuality—in other words, the legendary virtues of the poet H.D. But the Hippolyta of H.D.'s poem is highly sexual:

> She was mad—
> as no priest, no lover's cult
> could grant madness;
> the wine that entered her throat
> with the touch of the mountain rocks
> was white, intoxicant:
> she, the chaste,
> was betrayed by the glint
> of light on the hills,
> the granite splinter of rocks,
> the touch of the stone
> where heat melts
> toward the shadow-side of the rocks.

Here H.D. betrays that cult of herself, a bodiless, virginal ice maiden. These poems, written from her study of Euripides' *Hippolytus,* are sensuous, flagrantly so, as are most of the poems in the book in which they appeared—*Hymen.* There is a contradiction between the youth Hippolytus, who, once he had found what he thought was sex with the unobtainable Artemis, was wildly happy, and the dreary, puritanical Hippolytus, who was flung from his chariot when he discovered that his sex had been betrayed to a mortal, earthly woman not of his choosing.

"Murex" ("who fished the Murex up" is what H.D. quotes, eliminating the next line, "what porridge had John Keats?") could easily be passed over as the least interesting of the three stories of *Palimpsest.* It can be criticized as an unsuccessful attempt to write a "modern" story. Yet "Murex" is a definite illustration of the palimpsest principle, whereupon one impression erases another, yet the original imprint is seen clearly beneath the attempted obliteration. The original "stone" in all these stories consists in the obsessive telling of the Aldington-H.D. marriage and its dissolution.

In "Murex" H.D. gives an excuse why she believed it was necessary to eliminate Brigit from her life. (Actually at about this time, 1925, Mrs. Doolittle had remarked that Brigit looked "fast" and was worried about her influence on Perdita!) H.D. was still grateful for Brigit's role as protector and friend. She had been in love with her, as Brigit had loved her. Yet Brigit sacrificed H.D. for Aldington. When she wrote "Murex," H.D. did not yet know that Brigit would succeed to Dorothy Yorke's role in Aldington's life. During the Great War she had seduced Aldington with her beauty and charm.

"Murex" begins with Ermentrude Solomon, a young Jewish girl who lives in Hampstead, sent by a friend to ask H.D. for addresses of people she knows in Florence. The real reason for coming to H.D. is that she wants to be consoled because her lover has been snatched from her by a mutual friend, Mavis Landour (Brigit Patmore). In the long afternoon that follows, in which the two women share tea and cigarettes above the fog of London, H.D. (known in this story to her familiars as Ray Bart, and to her public as the poet Raymonde Ransome (oh, fearsome H.D. names!) is equally bored, annoyed, pitying, sympathetic, and finally enchanted with the young Ermentrude. The real person from whom Ermentrude is drawn was H.D.'s friend, known as "Oppie," from her maiden name, Oppenheimer. She became the well-known British novelist and biographer Doris Leslie, who through marriage became Lady Hannay. She appears again in H.D.'s later novel *The Usual Star.*

The poet, Ray Bart, recalls the hospital scenes where she had lost her child, remembering how consistently sympathetic Mavis had been, especially when the poet had asked Mavis to look after her husband. Mavis had wondered how she could possibly help the husband when he must

only be thinking of the lovely, suffering poet—she comforted the husband
by seducing him.

Comparing notes, Ray and Ermentrude learn that Mavis had taught
both how to dress, to choose colors, rouge, earrings, and how to appreciate themselves. Each has been betrayed by the admiring woman who
had handed them a mirror.

Finally after Ermentrude has left, Ray Bart begins a poem that first
praises the loveliness of Ermentrude, and then returns to the remembered beauty of Mavis.

> Now she may say
> that I adore her face,
> O brave, O true,
> For looking on the ruin of her grace,
>
> I shall see mirrored back
> my sun, just you,
> all grave and decorous
> and very rare,
>
> as one set with dull gold and amber
> and with fair
> Tyrian-blue hyacinths
> against hyacinth hair . . .

Finally she thanks Mavis for having sent her Ermentrude, who could
evoke a painful, yet colorful, past. Now she is in London, but soon she
must be off to her castle, Cret-d'y-Vau, which can be recognized as Territet in the canton of Vaud. H.D. then reminds herself of the power of the
poet's lance, which no one can escape, not even the charmed Mavis. The
poet has gone within herself to fish up the murex, the poem, whose
power consumes. She then writes:

> no rust shall stain my sword,
> it shall gleam gracious,
> silver-white for her,
> deadly intriguant,
>
> poisonous, with power
> I hated; see—I worship,
> more, more, more—I love her
> who has sent you to my door.

In the poem H.D. reverts to a more Elizabethan form, even translated
into a late Georgian one, in writing of Brigit. She recognized that Brigit
would not fit into her Grecian model. Brigit's beauty, in real life exceptional, was closer to the Pre-Raphaelite ideal.

In Brigit's own book, *No Tomorrow*, published in 1929, H.D. appears as the heroine. Here a man friendly with H.D. asks Brigit if she knows any other woman than H.D. "who seems to have an internal battle—not with passion or desires—but with some invisible antagonist whom she loves but cannot subdue?" Earlier, Brigit had visited Aldington at Port-Cros, where he and Dorothy had been staying and where the Lawrences also were guests. This unknown man in the novel remarks of H.D.—and it is highly likely that we are hearing Lawrence's voice—that "she has a peculiar weakness and avoidance of people—although she likes to hear about them and wants to know them . . . Her work bears marks of this struggle; she has a supremely fine poetic mind . . . but her words are those of someone who knows but two elements only, fire and air . . ." He also goes on to say that she had "*a power of dissatisfaction with herself and life and a terror of other people.*" (my italics)

When asked what Helga (H.D.) is suffering from, he answers that it is "imaginary love. She loves—no, it is not love so much as a desire for transference—*she looks at men and loves them as the Irish imagine fairies love human beings—with an envy to live in them . . . But her body, why —she hates it, she only likes womanhood in other women . . .* [my italics] She is at once a man and a girl-child and she fears the girl-child will be hurt and puts barriers around her." That last sentence sounds more like Aldington discussing H.D. with Brigit. This leaves us with the question as to which of the alarmingly candid writers fished the Murex up.

PART THREE

Coppet was . . . a literary and dramatic
workshop, a permanent seminar and debat-
ing Club, a laboratory of ideas, and a Circean
menagerie. Like a capricious and tyrannical
fairy queen, Germaine held sway over the
most ill-assorted crowd of admirers, lovers,
friends, and slaves ever assembled in a castle. Under the majestic and eternal calm
of the Alps they argued, quarreled, loved,
hated, wrote, acted plays . . . rebelled, sub-
mitted, intrigued and agitated themselves
. . . What characterized these years, then,
was not Coppet but the restless straying from
it; and what characterized Coppet while she
was there was her desperate effort to forget
she was there.

> J. Christopher Herold,
> *Mistress to an Age:*
> *A Life of Madame de Staël*

CHAPTER SIXTEEN

The Return of Frances Gregg

The H.D.-Bryher anniversary was celebrated in 1925 by the poem "Halcyon," dedicated to Bryher, "For July 17, 1925 Because of July 17, 1918."

Then in August of the same year, H.D. took over the lease of a flat at 169 Sloane Street for seven years.[1] This flat was theoretically to belong solely to H.D. From now on no more sharing or Hotel Washington tearful quarters. Her first purchase was a "romany pot." A description of the flat exists in "Murex." The apartment has a room on one floor and little curved stairs lead upward to a sort of attic alcove. She entertained in the downstairs room and worked in the room above. There was a handsome desk, a sofa, candles were always lit for the late afternoons and evenings, expensive flowers everywhere. The room indicated a sensitive, sensuous person, one to whom secrets might be whispered, problems and difficulties referred. Sybilline, it was dominated by the personage of H.D. She wore interesting dresses, amber beads, antique rings. Her dress still had a hint of the flea market, which she had discovered long before thrift shops became chic. There would be the added luxury of furs in the closet. There was scarcely anything to eat; the woman who lived there did not like to cook. Bread, some olives. Always tea and cigarettes; without being a chain smoker, H.D. loved her cigarettes. Then there was a fireplace.

Bryher and McAlmon either stayed at South Audley Street or across the street from H.D. at Herbert Mansions, where McAlmon kept a separate apartment. Perdita was boarded out with her nurse-governess. H.D. had found it "simply too much to have the child there." It was arranged that Perdita and the governess stay at a pension opposite the Brompton Oratory, where Mrs. Doolittle and other members of the Doolittle family would stay when they visited London. It was all conveniently in the neighborhood of Knightsbridge and South Kensington. It was at this time, in 1925, that H.D.'s mother and Aunt Laura returned to America. H.D. saw them off at the station for what would be the last time; Mrs. Doolittle died in 1927.

A reminder from her past now returned to haunt H.D. Frances Gregg

---

[1] She kept this flat until she moved in 1932 to 26 Sloane Street. She was there until 1934, when she and Bryher leased 49 Lowndes Square, which would remain their London address.

and her mother were living in London, Frances having separated from her husband. The Wilkinsons' life together had been one of a peregrine wandering to and from lecture posts in England, America, and the Continent. A description of one of the posts taken by Louis at a later date, but certainly similar to those he had been engaged in while married to Frances, is detailed by Malcolm Muggeridge in his autobiography, *Chronicles of Wasted Time.*

Both Muggeridge and Wilkinson had been employed by Sir Harry Lunn's Tours, the earliest organized company for tourism, a sort of middle-class anticipator of Swan's Hellenic Tours, and indeed one of the pioneers in the vast industry of holiday and tourist travel. Muggeridge explains that he and Wilkinson were hired as lecturers to educate the tourists. Muggeridge had met a director of Lunn's Tours, Leonard Dobbs, and subsequently had married his daughter. Mrs. Muggeridge's aunt was Beatrice Webb, and her uncle the much-loved writer Hugh (Lunn) Kingsmill. Muggeridge and Wilkinson had become great friends.

The two Gregg ladies now shared a single room. H.D. had spotted Frances in the neighborhood, but, to her discredit, had been so shocked at the circumstances in which she had found Frances that she tried to avoid her. She even wrote to Bryher, in reference to Frances, how much she hated poverty. She wondered how two women could live in one room; it was so uncivilized!

But Frances refused to go under. She continued to write stories. She was sustained spiritually by her friendship and correspondence with her old admirer, the now famous John Cowper Powys. She had courage and an intensity that under the most tedious circumstances would not burn itself out.

H.D. had other reasons for wishing to avoid Frances, and they were complicated ones. Frances represented an episode of her youth, a love from which she had never detached herself. Further, Frances, who was the closest observer of the original H.D., would not be a likely person to permit the present H.D. to escape her stern and critical eye. H.D. could neither vamp, nor pretend, nor cast any more spells with one of the former conspirators of her theatrics. Frances had wounded H.D. by helping Wilkinson write *The Buffoon* (1916) with its brutal distortions of her friend. More than anyone else, Frances was seen by H.D. as a shadow goddess of herself. H.D. must have reasoned that Frances was content to live in poverty, so long as her values remained intact, while she had come to terms with life and made her bargain. For this she would eventually be abused by Frances. There were frightening aspects to this alert purity of Frances. There are two stories by Frances published in *The Second American Caravan* in 1928, where by chance H.D.'s story "Narthex" also appears. In "The Unknown Face" we can find reasons for

H.D.'s ambivalent feelings of love and fear toward Frances, who had written:

> I have lived as a spectator, refusing to yield myself, to commit myself in any way to life. I have deliberately wilfully kept myself apart. Relentlessly, I have followed my idea; every event, every glance, every emotion, every sensation, every person has been weighed, estimated, judged and eventually, either rejected or dedicated to my idea,—but always impersonally, as though I were the Priestess of some Cult too abstruse to be grasped by the human intelligence, but to be served blindly by certain given rules. And that idea was Beauty, though, in certain ways it is more exactly expressed as God.
>
> `I could not let anything alone. My instinct was to draw a thing to me, then strip it of every defence, every self-illusion, every self-deception . . .
>
> Certainly there was a fury in me, a bitter hatred of people, and a vindictive malice toward life,—but there was too, a love, and a pity that broke my heart. I am queer. I am solitary.

In the second story, "The Apartment," Frances writes of meeting Kenneth Macpherson and his family. She is immediately attracted to him because she recognizes in him a special awareness for beauty. He is bold, licentious, and at the same time, "sweet, sweet . . ." She felt for Kenneth "a great tenderness . . . but how could one be tender and cherish that cold, small, aggressive soul?" She is both repelled by him and in love with his beauty. "Something pitiful and horrible about this mind which made me feel ashamed as though I were spying upon someone's deformity." She feared that despite his potentialities corruption would destroy him unless he was saved by a stronger force.

Oliver Wilkinson, Frances' son, has explained the background to this story in his letter to the author, July 14, 1980:

> My mother met Kenneth Macpherson in London during 1924. His family and the whole episode made the basis for my mother's story "The Apartment House." . . . There is no doubt that my mother was in love with Kenneth Macpherson . . . Kenneth Macpherson was in love with her, and she had a great influence on him . . . My mother introduced him to Hilda Doolittle, and he fell in love with Hilda. This must have been ironic; and I imagine, a bitter result of Frances' efforts to awaken Kenneth Macpherson's imagination and talent and further his career . . .

By 1926 when Frances introduced Kenneth to her, H.D. and Frances, despite H.D.'s trepidations, were seeing one another fairly often. H.D. had just turned forty. In America her *Collected Poems* had been published by Boni & Liveright the previous year. Her life was more orderly and satisfying than it had been for a long time, enabling her to concentrate on her poetry. Now a love affair—perhaps two—would intrude. She was first captivated by Kenneth, a young man of twenty-four, whose

beauty attracted her as it had Frances. Then Frances introduced her to
Andrew Gibson, a young schoolmaster from Suffolk who had lived near
the Greggs and who would, despite his marriage, continue to be in love
with Frances as long as she lived. He also had charm and good looks;
there is the possibility that he and H.D. had an affair. H.D. had also contacted Rodeck, the van Eck of her stories, the man who had sent her the
crystal she cherished and consulted. She claimed now that Rodeck was
scarcely recognizable from the man she had met on the *Borodino* in
1920. There were two meetings with Rodeck, carefully noted in her diary.
Kenneth Macpherson soon became more important than a distant Rodeck, a young schoolmaster, or a spectral shipboard encounter.

In 1934 from Norfolk, England, Frances wrote to H.D.:

> I think and I am afraid will always think that Kenneth was a nasty bit. I
> think he had the beauty of the gods and the fits of the gods, but I could
> never bear that great moving, writhing, maw of a family in the back-
> ground. They were truly unclean and obscene. I don't know how it is that
> I can see people in that way and still love them, for if wanting a person
> to succeed, and come clean is loving them, then I still love Kenneth . . .
> Kenneth was, I think, the original slug that poked its head above slime
> . . . I wanted the original woman who poked her head through the
> womb of time. You are it, and I am your still born twin . . .

Heavy words. H.D. would come to agree in part with Frances. Now
she was infatuated with Kenneth, and it is the first time H.D. can be seen
as a woman simply and truly in love, without her life or career at stake.
Desperation did not, for once, force her to rush into an affair. At last it
would appear that she could ask, "What can I do for Kenneth?" This
fresh approach must have been what endeared Kenneth to her, and what
made her continue to cling to him so long as she did. Also he was not a
competitive peer; he was wistfully and fearfully young.

It was at the beginning of her affair with Kenneth that H.D. was writing the "Choros Sequence from Morpheus" to appear in *Red Roses for
Bronze*. This long poem has in its Xth section the lines:

> O let me say the things
> that Thetis said
> to him when he had grown to lustihood
> of warrior grandeur:
> let me be the lover-mother,
> lay again
> your head here, here;
>
> . . .
>
> see I tell
> and tell and tell the same thing over again,
> over and over

in monotonous tone,
I love you,
love you,
love you,
dear-my-own.

These words, whatever the questionable poetics of the last stanza, are a rare confession from the poet. In case she has overreached herself, H.D. writes at the end of the next section:

I would be free,
be free;
go
for I fear
lest I strike swift
as she, the lynx and bear;
the Huntress claims me even amid the dream,
the breath of Artemis
stays this latter kiss.

A letter from Kenneth written at this time begins: "This thing has actually come to pass . . ." He tells her how he had

glimpsed your spirit behind you and watched and wanted . . . Then suddenly I was shielded and loved—It was more than I could believe or bear. Please—if you can stay near me. I see now how exactly that is what I need. I would do anything for you. I do not want you to feel that I threaten you . . . I have a strength in guarding others—somehow I might be a protection. You need something of the sort. Some desperate hurt looks out of your eyes . . . As things are now all that you were to me yesterday is all that I want or ask—all that anyone could want or ask—it came so swiftly after you had spoken of gods upon earth, and I knew that I had seen god or goddess in you then. God but you have in you that swift, impetuous, sudden divinity . . . Love me if you can . . . Hilda, I need you. But be free!

In *The Usual Star*, a book H.D. wrote in 1928, printed by Darantière, and issued in 1934 by Bryher's Pool Editions, Katherine (Frances) asks about Daniel (Kenneth). "O he goes on," said Raymonde (H.D.), "the usual star about the usual forehead." And Katherine adds to this, "He is the most beautiful thing . . . in the whole world."

Kenneth Macpherson's parents were Scots and his ancestry was Scots. His father was a painter of flowers. His mother, beautiful, overly solicitous of her son and her daughter, Eileen, was given, to everyone's embarrassment, to falling seriously in love with young men, frequently friends of her son. Dr. Hanns Sachs, whom Kenneth went to briefly, easily concluded that Kenneth had a mother fixation.

Kenneth was quick, intuitive, with a natural nobility that caused admirers, such as Stephen Guest, to look upon him as a "Prince."
He was devoted to beauty, whether that of a villa that he could furnish with a touch of genius. Although a cultivated narcissist, he was
able to cover his more questionable actions with an affection that
soon brought forgiveness. His letters are fun; he must have been a
marvelous companion when he chose. He was capable of repaying
generosity in a singularly gracious manner. No one, even those who
witnessed him when most imperiled, ever accused him of vulgarity.
He probably was starlike to those who were attracted to a star's brilliance. H.D. for a long time felt that attraction. She said she would
always protect her early memories of Kenneth. When ultimately she
became disillusioned with him, she regretted his loss and was permanently
wounded.

This then was Kenneth who leaped into the Bryher-H.D. alliance.
From her rooms across the street Bryher must have witnessed love's
progress proved by the masses of flowers sent to H.D., formerly a prerog-
ative of Bryher's. So strong then was Kenneth's attraction for H.D. that
even at the time of her mother's death, she was able to carry on and go
out to the theater with Kenneth, coming home with him by moonlight
across the rooftops to let him into her rooms.

Bryher, at that time, had a definite problem all her own. She wanted
to rid herself of McAlmon. Bryher was not only bored with McAlmon's
drinking, his scenes and his companions, but gradually she had decided
that Paris, where McAlmon insisted on living, was not her proper environment. She liked England now, especially since H.D. had set up an inviting apartment across the way and was entertaining friends and writers
whom Bryher liked to meet. Surprisingly, she liked Kenneth, who bright-
ened any atmosphere into which he entered. Bryher had never even
liked French food. She was very British in her tastes. She liked to pop
into little bun shops where she could have all the water she wished without explaining that she did not want any spirits. H.D.'s new setup became increasingly attractive to Bryher. The problem was in order to
maintain her British residence, it would be necessary to substitute a British passport for her American one.

McAlmon came over to London and disrupted Bryher's maidenly life.
He began to give wild drinking parties at Herbert Mansions, which Kenneth now attended. Kenneth had quickly learned that his affair with
H.D. must adjust itself to H.D.'s relationship with Bryher. He set out to
attract Bryher, consoling her for McAlmon's antics and flattering her intellect. He succeeded so well that Bryher asked McAlmon for a divorce.

To Bryher's annoyance, McAlmon went off to New York with Djuna
Barnes, thus postponing any immediate divorce plans, so she invited
Kenneth to visit her and H.D. at Territet. Kenneth eagerly accepted the

invitation, as it would include a stopover in Paris, which he had never seen. Perdita, Bryher, H.D., and Kenneth found themselves in another train compartment, setting out to Paris on the Orient Express. H.D., the veteran traveler, noted that Kenneth seemed "very un-travelled"! Kenneth was scarcely out of the Highlands, but he caught on rapidly. He entertained all three of them and quickly became an addition to their lives, particularly in his ability to amuse and look after Perdita.

He would be tactful amid the acrimonious scenes; whereas McAlmon had been angry, Kenneth was eager to create harmony in his dauphinlike way. This harmony was not easily achieved, but he was more adept than anyone else at soothing the frenzied women. In 1927 he wrote to H.D. (My Darling):

> Please, please don't get caught up into the Bryher blunderbuss manner. All is simple and all is perfect and everything can adjust and be adjusted . . . I have infinite faith in the good, the goodness and the simple beauty of our lives together. I don't want you to feel lost, harassed, browbeaten, separated from us, from yourself, from Bryher . . . You do have really . . . (for all it is worth) your silver curtain. Leave it down. Let it be a portcullis to your vulnerability. Don't be vulnerable. Just this thing has Bryher set up before you: her own fortress. Justly so. We all have to. But because she has a fort, has to have a fort, in some way BE a fort, so must you be armed and able to fall back on simple strength reserved for protection—rely on your armies . . . She'll talk, she'll say this, this in a manner of cold, rather quietly tragic conviction. And you'll have to recognize that incredible as some of the things she says are, they aren't dishonest . . . I think she doesn't really know quite what she is doing, except acting; reacting instinctually to some family-protective, almost small-child reliance on what she calls "my world" the mathematical, repressed, rather ungodly life of her genius father and crazy mother.

In Paris Bryher was reprimanded by Sylvia Beach, who despite her disapproval of McAlmon told Bryher she should not have "meddled with human psychology." Bryher protested that she had in no way wronged McAlmon. She did believe herself innocent. Astonishingly rigid in her attitudes, she believed that she had carried out her part of the bargain and was the injured party. Childlike emotionally, she could not understand how McAlmon possibly could have been hurt. The practical Adrienne Monnier chided her, "Ce pauvre McAlmon, he should be put in the far far Ouest and left there. Europe l'a complètement pervertie." A remark that amused Bryher sufficiently for her to repeat it to H.D.

The divorce finally took place in 1927, a year after McAlmon's press had published *Palimpsest*. McAlmon was given a handsome divorce settlement, enough for him to be known in Paris as Robert "McAlimony." The money did not make life any easier for McAlmon, as it vanished as quickly as the allotments arrived. Eventually he migrated back to the

"Ouest." He continued to write, but with the notable exceptions of *A Hasty Bunch, Being Geniuses Together,* and *Not Alone Lost* he remained unpublished. He had made his gesture for American letters by publishing the previously unrecognized talents of the Bunch. His efforts were insufficiently acclaimed, with the exception of an understanding Ezra Pound. Pound could empathize, having tilled many a furrow for an aspiring writer.

In Paris, while waiting out the divorce, which she imbued with fantasies of terror and persecution, Brýher had seen Marc Allégret, the nephew of André Gide. He had formerly been young John Ellerman's tutor, but now was making films. He would go on to make, with the assistance of his uncle, the famed *Voyage au Congo.* At his suggestion Bryher bought Kenneth a camera, a gift that would have a sequel.

Returned to Territet, where Kenneth and H.D. were waiting for her, Bryher collected the new menagerie; boarding the Oberland Express, they traveled back to London. There, with a suddenness that astonished her friends as much as had her previous marriage in New York to McAlmon, Bryher and Kenneth were married at the Chelsea Registry Office in September 1927. Young John Ellerman and H.D. were the witnesses.

Two questions naturally arise: Why this abrupt marriage to H.D.'s lover? And how did H.D. feel about this "other" alliance? Bryher's explanation of why she married Kenneth placed her in a role with which she was familiar, that of a benefactress. She said, quite simply, that Kenneth's mother was worried about her son, as he had little money and few prospects in an apprentice job as a commercial artist. A marriage to Bryher would furnish Kenneth with a safe future and, unselfishly added Bryher, the expensive time to continue his affair with H.D.

A more subtle answer to the first question may have been given inadvertently by Bryher herself when asked why her friend, the gifted and only recently acknowledged American painter Romaine Brooks, should have married the dilapidated, yet vestigially charming, John Brooks. Romaine, an expatriate since her youth, was the lover of Natalie Barney, the wealthy American settled in Paris. Preceding Natalie, her lover had been the poet Renée Vivien, whom Colette has written about as one of the most talented and fated of the group of women she joined after leaving M. Willy. Brooks was homosexual. Meryle Secrest, in her fascinating biography of Romaine Brooks, may have used her interview with Bryher to reach this conclusion:

What Romaine wanted was companionship . . . Romaine wanted to feel united with someone and marrying Brooks who knew how to keep a charming and friendly distance from a woman, who shared the same interests and had been the companion of many delightful hours . . . looked like the ideal solution. They would continue to lead separate lives. For Brooks, marriage . . . would make no demands of any kind . . . In marrying Brooks Romaine was making a deliberate break with conventional male-female relationships. She might even have expected Brooks to approve of her metamorphosis into a pseudo male.

There the parallel ends, as the Brooks marriage was disastrous. Kenneth and Bryher remained friends throughout his lifetime.

As has been noted, Bryher needed a British passport. She also had retained the hysterical notion that, in order to keep clear of the domination of her parents, she must have the protection of a husband. As in her choice of McAlmon, she had decided that Kenneth would help her socially. Lacking a personal magnetism that would attract people, Bryher liked to acquire them. Kenneth would be able to keep up with her restless pace. His bisexuality was also an asset.

Kenneth was willing to exchange his erratic family life for that of a Prince Consort. Bryher had written to H.D. that "Dog," or "Rover," as Kenneth would now be called, was very depressed: "I think he is beginning to see his family situation as the outside world sees it and not from the Brontë viewpoint of a haunted but majestic Scottish family." He had written about this family in Brontesque fashion in one of his very bad novels, *Gaunt Island* (1927), published by Bryher in her new Pool Editions (located in Territet, yet still printed by Darantière). The novel also contains characters based on two women who had been his lovers: Frances, and the ubiquitous Brigit. In 1926 he wrote *Poolreflection*. It would be wiser to ignore this novel if it did not present a variation on H.D.'s *Hedylus,* which he greatly admired. (He had consoled her for Pound's criticism of the book.) His repugnant tale is of a struggle between a woman and the father of her son for the love of the son. The son returns to the father, although warned by the mother (as Hedelye had tried to warn Hedylus) that his father desires not only his soul—and here H.D.'s version happily differs from Macpherson's—but his body as well. The story is garnished with silver-tipped walking canes, expensive suits, and villas.

In 1927 Kenneth was in the mature stages of his love for H.D. Marriage for him and H.D. was out of the question, but what better way for them to retain their separate identities and their shared love than for him to marry Bryher? H.D. may have reasoned in the same fashion.

H.D., thinking back on those early years with Kenneth, wrote: "There was beauty and companionship and a sort of strength that I needed in my relationship with Bryher and Perdita. Kenneth took over responsibility . . ." She often said that she would happily relive those first years with him of the late twenties and early thirties.

After the marriage the three shared a honeymoon in Venice. For all the optimistic analysis of a Macpherson-Bryher marriage, this honeymoon was not an auspicious one. What is known of it is told by H.D. in her story "Narthex." The atmosphere that surrounded these three intense personalities was one of varying nuance, concealed passion, compulsion, anger, and frustration.

To begin with, Venice must have been H.D.'s choice, her marriage gift to Kenneth. It conveyed the same magical properties to her as it did to Pound. Again and again she would return to Venice, and when she was not actually there, the city was a recurrent nostalgia. Venice represents enchantment for certain people, yet the ambivalence latent in that once excessively alive, and now museum-haunted, beauty causes others to turn distastefully away. Bryher's was the latter reaction. She did not like the place.

They were staying at the Hotel Danieli, the unhappy abode of Chopin and George Sand. Now H.D. took its name for Kenneth, whom she called Daniel in "Narthex." There was H.D., gay, costumed, excited; and across the table at Florian's sat a dour Bryher, whose severe dress betrayed her alarm of a city of sensuous activity. Between them sat the newly created cosmopolite, Kenneth Macpherson, already preening himself on the decadent felicities offered him.

A narthex is a wand carried by initiates. Originally it was the plant stalk Prometheus used to bring fire from heaven. In H.D.'s story, Daniel (Kenneth) with his personal beauty is the narthex. On the other hand, Gareth (Bryher) is secular, clerical, a mechanical little clockwork. "Her heart is where her brain is." The narrator (H.D.) continues to muse as they sit in St. Mark's Square: "Katherine [Frances] and I were happy. We talked, gouged each other's souls out . . . I mean Katherine made it possible to accept . . . Gareth. Without Gareth, there would have been no . . . Daniel. We're not three separate people. We're just one . . . And it was Katherine who could have married him who sent him to me. It was the act of Delphi."

The story concludes with Daniel and Raymonde (again H.D.) understanding Gareth's difficulties and the practical necessity of regulating their desires to her demands. Again there is the Jamesian analysis and atmosphere of three exacting personalities caught in a human trap. The story ends with a conspiracy: two adults agree to join together to protect a demanding child. If the adults are recognized as Kenneth and H.D., the plot is chilling.

Bryher, disliking Venice, wished to depart for Vienna in her new toy, the airplane, with Kenneth. Bryher loved airplanes. She wanted to own and pilot one. Bryher, who had never learned to drive a car! She was fearless, even in those early planes that normally made forced landings. H.D., whose dislike of ships mounted to a phobia, would prefer to fly when she crossed the Atlantic. Initiated by restlessness, this trip to Vienna turned into an event of consequence. Bryher made her first, albeit brief, contact with Freud.

H.D. returned alone to London where the Macphersons found her installed in her Sloane Street flat. As in her marriage with McAlmon, Bryher took Macpherson temporarily into the Ellerman mansion. For H.D. this Mayfair residence represented a kind of psychic estrangement from the Macphersons. Her reaction is reflected in the novel she wrote of this period, *The Usual Star*, privately published in 1934 by Bryher, but written in 1928. This book continues where "Narthex" left off, with Daniel, Raymonde, Gareth, Katherine, and the Ermentrude of "Murex," who is now reintroduced as a best-selling author. The title is taken from Raymonde's description of Daniel appearing with "the usual star about the usual forehead." She and Katherine have agreed that "he is the most beautiful thing, in the whole world."

We begin with Raymonde and Daniel leaving a film starring Greta Garbo. As they walk the twilight streets of Mayfair, they discuss how *each* resembles Greta Garbo! Daniel is on his way home to the luxurious address on Audley Street. (Here H.D. hints at an abandonment she could not help feeling when their marriage separates her from Bryher and Kenneth. Her nose now presses itself against the great house. Bryher is ensconced within the security and warmth of her father's mansion, and she has temporarily removed Kenneth from H.D.'s more modest orbit.) Daniel, decides Raymonde, will soon be "a distant voice on one of the house telephone extensions."

A nice touch later occurs when Lila (Lady Ellerman), seeing Raymonde on the street, offers her a lift home in her upholstered limousine. From a corner of the limousine, H.D. wonders how anyone could be loved as Gareth loved her mother. She fends Lila's questions about Gareth's marriage. Then these enemies side with one another, asking why Gareth hates all the things—"down pillows," a "polished escritoire," objects "plundered from Italian palaces"—they love. Raymonde whispers to herself, "How to get it across and get it across that Gareth was a sort of robot." Her mother believes marriage has changed Gareth. "Nothing would ever change Gareth," thinks Raymonde. Lila leans confidentially toward Raymonde and says, "I do *love* that boy." Raymonde answers, "We *both* love him." Then she extracts herself from the car and from an invitation to dinner. "I can't, I'm awfully sorry." Escaped, her thoughts run on: "Quick speed up of thought and sensations, not knowing why she said it. Some sort of revenge, something in her that stared aghast outside a misted window, something in her that had really wanted to run away, that would always run along bevelled cliff edges and that listened to sounds and scratches that gull wings make in passing."

Whenever Gareth appears in her story, H.D. interrupts the limp pathos of the passages and sharpens her wits. After she has returned home she allows herself to envisage what must be taking place at the mansion. Coffee would almost be over and some "paunchy person" would be in the dining room. Raymonde again sympathizes with Gareth's mother, who must find it difficult to have a daughter "who has skipped about two generations, who, in a sort of atavistic revenge for Lila's [Lady E.] maintained 1880-ishness, decides to construe herself into the sort of thing that might conceivably happen in 1980. *If girls progress in the astonishing way in which they are progressing, then Gareth is a sort of ready-made formula for 1980.*" (my italics)

Raymonde is not so lonely as she would lead one to believe. She has been invited to the first night of a play by a well-known playwright, who is a friend. Suffering from one of her self-pitying moods, she does not want to attend. She asks Ermentrude Solomon if she will go in her place, as Ermentrude newly rich will own, as Raymonde infers she herself does not, a dress expensive enough for the performance. Once it had been Ermentrude (Doris Leslie, Lady Hannay) who reached out to Raymonde for introductions. Now she has succeeded in a world that excludes Raymonde. H.D. did yearn for the world of the fashionable novelist. She would have liked, or so she fantasized, to have nibbled the cake of a best-selling novel. The lonely career of a poet left her undefined in a society modulated by public success. After Ermentrude has accepted the invitation, Raymonde settles down to the solitary biscuit and cigarette.

Lo! There is a knock at the door. It is Katherine! (Frances) Uninvited, shabby, scorned Katherine. The two settle down for a three-hour talking binge in which Frances—(it is easier now to use their real names)—asks why anyone should write at all. Beauty, the worship of it, is sufficient. H.D. admits that she can't help writing. She rushes to her typewriter "as to a morphine cupboard." Then follows a scene with destructive claws and scratches, criticisms and violent flares. After the battle the love between the two old friends is renewed, as H.D. reflects on the purity of Frances' rejection of those who do not pass her scrutiny, and whom she calls "apes." As this would include the world of Ermentrude, H.D. approves when Frances tells her that the values of these "apes" lie "in glitter on the edge of something catching something in a mirror, the ape joy of seeing one in the other; ape-face, ape-intelligence, matched with ape-face, ape-intelligence in a mirror." (H.D. here unconsciously catches the malice of D. H. Lawrence, or of Wyndham Lewis.)

Reconciled with Frances, now that Frances has proved how much finer the "witches" are than the depraved "apes," H.D. decides that "when Katherine [Frances] was like this, she was the most enchanting being she had ever met or ever would meet."

CHAPTER SEVENTEEN

Filmland

The newest menagerie of three returned to Territet. Sloane Street and its chimeras receded, to be replaced by the worldly shadows of filmland.

Bryher's recollection is that she and Kenneth were walking by Lake Geneva (like Shelley and his lass) when he remarked how cinematic the lights appeared upon the water. She recognized then that his talents, discouraged by the reception of his books, were turning more to film. He had used the camera she had brought from Paris to film the young John Ellerman wildly dancing in a reel called *Wingbeat*. Macpherson followed it, this July of 1927, with *Foothills*, the main role played by H.D. In this he attempted a film about telepathy, a subject of intense interest for him and H.D. The cinematic idea behind both films was to work with motion itself. The subject moves jerkily, or automatically, yet retains a normal identity while conveying a message, as if the subject were controlled by an electrical current. These films exist today only in fragments, but these fragments are evidence of Macpherson's first, almost Dadaist, camera work, in which a message that cannot be heard is repeated over and over. Macpherson's later work was allusive, not abstract in the way the Dadaist or surrealist films were. He was by nature too fond of a story to sacrifice its many traces. His inclination would be to follow the expressionist style of the Germans. These first films show him and his actors at "play," edging toward a professional filmmaking.

At the same time that Macpherson was shooting his first films, Bryher and he had come up with the idea of a film magazine. It would be called *Close-Up*. They rented an empty office space for the proposed magazine at nearby Clarens in the foothills of the Alps. They also took a studio at Lutry, just below Lausanne, in which to shoot their films. Next they named the film company POOL Productions, after the book of Kenneth's, published by Bryher, called *Poolreflections*.

Close-Up surprised everyone with its instant success, a signal that films were to be regarded not only as entertainment, but, as *Close-Up* emphasized, an art. As a magazine it was modest; a temperate beige color and a refreshingly noncommercial makeup concealed its iconoclasm. It first appeared as a monthly, then as a quarterly for six and a half years—years that would see the production of film "classics"—until its demise (along with much else that was experimental in films) in 1933.

Bryher and Kenneth rallied everyone they knew to write for the magazine, which Kenneth edited. Dorothy Richardson unabashedly wrote that sound ruined movies. Gertrude Stein wrote a "phylo-scenic-aria"; Barbara Low, the analyst, and aunt of H.D.'s friend Stephen Guest, wrote about education and films. *Close-Up* became a magazine in which professionals in fields not necessarily cinematic were called upon for their opinions. This editorial position, seeking radical ideas and personal reactions from fields outside the cinema, gave the magazine its verve. The magazine survived on its internationally known contributors and, surprisingly, on subscriptions. The Hollywood correspondent was Clifford Howard, cousin of H.D. from the Monrovia days, selected partly for his geographic nearness to Hollywood and also for his contributions to the Hollywood film magazines.

In his autobiography, *Ways of Escape,* the novelist Graham Greene mentions that when he was at Oxford and film critic for *The Oxford Outlook,* he was a passionate reader of *Close-Up.* He mentions especially the reviews from the Paris critic Marc Allégret and the remarks of the Soviet director V. I. Pudovkin, whose legacy to films was his insistence that the essential basis of cinematic art was the montage of individual shots, and not the histrionic abilities of the players.

Close-Up was the first magazine devoted to film. The German film director G. W. Pabst noticed that it would quite naturally come forth from England, where films were never made, instead of Germany, the heartland. There were remarkable, and multiple, photographs from the films reviewed. The magazine was an altogether opinionated, brilliant, amateurish, eager, entertaining, noncommercial venture. A relic of a vanished world. Its like has never been reproduced. The magazine has an air of bravada and discovery that indeed reflected the attitude of the two chief dogs—Fido and Rover—who gave the impression that *Close-Up* was sitting up with its paws waving in the air.

In particular, the magazine illustrated the interests of its editors, which were psychoanalysis and the cinema. As the cinéaste Anne Friedberg has pointed out in her pioneer study of *Borderline*—Kenneth's most important film—psychoanalysis, its methods and its study of deviations and madness, underlies many of the classic films. In his own work, Macpherson sought such a synthesis. (It is certain, however, that one of *Close-Up*'s reviewers, Marianne Moore, who reflected a certain skepticism toward psychoanalysis, was not exactly aware of the psychoanalytic undertone to the magazine. Had she recognized this aspect she might have hesitated to make her delightful contribution.)

Close-Up introduced Sergei Eisenstein to a public ignorant of his films. Bryher had become an authority on Russian film. In 1929 she published at her own press an inventive book called *Film Problems of Soviet Russia.* The dust jacket of this collector's item has a photograph in gray of a cameraman filming a moving tractor. The title of the book is boldly printed in red. The book itself is filled with photographs of the early Russian films. As would be expected, the text is biased and filled with personal criticisms, showing Bryher at her most formidable, arguing for what she believed in. Among many experiments she brings to her readers' attention was the Russian handling of mass scenes, illustrated by *The Battleship Potemkin,* which were more innovative than the techniques later used by Cecil B. De Mille. It is an intensely researched book, and after reading it there is difficulty in believing Bryher's later assertions that she cared nothing for film, that she had entered into the projects because of Kenneth's need to make use of his abilities. And yet she was a superb film critic and could use film to bring out her arsenal of arguments against prejudice, against England, against contemporary methods of education. She instinctively and, as her writing shows, temperamentally sided with Eisenstein. The two became friendly correspondents, and she later wrote to H.D. that she had heard from Eisenstein about his visit to England. He wrote her that he found England the funniest place in the world, that he couldn't stop laughing, and that he would like to make films in England. A proposed trip to Switzerland to visit Bryher never came off.

Instead, he had gone to Cambridge. From there he wrote Bryher that he wanted to write a book at Cambridge, because there were more young men there who knew nothing and more books that knew everything than anywhere else in the world. He had gone to the conference of bishops assembled to protest the antireligious propaganda in Russia, to the Lord Mayor's show, and after that to Eton. He couldn't stop laughing.

Close-Up received so much enthusiastic mail from Germany that Bryher and Kenneth took off for Berlin to show their film *Foothills.* Bryher decided she was in love with Berlin. For her, Berlin was like a person, calm and exciting, and at the same time fast-moving, as she phrased it. She began to acknowledge her German origins. She was at last at home, so she believed. She also remarked that, unlike herself, all the English film actors hated Berlin for the first three months and then never wanted to leave. On this first trip in 1927 she saw Berlin as "a big movie, like an impossible dream." She added that "Berlin was not like New York. It was New York." A comment many Berliners would make. Bryher would go back and forth to Germany in the early 1930s until she found the country so alarmingly fascist that she could no longer force herself to return to a place she had once yearned for as a "homeland."

Foothills was received rapturously (according to Bryher) by the man she considered the greatest of all German directors, G. W. Pabst. Bryher's comments on the cinema have been ignored by cinéastes, and they deserve an audience. She was received by the major directors and film companies and was in Berlin at an important time in the history of its filmmaking. She is humorous, wry, personal, and altogether modest; she knew everybody and deserves a chapter devoted to herself on the art of the film. (Unfortunately, this is not the place.) But there are some personal comments in letters to H.D. that bear repeating.

Bryher reported Pabst as saying about H.D.'s work in *Foothills:* "Pabst's one enthusiasm was *you*. You were strong, you showed up the fallacy of young [H.D. was over forty] American girls, you could act, look, in fact if possible he would like to go to bed with you, so to speak, tomorrow." Only fragments of the film exist, and are, along with *Wingbeat*, in the archives of the Museum of Modern Art in New York.

They also met Fritz Lang, who along with Pabst led the group of filmmakers. Both were Austrian. Lang specialized in horror films; later he would make the experimental *Metropolis*. At first Bryher liked Lang, but later decided that she and Kenneth should have nothing to do with him. "He is heavily homo and most conceited." Possibly their rejection of Lang was because Pabst had become so much a part of their Bunch. Describing Pabst, Bryher wrote:

> I saw a Fido, a fat, middle aged, but unmistakably Fido and we fell almost into each others paws saying together, but this is the greatest pleasure . . . My car, the studios, my films, my thoughts all are at your disposal. Ah how my friends and I have discussed Close-Up. It is so funny, so furchtbar funny, you permit that an Englishman should have written it . . . ha . . . ha . . . ha and tell me who IS H.D.? Who writes under those initials? Ah how he has understood "Joyless Street." And poor little Greta Garbo. Ah so sad. Ah, how funny that an Englishman should have started CLOSE UP . . . and exactly who is H.D.?

Bryher adored Pabst; she found he believed in hope, the people, pacifism, psychoanalysis. His great friend Dr. Hanns Sachs would become Bryher's psychiatrist, and one of the reasons she returned so frequently to Berlin was for her sessions with him. Fortunately, Sachs spent his summers conveniently near her in Switzerland.

The film that had made Pabst deservedly famous was *Joyless Street*, released in 1925. Bryher writes:

> It was made with French money in thirty four days in ten thousand feet. One time they worked thirty six hours without anyone leaving the set. Always they worked sixteen hours a day. In Vienna they cut out Werner Krauss completely. Somewhere else, Russia I think, they made the bourgeois the murderer instead of the girl. In France they cut the whole street out and the figures on it. In Germany one year after it was showing the censorship tried to forbid it. Pabst tried all over Germany and Europe to get Greta Garbo a job and nobody would take her so in desperation she

...neth Macpherson's drawings for an ...ning dress for H.D. *(Beinecke)*

Walter Schmideberg. *(Beinecke)*

Sigmund Freud in his office. *(Beinecke)*

Silvia Dobson, ca. 1950. *(Courtesy of Silvia Dobson)*

Church of Santa Maria dei Miracoli, Venice. "The church was cool, with a balcony of icy mermaids."

H.D.'s desk. *(Courtesy of Mervyn Dobson)*

Lord Dowding, hero of the Battle of Britain. (Photograph: Imperial War Museum, London)

M. Butler, author of The Fortunes of Faust. (Beinecke)

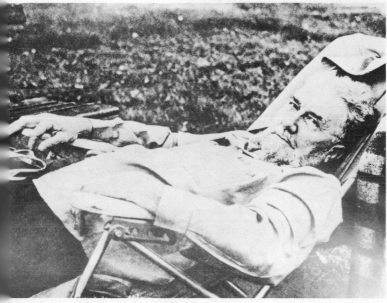

Ezra Pound, ca. 1950s. (Beinecke)

Hôtel de la Paix, Lausanne, where H.D. lived from 1946 to 1953.

The Stanhope Hotel, opposite the Metropolitan Museum, New York City. (*Photograph by Maeve Slavin*)

BELOW LEFT: 49 Lowndes Square, where H.D. and Bryher lived from 1934 to 1946. (*Photograph by Trumbull Higgins*)

BELOW RIGHT: Villa Verena, Küsnacht, Switzerland, where H.D. lived from 1956 to 1961. (*Beinecke*)

went to the States. She (Garbo) always likes to be a vamp, being as Pabst remarked, so entirely not one by nature. She *is* exactly twenty-one. Her last American pictures are a tragedy.

A summary of the plot of this pioneer film is needed because in every way Pabst influenced Macpherson. *Joyless Street* is a realistic and terrifying film of post-World War I Vienna reduced by inflation to poverty. Arthur Knight, the film historian, describes the film as:

reflecting the economic chaos and ruptured moral values of the day through the interlocking lives of the inhabitants of a single street—an impoverished professor and his daughter, an American Red Cross field worker, an oily procuress and the brutal, profiteering butcher who dominates them all. To convey . . . the psychological truth—and the horror—of these characters, Pabst began to explore and develop yet another power of the camera, the expressiveness of viewpoint and angle.

Joyless Street had been followed by the film that proved Pabst to be a master—*Secrets of a Soul*. It was the first film to make direct use of psychoanalysis, and was supervised by the eminent Freudians Dr. Hanns Sachs and Dr. Karl Abraham. It is not only the first serious treatment of psychiatry on film, but also the world of the dream image is used to introduce Symbolism. Like the earlier *The Cabinet of Dr. Caligari*, it is a film that combines psychoanalysis and Expressionism. Of course there is no doubt that the painting of the period, Symbolist, Expressionist, influenced this infant art.

Kenneth and Bryher were enjoying themselves going daily to the makeshift studios, spending evenings with the filmmasters, sampling the perverse Berlin cabaret world. Kenneth wrote H.D. one of his intimate comic letters urging her to join them: "Wish the lynx were here. Strutting down Unter den Linden with its whiskers in the air, getting an awful kick out of it and pretending to *hate* it, Oh this . . . I mean why go to New York to get watered down versions of the same thing? (Sniff sniff) Throwing three schizophrenic phits per day when asked to go anywhere, but always going."

H.D.'s reply must have been neither joyous nor amused. Much as Aldington must have felt when he was at the Front writing to his "Astraea," so did Kenneth, who, although he had worried about his Cat getting her big paws caught in windows, had not foreseen that the next letter would tell him that Cat was pregnant. He immediately wrote her that under no circumstances must she have the "Pup." He reassured her that Dr. Sachs would give her whatever help she needed if she would come to Berlin. In this most "Roverish" letter the dismayed and stricken Kenneth writes: "Brave, handsome, beautiful, sad, noble, furry dignified kitten, hurry up and come and have that star or starfish or star maiden or whatever it is removed . . . Just get on that train and tell itself its troubles are almost

over, and tell itself it myst bye a N A I C E woman from now on." H.D.'s
letter to Kenneth must have made him distinctly aware that it was he
who was the father, because in the same letter of reassurance he says,
"No more 'Normal' for Rover!" And he adds that "Fido has been tearing
me about being a grown-up Dog, but we both nearly vomited our
lunches until *chocolate cake* miraculously calmed our nerves." He was
determined that she not be "phobed," that she be sensible and let them
take care of her in Berlin.

Of course, it must have crossed Kenneth's mind that she had been seeing Andrew Gibson in London, also Stephen Guest and Peter Rodeck.
His first reaction was that the pregnancy might not have been his responsibility. During further correspondence it must have been brought home
clearly to him that it was his child. H.D. and Kenneth had evidently continued their affair after the Bryher marriage, as the pregnancy was in
1928. There is an important confirmation of Kenneth's involvement in a
letter H.D. wrote to Bryher while she was under analysis with Freud.
She wrote: *"My triangle is mother-brother-self . . . I have HAD the
baby with the brother, hence R.A., Cecil Gray, Kenneth."* (my italics)

H.D. obediently took the train to Berlin. All was taken care of. H.D.,
however, had scored a point. She had proved that, even in the cinema
capital of the world, real life could triumph over the silver screen. The
Macphersons left H.D. in a pension to recuperate from the effects of her
private melodrama while they returned to their duties in Switzerland.
This would include not only filmmaking, but also plans for building a
permanent home near Territet.

Recuperation turned out to be not so onerous after all. Although weak
and taking medical treatment, H.D. found that Berlin lifted her spirits.
First she went to the zoo. Visiting zoos was a required pilgrimage for
Bryher and H.D., as it later would be for Perdita. She enjoyed weeping
in front of the dead tiger's cage. She also enjoyed sitting in cafés, watching people pass on the sidewalk under the glinty frost gray night lights of
winter Berlin. She found the Berliners humane. She found generosity and
what she called "brotherly love."

The outrageous poverty, the perilous existences, the tragic elements reduced to the ridiculous were what comforted H.D. in the Berlin of 1928.
She was now in an exalted state, released from personal worry; and everything appeared to be more alive in Berlin, where death was nearer
than anywhere else. She noticed that the snow did not melt, but retained
its glittering powder. "If ever there was a 'people' it is the German 'people.'" What she was really discovering and reveling in was an exile's adventure outside the formality and organized social structure of England
(a social stratification that would be a constant reminder she was an
alien). Berlin was destructified, anarchic, a place where Heinrich Mann,
the brilliant novelist brother of Thomas Mann, could publish his tragic

The Blue Angel, a Berlin saga filmed by Josef von Sternberg, which became a classic.

There hovered over her a special hospitality that was not due to the generosity of the German people per se. She had been feted, invited everywhere by German film society, treated like a star, admired, compared to Greta Garbo and Louise Brooks; even the leading male star Werner Krauss had invited her to dinner! No wonder she was able to conclude:

> . . . the whole experience brought me near to you both, brought us into some exquisite psychic rapport and certainly brought me to my senses as far as London is concerned . . . it was ALL FOR THE GOOD. Your tenderness and sweetness will always now be a part of my life and I don't want playing about with any "and ors" and things, old or new fashioned it may be. I am getting a real old cat, it wants its mat, its dish, its owners . . .

A miraculous, guiltless recovery from what could have been a rotten scene. But such turnabouts were normal to the H.D. psyche.

If ever fresh proof were needed of H.D.'s continued dependence on Bryher, if ever there were a psychic kingdom in need of its Napoleon, H.D.'s unscheduled trip in 1928 to Berlin provides its own close-up.

CHAPTER EIGHTEEN

Borderline

In the fall of 1929, POOL Productions commuted each day along the lake to Lutry. H.D. describes the plot of their projected film, which they called *Borderline:*

There are in Europe many just such little towns as this particular border-line town of some indefinite mid-European mountain district. There are trains coming and trains going. One of these trains has already deposited the half-world mondaine, Astrid with Thorne, her lover. They have come here because of some specific nerve-problem, perhaps to rest, perhaps to recuperate, perhaps to economise, perhaps simply in hope of some emotional convalescence . . . They are borderline social cases, not out of life, not in life; the woman is a sensitive neurotic, the man, a handsome degenerate dipsomaniac. Thorne has not reached the end of his cravings, may seep this side, that side of the border; Astrid, the white-cerebral is and is not outcast, is and is not a social alien, is and is not a normal human being, she is borderline. These two are specifically chosen to offset another borderline couple of more dominant integrity. These last, Pete and his sweetheart Adah, have a less intensive problem, but border; they dwell on the cosmic racial borderline. They are black people among white people.

The "company" consisted of Bryher and local friends. The man who worked the lights was Kenneth's father, called "Pop." Gavin Arthur played the degenerate Thorne. Gavin was the nephew of a friend of Bryher's, and at this time Mrs. Macpherson was "in love" with him. H.D. was the neurotic Astrid; Bryher played herself in the role of the proprietor of a dubious hotel!

An international star drawn from the outside was Paul Robeson, who with his wife Eslanda Goode was traveling in Europe after a successful visit to Russia. (In the 1930s while the Robesons lived in London, Eslanda would attend the London School of Economics and Political Science.) Whatever it was that seduced him and his wife to the out-of-the-way canton of Vaud in Switzerland—possibly an urge to be in an experimental film, or possibly he was one of Kenneth's many black friends—it was he who gave style to an otherwise awkward film. Of course, Robeson does not fit in. He is too much himself. He is not a "borderline" person, even if it is rationalized that being black makes him so. He is very much a part of the world. His personal beauty and the strength of his character tend to dominate the film, mostly because Robeson seems unaware of the psychological overtones of the film. He must have been a great admirer of Eisenstein, and may have been suggested by that director for the role, but he has no concept of the scenario of the film, nebulous as it was. The same is true of his beautiful wife Eslanda. They are two stand-outs or outsiders among a group of borderliners and they change the sense of balance of the film, as Dorothy Richardson observed in her review of the film in *Close-Up.*

Macpherson had seen too many films for his own good. He is like an artist who understands what kind of a painting he wishes to make, but does not know how to mix the paint. He focuses on chiaroscuro. And in the cinema the lighting must be phenomenally professional to attain the degrees of dark and light that are intended to suggest the subjective states of the artists. It would have been impossible to have assimilated the technical knowledge he needed in so short a time.

Borderline does, however, succeed in suggesting the influences Macpherson had attempted to assimilate. In particular he must have been influenced by Pabst's superb film *The Love of Jeanne Ney.* In that film Pabst uses ordinary objects in a room to intensify the personality of his characters. Just so does Macpherson clutter, or leave bare, the rooms in *Borderline.* As an example, he focuses on a white shawl that indicates the degrees of anxiety of H.D., who clutches and unclutches the shawl.

The film is a melee of emotional difficulties, threats of departure, false loves, exaggerated despair. The comic relief is supplied by Bryher, who is quite at home with a fat black cigar in her mouth, going about the business of adding up the cash, while the others seek to destroy themselves. Through it all stalk the sincere and loving couple, Robeson and his Essie. The Robesons finally get out of the film by walking off into the mountain while H.D. writhes upon the floor in a death agony in imitation of the final act of *Jeanne Ney.*

This is not an altogether just summary of the film. There is a sadness attached to *Borderline,* quite apart from its actual filming. Macpherson wished to accomplish so much. Intelligent and an artist of sorts, he yet was an amateur. When the actual cutting of the film was to take place, Kenneth developed a "bad throat" and took to his bed. (Yet it was Kenneth who had published the Russian master V. I. Pudovkin on the art of cutting and editing in *Close-Up.*) H.D. and Bryher were left alone to assemble and even cut the film. No one knew where anything was. When stills were needed to send to Berlin, Bryher wrote exasperatedly to H.D. to ask if she knew where they had been placed. They had been grown-up children playing in an expensive (although Bryher claimed the picture was made for only eight hundred pounds) charade. With all their theoretical understanding of film, they still remained outside that world.

And yet when Bryher went to Germany to show *Borderline* she reported that Elisabeth Bergner's husband, the director Paul Czinner, had said that *Borderline* was not only the film of the year, but one of the greatest films he has ever seen! "He is," she wrote H.D., "threatening dire things to the Press for merely stating it is an excellent and psychological film." And Lotte Lenya, when she visited Bryher at Vaud, told her that the most important thing in the film was H.D.'s work and that she ought to do nothing but films. Macpherson was already excitedly proposing that Pabst replace Louise Brooks with H.D. in *Pandora's Box*.

Yet when *Borderline* was shown in England the British did not like it. Friends admired it. Frances thought it pretentious. Bryher resolved its comparative failure by deciding that the problem in Britain had been one of race prejudice. Actually the film's faulty technique caused much of the criticism. The English psychoanalytic movement, always at odds with the German one, may also have expressed its bias.

Bryher concluded that film work had been magnificent training, "because it taught me speed, not to hang about looking at my characters in a novel, but to get them moving and to try to fix a landscape in a sentence as if it were a few feet of film."

As for H.D., she had enjoyed herself immensely. *Borderline* gave her a way of releasing the dramatic personality within herself. She had lived, dressed, spoken the role of poet; now she could find a physical expression for the combination of sensitive poet and worldly woman. Her private suffering now could be used as a force, as symbolic of the response of a passionate nature. The portrait she had given of herself to her friends had been that of a retiring, reclusive, and secretive person. When the camera focused on her, she could forget that previous image and project her secret self.

Like many actresses, H.D. was in love with her director, Kenneth Macpherson. For him and Bryher, she was their swan, their own Garbo. And behind the scenes another drama was going on. Not only was H.D. in love with her director, but with a fellow actor, Paul Robeson. In a brief story called "Two Americans,"[1] written at Vaud in 1930 in the midst of the filming, and at the time she was completing her long commentary on the film *Borderline* for the Mercury Press[2] (which would be used in an attempt to explain and popularize the film), H.D. writes of two Americans in Europe. They are the Robesons. H.D. believes herself to be closer to them because she is an American and can understand their position and struggle there. Actually what the Robesons did was to revive a nostalgia within her for the America she had left. From that time on she would begin to collect Negro songs of the American past and would use them

---

[1] She included this story in *The Usual Star* (1934).
[2] A subsidiary of Bryher's publications.

later when she wrote of her childhood. In other words, the Robesons brought her back to the identity of the early H.D. and to the country she now longed for. In the story a panegyric is addressed to Robeson, who is here called Saul Howard:

> His least movement was so gracious, he didn't have to think things out. Nevertheless with an astonishing analytical power, he did think. That was the odd thing about Saul Howard, he did think. He had a mind, a steadfast sort of burning, a thing that glowed like a whole red sunset or like a coal mine, it was steady, a steady sort of warmth and heat, yet all the time intellectual; he thought not as a man thinks. Paula Howard, his wife, thought more as white folks, consistently, being more than half white . . .
>
> Daniel [Kenneth] said, "I can see the man has an incredible fascination for you." Raymonde said, "fascination?" Daniel said . . . "I can see how you reach out to him." After all she had never talked about America except to execrate its horrors, as they all did . . . Home? Raymonde Ransome had found that; her spiritual home was Gareth, was Daniel . . . They were related to her as Katherine had been related . . . she was surprised herself to hear what she said, "he's removed a silver thorn out of my side, called Daniel."

(Again the exile speaks: "Can you be more American than America in Europe?")

For the period from the first issue of *Close-Up* in 1927 until the filming of *Borderline* in 1930, H.D. had been buoyed by the Ariel wings of film. The chore of writing had no attendant glamour. Here had been the dream world in which her friends told her she belonged. Freud would tell her that one of the reasons her writing gave her so little satisfaction was that she wished to become an actress.

In 1929 Margaret Anderson had sent out from Paris a questionnaire to her contributors to *The Little Review*. The first question had been: What should you most like to do, to know, to be? (In case you are not satisfied.)

H.D. had answered:

> I am involved with pictures. We have almost finished a slight lyrical four reel little drama, done in and about the villages here . . . the work has been enchanting, never anything such fun . . . I want to go on in this medium working with and around pure types, pure artists, pure people, experimenting with faces and shadows and corners . . . I feel like a cat playing . . . I should like to work the Debrie camera . . .

When asked why she went on living, H.D. replied: "I go on living now because I am happy and want to get the most there is to be got out of existence. I did go on living for years out of spite or pique." She added that although she was "very vain and have an inordinate inferiority complex . . . I am loyal literally to death."

Borderline, although it may have failed as a film, had created an aura of excitement in the preparation and planning. In living this film life, H.D. was elevated from her morbid fears of isolation and disapproval.

Yet even this escape into filmmaking could not convince her for long that the world was a camera. Despite the applause of her beauty and grace, one unavoidably sees in this film a woman whose beauty is outlined by suffering. The handsome jaw is now gaunt, the eyes are hollowed. Her physical clumsiness, a withholding, an inhibition, would never let her move gracefully; she was too intense to move freely, with that same intensity of Garbo, whose body betrays an inner conflict, and with whom H.D. was always being compared by her admirers. Despite the elegant clothes, the pearls and furs, there is, even more than called for in the script, the suggestion of an anxious life.

It must have been in these supposedly glamorous years of the late twenties, when H.D. was nearing forty-four, that Ezra Pound wrote to her at the Riant Château. In her plaintive reply, we hear the echo of regret for the past, despite her declaration of present happiness in working in a new medium.

> I am very old and very, very tired. I put down a lot of myself after Perdita's birth. I loved Richard very much and you know he had threatened to use Perdita to divorce me and to have me locked up if I registered her as legitimate . . . I mean, anything in the way of a shock brings that back and I go to pieces . . . that is why I have kept away from you all. I was growing a sort of wall between myself and myself and when I heard R. and A. had parted, for some reason the wall fell down . . . One side of me is rich and creative, the other has not yet had time to let the Sun get to it.
>
> But O Ezra . . . I am so old, and I look so different. I am so ashamed of myself, of my face and even my body sometimes . . . I seem to remember always the indignity of being unsheltered and then the treachery of the betrayal. It doesn't make any difference to my LOVE and I will always love Richard.

They were corresponding because H.D. had seen Pound, Brigit, and Richard briefly in Paris. Pound had attempted to bring about an amicable meeting with Richard. His efforts had not been appreciated by Richard, who considered him a busybody. Richard and H.D. eventually mended their fences. Brigit and H.D., prompted by Richard, had renewed, however briefly it would prove, their friendship. There had been a gallantry about the meeting of the old friends. H.D. explained to Pound that she had not clung onto Richard for any ulterior purposes. "I was hanging on because I was 'winged.' I had no place in the air and no place on earth. Now maybe I have a place in the air and a place on the earth."

She wants to impress on Ezra that she now has a home and a peaceful relationship with Macpherson and Bryher. She admits to being lonely, because the others are of "another cycle." Despite her shelter and friends, she reminds him of their lost prewar London world. This theme of a "never never" past would run through her letters. It explains why there could never be a clear break between the three—Pound, H.D., Aldington. Although here it is H.D. who admits it, the feeling was certainly shared by the others.

It was always necessary to apologize to Ezra for her relationship with Bryher. Not only explain, but pacify Ezra, who detested Bryher. Here she does not hesitate to sacrifice Bryher in order to console Pound.

> Bryher, between ourselves, has been in a very difficult way and is going through a trying "analysis." She is a borderline case, so that sometimes I seem actuated by weakness in giving in to her, when I alone knew what she was and what terror came into my heart at her peculiar kind of suffering. Then I had nothing anyway . . . and Ezra, you know as well as I, that you might as well be killed for a sheep as a lamb. Bryher looked after Perdita and that seemed to be the only thing I was hanging on for . . . I looked after Bryher. Of course this is all very bald.

As it is indeed. The letter reads like a variation on the one she had written to Cournos in 1919. A now habitual need to apologize and explain after all those years!

She had her own protective devices and was not going to put herself into a position to defend herself from the complications of Ezra's presence. When he wrote asking to visit her at Territet at that inconvenient time of the filming, she refused to see him. Her excuse may be a real one. It was that much as she loved Ezra, she was fearful that he and Kenneth Macpherson would not get along (and Macpherson had been "very beautiful" to her). She was not going to mix old and new lovers, despite nostalgia. She may have believed, and rightly, that Ezra wanted to visit Territet to satisfy his own roving curiosity. About Macpherson, she wrote to Ezra: "You could so easily see in him the plaster-of-cast . . . I don't know he is Highland and presents such a very well-done portrait of himself . . . waiting back of himself and watching, always watching with almost clairvoyant intensity."

Pound must have privately commented about that "clairvoyant intensity," as she always signed herself to him "Dryad," and he may have felt a certain responsibility on his own for encouraging the dryad propensities. She, dryadlike, intended to slip behind the weeds and hold onto her present mortal lover. She was determined not to submit herself to the prescience of the river god.

CHAPTER NINETEEN

Kenwin

Taxes, a need to escape family surveillance, a bolt-hole for friends and activities, a point of departure for travel, primarily a need for a fortress of her own—determined Bryher to decide to build in Switzerland near the familiar Riant Château. Sir John urged her to do so, foreseeing future tax benefits. For Kenneth the building of Kenwin—Kenneth-Winifred—would be the beginning of a lifelong pleasure in the development of villas, apartments, town houses. He had already proved his decorative talents in the London flats.

POOL Productions had been spawned by German and European experimentation. The psychiatrists they had consulted were German or Austrian. No hint of British Tudor or Swiss chalet, except as horrifying representatives of bourgeois disapproval, had ever entered their orbit—why not choose an architect from the deaconry of the avant-garde, the Bauhaus? Further, Hans Henselmann arrived with credentials supplied by Dr. Hanns Sachs, Bryher's psychiatrist.

The alarm among the local Vaudois can be easily imagined. There near the Château of Chillon, already desecrated by an unregenerate British poet (although its official address is Burier-la-Tour, which one cannot resist translating as "Bryher's Tower") above Lake Geneva, in the foothills that feature in so many of H.D.'s stories, the cubistic structure was begun. As a further irony, the lot selected was next door to the famed geriatic specialist Dr. Niehans, whose patients would include Yeats, Somerset Maugham, one of the popes; on his grounds, like the patients indoors, peacocks flaunted their plumage.[1]

The architecture of Kenwin, which was built during 1930–31, is late Bauhaus, or Lac Leman international. Given the creative demands of its owners, Kenwin survives with a distinction all its own, blunt, crabbed, cubed, eccentric. The architect was subject to fits of depression, which he claimed could only be calmed by a remembrance of the beauty of H.D. as Astrid in *Borderline*, which had been in process at the time of the building—a poetic augury for a new house. Originally the house was to be a long low cube, a studio where Kenneth might perform his miracles.

---

[1] Fifty-three years after the controversy involved in its construction, and following the death in January 1983 of Bryher, the Swiss authorities declared Kenwin a landmark.

Two difficulties presented themselves. Kenneth was no longer interested in making films; he liked making houses better. And the Swiss, having decided that given the modernity of the building its owners intended to use it for pornographic films, forbade them to film there.

The large main room with its projection room vaulted under the ceiling, projecting into the studio, today is empty, save for some embalmed furniture from cast-off villas of friends. On another level are cabinlike bedrooms facing the low mountains and the lake. There is an inside room, much too small for its purposes, where conventional gatherings, such as after-dinner coffee, cocktails, and conversations, might be held. The aspect of the building today is of an elderly, eccentric ship. A formidable, hygienic, and ill-equipped kitchen is placed beside the breakfast nook where Bryher took her British meals. H.D. had worked on one of the interior balconies that overlooked the long studio. Outside are empty decks or balconies. At one time there may have been comfort and elegance. Today there is a dilapidated, saddening expensiveness. The main feature, which was proudly pointed out by Bryher, is the red extrovert furnace room.

The aspect of Kenwin in its day was pleasant, not too Alpine, and yet still not suburban, like nearby Montreux or Vevey. It is the only modern house in the area. Nestlé has its presumably efficient factory. When last seen the "Emperor" reigned solitary from a lonely, original Marcel Breuer chair. The splendid library (not formally equipped as in great houses, but built with ordinary shelves) with its Elizabethan acquisitions is elsewhere. Novels from the twenties up until today are to be found, as well as an extensive history of the canton of Vaud. Bryher's necessary historical books are still there. No cameras turn. Nor poems.

Kenwin became both a home and a prison. It was a place for the young Perdita to return from her schools in England. It was a schoolroom where Bryher could carry out her educational program with Perdita as experiment-subject. Kenwin coincided with Perdita's adoption by Kenneth and Bryher. Thus, Kenneth had his Scottish keep and Bryher her Eastbourne. For H.D., Kenwin was a retreat, yet (it is sensed) never a haven.

There were many visitors and semipermanent guests, not only Norman Douglas and pals for Kenneth, but also Stephen Guest, eldest son of the First Baron Haden-Guest of Saling, the former Dr. Leslie Haden-Guest of *The New Age,* and for thirty-five years a member of the House of Commons. Stephen's aunt, Barbara Low, was a psychoanalyst practicing in London, a former analysand of Sachs. She had been a close friend of the Lawrences, and Stephen had known D. H. Lawrence when he was young and often spoke of the intensity of his brilliant blue eyes. Lawrence gave Barbara the manuscript of *Sea and Sardinia* to pay for her training-analysis with Dr. Ernest Jones, as she wanted to prepare herself to become an analyst. (She was eventually very successful in working with the blind.) Barbara Low was cautious of H.D., and H.D. never liked her. She would claim that whenever she saw Barbara on the staircase of the house in Regent's Park where Dr. Walter Schmideberg practiced, she would come home with a nosebleed.

Stephen, by the 1930s, was a young man recently graduated from the University of London who had fallen in love with H.D. A difficult friend, she was kind to him; he and Perdita were great companions. He had been a lover of Brigit Patmore, after which he refused to meet Frances Gregg, claiming he had lived out the particular phase Frances would represent through Brigit. H.D. believed Stephen had a "rare kind of oriental magnetism." She described so aptly that "queer round paw gesture he had like a small lion rampant." During the early days of Kenwin and H.D.'s later retreat to London, there was an affair changing into a tender relationship. Later in retrospect he worshiped her. He liked her way of dressing in clothes found in the flea market. He thought her a genius. He betrayed her by taking letters from her, keeping manuscripts, and breaking appointments, a pattern he would reenact with others. Yet Stephen, brilliant and erratic, was just the sort of man she would be attracted to. It was his pattern to drop in at all hours and have long, difficult occult or psychoanalytic talks with her. She appreciated his capacity to see around and through people; further, his attraction to mysticism appealed to her. It was Stephen who brought Lawrence's *The Man Who Died* to H.D. and told her the book must have been written about her. She was the priestess, Isis. This conclusion, based on no factual evidence, is typical of Stephen, an extension of his "mystical" perception.

A glimpse of the early Kenwin can be found in H.D.'s short novel *Nights,* which she wrote under the name of John Helforth. Macpherson foolishly wrote to her that *Nights* was "Garbo in writing." After the house was completed, one of the early visitors was Elisabeth Bergner, who would soon star in *Escape Me Never,* adapted from Margaret Kennedy's popular novel. She was Bryher's current interest, and complicated scenes took place, as one would expect. Bergner was also fond of H.D. So much so that H.D. was forced to comment that both Kenneth's and Bryher's lovers turned to her for comfort. Bergner in this story appears offstage, but her presence enables a fictitious Bryher to look askance at a disappointing affair that H.D., the narrator of the story, is conducting with a probable lover of the holidaying Kenneth (Neil). The story may be a portrait of H.D. as she sees herself as unfulfilled mistress-wife, her role complicated by her attraction to women. The lover, as in all her stories, is a likeness of Aldington. He may in actual life have been Dan Burt, the nephew of Mary Chadwick, who was closely connected to H.D. as an analyst. In *Nights* she indicates the fantasies the narrator still has for Kenneth, or Neil. She attempts to get to the essence of her own bisexuality as she conducts her illicit heterosexual affair. The figures of Bergner and Bryher do intrude, and Bryher drops her usual intellectualisms, her commonsensical abbreviations of life. There is the duennalike presence of Kenwin's housekeeper, whom H.D. disliked.

H.D., despite all the unhappy nuances in *Nights*—and there is an eventual suicide—has her heroine say (referring to Kenwin), "The house was her spirit—she had never so loved any house—in the sparse and geometric contour of the house there was all wisdom."

What puzzles one about this remark, although it introduces a literary scene, is that H.D. was never successfully "at home" at Kenwin, despite the romance of her words. For one thing, she required, as had been noted, more intimacy in her living arrangements. Kenwin actually was a set for an unfilmed scenario; it was not a home. For another, household staffs—such as were necessary at Kenwin: governess, gardener, chauffeur, cook, maid—disturbed her. She had largely imaginary difficulties with all the domestics. The expensive cars chosen by Kenneth required a chauffeur, as no one ever seemed able to drive one of these valuable cars. Then, brought up as she had been with one servant in a professor's household, she could not accommodate herself to houses run by staffs. At Kenwin, most importantly, she was neither mistress of the establishment nor guest. She was very conscious of the ambiguity of her position. It may have reminded her of South Audley Street. In her own digs she had the devoted charlady Mrs. Ash, a friend on whom she could lean and who, thankfully, spoke English. At Kenwin, Bryher was the helmswoman, and her husband Kenneth was accepted as an assistant-squire. But who was H.D.? It was a sad question she asked herself all her life. An unanswerable question at this point, given the alien setting and the incongruities of her circumstances.

In 1929 Bryher, Robert Herring, a writer for *Close-Up*, and Kenneth had gone off to Iceland. They had intended going to Newfoundland, but that was for some reason forbidden. After 1929, although they didn't know it, Iceland would become more fashionable, particularly after the much-publicized Auden-Isherwood trip. Now it was "indicated" (a word H.D. would often use) that a journey might be taken to avoid the new domesticity and assert the H.D. kingdom of the Hellenes. She and Perdita set out in 1932 on a cruise similar to today's Swan's tours. There were lecturers of distinction, and archaeological sites would be visited. This cruise to Greece would in no way resemble the former hysterical and uncertain voyage of the early Bryher-H.D. period. It would be a private H.D. venture, with Pup (Perdita's childhood name) as family.

H.D. presents herself on this cruise as a standoffish, lone figure, fragile and inaccessible, carefully, like a good schoolgirl, taking her "notes," accompanied by her venturesome daughter. It was a sacred voyage for

H.D., asserting as it did her independence and "settler's rights" to Greece. She was also going toward the Delphic mysteries. Her way was strewn with flowers and plants whose names she carefully wrote down. She was gathering another botanical hoard into which she might dip for her future writing. As for her fellow voyagers, she did not reach out toward them, nor were they friendly with her. No one recognized the translator of Euripides! Whatever H.D. found among the mountains and ruins of Greece would remain a secret until carefully sifted down to one short word or a pebble for the track to her imaginary sea.

CHAPTER TWENTY

Bergasse 19

"Oh that awful Kat. She has got in, hasn't she. She'll be unbearable. A pupil of Freud. She'll live on that till she dies," Kenneth Macpherson wrote prophetically to Bryher in March 1933.

Urged by Bryher, Dr. Hanns Sachs had written to Freud about H.D.'s wish to work with him. Havelock Ellis, with whom H.D. had been corresponding over the years, and with whom she lunched in 1932 to discuss her hope of being accepted by Freud, also recommended H.D. There was Bryher herself, who had been financially aiding the psychoanalytic movement in Vienna. Formally, a letter came from Dr. Freud informing H.D. that she should be ready to go to Vienna in March and stay through May of 1933. Herr Doktor Freud would be pleased to welcome her as an analysand. Or, as H.D. chose to phrase it, "a pupil." H.D. was then forty-seven, Freud, seventy-seven.

She said she needed to see Freud because she "wanted to dig down and dig out, root out my personal weeds, strengthen my purpose, reaffirm my beliefs, canalize my energies." It is a rare analysand who is able to summarize the exact needs for a psychiatrist. H.D. was better informed than most. There was so much talk and emphasis on psychiatry in any household of Bryher's. H.D. had had her initiation with Ellis and a brief analysis with Hanns Sachs. She knew that she was still bound to the prewar period, which she found was suffocating her and causing her to carry endlessly the thread of those prewar days through her short stories and novels.

She has said two things: that she would be both a pupil, and, controversially, she would be an analysand. Throughout her sessions with the doctor there is this mixture of patient and pupil. She never fully relinquished herself to the doctor. She insisted that he was not always right. Right in his judgments, "but my form of rightness, my intuition sometimes function by the split-second (that makes all the difference in spiritual time-computations) the quicker." She wanted Freud to help her and at the same time she wanted to learn his "technique."

H.D.'s analysis with Freud is a curious mixture of Freud's scientific technique and H.D.'s belief in magic. In theory, she believed in psychoanalysis; actually, she wanted to go to the original magician, the Merlin, or the Theseus, as she would later call him. Superstition and intuition were the controls under which she worked, which Freud instantaneously must have recognized.

The letters H.D. wrote to Bryher from Vienna in 1933 differ from H.D.'s account of the first meeting with Freud in her book *Tribute to Freud*. In her book she says that Freud angrily pounded the chair and said to her, "The trouble is—I am an old man—you do not think it worth your while to love me."

In her letters she describes Freud opening the door, saying, "Enter fair madame." A small, furry chow got up and stood at her feet.

> I shook all over, he said I must take off my coat, I said I was cold, he led me around the room and I admired bits of Pompeii in red, a bit of Egyptian cloth and some authentic coffin paintings. A sphynx faces the bed. I did not want to go to bed, the white "napkin for the head" was the only professional touch, there were dim lights, like an opium dive. I started to talk about Sachs and Chaddie and my experience with ps-a [psychoanalysis]. He said he would prefer me to recline. He has a real fur rug and I started to tell him how Sachs had none, he seemed vaguely shocked, then remarked, "I see you are going to be very difficult. Now although it is against the rules, I will tell you something: YOU WERE DISAPPOINTED AND YOU ARE DISAPPOINTED IN ME." I then let out a howl, and screamed but you do not realize you are everything, you are priest, you are magician. I then cried so I could hardly utter and he said that I had looked at the pictures, preferring the mere dead shreds of antiquity to his living presence.

Later Freud made her stand beside him and told her he was nearly as tall as she. She confessed that she may have been disappointed he was not a giant, as being taller made her grown up; in dreams she was always a child.

She pointed out to him that she certainly liked him; as proof, hadn't Freud's chow dog, Yo-Fi, come over to her to be patted? They decided there was an English phrase "Love me, love my dog." Freud had first said, "Like me," and she had corrected him. This was the level on which they began the sessions. H.D. lay back on the couch and began to cry. She cried and cried, as she never had before in sessions with her psychoanalyst friend Mary Chadwick. Only at that first session. And when she was ready to leave, Freud pointed out to her she had left one of her string bags. "So he won, after all," wrote H.D. to Bryher. "I had forgotten I had two bags and was leaving with only one." It would be indicative of a struggle between analyst and analysand in which, as she had pointed out, certain intuitive strengths were hers. A curious way to begin an analysis, and one Freud would beautifully handle. He would permit the sessions to go from mythical excursions to antique countries, and then his control would change the subject back to H.D.'s particular problem.

In *Tribute to Freud* she also elaborates on her first session with Freud

by describing her entrance into his private chambers so filled with antique objects that her first delighted glance was at them, rather than the
professor. She tells us that Freud "sadly" remarked, "You are the only
person who has ever come into the room and looked at the things in the
room before looking at me." On March 13, 1933, reporting on this scene
in a letter from Vienna to Havelock Ellis, she writes: "He let me wander
about and then remarked rather whimsically and ironically that he saw
that I was not really interested in him, *nor in humanity* [my italics], that
the FIRST entrance of the analysand was most important, and my first
instinct was to look at the Greek and Egyptian collection and not at
HIM . . ."

Some ten years previously, Harriet Monroe had remarked of H.D. that
"she is quite unconsciously, a lithe, hard, bright-winged spirit of nature
to whom humanity is but an incident." (my italics)

First she learned that Freud was disappointed that she would make
her transference to him as a mother. The original transference had been
to Ellis, who had been, to her surprise, the father image. Freud told her
that she was the perfect example of the bisexual. She had "got stuck at
the earliest pre-oedipal stage, and back to the womb seems to be my only
solution. Hence islands, sea, Greek primitives and so on . . . My triangle
is mother-brother-self." As she once said, "I have had the baby with the
brother, hence Richard Aldington, Cecil Gray, Kenneth, etc." He next explained that she had "two things to hide, one that you were a girl, the
other that you were a boy." She wrote Bryher that in speaking of her
writing Freud explained that "the conflict consists partly that what I
write commits me to one sex or the other, I no longer hide." This explanation had followed a previous session in which Freud had told her that
her dreams were what he would expect of a woman poet. When H.D.
told Freud that her friendship with Bryher and Kenneth had adjusted
her to normal conditions of life, he had quickly replied, "Not normal, so
much as ideal." Freud told her that not only did she want to be a boy,
but she wanted to be a hero. And finally he explained that all along in
her unconscious she had wanted to be an actress. That is one reason she
was never satisfied with writing. He had treated the Corfu episode as a
hallucination and also had indicated that she had enjoyed acting out
some of its scenes, as a charade. Freud beautifully interpreted the Corfu
incident as "a poem sequence that was not written." The pictures she
saw on the wall he believed were a "sort of unclassified 'delirium,'" in
other words, a hallucination.

These are the kernels out of which bloomed that magical tale H.D.
called *Tribute to Freud*.

H.D. was living at the Hotel Regina on what was then known as the
Freiheitsplatz. The street is now named for the Votive Church, a nineteenth-century church near her hotel. The Regina was the favorite of

visiting psychoanalysts, as it was about half a block just around the
corner from Freud's apartment at Bergasse 19, which was on a respectable residential street within the Ring. Across the *Platz* from the church
was the university. Thus H.D. was able to consider herself living in the
"student quarter," although Vienna, unlike most cities, has no proper student quarter.

She loved Vienna, it reminded her of her old Paris. She also referred
to it as "the Moravian town of Vienna," because Freud's mother came
from Moravia. She changed her clothes to blend into the surroundings,
dressing in old tweeds and scarves. She asked that a leather handbag
Kenneth had bought her in Venice be sent to her, because all the students and professors carried leather cases; she had romantically brought
a string bag from Greece! She enjoyed, addictively, the coffee and cream,
saving some of the cream from her nightly apple strudel to put into her
morning hotel coffee. It was a Viennese repetition of her old days after
the British Museum, refreshing herself with tea and buns. She went to
concerts and the opera. The hotel staff, admirers of Freud, treated her
royally.

She was beginning to observe her surroundings as useful material for a
novel, which indeed she did write. H.D. went to Freud six days a week
at her favorite hour of five in the afternoon. It was her usual "tea" hour
at home, when the day could be summed up and warmth permitted from
the hearth. She explained this to Freud when he asked her why she preferred this hour. After the hour was over and she had taken coffee, she
would sometimes proceed to a certain "shop." There, on orders from
Bryher, she would choose nude photographs of actresses for Bryher's collection. She especially looked for Bergner in the nude or, as H.D. pointed
out to Bryher, ever so much better, dressed in chiffon. She disliked this
task, but then would come her own consolation, films. She saw Constance
Bennett. She went to Le Moulin Rouge where she could view "the rosy
bottoms" of the chorus. She saw movies, French in particular, nearly
every day. When not at the coffee shop, concerts, or films, she wrote in
her journal. This would eventually be published as "Advent." She was
happy. She was, as she wrote Bryher, "sane, sobbing, happy."

Throughout her analysis H.D. was aware of the unseen presence of
Freud's disciple and admirer Marie Bonaparte, who by marriage became
Princess George of Greece. Marie Bonaparte was so close to Freud that
H.D. realized that never could she, despite Freud's interest in her as patient and poet, partake of the same rapport they shared. She even admitted her jealousy, and she certainly felt it. She told her friend Silvia Dobson that everything she wrote had Marie Bonaparte in mind. She must
have meant everything she wrote in Vienna ("Advent"). It was Marie
Bonaparte who, in her seminal book *Female Sexuality*, wrote: "In any
case, clitoridal women who, whether manifestly homosexual or, having

passed from the mother to the father, succeed in developing the object relation proper to the female, have always unconsciously remained most passively fixated, cloacally and phallically, on the mother they knew when a child."

H.D. shares in *Tribute to Freud* a dream she had while in Vienna in which a woman, like a princess, is descending a staircase watched by another person, the dreamer. There at the lowest step in the water is a shallow basket or ark or box or boat. There is, of course, a baby nested in it. "The Princess must find the baby. I know that she will find this child. I know that the baby will be protected and sheltered by her and that is all that matters." H.D. associates this dream with an etching she had seen as a child of Moses in the bulrushes, and then she asked Freud, "Do I wish myself, in the deepest layers of my being, to be the founder of a new religion?" (Bryher was familiar with what she called, either sarcastically or jokingly, H.D.'s "religious mania.")

This is a surprising association. But does she not mean that the "Princess" is her mother, and that she, a little girl, is watching her mother pick up a baby—a baby brother? Could she not have witnessed this as a child? Whether or not this is a correct interpretation, the story illustrates the leap in H.D.'s thinking, showing that she was capable of unanticipated associations, and that she much preferred the exotic to the ordinary. Naturally, she would be interested in Princess George with her singular background and active intellect, a natural confrere for Freud, who liked strong-minded women. H.D. would not call Freud a magician, or Moses (did she know about his proposed book *Moses and Monotheism?*). She was beginning to call him "little papa," over and over "little papa," supplanting the early "little white ghost." He also was "Oedipus Rex" in her letters.

H.D.'s difficulties over money were not solved by Freud. She would be haunted by them all her life. Freud explained to her that a dream she had revealed she had an unconscious worry over Bryher's paying her bills in Vienna. Bryher was paying at this time one hundred pounds a month for a six-day week, or about twenty-seven hundred schillings. Freud wanted the money in pounds. That would be the equivalent of twenty-five dollars a session, which for that time would be quite high. Freud explained that he was forced to charge his wealthy and foreign clients more, so that he might charge the Viennese less. Bryher was quite willing to pay this rate. Vienna was controlled by a Social Democrat party; the city was rent-controlled and rent took only 5 to 15 percent of an income. Medical care was practically free. Public transportation was cheap. A secretary would earn about twenty dollars a month. On this scale it can be seen that Freud's fee was high; although he insisted, and believably so, that he would prefer not to charge his patients. This Socialist government would come to an end with the election of Dolfuss, who toppled the liberal Social Democrats and put in his own right-wing Christian Democratic power.

Ever since her analysis with Sachs, Bryher had been financially aiding the psychoanalytic movement in Vienna. She had deposited a sum to be used to publish their *Psychoanalytic Review*. She would transfer a sum to be managed by Martin, Freud's son, which would protect those needy analysts during the days of the Viennese money crisis. Emergency funds were finally, at the end of H.D.'s analysis, put at Freud's disposal. Bryher was frighteningly aware of the Nazi threat.[1] She did not for one moment believe Freud's surprisingly sanguine analysis that the "Austrians are really very kind people so we do not expect any real danger." Freud might have arrived at this conclusion because he was living in town, and the townspeople of Vienna were liberal and less anti-Semitic; it was the countryside outside Vienna that was notoriously fascist. More so than in Berlin.

Bryher expected a war and wanted to be in a position where she could help those who would need her. Although she had never emphasized that she was part Jewish, Bryher was ideologically opposed to fascism and the anti-Semitism that rode in its wake. She was prepared to aid all its victims. At the moment she had addressed herself to the Freudians. All this was quietly accomplished. Funds were transferred. Freud was notified. And just in time would Martin Freud be able to continue the *Psychoanalytic Review,* as he would soon lose his job in the bank in Vienna as the Nazis began to take over. Neither H.D. nor Bryher could understand what they believed was the silence on the part of the British psychoanalysts toward the disaster Freud might be facing. H.D. wrote to Bryher:

> I feel for all papa's renown, there is a little rescue work indicated. I think people are too inclined to treat him like Gawd a'mighty and forget he might like a little breezy gossip. I went over the chief points, how England was pledged to France . . . and H. would hardly dare the powers like in the old days. He says, "Yes, but before he has time to think many many people will be murdered." (He meant Jews.) I said I didn't think massacre was possible, there was still open sympathy in the world. Poor old, old little old papa. However, he gave a flea shake to his shoulders and said, "well we had better go on with your analysis. It is the only thing now."

Freud never seems to have delved into the main problem of H.D.'s financial reliance on Bryher when her own income, after an early judi-

---

[1] Bryher's continual references to the threat of war must have irritated H.D., preoccupied with her analysis. She wrote Bryher: "I don't give a damn who goes and who doesn't to war. All I want is to pick up the pieces, to know how I feel, not to be badgered by conflict." When war actually came she was as involved as anyone else, but in those days it was still the Great War that haunted her.

cious settlement of funds by Bryher, together with her brother Harold's careful investments of her money, freed H.D. from any financial strain. Freud was more worried, in a personal way, as to how he might repay Bryher's help. The solution he came upon can be explained by those qualified in Freudian terms. He offered Bryher one of the expected Yo-Fi puppies. The original litter had contained only one puppy, who had died. Yo-Fi was expecting more, and Bryher could have one. There is a certain parallel here to H.D.'s loss of her first child, and then her turning Perdita over to Bryher to take care of, in her own words, "just like a puppy." H.D. does not mention having repeated those words to Freud, and there is no evidence of them in her book. Yet it was rather unusual of Freud to offer a puppy to Bryher. Little did he expect the consternation of Kenneth and the upset in Kenwin. Kenneth refused to have anything to do with a chow puppy. He claimed they were terrible, mean dogs. Poor Bryher, who by now had an establishment at Kenwin of monkeys and dogs, did not need another dog. She also did not want to hurt the man she respected most in all the world next to her own Dr. Sachs, so she composed a letter to Freud that is half child, half businesswoman, half disciple, half worshiper, explaining that, to her terrible sorrow, she could not accept the puppy. The denouement was that, after giving birth, Yo-Fi ate part of the litter, and the one designated for Bryher bit someone and came to an early demise.

Freud liked to gossip and so did H.D. They talked about Havelock Ellis, and it was H.D. who told Freud that Ellis' wife had been a lesbian. This did not surprise Freud. Freud, also sympathizing with H.D. in her relations with Ellis, remarked, "Ah, I always thought between OUR-SELVES that that man's work was inconclusive and in some way he must be unusually immature. AND NOW I KNOW." Or so wrote H.D. to Bryher. She also added that "So far I have contributed to the occult and arcane and most secret gayety of nations BUT you know you must be careful as papa is most slimely dirtful and says, 'now you have been so frank with me, I will be frank with you between ourselves' and out comes some scrap of flea morsel." Later she learned from an English friend in confidence that Freud would leave his wife and small children to go on long journeys with his sister-in-law. This news delighted H.D., who decided that "Vienna is oak," meaning, one supposes, that all psycho-organic roots could be found there. Including much gossip. On the other hand, in the same letter of March 13 to Ellis, she is delighted to tell Ellis that Freud has his framed picture in his waiting room and "a little volume celebrating his birthday on a special shelf in the corner." She also writes that Freud one day had said to her, "You see I looove Havelock Ellis." This remark, which contradicts the previous attitude toward Ellis she had conveyed to Bryher, concludes with a hope that she may meet Ellis in the late summer and talk to him about her sessions with Freud.

At the same time the letter is proof that her friendship with Ellis had continued and was not interrupted, as would have been expected, by the personal conflicts that had interfered with their Greek journey. Ellis was a most forgiving human being, and understanding this, H.D. was able to write to him that she was "so happy to continue the 'thread' of our friendship right on into this strange experience."

An earlier letter in January 1933 to Ellis gives us a glimpse of the disarming ability of H.D. to confide her frailties in letters, if seldom in a personal confrontation. She again goes into the accident to her father. Explaining that she had not been able to speak of her father's accident previously, she writes:

> And with it, with you, there was some link or bond, you were of course utterly different . . . but my father was the upright, lean sea-faring type too . . . I mention this, only as a side-issue, but all this was at work in the under-mind or unconscious. I had such terror of letting this out. I am now in fact, hardly able to see as I type. This is a drab explanation of a lot of things but I want you to realize how deeply I am indebted to you, not only for my life but for my reason. If you had not been kind those days or if you had shut your door on me, I might very easily simply have lost the will to live (it was a struggle) . . . Well I will say this of myself I recognized the BEST and went straight for it. I now wonder at the courage . . . it was the courage of a battered gull, of course . . . to rest on the ledge of a light-house. I had to fly away again.

The letter to Ellis confirms Freud's opinion that H.D. had made the father transference to Ellis before coming to him. H.D. continues to assure Ellis of her eternal gratitude. She confides that "I do not so far, consider my work at all . . . anything. Here and there, yes, a peak, an ice-flower. But if I can manage to straighten this out, to gain strength or power, it will be partly in order to return in some literary form, the debt I owe to the few . . . to you, among those 'very few.'" She then goes on to say that Dr. Sachs had believed that she might contribute something in the way of writing and held open the possibility that she might "help others when and if needed." Evidently in her correspondence with Freud about coming to see him, or so she tells Ellis, Freud had taken the same attitude. "In fact, Freud says openly, he cannot take on people who have nothing to offer in return, any more . . . or words to that effect." (my italics)

Bryher came to Vienna in April of 1933 and stayed with H.D. at the Regina. Freud sent her a large bunch of flowers with a card bearing a small photograph of Freud and "thanks from Yo-Fi." She had congratulated Yo-Fi on the birth of her puppies. Kenneth's sister Eileen, known as "Egon," arrived with a governess and the fourteen-year-old Perdita. H.D. had all the comforts and discomforts of home. She had postponed Bryher's arrival as long as possible, but Bryher was eager to be in on the scene, and Perdita, now returned from a trip to Greece, which Freud had envied her, would necessarily need to be with her two mothers.

Freud and Bryher met. He told her that she was very practical and perhaps overinterested in business. Privately he told H.D. that she must find Bryher very tiring because of her overabundance of energy! He also encouraged H.D. to use the real influence she had on Bryher to help her.

Bryher observed to H.D. that "Freud saw analysis as a philosophical system applicable to some earnest thinkers who might influence the great wave of life." She herself viewed the process as a medicine—an antidote against illness. Freud, in turn, told Bryher that she would like analysis to continue forever. That was certainly true. She was elated while in analysis, in contrast to her depressions, which resulted from a lack of sufficient physical activity.

Bryher's excited entrance into the psychoanalytic world of Vienna, a preserve dutifully trodden by H.D., caused H.D. to become ill. She decided that she would leave in June of 1933, with a return date to be worked out.

At this time there occurred a parenthesis in the H.D. analysis that is worth noting. She was attempting to convince a depressed Conrad Aiken to become an analysand of Freud. In biographies of Freud it has been noted that Aiken's book *The Great Circle* lay on a table in Freud's reception room. This book was presented to Freud by H.D.

While with Freud, H.D. had a dream that was based on the story of the Aiken family. Aiken's father had murdered his wife and then killed himself, leaving Aiken orphaned. H.D. had dreamed that she and Aldington had been in bed together. He had shot Bryher and then he had killed himself. H.D. linked up all this with the grief she felt for those she knew who had committed suicide, been blackmailed and destroyed, and her fear of becoming such a victim. (There is a mysterious story about a drug ring surrounding Heseltine and Mary Butts into which H.D. might have very early been introduced; the subject is never made explicit, but there was always uppermost in her mind the fear of blackmail.) H.D. would always suffer a paranoiac concern over her privacy being intruded upon and something "discovered."

Regarding this dream and Freud's interpretation (which was thorough, considering he shortly before had told her that she had "become so independent and clear in my head that there was no need for him to speak at all"), she wrote Bryher:

> Evidently that was THE primal scene, and all the rest, mstn. [H.D.'s private shorthand for "masturbation"], later affairs, all the . . . terrors of war and that sort of thing is built on that first scene. (where R.A. shoots you, à la Aiken menage, then shoots himself in bed) Also usually a child decides for or against one or other parent, or identifies himself with one. But to me, it was simply the loss of both parents and a sort of perfect bi-sexual attitude arises, loss and independance. I have tried to be man or woman

but I have to be both. But it will work out papa says and I said, now in writing. Mstn. with me only breaks down the perfection, I have to be perfect, I get that in my writing . . .

Aiken had a practical use also. He had reviewed *Palimpsest* in *The New Republic* in 1927 in the very words she had been longing to hear, as the work of a poet who was trying to break away from the Imagist mold into which she had been frozen. He had written:

> . . . one cannot evade the feeling that in prose H.D. is a much more disturbing person than in verse: which is tantamount to saying that she had a great deal more to express than she found it remotely possible to express in the somewhat narrow, somewhat previous, poetic mode which she had invented for herself.
> . . . And the result is a novel which invites comparison with the very best fiction which has been written, in any language, in this century.

A critic who would load her with such praise was worth saving. Aiken was a contact with America, the America she constantly believed was slipping away from her.

She wrote to Aiken that she believed Freud needed people—perceptive, creative people like herself and him—to carry on his work. And Aiken wasn't even certain he wished to go into analysis!

The matter was ended by a letter from Anna Freud saying that Freud had suffered a heart attack and would be taking no patients at that time. Later Aiken would consult Dr. Sachs in Boston.

Then, shortly after H.D.'s departure from Vienna on the Bryher-H.D. anniversary in July, Bryher having sent lilies and H.D. writing her usual grateful letter, Sir John Ellerman died. He had been in France at the time, and one of his own ships came to take him back to England, where the family faced cameras, reporters, all the notoriety surrounding one of the wealthiest men of his era. Dr. Sachs came straight to Kenwin from his own holiday.

The newspapers reported that Ellerman had left "the biggest fortune ever dealt with at Somerset House. It does not include any of Sir John's large holdings in shipping and other interests." The Dictionary of National Biography noted that because his estate had been so efficiently managed "his death created scarcely a ripple of disturbance on the surface of London finance, and his organization continues to function almost automatically today from the same headquarters." He left £17,223,977, not including large holdings in shipping and other interests. The *Telegraph* reported that "the total estate is expected to be £30,000,000. Duty will be £15,000,000. His son, Sir John Ellerman would receive £600,000 absolute and £2,000,000 upon trust for him and his issue. His daughter would receive £600,000 absolutely and £600,000 upon trust." Translated into today's monetary sums, Sir John had left over $800 million.

Kenwin and its surviving ménages would thus be safe for several dec-

ades. And it was to Kenwin H.D. returned from Vienna. She remained
there working on *Ion,* which would become her finest translation, a work
that had been in progress over many years. She did suffer some kind of
breakdown during the early summer of 1934 at Kenwin, while waiting
for her sessions to begin in the fall in Vienna. She had been estranged
from friends, working extremely hard, and then she received news of
the death of the analysand who had preceded her hour with Freud, J. J.
van der Leeuw.

H.D. makes a great mystery of this figure she had watched on the
stairs at 19 Bergasse. He was another "Blue Nile" man. She was curious
about him, and Freud had indicated that van der Leeuw was interested
in applying principles of psychoanalysis to general education (an idea
also of Bryher's). Therefore the Dutchman, or Flying Dutchman, as she
called him because he had an airplane, was more a disciple of Freud's, as
she considered herself, than a patient. In *Tribute to Freud* she describes
him carefully as being handsome, young, appearing intelligent and capable. In fact, she envied his atmosphere of efficiency and worldliness. She
was creating another Peter Rodeck. She had a mystery man in her life.
But it is still unaccountable why she should have broken down almost severely when she learned of his death while at Kenwin. And why in *Tribute to Freud* she creates a heroic atmosphere around him. She includes
the lost Dutchman as one of the "victims" of life, along with those other
"victims" of her past, including the mysterious group around Mary Butts
of blackmailers and Aleister Crowley disciples. She, in other words,
identifies with the Dutchman as part of her own fears of death. On another level she must have been considerably attracted to him physically
and retained him unconsciously as one of her mythic lovers. A discussion
of the Dutchman took place when she returned to Freud in the fall of
1934, her second visit to Freud.

This second meeting with Freud does not appear to have been as fruit-
ful as the first. There is more resistance, and evidence of a deeper sort of
unhappiness. It is almost as if she has used up her earlier enthusiasm. By
December of 1934 Freud told her (according to her account) that her
analysis was "finished." Formerly he had said that an analysis is never
finished, it is only broken off. But now she assumes that she has passed
her pupil stage and is ready to take on patients from friends of her own.
She had learned, so she believed, enough of Freud's technique to establish herself in London with patients!

The inevitable question now arrives: Of what benefit was her analysis
with Freud? This was no ordinary analysis. There are times when patient
and doctor appear to be acting roles outside the analysis. Her fantasy life
was approved of, supported, found reasonable. Freud's position can be
looked upon as ambiguous. (At least here.) He told her that he could not
"read" her face. He certainly could read her mind. There are moments
when an uncertain feeling, an uneasiness overcomes the reader of *Trib-*

ute to Freud. There is so much drama, so much sensibility. Freud was not a "little white ghost," a "little papa," nor was he a "magician," as she called him. He was a scientist and a diagnostician, one of the best of his time. Freud must have realized H.D. was responsive when he addressed the artist in her. He told her she had *the sort of dreams he would expect from a woman poet!* (my italics) He also got around her "magic complex," as she called it, by explaining that "magic is poetry, poetry is magic," and, she adds in writing to Bryher, "which is all very Wien somehow. But stabilizing."

The question remains: What did Freud do for her? He restored a *dignity* to her she had somewhere mislaid. Freud gave her confidence, not only in her work but in her dedication to her work. From this time on dates a freedom in H.D.'s writing that had not been there before. She is free to be the kind of writer she wants to be. Not that she will be free of her need of Bryher's encouragement, but she appears to have escaped a yoke. The yoke of Imagism. The yoke of perfectionism. The Bryher work yoke. She certainly was not freed of her phobias. She was not "healed" as a person. She would need to have a psychiatrist in attendance all her life. And she would suffer a complete breakdown. It was her creative, more than her psychic, world that Freud helped.

In the middle of the final sessions in November of 1934, H.D. wrote to Bryher:

> Please Fido, if you love me, and love my work, leave that to work its own will in its own way . . . If I can rest it will be all right. If I can go on my own two rails it will be all right but do not probe me or try to make me angry. I might die Fido—literally die. My whole life literally [*sic*] is one pure and perfect crucifiction [*sic*] . . . I am not, except in certain hours of writing and in certain hours of FORGETTING writing ever free. Let me write, then let me FORGET my writing . . . Please for six months or a year do not probe me about writing.

H.D. was announcing, along with her Freudian slips, her independence of Bryher. She was telling her that she was going to make it on her own; she was shaking off the Fido paws. Freud gave her this courage.

H.D. returned to Kenwin from Vienna determined to complete *Ion.* What she had to combat was not only the work, but extreme loneliness and isolation. Indeed, she had several near crises, but she recognized that she had begun *Ion* in the last war and she had dropped it. Her analysis with Freud had supposedly helped her through the repressed anxieties of that war, and therefore she must prove herself free now to complete the work. She had already written Bryher that she did not want her to dictate to her. Now again she wrote Bryher a letter within which are signal messianic signs:

> 1. My work is creative and reconstructive, war or no war, if I can get across the Greek spirit at its highest I am helping the world, and the future. It is the highest spiritual neutrality.

2. Apart from all that actual inner urge, this is the ONE thing that my public, my "fans" have been clamouring for.

3. In case of any breakdown, if we were all separated, this would give me carte-blanche to the sort of America I did not have in my youth.

4. This is a sort of counter to P.R. [Peter Rodeck] and his church—this is my church. [Didn't Freud believe that in the Moses dream she wanted to be a hero, wanted to even found a church?]

5. This work I was doing after the first confinement and during my preg. with old Pups. Probably I have it linked up with my physical creative force. As that is going, I translate it into this output of plays. The attitude one takes at this time is all important for the rest of ones life . . . I plan completeing [*sic*] *Ion* for a publisher—I have written Boston before leaving here and probably starting on the Helen. That will take me over the London winter.

. . . The Greek will hold me to my centre, now whether here or in London.

signed with
Star

The translation of *Ion* was such a burden. It was linked with H.D.'s phobias, her life in World War I, her repressions, her desires both to live with and to break away from Bryher; further, she did want to reach a public approving her Greek hieratics, but demanding something new. She was now in an agitated emotional state wherein she was continuing within herself the remembered sessions with Freud, which would encourage her finally to finish *Ion.* She believed that *Ion* would "break the backbone of my H.D. repression." She wrote on to Bryher: "I feel this ION is a sort of fancy dress edition of my phallic phantasy. Also all the sun-god stuff and the Delphic, hitches on to us in Corfu." Then she continues with what is typical of the artist, a description of her method. She was beating out the Greek prologue to more or less chant rhythm, a new method, "a wonderful idea, I just thought of it," as Stein would say. After an inferno she is able to exclaim, "I am, I am, I AM a POET." She had never felt it necessary to repeat her idea of herself so intensely before. "It is God or Mammon, no halfway . . . straight into the maw of the Delphic oracle."

The Delphic Oracle in Vienna had pronounced these words of freedom to her; she had listened. She retained her identity as a poet, developed that identity in her sessions with Freud; the human being, the anxious suffering woman would now have to wail outside the gates. She was going to dedicate *Ion* to Bryher Macpherson and Perdita Macpherson, Athens 1920–Delphi 1932. She would write *Tribute to Freud* and dedicate it to "the blameless physician."

Hugh Kenner has written of *Ion:* "What we do possess with regard to the tragedies is a record of their recurrent discovery by poets in crisis, the very pedantry of the form permitting the indulgence of self-expression. Thus H.D. forcing every occasion to dilate on her preferred imagery of weeds and sandy shores, turned choruses from Euripides into statements of her own impassioned sterility."

Herbert Howarth in *Notes on Some Figures Behind T. S. Eliot* writes that, for the foundation of *Family Reunion,* Eliot adapted *Ion,* inspired by H.D.'s translation, which had recently appeared. It is doubtful she was ever aware of this. She would have been pleased, as she counted him among her friends from the old days, and whenever a visiting poet from the United States came to see her, or whenever she specially wanted to brighten a group in for tea, she would invite Eliot. After all, he had once in *The Egoist* praised her translations beyond those of Gilbert Murray. *Ion* proved that she could rely on what Freud had protected and encouraged, her art; she now was determined to make her way once more in London.

"The reason why they do not know why they love me so is because everybody has to begin a thing." By 1934 there would no longer be a writer like Gertrude Stein whipping up a scenario called "Three Sitting Here" for *Close-Up.* That magazine was now discontinued. Its day had ended when Nazi threats sent Pabst and Lang to Hollywood. Where would one now find an advertisement for the film *Wingbeat:* "Free verse poem. Telepathy and attraction, the reaching out, the very edge of dimensions, the chemistry of actual attraction, of will shivering and quavering on a frail, too high, too inaccessible brink." Nothing in film writing would ever be so clear in such a complicated way as that which had appeared in *Close-Up.*

To console themselves after the demise of *Close-Up,* Bryher and Kenneth had gone off to America. Now it was the Waldorf Hotel Bryher disliked; it was too expensive. She preferred Boston to New York. But first she had to pay her duty call on Marianne Moore and her mother—a dinner preceded by a long grace, followed by a dismaying, for Bryher, religious discussion. The Moores stressed that they never paid calls; they only received. They did not even go out to the theater.

The high point of Bryher's days in New York was not literary at all. She went to see a play starring Katharine Hepburn and immediately fell in love with her. She declared that Hepburn was the only rival of Bergner. Hepburn, also, was "a slightly older [!] and wiser Cat, but not so exciting." Even the bangs she wore at that time gave her the look of H.D. However, Bryher preferred Bergner because she was "more boy," more mischievous, more of a piece. "You," she wrote H.D., "if you saw Hepburn would never leave New York, so I think it is just as well you are NOT here." Hepburn represented to Bryher the rebel, the woman against the Establishment, all the issues close to Bryher. Needless to say, these letters of Bryher's infuriated H.D.

After seeing Dr. Sachs in Boston, Bryher continued on to Chicago to visit Harriet Monroe, who, she decided, must be a little mad, as would anyone who lived on the eleventh floor of a tower building. Careful to keep in touch with H.D.'s former school friends, Bryher visited Mary Herr, who was librarian in Chicago at the Girls' Latin School.

Through Harriet Monroe, Bryher was able to arrange to meet the writers Horace and Marya (Zaturenska) Gregory, whose work she had liked. Horace Gregory in his autobiography, *The House on Jefferson Street,* has described their first meeting with Bryher: "The setting for our meeting was Rumpelmayer's tearoom on the ground floor of the St. Moritz Hotel on Central Park South . . . Bryher moved toward us, a compact, small-boned figure in navy blue: navy blue beret, navy blue topcoat. As she approached, her right hand shyly extended in welcome, one remarked her amazingly clear blue eyes . . ."

As the Gregorys were leaving, Bryher handed Horace an envelope to be opened when he returned home. In it was an invitation to visit London the next summer, and a check to pay their passage.

The Gregorys were established writers in the New York literary community. Not only were they gifted poets, but they had a talent for friendship, which made them much loved. They had two small children and lived in the first planned "garden suburb," now the renowned, if shabby, Sunnyside, on Long Island, a short journey from New York City. They had little money, and Horace Gregory, who would become ill with Parkinson's disease, was frail. He was a slight, handsome, meticulously groomed man who set off the beautiful and more exotic Marya.

Horace Gregory has described their trip to Europe in his autobiography, including their arrival in London, where, after spending the night in what turned out to be a most disreputable hostelry, Bryher rushed them off to a proper hotel and engaged a governess for the children. He continues: "One day that summer we received an invitation to join Bryher and H.D. at a performance of Bergner in 'Escape Me Never!'" (The original film version also starred Bergner. It is possible that it was financially backed by Bryher, although the book was a best-seller.) Presumably the story had been an adaptation of the gypsy life of the Augustus John family, although the father in the story had been changed from an artist to a musician and the setting changed to Switzerland.

Augustus John and Dorelia were furious with the play, possibly because of the emphasis on the free sexual atmosphere, which they would consider, for reasons best known to themselves, libelous. Gregory continues with his description of their first meeting with H.D.

> I remember her most clearly, standing in the lobby of a Shaftesbury Avenue theater, waving me a greeting with a cigarette in her hand. She was, so I thought, an American Aphrodite, taller and less sensuous than her

Greek ancestress, but with the same powers to attract and charm: she moved with an ease and brilliance that outshone all those who surrounded our small company of four. In contrast to her, how middle-class, how drab other people in the lobby looked—how cumbersome and ill at ease they seemed in evening dress: How hopelessly *English*. H.D.'s talk was like her verse, angular and swift, with small rushes of words. Her accent, like Ezra Pound's was British-American-on-the-Riviera. She spoke of poetry, the stage, and how Elisabeth Bergner's performance in the play had recreated the illusion of youth. [Actually, Bergner might have been thought too old by this time to play a very young girl, and H.D.'s remark might be considered somewhat caustic.]

There was rather more than a touch of the transcendental Moravian Puritan in H.D. that lifted conversation off its feet, swaying in short flights, with a bright laugh, or a suspended sentence wavering in the air. Yet those who, even today associate her solely with Pound's Imagist verse, are wrong. When I met her in 1934, she had been reading William Morris with her characteristic enthusiasm—and she was about to reread the devotional poets of the 17th century. She had probably reawakened her interest in the Pre-Raphaelites, and therefore in William Morris, through her friendship with Violet Hunt, for she was among the most extraordinary of H.D.'s London friends.

The friendship that developed with the Gregorys was one of the most fortunate for H.D. in a life of many meetings with many friends. It was through Horace Gregory that Grove Press, where he was an editor, decided on his recommendation to print H.D.'s *Selected Poems,* her autobiographical novel *Bid Me to Live,* and *Helen in Egypt.* Such was the unexpected conclusion to Bryher's trip to America in 1934.

A footnote can also be added to this spontaneous trip of Bryher and Kenneth's. She and Kenneth went to Hartford, Connecticut, for the performance of Gertrude Stein's opera *Four Saints in Three Acts,* with music by Virgil Thomson. Wallace Stevens was also present. Although they did not meet, Bryher sent him a note. In a letter to Harriet Monroe he mentioned this, saying that he had been with some "pretty awful people," and how easy it would have been to have met Kenneth and Bryher, only the exigencies of Hartford had kept them apart. And when Bryher learned that Stevens had admired some watercolors by the writer Herman Hesse, she arranged to have them sent from Hesse to the now famous American poet. Stevens wrote a graceful note of thanks to Hesse mentioning the "private charity" of Bryher. There is one other connection between Stevens and H.D., who, although contemporaries and Pennsylvanians, were never friends. In 1907 (before H.D. had dedicated herself to her Greeks) in a letter to his fiancée, Stevens had mentioned that he was reading about Greece. He had uncovered and been blessed by "a pagan world of passion and love of beauty and life. It is a white world under a blue sky, still standing erect in remote sunshine."

CHAPTER TWENTY-ONE

Beginning Again in London

A new flat was leased in 1934 at 49 Lowndes Square, a modish step away from the Sloane Street flat. The neighborhood and its apparent propriety indicated that Bryher would be in residence. There were two bedrooms, kitchen, bathroom, hallway. Bookcases lined the wall of the sitting room. There were large windows with a view of the plane trees in the garden of the square. Flowers always filled the rooms—lilies, roses, anemones. Both Bryher and H.D. loved snowdrops, violets, and bluebells, delicate flowers. Kenneth had decorated the flat, adding his own touch of exotic luxury with a leopard-skin rug.

Yet always the apartments in which H.D. lived gave off the atmosphere of an abode, a haven, a shrine. Maidens and devotees gathered there; H.D. was their goddess. "She was always surrounded by a guard," a friend had noted to her son-in-law, John Schaffner, adding that "it would have been easier to arrange for an interview with the Pope." At the same time she remained solitaire. There would be several H.D.s: The schoolgirl giggling with her friend, the faun startled in a brake, the priestess of letters.

The present Bunch included Gerald and Dorothy Henderson, the only married couple in their circle. He was the librarian at St. Paul's, whom Perdita remembers as being so identified with his work that he wore seventeenth-century buckles on his shoes. His wife was a novelist (always referred to by her maiden name, Cole, among themselves). For a time Cornelia Brookfield would be one of a number of strange and devilish young women who fascinated H.D. There was Robert Herring, formerly a contributor to *Close-Up*. Kenneth had brought in H.D.'s friend George Plank, an illustrator and another Philadelphian. Plank, also a friend of the novelist Patrick White (a future Nobel Prize winner), designed H.D.'s letterheads, and her bookmarks. Dr. Elizabeth Ashby was around, adding her astrological notations to those of H.D. In the permanent background was Dr. Walter Schmideberg, H.D.'s psychoanalyst, whom Freud had known when Schmideberg was a student in Vienna, preparing for his career in psychiatry. When he was inducted into the Austrian Army, Schmideberg had managed faithfully to smuggle cigars in to Freud. In their "gossip" sessions Freud had described the attractiveness and intelligence of Schmideberg. Finally, there was the reigning favorite, a young woman, Silvia Dobson, just settled in London. Indeed, H.D. had her court, her attendants faithfully serving her, and Bryher acting as majordomo.

Establishing herself in London did not mean that H.D.'s life would become severed or disentwined from Bryher, only that the tempo would be set by herself. Kenwin would be a place to visit, a place where work could be accomplished in quiet, not merely a villa on the lake for relaxation. At Kenwin were installed, it might seem forever, the baboons, the monkeys, and the dogs, along with the flitting presence of Elisabeth Bergner. Bergner was so petite that Bryher had cautioned H.D. not to come over all tall and commanding, "the way you can." Bergner was someone whom Bryher could tease, command, and be amused by. In temperament they were somewhat alike. H.D. was not supplanted. Bryher and H.D. would constantly write to one another "Save Me the Waltz," which had become the Fitzgeralds' favorite tune and would be a tune that evoked that era of the 1930s when Paris was becoming dim and *triste* to the expatriates. As Bryher remarked, by the early 1930s Paris was "finished." Another Americanism of the era, a favorite to be used on special occasions in their letters to describe a favorable reaction, was "swep away." "Jes swep away." Zelda Fitzgerald. Coming across it is startling, suddenly amid the intimacy of their conversing letters. The world's proffered amusements might be fun. Their private language continued to keep them close, even when Bryher would be in Switzerland or traveling. Then after a few days with Bryher in London, H.D. would retire to Kenwin. Separation would be a ruse that would keep their affection constant.

For much of the information about this period in H.D.'s life we are indebted to the letters she wrote to Silvia Dobson. Silvia was newly arrived in London and living on Glebe Place near Violet Hunt. She had taken a job as an elementary school mistress when she first met H.D., who was living then on Sloane Street. Silvia was twenty-six when they first met; H.D., forty-eight. H.D. grew more beautiful as she aged, thought Silvia. Talented and distressed, the young woman fell under the spell of H.D. She had the emotional problems of a sister who had suffered the death of a promising younger brother to whom she was much attached. Probably unsure of her own future, she clothed H.D. in all sorts of miraculous garments. Not only did she become a disciple but, having the gift of love, she gave freely to H.D. In turn, H.D. needed the support of this sturdy, yet dependent, young woman who would support her own trembling ego. Silvia could construct zodiacal charts, and this ability H.D. found useful. Silvia drew up H.D.'s chart and presented it as a birthday present to H.D. showing Sagittarius in ascendant over the Virgo birth sign. After returning from her sessions with Freud, H.D. took on Silvia as a sort of analysand, although the hour extended itself into long talkative evenings, as it would with other friends who came to H.D. with their problems.

H.D. wrote to Silvia that she wished she could "HELP all the time everyone like you. But after the war it was Sauve qui peut and having saved my hide by the skin of its teeth, I hold on to it, there's no preaching to the young, I know. I would not have it at your age. Only just eating now and again doesn't hurt the Soul."

To repeat, the life of H.D. cannot be scrutinized without taking into consideration her various brews of Egyptology, Hellenic studies, tarot, astrology, numerology, and psychoanalysis. She used bits and pieces of each to arrange a working logic that was both mystical and confusing.

For instance, her letters to Silvia (known as "Dragon," and privately between H.D. and Kenneth, as "Robin Hood") were about the fusion of electricity that emanated from the crossing of the wires of Frances' remembered ego with that of Silvia's. Those letters to Bryher, who had asked her to come out to Kenwin, concentrated on the difference between their generations. These disparities between generations became more apparent to H.D. as she saw younger people in London, such as Silvia, who had been untouched by the Great War. They were outside those ruins that still smoldered for H.D., and where still, despite all her psychoanalysis, was her crater. She explained to Bryher that when she was in Vaud at Kenwin working she became so lonely with only Bryher's new housekeeper-secretary Miss Volkart—who would remain a fixture for many years—that she got into a real "Ka" state. Then after she removed herself to London, "the poor Ka let out a yelp." She went on to say that she had to "weave a sort of garment for the naked spirit, the Ka, if only it is to survive at all." Meaning, more simply, that she found herself getting into an extremely intense state at Kenwin, a state heightened by the isolation, and that she would find it necessary to return to London, so that the Ka, or the intense cerebrality that raged within her, might be released and relaxed amid her own surroundings. There is much guesswork involved at discovering just what H.D. is getting at. In simple terms it was probably that at Kenwin under Bryher's dominance, and also that of Miss Volkart, whom H.D. did not particularly like, she found herself in a highly nervous state. She needed her own lair to comfort her, and the support to her ego of her circle of friends.

At this time, 1935, she wrote Bryher, in one of her mystic-astrological-prophetic states, that Bryher possessed

> the rare and dangerous gift of bringing the soul to life, and yet one must protect the naked soul, the naked truth. You have your own protection . . . The whole quarrel is a matter of protective colouration. Probably our Neptunes come in here too. I am Taurus; my Neptune, or Ka, I mean. That is the oxen and calves and heifers are literally slaughtered, holocaust of the war; having survived that, I feel I must "carry on." You are a

half person, all of you, Ken [Kenneth], Eileen and so on. You can be two
people and one of them is dead or inspired or crazy. Hamlet is the prototype of the Ka of your generation. But I am ONE person, one heifer or
calf that just escaped the pyre . . . Ka that is in the Ox that has escaped
slaughter, attracts the Twins who are half seeking slaughter, suicided,
Hamlet . . . But there comes a point when an escaped Ox becomes a sort
of sacred Ox or Apis, maybe I have reached that stage or am reaching it.
Obviously it is what Rodeck is doing—browsing in an outgrown conven-
tion of the church . . . To you it is NATURAL TO TALK and think of
war but once slaughtered as my generation was, and I was—and I am sick
of that and must only think out how I can do the best I can and be philosophical and escape if possible. But it is the whole reality to me and not a
half one as to you Gemini-Ka people. Pluto my searchlight links up my
Saturn, Wisdom and Neptune, the Soul, so probably this Ka talk is my
mission . . .

At this period Silvia was working out the astrological charts of their
friends. Silvia realized that to be one of H.D.'s circle she must be clever
in a way different from the others. Therefore, she rather unwillingly
drew up these charts. Her dilemma was that she found it a great strain
to concentrate so much on astrology when instead she wanted to
write. The work was too intense for her, drawing, as it did, both on
mathematics and intuition, and she was forced to give up the charts.
H.D. unexpectedly encouraged Silvia in this and understood Silvia's need
to write. H.D. recognized the essential need a person might have to write
in order to keep on the track, that is, both to invite visions and to recognize reality.

H.D.'s previous letter to Bryher does illustrate the extreme positions
she could take, treading in her unconscious far from the Freudian path.
She may have been discouraging Bryher from the continually pessimistic
prophecies Bryher was making about an approaching war. There is a lot
of the big Cat using her claws on a small Dog. Reminding Bryher that
life was not all pragmatic foresight, but spiritual vision as well.

Silvia Dobson served at this time both as confessor and confessional.
H.D. could subject the younger woman to her prophetic and sibylline
states, from which Bryher by now had rebelled. H.D., although now
more cautiously, liked to wander into her Corfu trances; Silvia was now
the spectator. Yet although H.D. did recognize the need Silvia had to
protect her own ego, this did not prevent her from establishing Perdita
for a time at Silvia's flat on Tite Street, the very one, coincidentally, in
which Heseltine-Warlock had lived and had committed suicide. She did
not inform Silvia of this, but Silvia claims to have had some very odd
psychic experiences in that flat, of whose possible haunt H.D. had not
warned her.

Then, blissfully, H.D. whisked Silvia off to Venice, "a fairy city of the heart," as Byron had written. It was a honeymoon trip. They were lovers under H.D.'s special conditions. It was, said Silvia, "cerebral sex." There was no sleeping through the night in a lover's arms for H.D. Just as she had written in *Nights*, the lover must leave the lady before dawn. Coincidentally, they stayed at a pension on the Zattere near the flat shared by Pound and Olga Rudge.

H.D. would see the person with whom she traveled only at special times of the day. Appointments had to be made in advance. It is both whimsical and touching to think of Silvia scurrying along the narrow Venetian ways as she pretended not to see the tall poet stalking her dreamlike path, past stalls of scarves and rings, her head held high, listening for the rush of Gabriel's wings (or Mercury's), and the commanding bell notes that would be summoned one day to echo in her poems.

Their rendezvous would usually take place at Quadri's café. They had a special table with a "Byron chair," so called because one of the waiters insisted Silvia looked like Byron. Then there would be the shopping for rings and bracelets, which H.D. loved. According to Silvia she loaned these to her friends for a period of two or three years and then would recall them and lend them to other friends.

In Venice she went to the church Pound so particularly loved, Santa Maria dei Miracoli, of which he had written in his cantos of the sea-mermaids inside on the columns of the nave. The church became one of her favorites. She succeeded so well in the transubstantiation of Santa Maria dei Miracoli that it became not only Pound's church of the mermaid song, but hers as well. She changed it into Saint Mary of the Miracles. The Virgin Saint, Virgo, the planet of H.D.

From Vienna when she was with Freud, H.D. had written to Silvia that she was "very happy now . . . I had some dreadful resistances, but I think I have burst the dam at last. One goes on, very Aquarian, like a river must get to the sea." After their Venice trip she wrote Silvia that she felt there should be a "Libra wedding of St. Mark's Catholicism and Zodiac Beasts and Greek Legend, a new book of prayers for all Aquarians. [Those who had embraced psychoanalysis.]" She repeated that she believed that psychoanalysis was a "true Aquarian science, along with X-ray and television and those things—science plus something uncanny or supernatural, not science in the old sense of the word."

So much of this delving into esoteric sources reveals that H.D. was released from Bryher's commonsensical restrictions and her dominance. It would have been supposed that after her sessions with Freud, "reality" might have been more consistently present. Instead, she seems to have explored her unconscious, using those methods she believed might direct the unconscious, methods largely esoteric.

For instance, in writing to Silvia to thank her for flowers she had sent, she says about the lilies that would "protect the household" that "it has

five buds and flowers and five is the pentacle—to keep off witches. Five is
Mercury and Mercury is the Messenger or Gabriel of the Zodiac, isn't he
to Virgo?" She was experiencing very intense states and then would become ill with "suppressed flu" and would feel weepy. The weeping
pleased her, because she said that for years she could not squeeze a tear.

That H.D. was capable of possessiveness and jealousy is illustrated by
her reaction to a visit to Kenwin, where H.D. was staying with Bryher,
Silvia Dobson made with a friend after the two young women had been
hiking in the Black Forest. H.D. had written to Silvia, half-jokingly:

> Why do they stand me up like a Saint Sebastian [sic] and shoot all the
> arrows at ME, the arrows of love-hate that they haven't the courage—the
> brats—to aim at their mothers????? Damn them, damn them. Damn Ken-
> neth and Bryher and now this brat Silvia—who is just repeating a sicken-
> ing old theme. I am NOT their mother. I will NOT be the Aunt Sally for
> their coconut shy—I am not—I AM NOT etc. You see?????? Well, perhaps
> I AM.

And then she added teasingly how thrilling it all was, what they were
doing with the Zodiac and ps-a sessions, that she did not have these reactions from others—"so I suppose there IS something very poignant, really
between us . . ."

After such a communication from H.D., when Silvia arrived with her
friend, she was not prepared to be pounced on, nor to have her friend
told to "go play with your rocking horse." This behavior may have been
more common with H.D. than supposed. The usual idea, as with most
writers, is that she brought her suppressed jealousies into her novels and
poems.

She now sent her Darantière—"Peter Rabbit," she called them—books
(*The Usual Star, Nights, Kora and Ka*) to Frances, who was now living
in Norfolk. She may have been prompted by her identification of Silvia
with Frances. Silvia, Frances, and Peter Rodeck had those "strange"
eyes. She had hoped Silvia would break the Frances spell.

"These things happen," H.D. had written to Silvia.

> Love terrible with banners only emerges or materializes once or twice in a
> life-time and my "terrible with banners" is being lived down. . . . But if I
> materialize you, I firmly and neatly super-impose you on that Frances
> whose mother . . . was also half Scot who "saw" things. She [Frances]
> would tease me with her clairvoyance, go over the edge and pretend she
> had found some choice dragon morsel which she would not share . . .

Are those "morsels" reminiscent of the Corfu "dots" on the wall with
which H.D. "teased" Bryher? H.D. emphasized to Silvia that she had
loved and always would love Frances, although it was wrong of her to
put Silvia in her place.

A few remarkable letters from Frances to H.D. at this time have sur-

vived. They were entrusted to Silvia by H.D., who asked her to preserve
them, as she did not know what to do with them. She must have been
fearful that Bryher would come across them and certainly preferred that
she not read these letters. The faithful Silvia still possesses them.

Frances wrote H.D., thanking her for the books, which she liked better
than anything else she had read of H.D.'s, including the poetry. She
called H.D. "daughter of many miscarriages of Henry James."

Frances wrote to H.D. that November of 1934:

> I am glad this shimmering coat of sanity is falling about you. Your naked-
> ness was never lovely to me. You had such ugly feet. You say that all the
> gods are yours and that none linger on that Jacob's ladder where beggars
> mount to you, and that all the golden spaces of heaven are yours too, so
> that there is no place left for me save this cold stone, and here I pray that
> Hilda may grow in grace and sanity, and give at long last to the world, to
> the world and not to her hundred friends—the beauty that I knew, the joy
> that she was to me. I do not, even now, find anything stronger to say of
> beautiful things, than "It is like Hilda."

Frances was then living "in a row of wooden bungalows on a shallow
cliff directly overlooking the beach and the sea. It is very stark and bare,
with nothing picturesque. The gulls mewl all day, cleave the fog and
disappear in the sun." Her mother lived in a wooden hut on the property; her daughter, Betty, was sleeping in a hammock; and her son,
Oliver, "the god," is there "in his room, but already going off to see his
father, Louis Marlow [Wilkinson] and planning films and plays." She is
in debt, she is impoverished. But more important than all that, she is seeing John Cowper Powys, whom she has been pursuing "literally yowling
down all these many years." After five years he has returned to her, saying he enjoys being with her, despite their quarrels. She calls him "the
great man."

In a later letter Frances suggested that Oliver meet Perdita. From
H.D.'s reply it became apparent to Frances that this suggestion upset
H.D., that she was determined the two should not meet. Frances laughed
at her for not wanting to lose her daughter, but never mind, would she
only obtain two tickets for the Elisabeth Bergner play for Oliver?

The letters from Frances are emotional, defensive, courageous. They
are also protective letters. She worries that H.D. is working too hard. She
tells her she would like to invite her to Norfolk for a rest, except that
while she likes her house, she fears it is too "mean" for H.D. The final
picture we have of Frances is what she wrote of herself: ". . . reading
the last of Kora and Ka, while I ate sausage in my fingers and drank lots
and lots of tea and gave a side glance to the sun rising over the sea and
was very happy."

When H.D. had given Frances' letters to Silvia for safekeeping, she had written that there was such a charge in the atmosphere around Frances that it "caused an explosion and without exception destroyed something near it." H.D. had considered moving Frances and family into town, but she claimed that it would cause so much trouble and there would be difficulty about money, etc. But the letters she wanted kept. "I simply do not want quite all of F. to burn into high-explosive." These last letters from Frances to H.D. were written in 1934. When Plymouth was bombed in 1941, Frances, her mother, and her daughter were killed— exploded.

Their house was the only direct hit in that section of Plymouth. Afterward, neighbors gathered in memory of the perished family. Over the empty hole of earth where once the house had stood, British flags were laid.

CHAPTER TWENTY-TWO

Life and Letters Today

An intelligence such as Bryher's could never permit itself to idle for long. She liked very much to give advice. Knowing how little domesticity concerned H.D., she offered the following:

> On the whole I believe the frig is more for fruit and milk and butter, but we keep cold meat in ours, I *believe* uncovered. I should get off stews for a bit, why not ask Mrs Ash to stew you a little *I think* it is the heart of lamb, a great standby for English spinsters. Also very small soles to be got at Harrods are easy to fry yourself at night. Also very tiny cutlets or English bacon and an egg, these are really better than continental stew. I believe it is not supposed to be terribly good to eat them too much, particularly in the summer.

Following up her domestic advice, Bryher shortly demonstrated those other aspects of her mind, most commendable: her keenness in literary matters and disregard of current fashion. This letter was evidently written to ease H.D.'s worry about her work being out of fashion at a time when Auden & Co., whose work with its overtures of social consciousness in art and literature represented the zeitgeist—a favorite word—of the period. This era of social concern ruled out the lapidary world of antiquity, unless it applied to the economic disasters of a Caligula or Claudius. Bryher's dedication to what was becoming increasingly important to her, historical research, ruled out any confusion of epoch or fashion. She admonished H.D.:

> 1. Writers pre say 1925 should concern themselves with art as they understand it and concentrate upon doing what they should themselves produce. It is fatal and absurd to suggest that they sit down and turn out proletarian literature.
>
> 2. Young writers, or actors or painters, have equally no right not to be politically minded. It is useless grumbling at Browning or Swinburne, for example, because they knew nothing of the Oedipus complex, but they kept their place just as Walt Whitman does. Therefore it seems to me that the important thing is that you should get on with your Mss. Don't destroy old stuff. It may be valuable later.

She then added:

I do not think merely to write is good for the young; that is especially a pleasure to be deferred to middle age. [This remark would eventually apply directly to her.]

By 1935 the energetic Bryher was frustrated and bored by her life at remote Kenwin with its menagerie of animals. Realizing that she could not lure H.D. away to Switzerland as frequently as she liked, that Kenneth's idleness led him into a series of unsatisfactory affairs, Bryher made a radical decision. She bought a literary review. It was the esteemed *Life and Letters*, which had been edited by Desmond MacCarthy. She changed its name to *Life and Letters Today* and incorporated it with *The London Mercury*.

Bryher selected her friend from *Close-Up* days, Robert Herring, an unfortunate choice, to be the editor. If H.D. were worried about her neglect by the literary scene (and this was not an unreal fear, for recently she had indeed been excluded from the 1930s anthology compiled by Robert Graves and Laura Riding, who disliked Imagism), Bryher would provide a publication in which H.D.'s poetry and prose could once more find its readers. Bryher decided that again, like *Close-Up*, she would publish work with an international bias. The question also remains as to why with all the intellectual resources, as well as financial ones, Bryher should have chosen to remain behind the scenes, permitting others to edit what she could have done so much better herself. It was she who possessed the necessary contacts so useful for a publication.

Among the distinguished foreign writers who appeared in the magazine were Louis Aragon, André Gide, Henri Michaux, Jacques Prévert, Jules Romain, Jean-Paul Sartre, Paul Valéry; and in 1937, anticipating other reviews, she published the work of Franz Kafka. The British scene was controlled more or less by intimate friends. Silvia Dobson wrote reviews; Kenneth contributed, as did sixteen-year-old Perdita (under a pseudonym), Dorothy Richardson, Oswell Blakeston, Mary Butts, Siegfried Sassoon, Michael Roberts, the translator Scott-Montcrieff. And later the Sitwells brought in Dylan Thomas and Bryher's discovery, the Australian novelist Patrick White. Among the American poets were Marianne Moore, Jean Starr Untermeyer, Marya Zaturenska, Elizabeth Bishop, May Sarton, Muriel Rukeyser—a circlet of women.

The review was published from 1935 until 1950. Providentially, Bryher had bought enough paper to last throughout the war when other magazines were forced out. During the war the sales were unexpectedly high. The explanation for the sale of a magazine of the quality of *Life and Letters Today* was that there were few magazines left to buy. Those competitors that survived—*Horizon, Penguin New Writing, Poetry London*—also sold fantastically. A public deprived of print reached out for whatever was on the market.

The original plan for the magazine was to have articles, stories, poetry, music and theater reviews, a cinema section, and book reviews. The magazine would not be insular, but international in intent. Bryher not only summoned good writers, but she was able to pay them. The major difficulty centered on the editor Robert Herring, who had none of Desmond MacCarthy's genius for editorship. With all the material at hand, the magazine should have made a more professional impact. The freshness of *Close-Up,* with its deliberately cultivated amateurishness, was here dissipated into incompetency. Bryher permitted Herring too free a hand, as was her habit with all those to whom she was personally attached. For posterity the magazine is invaluable, as it indicates both the scope of international writing at that time, and the assortment of books that were published in Britain, even during the war—books that could not be assured of a commercial success, or even a review. Still, the quirkiness of *Close-Up,* although here strained, gave a savor to *Life and Letters Today* that was not located elsewhere in the literary machinery.

The magazine presented H.D. with that providential shelter every writer longs for, a place in which to write and publish as she pleased. There she published serially her impressions of Freud, titled at that time "Writing on the Wall." Her poems "The Dancer" and "The Poet" came out in 1935. Then those selections from what she called "The Temple of the Sun" were published in 1939. Much of her World War II poetry (collected in the books *The Walls Do Not Fall* and *Tribute to the Angels*) first appeared in *Life and Letters Today* throughout the 1930s, together with Parts I and II of "Good Friend."

H.D. was now able to emerge from her seclusion and publish again, without any of the encumbering process of sending out work to questionable or unfamiliar editors. She was appearing in a prominent magazine backed by friends and allies. The proprietorship of a magazine naturally strengthened Bryher's hand in publishing circles along with its corollary help to H.D.'s career.

In 1935 T. S. Eliot, also a contributor to *Life and Letters Today,* mentioned H.D. in his introduction to the *Selected Poems of Marianne Moore.* Having been sent the book, H.D. reacted in an honest, if surprising, manner: "I do like Marianne Moore's poems, but they leave me a little stricken or shriven or shrivelled, somehow. It is very 'crab' world, collecting junk under the sea from old hulks; it sometimes reminds me of myself—much that is exquisite." Here is an indication that she would be turning away from the tightness of her Imagist style, stretching further than those frequented shell-washed shores.

Then came 1936 and the death of George V and the subsequent abdication of Edward VIII. Now, these kingships, deaths, and anticipated crownings fascinated H.D. She was very much intrigued by all the proceedings. She and her friends were emotionally overcome by the fate of

Edward VIII. It all went back to George V, who had represented in
H.D.'s "UNK" (unconscious) all the disasters of her youth, with the
Great War, the minor battle with the Georgian poets who had stood in
the way of her own recognition. She received the death of George V personally. Despite her dislike of all he had stood for, she was so moved by
the idea of a royal ceremony at Westminster Abbey that she stood in a
mourners' line to view the royal body. H.D. was rather proud of her action and congratulated herself for having gathered the necessary courage
to leave her flat and join the great crowd. Then she did an odd thing. She
sent a note of condolence to Lady Ellerman. She also dressed in black.

After this began the conversations with and letters to friends concerning the personality of the new king. The circle around H.D. was enchanted with Edward. Not only was he attractive, especially to the men,
but he represented, so H.D. decided, a new era in the arts. Traditions
would be attacked; a handsome, boyish king would bring an end to
repression and a new vision to the age. So H.D. romanticized about a
semiliterate, spoiled, frightened, if gallant, shy prince. How she arrived
at such conclusions remained her secret. Yet her friends all had high
hopes; it would be just as it had been earlier when Edward VII had
swept out Victorianism. They all neglected the greater sophistication implicit in the age difference. And what aspect of repression H.D. believed
herself to be suffering from would be anyone's guess. The grief when Edward abdicated! It affected all her Bunch, including Dr. Schmideberg,
who claimed an acquaintance with the prince (made in the Turkish
baths). Rakishness of the sort they approved of would be ousted; respect-
ability would again ascend. Osbert Sitwell startled H.D. when he announced that it had been wise of Edward to abdicate. These royal affairs
occupied H.D. for months, longer than the completion of a poem.

In 1936 H.D. found herself addressed by an advocate of the new,
American left; a politically conscious young poet arrived at her door.
Muriel Rukeyser was in London, claiming that she was in England looking for outlets for chain stores! It is probable that she was soliciting
funds for the Spanish Republican cause. Such a connection would never
have been made by H.D., as to all intents she was oblivious to the
Spanish Civil War. The nearest she did come to being involved in any
way was through Stephen Guest, whose brilliant mathematician brother,
David, was killed shortly after he had arrived in Spain. (Today a gate at
Cambridge named in his honor marks the promise of his brief life.) H.D.
had not mourned David's self-sacrifice, instead she psychoanalyzed the
effect David's death would have on the inferiority complex he had given
Stephen.

Meeting Rukeyser was at first exciting for H.D. The twenty-three-year-
old woman was enthusiastic and strongly American, and H.D. had need

of both those qualities. Muriel wanted to meet "everyone." H.D. invited the literary set she knew because she sympathized with Muriel and liked her. Rukeyser had departed Vassar abruptly, just as H.D. had left Bryn Mawr. Muriel's friendship with the poet Elizabeth Bishop paralleled that of H.D.'s with Marianne Moore. All went superbly. H.D. roguishly called Muriel very "Leo-ish" and decided Muriel and her poetry would be a helpful association when she visited America, as she soon planned to do. It would be a good idea to be in touch with the young. Then disillusionment set in. Wasn't Muriel too Vassarish-Millayish? She had sent a "vulgar" little poem to Robert Herring about "not sleeping alone." And by now H.D. had learned about those "left-wing tendencies." Muriel was probably too dynamic for H.D. She made H.D. worry if the young poets were all like that.

All she wanted from America, so H.D. claimed, would be the weather, the snow, and the New England coast. More strictly, she wanted to meet new poets in America. Bryher had encountered Elizabeth Bishop recently in Paris and had pronounced that she "out Marianned, Marianne." Would Bishop be friend, or competitor? The question may have been settled when Bryher published Bishop in *Life and Letters Today*. She also published Rukeyser. Perhaps Bryher at first liked Muriel a little too much, each sharing an excitement about action and airplanes. Rukeyser was not invited to Kenwin. H.D.'s final comment on her was that it was difficult to concentrate on the trial of the Scottsboro boys during a Mozart ballet. Principally she was frightened by the younger poet's closeness to political causes, comparing her with Auden and his followers, and the tactics of the new left in poetry.

H.D. was willing, and even eager, to welcome other poets from America. Hilda Morley, then a young poet caught up in the meshes of an adventuresome life, found H.D. most helpful when she needed money, advice, and a doctor. H.D.'s sympathies would always be called upon when personal difficulties were involved. Rukeyser—who all her life would expend her energy on causes while at the same time devoting herself to her craft, leaving a legacy of respect for her talents and dedication —was perhaps too strong a personality for H.D. H.D. preferred the seemingly frail, the innocently needy.

The Belgian-American poet May Sarton, in her last trip to Europe before the war, visited H.D., in part because H.D. had sent her an admiring letter about Sarton's first novel, *The Single Hound*.

As an outsider, Sarton was more susceptible to the vibrations of the Lowndes Square ménage. She describes arriving at the flat, climbing the staircase, and seeing Bryher and H.D. peering down at her. The apartment, she decided, was distinctly "posh." It was lit by a round blue lamp that cast a dim light. Light enough for her to notice the "tiger skin plushy carpet." Kenneth's decorative schemes were more exotic to her than to the initiates. She also heard either Bryher or H.D. say in an aside, "She'll do."

Sarton says of H.D. that "she was certainly not a warm person, perhaps because she was very self-conscious and shy." She also wondered whether the protection of Bryher was altogether helpful; whether or not she screened H.D. too much from ordinary life and ordinary people. This is an acute comment on May Sarton's part, and certainly contains much truth. H.D., of course, paid in indefinable ways for Bryher's "protection," yet the question remains: What else could she have done? There is a danger that she might have disappeared from the world of letters altogether had there been no protectors or advisors. May Sarton possibly was comparing H.D. with her own friend Elizabeth Bowen, who competently made her difficult way in the world of letters. Bowen was overtly more mondaine and social than H.D. Bowen, about whom Sarton was enthusiastic, must have been discussed, because Sarton gave H.D. an introduction to her, which H.D. uncharacteristically made use of after she returned from her projected trip to America.

In comparing the work of the writers in *Life and Letters Today*, H.D. had discovered that she missed the American timbre in almost all English writing. She had been reading William Faulkner's *Pylon* and noted that the British prose lacked "its drive and velocity and depth." She admired Faulkner's move from a Jamesian dominance into

> skyrockets of prose that without James would probably remain inchoate, but with that as Background are consummate Art. One thinks and wonders at the language, itself. How Americans do put drive and push and punch into it—yet how what is back of it must remain as unintelligible as French to the good average intellectual here—I mean above average, the highbrow almost. And how a French man would stand breathless—so there is a spiritual or logical reason for "Lafayette we are here" sort of thing.

She frequently considered the career of T. S. Eliot, and after reading Faulkner, she decided that "T. S. Eliot is so terribly wrong—yet is saving his skin, I suppose simply." Meaning that he was not wrong in his poetic attitude, but possibly wrong in clinging to the British tradition. For herself, she was trying to maintain a balance between "these two vibrations and that is what is so deadly to me," she wrote to Bryher, "when YOU come back and tell Me how much energy there is in the States."

Bryher had become the social guide to the American scene. She was now hoping to make frequent trips to America, which H.D. encouraged. If she herself did not choose to commute, she wanted some of the American atmosphere imported. But this time, in 1937, she decided to accompany Bryher to New York. They stayed with Kenneth in a flat he had taken for himself—a sort of beachhead he would establish for the war years, which he would spend in New York.

It turned out that the most important event that occurred on the trip was a meeting with the young Norman Holmes Pearson at the home of William Rose Benét. Almost from this moment Pearson would begin to assume a major role in their lives. Bryher had carefully escorted H.D. to the Benéts, as she knew that William was influential in American literary politics. He gathered around him those who compiled anthologies, those on the lookout for talent, young men, such as Pearson, who would spend their lives in an academic pursuit of literature, who finally would assume strategic positions in universities, enabling them to enrich the careers of those writers whom they admired.

Bryher, having arranged the politics of the evening, in her usual silent way regarded the group. She had already decided that Pearson "would do." Elinor Wylie, the late wife of Benét, had distressed her when Bryher had met her in London, before her death in 1928. She had wondered what the States did to women. She guessed that Elinor was older than she pretended, because she seemed to Bryher to be Victorian in so many ways. (After reading a book of Wylie's, she said that it was H.D. at her worst. When H.D. read *The Orphan Angel*, she liked it.) Later, Benét would include H.D. in several of his many anthologies.

And of course once again they saw Marianne Moore. She and her mother were rejoicing that Alfred Landon was running for president. This so riled Bryher that she told H.D. that it was a pity the Moores couldn't join the Primrose League and the Conservative Party. Marianne and her mother were just as adept at quips as Bryher, and one longs to know what they had to say about Bryher and H.D., although on the surface the two poets were the most admiring of friends. What a feast of wit the two Moores might have made of Kenwin, its menagerie, and the current diet there of roots and berries.

On this visit Bryher changed her mind about civilized Boston and finally concluded that the only place in the States was New York, "unless you are interested in farming." She emphasized to H.D. that it was *not* her world any more than it was George Plank's or Marianne's or even Ezra's. "It is a totally different thing for me, because I'm fundamentally interested in dirt and politics . . . You stick quietly to Europe." Nevertheless, Bryher found her "dog run." She watched the Farr-Braddock fight, which she enjoyed more than she had anything in a long time. "Frankly," she said, "I think it [boxing] is as much art as any poem."

Poetry magazine showed its esteem for H.D. by awarding her its 1938 prize. It was twenty-one pounds, and at first she was undecided what to do with the money. She finally sent red roses to Freud and did "other poetical things."

The heartiness, the welcome of America had reassured H.D., had even added a feather or two to a plumage she liked to consider drab. Contrary to May Sarton's opinion, in London H.D. did not often move in spectacularly social or literary circles. Her friends were selected because of the intimacy they provided and the kindness they would distribute. True, she had old friends, like Eliot, who were now famous. She had known many men and women who had become successful and acclaimed. And yet her inner circle was composed of those whom she could love and, most importantly, who would construct around her a deferential family circle.

After the gaudy American days she may have wished to extend her London borders. There must have been a hint from Sarton at the fascination Elizabeth Bowen might exert, should she care to do so. Although it was not until 1940, H.D. made a first overture to Bowen. From then, with Bowen's acceptance of an invitation for tea, began one of H.D.'s crushes. H.D. was smitten with her. From 1940 until 1944 she kept a notebook with the exact dates of her meetings with Bowen. In the same way she kept dates of her meetings with other crushes, Rodeck, and later Lord Dowding.

Elizabeth Bowen represented a combination of rakishness and conventionality that appealed to H.D. It may have been the way she would have liked to think of herself, as once she had hinted to Marianne Moore. Her snobbishness was satisfied by the material surroundings of Bowen. At that time Bowen lived in a handsome house in a correct neighborhood. In the background was the agreeable, rather conventional husband. Bowen was part of that social-literary group that had never accepted H.D. Although allied with a powerful benefactress, for several reasons, in part psychological, H.D. had never become part of the London literary axis, one section of which was certainly dominated by Bloomsbury. Bowen appeared to have an entrée to several worlds.

At the heart of the matter, H.D. was convinced that Bowen's male lovers were only a "smokescreen," that on the deepest level she preferred women. This made Bowen particularly alluring. Also H.D. identified with Bowen's mixed parentage. "She doesn't feel apparently Irish and not wholly English, rather like myself being from America that is not 'American.'" Here, for the first time, H.D. refers to her secret feelings about a Moravian background, which she believed set her apart from her "American" friends.

She found Bowen kind, intelligent, and not too highbrow. This must have been a relief from the exceedingly highbrow atmosphere of the Sitwells that by 1940 Bryher was edging her way into. Elizabeth Bowen was "tall, sturdy, handsome, not beautiful, very good altogether."

This was in the early days. Later H.D. learned, to her misery, that Bowen would forget appointments she had made with her; that she had a tendency to dash in and out. That, indeed, although an "authentic friend," and one who reminded her of Romaine Brooks, Bowen intended to keep herself removed from H.D. She was not to be entertained by the intense conversations that intimacy with H.D. demanded. She was, however, willing to gossip. For instance, Bowen did not like the decorator Ernest Freud. H.D. was pleased to learn from her that Bowen would have had him decorate her house as he had wanted to do, but that she was depressed by his work because there was an "absolute lack of any trace of vulgarity."

Bryher surprised H.D. by getting along with Bowen rather better than had H.D., who decided this was because Bowen evidently liked the sort of quick-fire intelligence Bryher could release when she chose. Later on Bryher wrote to H.D. a dialogue that may have explained Bryher's attraction more consistently.

> Elizabeth Bowen calls us and asks if BBBryher [Bowen stuttered] could lend her thirty pounds.
> B.   Nothing would give me greater pleasure.
> E.B.   I couldn't ask Alan [her husband].
> B.   Of course no, dear, now come right over, or shall I bring it to you?
> E.B.   (Stammering) Not here, not here, you see Ireland . . .
> B.   (Tail flapping up and down) Of course, of course . . .
> Bowen arrived in her best clothes. What does it mean? A new boy friend?

Typically, Bryher never again refers to the loan. She did remark to H.D. that Bowen was "too Latin in temperament for me." It was the Edith Sitwellian remoteness and artistic dignity that appealed to Bryher. Bryher liked a certain style in ladyhood, whether it grew at Renishaw or burned in Capri among the Compton Mackenzie "vestal fires." She had always loved Romaine Brooks and Natalie Barney. Her hesitancy about Elizabeth Bowen may have sheltered a certain jealousy. She knew her Cat.

In a letter to May Sarton, H.D. described a visit to Bowen in which "Bowen spent all her time on the phone with a long distance call to Ireland, then had people in." H.D. was outraged and told Sarton that she would not "pay any attention to *Suburban* and *rather cruel snubs* . . . She has got me straight—maybe she thought I was stand-offish and 'respectable' in the wrong way . . . she is delightful but I am *too old* to take crude snubs *you know really old and too sad.* O.K. The snubs don't matter only I hated it for HER. SHE SHOULD NOT." Thus spoke Bethlehem and Philadelphia.

And there goes disappointed love, of which this digression is another example in H.D.'s life. It could happen with women, just as well as with men. H.D. finally concluded that Bowen would not accept her attraction to women; that she was "somehow broken inside"; and finally that Bowen was such a problem to the ambivalent HER. "So very attractive. So very!"

CHAPTER TWENTY-THREE

Divorce, Psychoanalysts, Parents

When she was divorcing McAlmon, Bryher said that "you could only enter the law courts if you were pure as driven snow." Now it was January 1937. Aldington was writing to H.D. from the ship that was bringing him back to England from America that he had left Brigit Patmore and was "madly in love" with her daughter-in-law, Netta. He wanted to marry Netta and they both wanted a child. When he reached England he and Netta planned to go to Italy. Before going to Italy, however, he wanted to consult with H.D., whom he was calling his "Dooley," as she would so well understand the feelings of a man in love and would agree, he prayed, to a divorce. Writing Bryher about Richard's new romance, H.D. noted caustically: "It was Richard's fourth honeymoon in the heel and toe of Italy and environs, very Byron?"

As could be expected, drama broke out on all sides. Legally, there was a complication in that Aldington's connection with the publisher William Heinemann was Mr. Frere-Reeves. A Mr. Brooks, who became H.D.'s solicitor, by coincidence represented a firm who handled the financial affairs of Frere-Reeves' wife, the daughter of the novelist Edgar Wallace! Literary caution was needed on both sides.

By the fall of 1937 Aldington was determined to force through the divorce, as Netta was now pregnant and expected a child in the summer of 1938. H.D., recognizing the seriousness and speed with which events had now proceeded, promised Aldington the divorce. She was particularly sympathetic about the expected child and its legitimacy, having experienced so much pain regarding Perdita's parentage, as Aldington well knew. There was some backbiting on her part, but it was done with a sense of humor. She definitely was not out to get even. She did not want Aldington to suffer unduly. What happened was that H.D. began simultaneously to suffer from and to enjoy the fancy drama of the forsaken wife who now controlled the fate of the negligent husband. H.D. may have made malicious remarks, but she did not behave maliciously. It was simply not her way.

She wrote constantly to Bryher for advice on legal processes. Bryher was also enjoying herself, for different reasons. She did appreciate a good legal battle. She was available for advice and comfort. Discreetly she remained at Kenwin so that no scandal of the unknown "Mrs. M."

would confuse the issues, but she couldn't resist shocking the solicitor by remarking that there was no trouble that a good piece of bribery couldn't cure. The wisest advice she gave H.D., acutely sensible as she was to H.D.'s moods, was to go to a psychoanalyst.

H.D. was definitely in danger of reliving the old war days with their anxieties and sorrows. She became alternately hysterical, paranoid, and euphoric. Serious opera needed to be avoided, and so, harkening to Bryher's advice, she went to a psychoanalyst, Dr. Walter Schmideberg, whom she had met at Kenwin. He had already unofficially entered the Kenwin–Lowndes Street saga, and been given the familial name of "Bear."

She trusted Schmideberg and relied on his Freudian help throughout the difficult period with Aldington. She had been seeing him off and on since 1935. She would always need the presence of a psychoanalyst to tide her over the various crises that threatened her. Bryher willingly paid the fees, and unlike so many spouses, thoroughly approved. She herself was in constant touch with Dr. Sachs in Boston up until his death. Perdita was sent to Schmideberg, briefly, so that she might consult someone who might be regarded as a father figure, one with rather more authoritativeness than Kenneth, who had proved himself as much her friend as her father.

As could be expected, there were meetings with the solicitors, sessions with Schmideberg, collapses, accusations, nightmares, euphoria. A landlady was brought from Corfe as witness to Aldington's adulterous behavior, in case he tried to prove H.D. the guilty party. To add to the confusion and high jinks, H.D. had one of her crushes on her young solicitor! She also went to films to take her mind off events. She liked the Marlene Dietrich films and decided she liked Dietrich, although she became more and more "doll." Such was the way her mind ran. Films at the theater, scenarios at home.

Finally, on June 22, 1938, she was awarded the divorce decree. Aldington was declared the guilty party. Damages were to be paid by him.

In H.D.'s Petitioner's Statement at the High Court of Justice, Probate Divorce and Admiralty Division, she testifies that she was living with Gray in Cornwall for about six months, during which time "misconduct took place between us on several occasions. *About the end of July I found I was going to have a baby, whose father would be Cecil Gray.*" (my italics) In her statement H.D. quotes Gray as asking her to divorce Aldington and marry him. She, however, "decided to accede to my husband's request and return to him as soon as the baby was born." H.D.'s statement includes a description of Aldington's rage when he discovered that after the child's birth, and when she was living with him at the Hotel du Littoral, she had gone out and registered the child in his name. Then, H.D. testified, she had consulted a psychiatrist, who when he learned how Aldington had behaved toward her, advised her that it would be hopeless to continue living with him, as "his conduct was due to the nervous strain and shock from his experiences at the Front." This, although a common diagnosis of returned soldiers, might well have been a true explanation for Aldington's erratic and "spurious" behavior. The consensus of her friends who had accompanied her to the courtroom was that she had looked beautiful in the witness-box, had behaved like a lady, and nearly had the courtroom in a swoon. Once more she had starred.

There next followed a scene so typical of the actors and so enjoyable, in retrospect, to those who had followed their careers. A heavier, older, tousled, repentant Aldington showed up at H.D.'s charming flat. He stayed long enough to drink eleven cups of tea. The two were alone together for the first time in years. He proceeded to throw himself on her mercy. He had no money to pay the court damages, charges, or lawyers. The baby was expected any day. Would she waive charges or, more accurately, would she pay off the lawyers for both sides herself? A special plea had been placed that the divorce decree be made active immediately, so that when the baby arrived it would be legitimate. All was now in jeopardy.

Aldington had expected his book *Death of a Hero,* first published in 1929 by Doubleday and later by Penguin Books in 1936, to have been made into a film. It had been such a successful novel. He had also expected the book to bring in additional money by serialization in the *Daily Mail.* Both deals had fallen through. What irony that at this stage of their lives the book that had made him famous should have been based on a heroic young Aldington, whom H.D. had first loved, and whom she was now divorcing; and that she, the unnamed heroine of his book, should now be expected to pay the divorce expenses of a marriage whose failure the "hero" had regretted.

H.D., fearful only of Bryher's reprimands, paid the expenses. She believed Aldington when he told her that if the Patmores succeeded in their suit for alienation of affection (and they did), he would be forced to pay every penny he earned to them, or otherwise leave the country. (He left the country, not unwillingly.) H.D. may have given him a little extra cash, who knows? It would have been like her. Aldington was a section of a past that would never be severed.[1] True, she believed that she no longer loved him, yet she could give him her blessing as the present knelt before the past. So ended a drawn-out, and what might have become a disastrous, experience in court. Richard's charm had exerted

---

[1] Back in 1929 she had written to George Plank: "Richard may be a be-sotted fat sentimentalist . . . nothing can cut across what my 'psyche' self or 'core' feels toward him."

itself; H.D.'s generosity had prevailed. Frere-Reeves told him that "H.D. is the only gentleman in your life."

As the divorce proceedings had continued, Edith Sitwell, who could be critical and quarrelsome in many ways, exhibited a kindness and thoughtfulness toward H.D. Edith Sitwell lived more vicariously than H.D., so it is possible she shared more of the world's problems. From her own experience she wrote to H.D. not to let ghosts haunt her, to drive them away. She cautioned her that ghosts were no longer a part of her life and could no longer feed on her real life, which was the life of poetry, and the love she received from her friends. She wanted H.D., whom she called Hilda, to know that they all valued her. This letter must have upheld H.D. in darker moments when she questioned her early behavior with Aldington and the reasons for their separation. She wrote to Bryher that "Edith knows, is more aware of everything and shirks nothing." Then she sighed, "Anyhow she is my own age."

One of H.D.'s pleasures at this time was to be driven by Perdita in her little car about and around London. On a particular day after the divorce the two had driven out to Hampton Court. Then Perdita had asked about "Cornwall." H.D.'s answer may have been her final one. "Most people," she said, "had found it [and "it" meant the birth of Perdita] romantic." Still, for the young woman the existence of several names—from Perdita Aldington to McAlmon, finally to Perdita Macpherson—might have been more confusing than romantic. And that same confusion might have followed her into the various housing arrangements made by this poet-mother. First there had been the Norland Nursery, then South Audley Street. H.D. rationalized this stay by explaining that Perdita was accustomed to large houses, and the Sloane Street flat was too small! Later there had been Switzerland, the Riant Château, and Kenwin, followed by the abrupt decision to send Perdita to live with Silvia Dobson. This was an unsatisfactory arrangement all around, as Silvia was too young for the responsibility; further, there was a hidden competition between the two for the affection of H.D. These separations, the result of her mother's demand for privacy, must have been extremely hard on the young girl. Bryher, despite her support of liberal educational ideas, definitely did not want to experiment with the local Vaudois schools. Who was there nearby who would be on a social level with the girl? With whom would she share her time and thoughts? Bryher never discovered anyone. What Perdita especially wanted, as she grew older, was her mother's presence, a mother more experienced in life than Bryher.

At one time Bryher had sent Perdita to a vocational school where she was instructed in cooking, housekeeping, etc., so that she would be prepared to cope with the world in the event the Communists took over! After that she was sent to a proper girls' school, but Bryher then disapproved of the "county" accent Perdita had acquired. Perdita was then shuttled back and forth from Kenwin to London. To do her justice, Bryher did not want to keep her a prisoner in Kenwin. Frequently she would ask H.D. if Perdita might stay with her. But H.D., whose affection for her daughter was uncompromising, still equivocated about having Perdita installed in the flat. Now an eighteen-year-old Perdita wished to settle in London to be near her mother.

The coming war would keep Perdita in England for its duration, but H.D. always held the hope that Perdita might finally settle in America. Her loved ones, i.e., her family, were associated with America, so indeed were her own largely neglected roots. At the time of the Hampton Court conversation it was decided that until Perdita took a flat of her own, she would live at South Audley Street. H.D. found housekeeping and making dinners, even with the assistance of the estimable Mrs. Ash, too much of a strain on her, in particular with the addition of a young person who naturally would want to play records and sprawl on sofas. This did not mean, she assured Schmideberg, that her love was any the less for Perdita. It was that she suffered from the mere physical presence of another person. Again arose the problem of H.D.'s need for friends, lovers, family, but of a necessity they must remain at a distance. She wished to maintain her position as a solitaire with her solitude inviolate, yet with friends within calling distance.

The original trio—Pound, Aldington, and Doolittle—were parents of daughters. Catherine, or "Catha," was born to Richard and Netta Aldington shortly after the H.D. divorce. But Pound? In 1938 H.D. was corresponding with him in an oblique *Winter's Tale* way about a photograph Pound had sent her of a child with lovely long hair. She offered herself as a legal guardian for this supposedly "unknown" child. She wrote that she would be "so honoured and happy, to have a distant hand in its fate." Earlier she had offered to send him a bank draft for his bank in Italy. He had suggested that she put the money in the safest place, which would be in an Italian state bond! This was just before H.D. was going to America, and he assumed that she would be lecturing there, making moncy, or was she "merely carrying sweetness and Light? To the Hesperian etc dockfronts?"

Now when he received her letter about a supposedly unknown child, Pound wrote: "Gawd a might / as for legenda / it is about as crazy as one of ole Ford's though one can vaguely trace the thread of fact under the carpet of hooey." He then made it clear that the child was his own and he was "if anything rather pleased at the sex of the product. Despite the Chinese traditions etc." Pound was converting his private correspondence into public legerdemain, obliqueness and intelligence running ahead of gossip's information. As H.D. had run to Pound long ago in 1919 at Perdita's birth, so he troubled to tell her about his newly born child.

He never could resist the slight taunt in his correspondence with her, urging her to "leave off the school room helenism [*sic*]." Nor could she ever reply without a slight catch in her throat. Pound couldn't resist teasing Marianne Moore, whom he now called "Marianna of heightening brow."

H.D. was supposed to remain Pound's student. He still must have wanted to draw her into his life. "Bring on yr / Aesclapius I dunno, in doing them traductions you may have found an intelligent student writing footnotes / question iz, have you?" In his own fashion he was more straightforward in his criticism of her writing than about the facts of his own life.

H.D. by 1938 was more than the intelligent student there at Kenwin, where she was writing to Pound in the last days before the war. She was also the sensitive, attenuated patient whose psychoanalyst, Dr. Walter Schmideberg, and his wife had followed her to Kenwin. H.D. would always be able to retain a peculiarly personal relationship with her doctors. It had begun with Havelock Ellis, then had followed Mary Chadwick, and then Dr. Elizabeth Ashby. They all had seen her through crises and breakdowns. With Freud, of course, the situation had been handled more carefully. His international status had separated her further from the personal aspect of her case than she had supposed. Freud found certain chemistries, such as hers, useful for his own explorations. Freud had retained the control, and she had been the patient-pupil. With her other consultants, despite her emotional reliance on them, one senses a more tenuous relationship. H.D.'s was a powerful presence. The chapters of her neuroses tended to usurp the variables of the analytic chamber.

The Walter Schmidebergs, now included in the "family," increasingly spent their vacations at Kenwin. Day after day, at Bryher's urging, H.D. had gone to the doctor during the Aldington divorce. The Schmideberg sessions were a necessary cushion for the years between 1935 and 1938. And thus the Schmidebergs gradually were introduced into the daily welfare of H.D. Melitta Schmideberg, in a letter to the author, wrote that when "I first saw Kenwin it struck me as the most beautiful place I had ever seen; the glorious view across the lake, with the lights glimmering at night. In the evening you could watch the peacocks displaying their feathers, they belonged to a neighbour, Dr. Niehans . . ."

Dr. Melitta Schmideberg, who after the death of her husband studied and worked in America and returned to London to practice as a psychoanalyst, has defined her relations with H.D. as somewhat uneasy because of H.D.'s having been her husband's analysand. This explanation simplified a more complicated situation. H.D. probably demanded more attention from Schmideberg than would please his wife.

I was always afraid of saying the wrong thing, partly because she intimidated me; she was a somewhat overwhelming personality, imposing in build, very lively and inclined to bursts of emotionalism—very much in contrast to Bryher's calm controlled behaviour. One had the impression that Hilda dominated Bryher, but I think this was a false impression. [letter to author]

And one gathers that H.D. and Melitta Schmideberg were not overly fond of one another. Melitta, the daughter of Melanie Klein, the famous psychiatrist, would not exactly be a simpleminded subject herself. H.D.'s attitude toward women was either a reach for total possession, a need to overwhelm them, as in her struggle with Bowen, or she remained critically aloof; she regarded those women who did not interest her as mere members of the tribe. And yet, H.D.'s boundaries could never be so clearly defined, she was too apt to cross them. She did have crushes and she did have dislikes, and they could often descend impetuously, without warning.

They were all thankful that Dr. Freud was safely in London. H.D. had visited him at his son's house in Hampstead, in June of 1938. "The Professor was sitting at a table just exactly like in Wien with a row of gods. I said, 'O—I am so glad you got these away.' He said, 'O, no, you see I was to be one day in Paris so the Princess got these for me so that I should feel at home.'" Princess George had brought from Greece about a dozen lovely authentic pieces of Tanagra sculpture. (Just as H.D. had once dreamed that she might obtain a special sculpture for the professor.) They had talked about the Friends' Relief Committee, for whom Anna and Ernest Freud were working, and H.D. for a brief moment considered helping out there, but as usual she would prefer not to associate herself with a public committee. She had mentioned German poets to Freud and he had looked unhappy when she said she liked them. Hastily she had added, "Not German poets, I mean Heine."

Afterwards she sent Freud gardenias, but privately she wrote to Bryher that the visit had been a great shock to her "UNK." "I simply feel he died this is his ressurected Pharaoh or Ka, all rather alarming to the UNK."

It was a time of old ghosts before the world's death. Very soon there came another letter from Pound telling H.D. that Olivia Shakespear had died. He would be coming over to settle the contents of her flat, as Dorothy was too ill to travel. Mrs. Shakespear had still been active, raising her grandson Omar Shakespear Pound, who had been born in 1926 at the American Hospital in Paris and subsequently taken up residence with his grandmother. Yeats had sympathized with Olivia's liking to be a grandmother, but he would never understand why Dorothy had given the child over to her mother. Such puzzling parenthoods "les jeunes" had formulated for themselves. Parenthood-by-proxy by now was an additional established Imagist credo.

Ezra asked H.D. to come to the flat in Kensington that had belonged to Mrs. Shakespear to help him sort out her effects. She arrived at the flat, which now witnessed the scene of another historic moment in their lives together. Mrs. Shakespear had been one of the first of his friends whom Ezra in 1912 had asked to be helpful to the newly arrived Hilda from America; she had consistently befriended H.D., in particular at the time of the birth of Perdita. And it had been at her house that H.D. had met Violet Hunt, Yeats, and so many others.

It may even have been Yeats who first encouraged H.D.'s interest and reliance on horoscopes, her gropings into the occult. Yeats would always rely, as did H.D., upon the casting of a horoscope to reveal the characteristics and instincts of his friends and associates.

While they rummaged, they talked. Ezra told her more completely about what had recently been happening to him; he explained the birth of Maria, whose mother was Olga Rudge. She learned that the daughter was being raised by a "friend" in the Tyrol. Then he found a carved ivory box with little Indian pieces as a souvenir of the past for H.D.

She began to find the intimacy of this scene more and more difficult, but she continued to listen to him calmly, hoping, in all events, he would not speak of his politics. He was stirring up memories, opening wounds. She began to believe now that Ezra had been cruelly blind to Dorothy, just as he had been to her. The combined effect of the Shakespear flat, the familiar objects, her enforced intimacy with Ezra began to create a kind of anger in her toward him. She would later write to Bryher that "it was the way Ezra did not seem to see what he might be doing to each and everyone of the crowd . . . It did upset me because I might have been landed in just such a mess if I had not broken out with that past. That was the nightmare—there but for the grace of God!"

It would not be until the war, after Pound had been arrested as a traitor and placed in the barbed wire enclosure at Pisa, that he would begin to write his finest poetry, poetry that would at last free him to disclose his inner feelings and show that now he understood that his concentration on his central self, his blindness to the emotional needs of those closest to him, had been wrong. He wrote in Canto LXXVI:

> J'ai eu pitié des autres
> probablement pas assez, and at moments that suited
> my own convenience.

H.D. might have considered that she had presented herself with somewhat of the same dilemma as Ezra: the threatened marriage, a child raised by others, the troubled marital life causing her to break with marriage and seek other consolations. H.D. believed that she had suffered for

her "crimes," as she would call them, but Ezra had gone free, allowing
others to suffer. She could not have known what the lares and penates
were holding out for him. An appointment was made to meet Ezra on his
last day in London. She broke the date. Once more she refused to forgive
his actions, his self-preoccupation, not recognizing that some such
selfishness was shared by herself.

The unseen heroine of that meeting with Pound had been Olivia
Shakespear, who must now be viewed as a more active figure in H.D.'s
life. In 1961, H.D. wrote to Aldington: "Am I the only person in the
world who didn't know about Olivia Shakespear or Diana Vernon, as he
called her! I don't know why this upset me—that affair discreet as it may
have been—one year and 'friendship' afterwards may have had repercussions in Dorothy aged about ten." H.D. was not referring to Pound; it
was to an affair between W. B. Yeats and Olivia Shakespear.

"Her beauty, dark and still, had the nobility of defeated things, and
how could it help but wring my heart," said Yeats, her first lover. When
Yeats asked Olivia to leave her husband, she refused to do so, and a discreet affair took place at 18 Woburn Buildings. The affair was brief; the
friendship, long. Yeats' biographer Frank Tuohy explains this by saying
that Yeats could not love her as he should because he believed she was
"too near my soul, too salutary and wholesome to my inmost being."
There were also the interrupting memories of Maud Gonne. Yet it is to
Olivia Shakespear that Yeats has written one of his most perfect love
poems, "The Lover Mourns for the Loss of Love":

> Pale brows, still hands and dim hair,
> I had a beautiful friend
> And dreamed that the old despair
> Would end in love in the end:
> She looked in my heart one day
> And saw your image was there;
> She has gone weeping away.

After she had died, Yeats wrote: "For more than forty years she has
been the centre of my life in London and during all the time we have
never had a quarrel, sadness sometimes but never a difference. When I
first met her she was in her late twenties but in looks a lovely young girl.
When she died she was a lovely old woman."[2]

Yeats—Ezra—H.D.—Olivia—the London flat disassembled. Ezra, even

---

[2] Yeats wrote to Dorothy Shakespear in 1934 when he was composing *Dramatis
Personae:* "I am just beginning on Woburn Buildings . . . alas the most significant
image of those years must be left out." Ian Fletcher (*An Honored Guest*) says that
"the reference is to the enmenagement with Mrs Shakespear in 1896 or that of 1903.
And since the unrecorded crises are the heart of much of his later poetry, the loss
is severe."

from his remoteness, reaching out to H.D., who broke their appointment. Now anger from H.D., creasing the memories.

It was Lady Ellerman who died next, in 1939, just before the outbreak of the war. Bryher distributed her personal effects. H.D. inherited furs, laces, Lalique glass. Robert Herring was given furniture from the Ellerman house to decorate a house in Eckington he had taken and where he would remain during the war, editing *Life and Letters Today*. When H.D. would visit him, surrounded by all his furniture, she declared that she was in a "proper house" for the first time since she had left Philadelphia.

Bryher, who had sincerely loved her mother, now mourned her as the one from whom she had inherited her sense of adventure, not, as she had once believed, from her buccaneer father. Lady Ellerman's character was one of many surprises and acceptances; her limitations only increased the gratitude of those whom she chose to accept and help. Bryher closed Kenwin briefly while she and H.D. returned to London. Then Bryher would return for the last days of Kenwin, before she was forced to flee to Portugal.

It is in those last days in Switzerland, dedicating her energy and money to refugee aid, that she was able to help over a hundred refugees escape over the border and place them in homes and countries. She only just managed to make it herself to Portugal, where she rather enjoyed her emergency exit to London. H.D. was waiting for her at Lowndes Square.

PART FOUR

"Taedet caeli convexa tueri"

[It becomes dispiriting constantly to watch the arch of heaven]

Virgil, *Aeneid*, Book IV, as quoted by Len Deighton, *Fighter. The True Story of the Battle of Britain*

CHAPTER TWENTY-FOUR

Notes from the War Years

The only time Bryher and H.D. lived together continuously was during the Second World War. The duration was unforeseen; its extensiveness caused difficulties and personal sacrifice. The war projected into the lives of these indulgent women a creative and personal tumult whose final errors, beyond all expectancy, left them charitable and loving toward one another. Their outward bonds were never changed. Inwardly, after the war, Bryher and H.D. reached toward separate horizons. Affections, gratitude, were fixed. At Lowndes Square, Bryher occupied the smallest room. She said, truthfully, she preferred this room. There the dark drew in so quickly, even when there was a new summer time for the clock. The black curtains must be drawn against the windows to shut out any gleam of light. It was dangerous to walk on the streets, not for fear of thieves, but of losing one's way or falling and hurting oneself. Bryher began to write on a little ledge by the window. H.D. was given the proper desk. H.D. believed that all during the war she deferred to Bryher so that she could entertain her friends in the flat. This was not entirely unselfish of H.D. The war encouraged a creativity in her that had been thwarted by the travels, extensive plans, the shifts of persons and places in the previous years. True, she had worked hard, but those "Peter Rabbit" books only intimated her possibilities. Concentrated living, squirreled away in a small apartment, fewer social activities, a narrowing of her dimensions would give her a concentrated world so necessary to her craft.

For one thing, this was a war that removed that projected and unreal war guilt from her. This war, after all, hadn't been an act of wrath aimed at her personally for her sins. Here was another generation upon which the same vindictiveness could be enacted. It was no longer her youth that was being consumed; it was the youth of others. So, in a sense, she was morally free. Free to create. Never had she felt so unfettered. She wrote now to prove that creativity could conquer death. She had not felt this way in the Great War. That war had crushed her just as she was beginning to bloom on an alien soil, so she would always believe.

How extraordinary that she could write of the 1940 Battle of Britain:

Now exaltation rises like sap in a tree. I am happy. I am happier than I
have ever been. It seems to me in my whole life . . . we were able, night
after night, to pass out of the unrealities and the chaos of night-battle and
see clear. If my mind at those moments had one regret, it was that I
might not be able to bear witness to this truth, I might be annihilated before I had time to bear witness. I wanted to say, "when things become
unbearable, a door swings open or a window."

There was the story—true or not—of H.D.'s fleeing to the roof of
Lowndes Square and flinging her clothes over the edge, preparing to
leap after them, yet fortunately prevented. Or of Bryher's taking a near
overdose of a drug and being saved by H.D. Yet these were the produc-
tive days. Bryher commenced her historical novels. She began *The Fourteenth of October* (the date of the Norman invasion of Britain) in recognition of this new near invasion. And H.D.'s triumph over circumstance
is celebrated in her *Trilogy*, which is an overture to her late poetry.

It is no wonder that H.D. wrote during an air raid: ". . . now that I
saw that Bryher was accepting the fury, we could accept the thing together. We had accepted many things together but this last trial, this last
acceptance, might still be the last . . . Bryher sitting there with her face
collected, ears set close to her head, the short-cropped head. What she
said was oracular and always had been."

Then follows the thread of despair: "But I didn't care about rules any
more. I didn't care about memories. I was sick to death of tension and
tiredness and distress and distorted values and the high-pitched level
and the fortitude which we had proved beyond doubt that we possessed.
I had passed the flame, I had had my initiation. I was tired of all that
. . . I was sick to death of being on the qui vive all the time."

H.D. wrote those stricken words in the last years of the war, at the
time she began her long account of her childhood growing up in the
Moravian faith, called *The Gift*. It was this faith that would carry her
through the last episodes of the war and would leave its evidence in her
war poetry. She needed to reconcile Europe and America. The Moravians started out in Europe, then settled in America; she had reversed
the process. There are many hints of homesickness too. In the early days
of the war H.D. wrote to her American friends that she was glad they
were out of it. Later when America entered, she welcomed them, as if
her native country could now share her battle fatigue.

The two women leaned on their London friends—"the Lowndes
Square Group," as Bryher called them in the dedication of her autobiographical *The Days of Mars*. The stars of this group were the Sitwells,
who especially enthralled Bryher. She liked all three, Edith, Osbert, and
Sacheverel. She helped them financially and they repaid her by inviting

her to Renishaw, their home, and by dedicating books to her. Osbert also presented Bryher with the manuscript of *Laughter in the Next Room,* a part of his series of memoirs. Bryher gave the Bryher Foundation Travelling Fellowship to their favorite poet, Dylan Thomas, and his wife, Caitlin, which enabled the Thomases to go to Italy.

The Sitwells appear to have been at their best and kindest with Bryher. Edith, under different circumstances, might have been a rival of H.D.'s, but not as a lover of Bryher—in that direction Bryher preferred actresses, such as Elisabeth Bergner and Lotte Reineger, the producer of silhouette films. The rivalry was in poetry. Bryher considered Edith a literary genius and she said she would rather hear Edith read her poetry more than any other poet except H.D. After listening to records of Edith Sitwell's voice, one can agree with Bryher. Like the recordings of H.D., the voice has great charm and dignity. Edith and H.D. admired one another, yet were more generally cautious in their personal approaches. Undoubtedly, Edith's war poems, "Song of the Cold," "Still Falls the Rain," and the copiousness of her wartime output affected H.D.; it may have, indeed, accelerated her own writing. Edith Sitwell, H.D., and Eliot were equally determined that the war should not defeat them, that poetry should shine its own lantern—even, as it turned out, to the gates of Buckingham Palace.

Bryher's interest in the Sitwells may have been based on her own precarious family tradition, or lack of one. Tradition was much celebrated at Renishaw. As an outsider, Bryher was prepared to attend its conservators. She said she had had five years of the war and was surprised to be alive; war had proved to her the strength of English tradition. Bryher was angry that Woolf and Sitwell had been taken to task for being so isolated from wartime activity. Bryher said she always had supposed that it was the poet who carried the banners into the fray!

In 1943 Bryher had a rather heavy run on the Elizabethans, so naturally she would be prepared to accept Edith Sitwell's claim to Plantagenet blood. Bryher even believed that she herself could speak Elizabethan. It is probable that with her own slight cocknified and non-upper-class accent she might not have been far from wrong! She attended the Shakespearean plays that were given in Regent's Park. (In one of her war stories, Elizabeth Bowen begins with a scene in Regent's Park: it is a concert where the eager and culturally starved Londoners gathered to hear music and plays; there they also liked to criticize the authenticity of the actors' speech.)

Bryher wandered the streets looking for Elizabethan sites, and attempted to locate Shakespeare's house on Silver Street. She began to gather from booksellers an exceptional library of the Elizabethans: she loaned this collection to Edith Sitwell for her work on Queen Elizabeth I. H.D. herself was helped by Bryher's library when she wrote *By Avon*

River. It is probable that the Sitwells evoked this favorite age in history for Bryher. In consorting with the Sitwells she may have subconsciously believed she was near "the real thing," the true monarchy, not snobbishly, but in a way her historical mind demanded.

And everywhere people were speaking the words from Shakespeare's King John:

> This England never did, nor never shall,
> Lie at the proud foot of a conqueror,
>
> . . .
>
> Come the three corners of the world in arms,
> And we shall shock them.

More of the Lowndes group. There was Silvia Dobson and her family, who were away in Kent, and Cole and Gerald Henderson. Bryher was grateful for Henderson's tours of Elizabethan London; they inspired her book *The Player's Boy.* During a bombing the Henderson flat received a direct hit and Gerald was seriously injured. Then there was Robert Herring, formerly on *Close-Up,* and now editing *Life and Letters Today;* also George Plank. During the war Plank served as part of the Home Guard, which was composed of civilians armed and instructed to save England in case of invasion. David Low, the cartoonist, has invented a name for a typical member (which George Plank was not)—men of the huntin', shootin', fishin' school of life known as "Colonel Blimps." George was to wear himself out in this service and become seriously ill before his eventual return to America. There was Philip Frere, the lawyer to the Sitwells, and now of much importance to them all; the cleaning woman, Mrs. Ash, who had been with them for years, and would remain throughout the war. She who was forbidden to pick up the petals of roses that must have strewn the room from H.D.'s many vases.

Then Norman Holmes Pearson arrived after the United States had entered the war to see war duty in England with the OSS. He would be H.D.'s friend, confidant, and admirer. It was he who rescued Perdita from a dismal war job as a typist at Bletchley Park,[1] sixty miles from London. He helped locate her in London at a job in which she was able to use her considerable capacities as a linguist. Perdita now would be near her mother. And so, in a way war, the destructive agent, helped unite mother and daughter.

Earlier Perdita had been in the thick of the raids, driving a volunteer canteen service that fed men engaged in digging out the bombed ruins. Later when she was transferred to the country, long hours of travel

---

[1] Bletchley Park, to cover its high-priority operations, was called a "counter communications center." Actually it was where the British were successfully breaking the code used by the German enciphering machine known as Enigma (an H.D.-like title).

meant infrequent intervals before she could rejoin the group in London. Now, stationed in London, Perdita writes of her work under the supervision of James Angleton, who later became well known in his role with the CIA until his dismissal in 1974. She had been assigned to the Italian desk in Counter-Intelligence and had been moved from Bletchley Park to London, thanks to Pearson and his OSS contacts. She describes the volatile, erudite Angleton, who in college had published a literary magazine. Recruited from Yale, when he first appeared and reorganized the office, he was a PFC who would quote Ezra Pound and Eliot. Perdita describes his work habits, his impatience, his sensitivity and charm. Underlying the story of those days, written by Perdita for the East Hampton *Star* (Long Island, N.Y.) in 1980, is a portrait of the twenty-one-year-old Perdita. She was eager to help, although encumbered by the details of her private life—the endless queueing for food and lodging, foraging for life in the city first endangered by buzz bombs and after D-day the more damaging V-bombs. Perdita was thoughtful of Angleton and in her conscientious way watched over him. There was time even then for this young woman to show compassion and interest in an American, for after all, she was half American. She says that after the war during her dolce vita days in Rome she saw him across a piazza. He grabbed her up and took her for a moonlit ride, and over drinks they reminisced. She must have been a most unusual secretary to have been assigned to an enigmatic PFC who would shortly be a lieutenant and who would end his working days with the CIA's Distinguished Intelligence Medal— "Mother" they called him in the press in 1975, his code name; but there is a mother role there, quietly hidden by Perdita . . .

Bryher said that she had a "bad war." From the beginning she was incensed that the British had not prevented the war by an early attack in 1933. To Mary Herr, H.D.'s schoolgirl friend, she wrote in February 1940:

I blame the English government intensely for not having stopped Hitler before German rearmament became serious. As it is, there is nothing now but to fight it out for were the Germans to triumph, there would be no more liberty, art or thought in Europe. It may be that this had to come as a beginning of a reorganization of the whole of Europe, but I think we have to win the war first and then get on to what will happen, for example, I do not believe in the stuff some English preach about their enemies being Hitler and not the German people. Most of the Germans elected Hitler and believe in him. I am intensely sorry for individuals there but I think the mass of the nation thinks in Nazi fashion.

Thus spoke Bryher, who had found some of her happiest moments in Berlin, and whose family had originated in Germany.

After the war began, what enraged her most was the inefficiency of the bureaucracy. She came to believe that business people should be running the government in matters such as rationing, food supplies, etc. Here she reflected the attitudes of her father, and she would have liked nothing better than to have helped Beaverbrook and others like him regulate England. Bryher should have had a job that would have employed her energy and abilities. She saw clearly from the earliest days that it would be the Russians who would in the end come out on top. She found that the elite believed in Russia, that the common people did not; the war had begun with fascism in Italy and she was firm in believing Communism would not be the answer. As her fears deepened during the long struggle, she became increasingly conservative. Her hopes were that the United States would enter the war with the strongest naval and air service in the world. She was certain that no American aid as of June 1940 could save France. In another letter to Herr in the summer of 1940, she wrote:

> The French held out for six days and six nights, outnumbered and without the kind of weapons that would stand up to German ones. I feel only that in a way it is just retribution for Spain. They let the Spanish die in shoals and it was there that Germany and Italy tried out the new methods of attack . . . Fascism as always meant the subordination of everything to war—then war and then plunder. I doubt very much now if much of Europe will survive but I do think that at the final end, it will be Russia who will walk in and pocket the spoils.

Any description of the actual day-by-day struggle of those war years must take into account the letters Bryher wrote to her friends in America. She needed letters, and she wrote them all the time, purveying just such views as she expressed to Mary Herr. Letter writing suited her method of thinking, and there was so much time now to write.

We do not have Mary Herr's replies to Bryher, but we do have accounts in Bryher's letters of the endless food parcels Mary sent. How much they enjoyed the honey, the sweets. How precious to H.D. was the American maple syrup. (Of course, everyone was preoccupied with food. One night Pearson brought a pineapple, and they had a party, dividing up the pineapple among six people.)

One of the few refuges outside London where H.D. could recover was in Cornwall at Trenoweth, St. Keverne, where Bryher had "gone shares" with a school friend and bought a farm. In Cornwall the flowers that were sold on the London streets, especially daffodils, were grown. During the war there were vegetables and rabbits. Bryher loved Trenoweth, and her friend Doris Banfield ran the farm with her new husband, John Long. H.D. went seldom, as the train ride was tedious and difficult, but she did once stay for six weeks.

To escape the intimacy that war thrust upon them, Bryher and H.D. always took separate vacations. One would remain in London while the other went away. Bryher was away more frequently—it was necessary for her to go to Eckington in Derbyshire, the village next to Renishaw, where Robert Herring was now living in a house partially furnished from relics of Bryher's old South Audley Street mansion. It was at Eckington that they put out the magazine *Life and Letters Today*. And nearby at Renishaw, Bryher was admitted into the Sitwell family circle, where she admired the garden "more than any other she had ever seen." Edith, as regally as the Elizabeth I she would soon write of, would draw Bryher aside and read to her from her poems. Possibly no one understood why this little woman with her short brushed hair, her shabby beret, her mannish suits, so adored going to Renishaw or why she would attend the new performance of "Facade" (there is no record of H.D. having been to it). At the theater everyone wondered where the rumored millionairess sat, not knowing that the shabby woman who was often thought to be a clerk when she shopped at Harrods was that person, dressed in her russets while the Sitwells paraded in their royal robes. However, all such events led to good things for H.D. The Sitwells were not ungrateful, and Edith would reward H.D. by including her in her anthology of poets; Osbert's introduction of H.D. to Sir Humphrey Milford of the Oxford University Press resulted in the publication of final poems of H.D.'s war years. Osbert wrote a rave review of the poems in the *Observer*.

H.D's private journeys away from London led to Woodhall in Kent, the house rented by the Dobsons. She seems to have found at Woodhall a part of her girlhood, long past, a simplicity, no promptings to play the role of the seeress, the oracular poet. She could play herself, Hilda Doolittle from Bethlehem, Pennsylvania. They gave her a simple spacious room of her own.

There was music. There was a garden, a pool, flowers. There was a separate oast house that she wrote to Bryher she wanted very much to buy and to keep for herself forever. This dream disappeared with the war's end, but for a while H.D. contented herself with the thought that she might live in the farmland in the oast house. Then there was a donkey; they would place H.D. in a wagon, then hitch it up to the donkey and off they would go to a nearby pub. Or off to the manor house—a house made famous by its original owner, who was the discoverer of the Gunpowder Plot—where the gardener would tell them when the hay was laid. They might go over and gather it for the animals.

There was the spontaneous affection of the Dobsons and the particular love of the gifted Silvia. Silvia writes that Woodhall was a "kat place, Bryher never came there." H.D.'s letters from Woodhall are her happiest of the war. Although not the elated ones of poetic accomplishment, they show her as more relaxed, less anxious than would be expected during a war. It was a pity that events would not provide her with the oast house.

Mervyn Dobson still owns H.D.'s desk. It was of the Empire period;

possibly this is the Empress Eugénie's desk bought at the Violet Hunt sale. It may have been at this desk that H.D. wrote her countless letters to Silvia, describing the events of her days, her stirrings of the "un-k," the difficulties with her friends. H.D. was able to confide to Silvia what she would read in the crystal given her by Peter Rodeck. She was able to talk to Silvia about this man on whom she had formed such a strange crush, who was now a priest. She would use the memories of her days with Silvia when they lived at a pension on the Zattere Santa Maria della Salute, near the Calle Querini, where Ezra Pound would finally return to Olga Rudge after his incarceration in St. Elizabeth's. From there Pound left by boat for the Venetian hospital in which he died.

H.D. had written to Silvia that she believed that "Ps-a [psychoanalysis] is a true aquarian science—along with X-ray and television and those things—science plus something uncanny or super-natural, not science in the old sense of the word." She found this "aquarian" element in Venice, where she attributed the egalitarianism of women to the Cult of the Virgin. In 1934 when they had been together in Venice, H.D. had bought a volume called *One Thousand Saints*. She wrote to Silvia: "I feel there should be a Libra wedding of St. Marks Catholicism and Zodiac beasts and Greek Legend—a new book of prayers for all Aquarians—for I bought a Latin book of psalms and invocations and it is exquisite in bits." Perhaps when she wrote her *Trilogy*, she was celebrating this wedding.

It was about this time in the early 1940s that she became interested in spiritualism. As in the Great War, there was a revival of spiritualism during the Second World War, understandably, because of all the deaths and disasters. At Silvia's she must have (thinks Silvia) talked to Emma Brown, their nanny, about Silvia's dead brother Hilyard and spiritualism. Hilyard was not one of the dead pilots that her hero of the war, Sir Hugh (later Lord) Dowding, wrote about, but a scientist. H.D. believed that after Hilyard's death he would be one of "a group of lovers or of brothers" warning about atomic warfare. This is the first indication of the wave of esoteric research, of magic, of spiritualism, that would engulf H.D. during the war. And perhaps it can be explained as part of the superstition and phenomenalism that arose all over England and is certainly explicit in the writing of poets and prose writers from that period. Elizabeth Bowen writes again and again of haunted houses and supernatural occurrences. The blitzed houses of London—silent, dead—would provoke this. Ghosts were everywhere. The world was a place where there were only the ghosts and the living, and the distinction between the two must have been close. Among those dedicated to the spiritual resurrection of the dead was the hero of the Battle of Britain, Air Chief Marshal Sir Hugh Dowding, who had lost his pilot son in combat.

The career of Air Chief Marshal and Fighter Commander Sir Hugh Dowding was one of the fatalities of the war. Made Air Chief Marshal in

1940, it was he who determined that British fighters would intercept the German bombers when they flew over Britain. This meant he had to throw almost the entire Air Force into defense. It also meant that the production of British fighter planes must be upped far beyond their current rate. Prime Minister Winston Churchill presented Max Beaverbrook with this problem of production and asked him to join the Cabinet. With his exceptional executive ability and control of propaganda, Lord Beaverbrook was able to accomplish the unbelievable. Between Lord Beaverbrook and Dowding there fortunately existed a comradeship based on a shared admiration. They believed in the same goals; they were companionable. The intellectual in Dowding also must have appealed to Beaverbrook. Dowding, who may now be called a contemporary Sir Francis Drake, was not always successful in his relationships. Usually he was known as "Stuffy" Dowding. He was a conservative, an isolationist. He was thankful when the French were out of the war because he wouldn't have to put up with them and their demands for British aircraft, so badly needed at home. Though he was remote, difficult, and self-opinionated, he was undoubtedly the most superior air chief marshal to be found. Despite the undisputed admission that his decisions had saved Britain that September of 1940 as bomber after bomber came over from Germany and was turned back by his pilots, he was dismissed from his post. First relegated to a fictitious position in Washington, thence to Canada, he was then allowed to disappear. He had made enemies, and Churchill did not like him. Such are the fortunes of war. The termination of his career was a personal tragedy, equal to the loss of his son and the early death of his wife. He was a greatly superior officer whose career had been terminated unnecessarily and probably spitefully. And yet to the public he was a hero. He certainly became one to H.D. He was more than a hero to her; he became an obsession.

She wrote: "To recall Ezra is to recall my father. To recall my father is to recall the cold, blazing intelligence of my 'last attachment' of the war years in London." He appears as "Lord Howell" in a book she was writing at this time, "The Sword Went Out to Sea." He is the Achilles of *Helen in Egypt.* He appears in the manuscripts called "The Rose" and "The Mystery." He was her war monument.

Lord Dowding wrote a book, *Many Mansions* (1943), in which he cited occasions on which "lost" sons, that is, dead sons, had been contacted through mediums. These airmen, for they were not combat soldiers, were in middle ground between earth and astral space and were helping their comrades to their astral haven. This is not an exact account of the book, but it will give some idea of the levels on which Lord Dowding, by this time, dwelt. He lists example after example of these happy dead-only-to-the-world airmen who were living out their lives on another stratum.

H.D. went to one of Dowding's lectures in 1943. She sent him three Christmas cards. He came to see her, she tells us, after they had been corresponding a year and a half. This, of course, is quite extraordinary, that a man in his position would correspond with an unknown woman. What would encourage their friendship was a belief in life after death. H.D. said, "There must be another world, but where was it? It was there somewhere. I had never doubted it." There we are back again at the center of her quarrel with Freud, who did not believe in life after death. But Dowding did. Perhaps he appeared to her as great a man as Freud; certainly his reputation at the time of their correspondence was in many circles greater than Freud's. Here again, the father figure.

The reason for Dowding's coming to visit her personally was that she had written him that she had received "messages" of where bombs were to fall. She had received these messages because she was attending seances by a Brahman Indian, Arthur Bhaduri. Either she would be alone in her flat, table tipping, or with Bhaduri, at a seance, where she gave him her "zodiac" ring that she cherished as a psychic touchstone that would inform them of where the bombs would land.

Here Dowding showed a certain sense when he told H.D. that she must be careful, that "beings of a lower order could get into communication." By now she must have been in an overwrought state. She had written to May Sarton that "we are all cracking up, in a way—really there is no place for us to go and really recuperate." There actually were places to which she could retreat, such as Bryher's Trenoweth in Cornwall, but by 1945 her life had become too intense for any normal recreation. She had turned to the Society for Psychic Research; she had found the magic of her ring and table tipping. The society had led her to Lord Dowding. She confided to him that she had also received messages from airmen, from a Viking ship. Her condition may have cautioned and frightened him. He urged her to "give up this work." She should have accepted his advice, but then she would not have gone on to write the books in which he figured as her hero. H.D.'s incredible ability to balance worlds and ideas is shown by her involvement in "psychic research," at the same time as she was writing her first poems for the *Trilogy—The Walls Do Not Fall.* Dowding and what he meant to her would continue until its exorcism in her book *Helen in Egypt.* Even when he remarried and they had been out of touch for years, she did not give him up. His address remained in her last address book: St. Mary's Rd., Wimbledon.

There was an immense response to literary work in wartime Britain. Their lives dulled by hardship, the public was eager for imaginative experiences. The Regent's Park performances of Shakespeare in the outdoors were crowded. Concerts were sold out. Of the magazines, only *Life and Letters Today, Horizon, Penguin New Writing,* and *Poetry*

London survived. Bryher was astonished that *Life and Letters Today,* placed on newsstands, sold out.

In April 1943 H.D. came in for a certain acclaim of her own. Her name, among those of other selected poets, appeared on notices placed around London. The Sitwells had the idea of promoting the value of the arts in wartime by arranging a "Reading of Famous Poets" to be given at the Aeolian Hall. Of more renown than the poets would be representatives of the royal family: Queen Elizabeth, and her daughters Princess Elizabeth and Princess Margaret. This became, in many aspects, both an eventful and hilarious occasion. Edith had consented to rehearse the poets, then despite her consent she reacted with her particular mixture of spite and kindness. The poets reacted with their mixture of ego, bravado, and hysterics. One of the women poets became drunk. Another poet decided that it would be an opportunity to read a good many of his works, going far beyond the allotted time. However, everyone was impressed with the solemnity of the occasion and the professional staging of the Sitwells.

Edith might chafe at the silliness of some of her poets as they rehearsed, yet she knew that this would be a moment for her, in her exotic dress, to triumph. She was right. Bryher described her as "stepping forward as if from some great tapestry." Edith read "Anne Boleyn's Song," which, with its overtones of the rise and fall of an era, fitted exactly into the moment's peril.

H.D., recalling events in the Greek past, read:

> who when the earth-quake shook their city
> when angry blast and fire
>
> broke open their frail door,
> did not forget
> beauty.

Rather inappropriately, Eliot read—in what Norman Holmes Pearson had called "that High Anglican asbestos voice of his"—from "The Waste Land," the lines ending with "London Bridge is falling down." John Masefield, Walter de la Mare, Vita Sackville-West, and others read. H.D. made her three curtsies.

Insecure about her personal appearance, H.D. had worried that her fingers were too nicotine-stained. In trying to remove the stain, she rubbed off most of the skin on her writing finger. She also got herself a perm, the first since the beginning of the war. She wore her hair shortish and tucked under at the neck in a roll, with two strands rolled on top of her head. This, she considered, gave her an "Edwardian" look. She was wildly excited about the parties that were given for the poets each day for a week, although she considered herself a "ravenant." When the excitement of the reading was over, she suffered from a gripping neuralgia. H.D. wrote to May Sarton in the United States:

> It was especially touching as the Queen came with the two Princesses—it made it so gay, like good Queen Bess times for a lot of assorted poets to read aloud—formal and informal at the same time as only England can manage things in War or Peace. When asked whom she wanted to act as escort to the children, the Queen said she would like them to have the poets near, so between the two poets of the programme, O.S. sat with the Queen, de la Mare with the big girl and Arthur Waley with the little girl. In the second part the Poet Laureate sat with the Queen, Bottomley with Princess E. and Eliot with Princess M. All this made a sort of fairy tale of it or charade . . .

Bryher wrote to Mary Herr:

> And then there was the Reading. It was a very great affair. Some of the poets from the last war read from their own works in aid of the French in Great Britain. The Queen and the two Princesses were present and spoke to the poets in the interval. H.D. and Eliot were the two representatives of the Anglo-American side. Hilda read a new poem most beautifully and it was then printed in the Times Literary Supplement. As for the audience it would be much easier to say who was not there than who was, and tickets were unobtainable days beforehand—even before it was known that the Queen might be present. I was delighted not only that Hilda was there, but that she was representing the bridge, as it were between the two countries.

In 1940 after she had returned to London from Switzerland, Bryher settled £70,000 on H.D. (today, about $2 million) with an income for life of £2,450 yearly. H.D. already had inherited money from her family. Her businessman brother Harold had invested wisely for her. Indeed, she was well off. And yet H.D. always considered herself impoverished—not exactly poor, but she feared to spend any money. Bryher had given her, and she carefully listed them, a seal-skin coat, one with a fox collar, and a sable cape inherited from Lady Ellerman. Her clothes were designed and made for her. Bryher had given her jewels. In 1942 on the anniversary of their twenty-four years together, Bryher also presented H.D. with a life membership to the London Library and a life membership in a society Bryher established for the promotion of Hellenic studies.

And yet, the picture she seems to have of herself is of a woman living in a fairly small flat—especially small after Kenneth Macpherson's father, affectionately called "Pop," came to live with them, sleeping in a little trunk room; she believed she lived a fairly marginal life, economically speaking. They paid £325 yearly for Lowndes Square. It was a design suited to H.D.'s own rhythm and personality, pared down, like her poetry, and in a carefully selected neighborhood. Her extravagances were the theater and flowers. She visited Renishaw infrequently, but as if it were a castle. Robert Herring's home in nearby Eckington she spoke of as filled with lovely old things—china, silverware, mahogany—the cherished possessions of a household, which she had not known since she was a girl living at home. She had the mentality of one to whom things are given, but are not earned, nor even rightfully inherited. Later she would speak of Bryher's furs as "the wages of sin."

H.D. did not find Lowndes Square oppressive. Certainly it was in a familiar borough; it was one of the more elegant squares. It was near Harrods, where she shopped. Bryher had said that she herself preferred small spaces; H.D. seemed only aware of atmospheres. She controlled the atmosphere of Lowndes Square, and it must have contributed to an elation that shows in her writing about her life. Having Pop in the flat gave her a feeling of family life when he might well have been a nuisance. Remarkably, she never complained, at least not until the end when she was breaking down. Previous to this she was more stimulated than she had been in years. She never expressed fear of the bombs. She wrote that "times were NEVER so exciting—the last war was not. It is simply a sheer mathematical problem of how much can the human frame stand and endure and we seem to get stronger as far as nerves go, as we go on." This was written just after Virginia Woolf's suicide.

H.D. believed that Virginia Woolf's suicide in 1941 was unnecessary. "The general attitude," she wrote to her war correspondent, May Sarton, "was 'poor thing—she went through such a lot' but having been through so much, I myself, did feel stricken to think she got away like that, just when really everything is very exciting and one longs to be able to live to see all the things that will be bound to happen later—think of not being here to look at France, to watch the whole shift of civilization." Here Bryher distinctly disagreed with her. She thought that Virginia Woolf had every right to take her own life and admired her courage in doing so.

H.D. likens herself to a trained seal who does all the right things, balances the ball and so forth, yet all the time is a creature of another element. She never assimilated into society. Poetry had become her country, and poetry was her weapon against the war. As such, she was impervious to the slings and arrows of the raging battle because she was not quite "of it"; she was a denizen of another world, a vapor in the atmospheric life of Lowndes Square, immune to bombs or death.

H.D. was shocked by the newspaper photographs of Ezra Pound—Lord Ga-Ga, as they called him, after Lord Haw-Haw, a much publicized traitor. She had not listened to Pound's wartime broadcasts; those who had heard him said they were idiotic, and this she quoted to Viola Jordan, Pound's loyal friend. Again, another source had told her they were clever and poisonous. She wrote Sarton that he was probably a little crazy, which was perhaps the kindest thing to think. The article she had read about him was called "Troubadour Traitor." She says suddenly that he had *bored* her very much, but that now she was interested in him, his "sheer psychology," now that he had been declared a traitor. It would not be too long before he would be captured and interned in Pisa.

H.D. was also thinking about Ezra because her mind was on the American scene. She was trying to write *The Gift*, the reconstruction of her childhood, the story of the Moravians, her family. Thus she wrote to Gretchen Wolle Baker, her girlhood friend and cousin, now living in Nova Scotia. She wanted to know about Uncle Fred, who had started the Bach festival in Bethlehem, Gretchen's father. She wondered where Count Zinzendorf's desk was, as it formerly had been among the family possessions. Gretchen replied that she had the desk, although it was really an oblong table with a drawer. They both agreed that the family inheritances relating to the Moravians should be returned to the Moravian museum in Bethlehem.

Toward both Aldington and Pound, H.D. was alternately angry and compassionate. Bryher was contemptuous of both men. Bryher was reading the life of James Joyce. More interested in Joyce than in H.D.'s former loves, she argued rightly that despite the conservative Eliot's defense of Joyce, it was the work of Joyce that marked the end—not the beginning—of literature, or the novel, as all previous generations had known it.

Kenneth was in New York. McAlmon was spending his last years in the American West. Past and present and future, Bryher had many concerns. She was worried about her old friend and literateur Norman Douglas. Her new admiration was for Compton Mackenzie. Bryher recommended his latest work, *The Red Tapeworm*, to everyone. She might have been biased, because she cared very much for both Sir Compton and his wife, Faith.

At Lowndes Square they had mince pie for Christmas, tree ornaments that had survived the Blitz, and a turkey sent up from the farm in Cornwall. And H.D. had her correspondence with Norman Pearson, her mentor now, and consultant. And like Arachne, she sewed on her tapestry—a consolation that would be with her the rest of her life—and thought of her books and what she would confide about them to Pearson.

It was Pearson who had supplanted Aldington, who had supplanted Amy Lowell, who had supplanted Pound. H.D.'s life is marked by these influences, both erotic and intellectual. All seem to have been, after their fashion, in love with her. All remained intrigued by her. And each one went out of his or her way to come to the aid of H.D. They formed campaigns, wrote about her, sent her work to publishers, criticized the work, encouraged it; always they stood loyally beside her. And, of course, there was Bryher, the firmest of foundations.

Pearson came on Sundays to visit while he was stationed in London during the war. A former student at Bowdoin College, he had been an economics major, then suddenly turned to a study of Nathaniel Hawthorne, who remained an interest (much to Bryher's disgust) throughout his life. Pearson transferred to English and won the William Strong Prize, one of the first of the many plums he would pocket. He attended Magdalen College at Oxford, and returned to Yale for his doctorate. After serving in the OSS in a superior position he returned again to Yale, where he was director of the undergraduate department of American studies. He became, most importantly, an advisor to the Yale Collection of American Literature. It was from this position that he first considered the work of H.D. and her group.

Pearson had endured much physical pain, most of his bones having been broken and reset, and a year spent in a hospital. He was a near cripple, supported by overwhelming ambition. It has been said of him that he was directed by his need for power. Pearson seems to have obtained this power indirectly by devotion and loyalty to the object he desired. He wished to increase the Yale holdings of contemporary American literature far beyond that of other universities. He schemed and maneuvered, and with a surprising show of strength he seems to have succeeded.

Pearson's relations with H.D. are mystifying. He did everything he could, without faltering, to further her career. It may have been that, in his fashion, he was in love with her, as certain of his letters to her exhibit a kind of adulation and regard, as if she were an extraordinarily special person both to him and to the world. From her he obtained much contact with a larger frame of interests, personal insights into the private world of artists he admired. He promised her a "shelf" at Yale, and she got it. Bryher seems to have been magnetized by him. She gave him correspondence, manuscripts, books, and probably would have given him Kenwin had he lived. Bryher never made a literary move in her own behalf without consulting him. This is an extraordinary aspect of Bryher, one never before witnessed. It has been said that she always had to be right, and gave up any literary agent who criticized her work. With Pearson she was submissive. It was he who altered and edited her texts; his word was law. But it is questionable how much help he actually was to her. His power to exert influence in public circles worked well for H.D., but his literary criticism was not always profitable for Bryher.

H.D. characteristically never wanted to be bothered by publisher's contracts or questionnaires, or any sort of mundane detail. Pearson handled it all for her. In return she gave him power of attorney for all her work. He was her literary executor, a position she had once considered for Marianne Moore. It was a chancy situation, but one that turned out quite well in the long run. With two different people, it could have been disastrous. Pearson even held a copyright to H.D.'s work.

All this gives one an example of Pearson's strength, and to H.D. and Bryher, his reliability. Certainly H.D.'s later work was helped by Pearson. He was someone to lean on, confide in, and he urged her to write in the most ingratiating manner, unlike the tactless prodding of Bryher. He continuously brought her work to the attention of his students. And it was he who would write the introduction to the *Trilogy*.

There is a description of Pearson given by Bryher that lends a piquancy to his legend. Bryher was relating to Pearson a trip H.D. had made to Stratford-upon-Avon, whereupon "Pearson became very chatty and gave me a monologue on his future career as professor . . . in politics, as writer, as critic." After speaking of Stratford "he gave me a lecture on the prologue of Romeo and quite forgetting himself said, 'now remember in the paper you bring me to . . .' so I suppose he felt I was one of his students."

Much poetry was being published during the war, partly because it took up less paper! People bought any book available; anything to *read*. Stephen Spender observed that even lesser-known poets could reckon their sales at between two and four thousand instead of in the hundreds, as would have been the case before the war.

It must be remembered that Eliot and H.D., both Americans, had chosen to remain in their adopted country during its time of mortal stress. They were repaid in that they wrote some of their best work, triumphing over circumstance, determined to continue in their profession. We have in Eliot's *Four Quartets*, "Little Gidding," his account of the bombing of London. "Burnt Norton," which had preceded these poems, was followed by the others in 1940, 1941, and 1943, written in disastrous years. H.D. wrote constantly throughout the war. Her published works were: *The Walls Do Not Fall*, dedicated to Bryher in 1942; *Tribute to the Angels*, dedicated to Osbert Sitwell in 1944; *The Flowering of the Rod*, dedicated to Norman Holmes Pearson, written in the last months of 1944. Aside from her published works, she had written *The Gift*, and begun the extraterrestrial work "The Sword Went Out to Sea." The same creative activity was shown by Edith Sitwell. It was extraordinary. Poets who had belonged to the World War I generation now found a second flowering, nourished by the great vacancies of bombed London. In 1949 *By Avon River* was published, and later dedicated to Bryher and to Robert Herring.

The Foreword to *The Walls Do Not Fall* was written by Norman Holmes Pearson. In the first paragraph he explains that "H.D. was at one time well known to all lovers of verse as one of the earliest Imagists." It was written on the publisher's statement on the page proofs and sent to H.D. She crossed out "was at one time," and wrote "IS." Ultimately the publisher's statement read: "H.D. came into prominence as one of the earliest Imagists." A more formally true declaration. Her dedication to Bryher was: "for Karnak the most perfect day of my life."

> Don't worry about your work . . . The fact is writing is the thing—it trains one to a sort of yogi or majic [*sic*] power, it is a sort of contemplation, it is living on another plane, it is "travelling in the astral" or whatever it is they are supposed to do. That is the thing.

No one else could have better described the world and work of H.D. than she herself did in this letter she wrote to a poet. She constantly nourished in her own mind what she called "the shifts and allusions" of what would become a poem. One work would give birth to another. Writing *The Gift* led to *The Walls Do Not Fall*, the first book of what would become a trilogy. This book, thanking Bryher for having taken her to Karnak in 1923, concentrates on H.D.'s interest in Egyptian history. Ending in London in 1942, it connects today and yesterday in what she called a spiritual etymology or "spiritual realism." She found no difficulty in making the association between Egypt and Bethlehem, Pennsylvania. To her they were one. "Ahead of Egypt was Christianity; Amen became, in the Bible, Christ." The book also marked her departure, rather her wish to separate herself, from her Imagist connection. She now said, "I do not want to pick out gems or be a 'clear-cut crystal.'" She enters the realm of mysteries, of oracular vision; her poetic tools are no longer evocations of Greece, or even Victorian Greece—no more the branch, the root, the stone—she is aiming for the seed and what will become the flowering of the rod. She has not "given up" Greece; she is adding Egypt and Christianity and the prophets, even the stars, to her etymology; she is searching for the Truth. She was fond of quoting from the Bible: ". . . and the truth shall make you free." As she had grown older, more and more she turned to the Bible, to Revelation, to the Gospels. Very much like Edith Sitwell, she was having apocalyptic visions.

Osbert Sitwell, reviewing *The Walls Do Not Fall* in the *Observer*, mentioned that more of this kind of work was needed. And she responded by writing in the last three weeks of May 1944, what she called a sort of "premature peace poem," *Tribute to the Angels*, dedicated to Osbert Sitwell. This was followed in December by the last book of the trilogy, *The Flowering of the Rod*. The poems were written in one emotive rush, as if she had been waiting all through the war on the walls of Troy or Thebes to proclaim "a new heaven and a new earth" she believed were about to materialize. *Tribute to the Angels* was written before D-day, before the doodlebugs fell. When they came, she loved the name of the bombs, probably making a connection with her old nickname—Dooley! When Bryher, who was frightened, sensibly wanted to leave London for Cornwall, H.D. refused, saying the bombs would not

drive her out. What she was doing was hoarding her own doodlebug; she
wanted to finish it before leaving for the safety of Cornwall. She wanted
the rod to flower. H.D. dedicated this last section to Pearson.

In "The Walls Do Not Fall" she exhorts the reader to "dare, seek, seek
further, dare more," and then

> here is the alchemist's key
> it unlocks secret doors,
>
> the present goes a step further
> toward fine distillation of emotion,
>
> the elixir of life, the philosopher's stone
> is yours if you surrender
>
> sterile logic, trivial reason;
> so mind dispersed, dared occult lore,
>
> found secret doors unlocked,
> floundered, was lost in sea-depth,
>
> sub-conscious ocean where Fish
> move two-ways, devour;
>
> when identity in the depth
> would emerge with the best
>
> octopus or shark rise
> from the sea-floor:
>
> illusion, reversion of old values,
> oneness lost, madness.
>
> Wistfulness, exaltation,
> a pure core of burning cerebration,
>
> jottings on a margin,
> indecipherable palimpsest scribbed over
>
> with too many contradictory emotions,
> search for finite definition
>
> of the infinite, stumbling toward
> vague cosmic expression
>
> . . .
>
> jottings of psychic numerical equations,
> runes, superstitions, evasions,

H.D. has written here a confession of the forays of her mind from the
past into the present when she and Arthur Bhaduri, the Brahman. had
engaged in table tipping over the William Morris table; this activity led
to Sir Hugh Dowding. She has the courage to continue the poem with a
comment on her own work:

> Depth of sub-conscious spews forth
> too many incongruent monsters
>
> and fixed indigestible matter
> such as shell, pearl; imagery
>
> done to death; perilous ascent
> ridiculous descent; rhyme, jungle,
>
> overworked assonance, nonsense
> juxtaposition of words for words' sake
>
> . . .
>
> over-sensitive, under-definitive,
> clash of opposites, fight of emotion
>
> and sterile invention—
> you find all this?

And then she offers a solution:

> Let us substitute
> enchantment for sentiment,
>
> re-dedicate our gifts
> to spiritual realism
>
> . . .
>
> prepare papyrus or parchment,
> offer incense to Thoth,
>
> the original Ancient-of-days,
> Hermes-thrice-great,
>
> let us entreat
> that he, by his tau-cross,
>
> invoke the true-magic,
> lead us back to the one-truth,
>
> . . .
>
> possibly we will reach haven,
> heaven.

After the success of the *Trilogy,* one questions why H.D. wrote *By Avon River,* later published in 1949. It is true that she went frequently to Warwickshire, and on Shakespeare's Day placed a flower in the chapel for her own Perdita. She seems to have become absorbed in this atmosphere of Shakespeare's setting: the plays that were performed were a necessity for her, a life source. She had gone to Stratford with Bryher and Robert Herring on Shakespeare's Day April 23, 1945, and to them she dedicated "Good Frend," which was included finally under the roof of *By Avon River,* along with a second part, "The Guest." "Good Friend" is based on *The Tempest.* Its uniqueness is that it stresses the character of Claribel, who is only mentioned briefly in Shakespeare's play. It was after attending Claribel's wedding in Tunis that the ship was wrecked on Prospero's shores. H.D. picks up on this and magically uses Claribel as her center. She may have identified with this Claribel, who was sent to marry a foreign king and live in a foreign land—Tunis—another exile like H.D., who came to England, married, and remained there. A second poem, "Claribel's Way to God," uses a Poor Clare nun as a starting point, yet she is the former Claribel now discovering God. This poem is much more an "arranged" figure piece, yet it contains the pearl that H.D. placed in many of her poems—Venice. It must have been on her visits to Venice that she thought so unceasingly of the Church, as symbol of the meaning of the Way, the Truth—not in any Catholic sense—but oddly, this Byzantine "La Serenissima" revived her Moravian memories. She transfigures the Byzantine and the Catholic into Moravian doctrines of the Bible and the New Testament. The very word "Claribel" carries with it a lightness. The poem may be said to correspond to Edith Sitwell's "Anne Boleyn's Song," in which two women live out their destiny, and H.D. may well have been influenced by Edith. Sitwell's poem, along with other lilting, bright, tender poems, was originally published in *Green Song, and Other Poems* (1944), dedicated to Bryher.

Certainly "The Guest" must have been written with a certain competitiveness toward Edith, as it purports to be a discussion of the sixteenth- and seventeenth-century poets, somewhat in the spirit of Sitwell's *The Queens and the Hive* or *Fanfare for Elizabeth,* extracts of which had appeared in *Life and Letters Today.* H.D. has really nothing of interest to say of her poets and she had a good deal of trouble even spelling their names, frequently consulting Pearson and Bryher. She was not in her depth in this section; she had not fancied herself Elizabethan, as did Edith Sitwell, and it shows.

It was Edith who wrote to her of *The Walls Do Not Fall* that they were "the poems of an atalanta—of a spiritual athlete." When she wrote to H.D. about her work, Edith quoted an eighteenth-century critic who said, "Wait till the words shine." Edith added, "Yours always do as if one saw them beneath deep water."

Writing from Le Lavandou, after the war where he finished his book on D. H. Lawrence, Aldington also questioned the value of *By Avon River.* He, too, liked the first poems, but told her: "With 'The Guest' you gave yourself a very difficult problem inasmuch as the texts you deal with are familiar household words to all students of poetry and you should have done as you intended, delivered it as an opening discourse to a university audience of students for whom it is admirably calculated." Then he equivocated by saying that she had gone beyond the usual scope of such a discourse and that "it really is a compact anthology of

Tudor-Stuart lyrics with a running commentary. You have extricated yourself with honour from a most difficult situation."

However, in 1955 H.D. admitted after she had been reading Wilson Knight and E. M. Butler: "They are grown-up established people. Technically, how ignorant I am, and what a bundle of dandelions my *Avon* is compared to their laurel. How happy I am with *Avon*." (And then she crossed that sentence out.) She continued: "But are they as happy as I am?"

These poems represent the high moments. In order to comprehend better what a triumph they mark, a look should be taken at the daily life of H.D. First the blackout. Then cooking over a small jet flame by candlelight. What irony that H.D., who aside from her flair at decorating a home was the least domestic of women, should now be relegated to the cooking and household chores, necessarily, by Bryher, who had not, and never did have, the simplest idea of cookery. Bryher now knew what went into an icebox and what an icebox could be used for, but she never mastered the stove. Mrs. Ash, the invaluable charlady, still did the cleaning up of the flat. Bryher was assigned the queueing and the washing up.

Evenings Perdita would come over from her flat across the street. She would darn. (Everyone during the war darned.) Bryher would polish furniture, this being before Bryher began her book *Beowulf*, no doubt. H.D. would sew on her tapestry while they listened to Mozart or Beethoven. In 1947 she wrote:

> I started a number of large ones in London while we sat around waiting for the last trump. I treasure them as they are mostly things that went off the market, three huge original Cluny designs meant for mantle-piece. They are copied from originals at Cluny museum . . . Bryher always said "but what will you DO with them?" I have just loved them and the designs of huge grape leaves, pomegranates and small animals, just kept me alive. But now I will try to finish off the odd bits and see them myself in wood frame.

It was the sort of cozy, comforting nest that H.D. reveled in. Perdita and Bryher, she was sensitive enough to realize, were desperately unhappy, each deprived of the kind of life she would have chosen. H.D. felt grateful for the uncomplicated life—uncomplicated amid bombs and destroyed buildings because she could live coolly in her cerebral dwelling surrounded by domestic objects, the sort of combination that ideally suited her. It is true that she did cast an angry eye in the direction of Richard Aldington, who was living in Hollywood at the Garden of Allah, escaping the war and basking in the sun.

"Bryher makes me laugh with her wonderful pessimism. Bryher has the 'Courage of her pessimism,' as someone said of Freud. I have not the

GUTS to be that depressed, or I would be swamped by the tide-wave," H.D. wrote to May Sarton in America.

Restless as ever, Bryher actually enjoyed venturing into the long queues, overhearing conversations, mingling with "ordinary" people, especially the tradespeople. Along with her snobbery there was a strong dash of democracy about her; it showed itself in an outward shabbiness. Restless, energetic, she divided her days between the search for food and utensils, long train trips to Eckington, where she helped select and edit *Life and Letters Today,* and finally when all other resources failed, she took up the study of Persian! It was the long evenings that literally nearly drove her crazy, the enforced confinement at night. As a song of the period went, "There's no place like home, but we see too much of it now."

Bryher, in a city pent, she whose heroes had been Sir Richard Burton, Charles Doughty—people who went out and did things—complained of the terrible boredom—not fear—boredom and inefficiency. She could no longer make her countless plans for travel, or reorganize lives. Bryher suffered from claustrophobia (this probably accounting for her dislike of snow; she, a denizen of Switzerland). One shivers at enforced confinement of even the closest of friends and lovers. But these two original, temperamental, self-indulgent, egotistical, and talented women must have suffered more than most through those long days and evenings together, a torturous time that had been most sedulously avoided in the past by H.D. Not only was H.D.'s health and mind to break down at the war's end, but something nearly unpreventable may have broken between the two, despite their continued shared dependency, loyalty, and affection. It is inevitable that suicide would be in each mind; wasn't the human race remorselessly pursuing it? Finding her literary form saved Bryher and changed the conditions of her life. She would no longer so damagingly lean on H.D. for a vision of the creative life.

A very Bryher activity was to keep chickens in London. In theory it might have worked, but in actuality the chickens ate the eggs.

"It is only sad to reflect that good intentions so frequently lead to negative results" was an axiom Bryher was to repeat from her own experience. She read in the paper that the camels in the zoo were shedding and that the zoo offered to sell clippings from their coats without coupons. Off to the zoo to the camels went Bryher and obtained clippings from the Dromedaries and Bactrians. (There she learned the camels didn't mind the air raids, but hated storms.) Off she went in a taxi with the very smelly sacks. H.D. refused to keep the sacks in the house, so they remained in the basement until Bryher was able to obtain the address of a firm in the Hebrides that would accept and weave the combings. Finally six skeins of rough and prickly wool arrived, but they proved to be too uncomfortable to wear. Osbert shared the wool with her and had a coat made that he later gave to a gamekeeper. Bryher's jacket of camel skein was too hot for her, so she finally gave it to a farming friend to wear during lambing season.

A consolation was that Bryher could write, from her intense feminism, that one good the war had done was to equalize men and women. Women had proved they could take over men's jobs. H.D., too, celebrated. "Women, WOMAN—this new aquarian age we have been told is well on the way—a woman's age, in a new sense of WOMAN."

The critical days of the war were at hand. V-bombs. One hit the London Library. Bryher, going over there to take out a book, saw the mess and immediately offered her services. They wanted to know if anyone read German. Bryher was given the task of cleaning the pages of a German encyclopedia. Despite the dust, the water, the smell of ash and wet paper, Bryher stoically helped. It was in the details of life that she was so good. The ice cream queue she found the most interesting place, "because the people in it were intent on pleasure."

There was one place special to H.D. and Bryher. It was a tea shop called the T Kettle, which H.D. had discovered when she was alone in London. It was a spinsterish sort of place except when it was patronized by shoppers from nearby Harrods, or secretaries from the offices; H.D. and Bryher ate there. Lunches and dinners were served with an emphasis on fresh well-cooked vegetables and the better cuts of meat. The T Kettle with its homely, wholesome food contrasted with the cosmopolite raffishness of their presences, their clothes, no doubt their conversation. It certainly represented their thrift. It was definitely not a Soho-style restaurant with wine and foreign food. It had simple British food that appealed to many single British ladies. Bryher became friends with the proprietors, and when during the course of the war she discovered they were losing their clientele, she gave them money to help run the shop. Finally it was forced to close. Bryher was repaid all her financial assistance, for she uses the T Kettle as the home base for the characters in the book she wrote of this period of the war, *Beowulf*. Beowulf was the name of a plaster bulldog Bryher saw in Harrods that typified for her the look and meaning of the British people under stress. In her book the dog is brought to the T Kettle, where it sits at the hearth, and even after the shop is hit directly by a bomb, the bulldog, that is, England, survives.

No greater contrast between the two friends can be found than that between *Beowulf* and the oracular poetry H.D. was writing. The important thing was that Bryher had found her medium. From now on she would write historical novels. From *Beowulf* she went to *The Fourteenth of October*, a book about the Battle of Hastings. The war had given her these two books, had inspired her to explore her own feelings about England. *Beowulf* is delightful. It brings out the human suffering amid the vivid scenes of wartime; above all, it is a story of survival, just as H.D.'s

Walls survived. Bryher had summoned all her knowledge of London war-time street life to incorporate in this book, and she does it simply and sparsely, but there is a common smell of the devastation of London and the desperate attempts of the ordinary people to survive.

Bryher wrote to a friend: "I think one arrives nowhere until one is intensely individual." With *Beowulf,* Bryher accepted her sense of herself as an individual. She also realized she could no longer go back to the old life with Kenneth Macpherson.

The hardships of war confirmed Bryher's belief that life should be easy:

> It seems to me that that is the really desirable ideal. We are all aggressive and the easier to get on with, I think, the least dangerous to our fellow citizens when we recognize this and have some aggressive outlet and then ease for the rest of the time. Most of the people I have known who have really helped have given a lot of thought to make their own days smooth, it gave them extra energy. True wisdom consists, I think, of working very hard to achieve all possible comfort and smoothness and then letting one's full energies into whatever work it is that one does.

This from the Spartan Bryher. But she always had said that "analysis was a process of learning how to conserve energy and discard the unimportant."

Until 1944 H.D. also shared the victories of the "simple" life. She continued to go to Woodhall to the Dobsons. They were using their garden as a market garden. From Woodhall they would take a cart of vegetables, eggs, flowers, fruits, and chickens up to London. First their friends would buy from them, then came a "widening circle of customers in Kensington, Chelsea, Park Lane, Berkeley Square, Knightsbridge, etc." Then in late 1944 petrol rationing tightened. The Dobsons appealed to the Lord Privy Seal, who was one of their customers, and he took it up with the Transport Minister, who turned down their plea for five gallons a week. And so it ended. But as Silvia Dobson describes it, it was a lovely funny sight to see H.D., the cautious recluse, draped atop the produce, riding into London in a cart. This was a side of H.D. she had concealed so long—the girl who had raced over fences, holding high her skirts. This was the tomboy, the careless girl who in her youth would have enjoyed just such a treat as riding on top of a cart.

It was a pity that these games releasing H.D. from her tension had to end. Silvia joined in relief work, the Save the Children Medical Mission, and sailed in convoy to Alexandria in 1944. The Greek revolution turned them back, and she went on to Egypt and Bari, working for the Yugoslav Medical Mission. Then came UNRRA (United Nations Relief and Rehabilitation Administration) in Rome, then Florence. She returned to a battered London in 1946 and continued with her market garden, writing novels and poetry. In 1957 she went to Spain and Portugal to write, helped by a private inheritance and later by Bryher's assistance. So the thread with H.D. continued.

During these last war years H.D. was telephoned by Logan Pearsall Smith, that "English bachelor from Philadelphia," as the Boston *Transcript* had called him, neglecting his frail, but elegant, contribution to literature and his connections through his sisters' marriages with Bertrand Russell and Bernard Berenson. He asked her if she would come to read John Donne to him at the apartment in Chelsea where he and his sister were staying. The exhausted, but amused, H.D. began to read to him "a page of the most gruesome worm-sermons." He asked her what she thought of it. In describing this episode to Aldington in 1951, she wrote: "Realizing he was not long for this life I felt a bit awkward—but said 'O I think it is the most COZY bit of writing I have ever come across . . . especially the worm bits." Thus ended another connection with Philadelphia and Bryn Mawr.

And then the Hendersons' flat was hit. Cole was away, but Gerald was at home. He was blinded in one eye. Bryher went immediately with friends, as was the custom, to help save bits and pieces from total destruction. Bryher writes of this in her autobiography, *The Days of Mars:* the salvaging of furniture and clothes, seeing jam pots lying broken, and silver and china destroyed—a lifetime of housekeeping. The Hendersons managed to survive the war; in 1961 and 1962 they died a year apart from one another.

H.D. claimed that Bryher had talked about suicide when they first met and she seems to have tried it in 1920 in Zermatt. H.D. told Pearson that she was always afraid Bryher would take her life during the war. One terrible night, according to H.D., Bryher "injected herself—and lay moaning on her bed." H.D. was there to help or, as she mysteriously implies, to save her.

Shortly after the war, on the anniversary of their meeting, July 17, Bryher wrote to H.D.:

> I shall be thinking of you with much gratitude for all the years, especially the blitz years, London would have been quite unendurable without the Kat and I doubt if I would ever have found my way to our work sans Kat. I miss you particularly after work, when there would be so much to discuss but I expect it is just as well we have our holidays in different places and then come back fresh . . .

All through 1945 H.D. was contributing "Writing on the Wall," chapters about her work with Freud, to *Life and Letters Today,* the last article appearing in January 1946. H.D. was increasingly taken up with her esoteric novel, "The Sword Went Out to Sea." The book had been an outgrowth of the table-tipping sessions with Bhaduri and of her near manic obsession with Lord Dowding. Nearly impossible to decipher, it is an upsetting book, as everywhere there is evidence of a disturbed consciousness. Neither *The Gift* nor "The Sword" was published in her lifetime. H.D. worked frantically on "The Sword" for years. By 1946, she had written *The Gift,* her *Trilogy,* and had begun to work on "The Guest." She had lived through a war.

Then came H.D.'s mental breakdown, in which Bryher proved her mettle and her ability to handle a very bad crisis when a woman whom she loved appeared to have lost her mind. There is no written evidence of events leading up to the breakdown; however, interpretations can be drawn from her writing. It is apparent that H.D. had overextended herself. Her euphoria is inexplicable given the wartime conditions under which she lived. Dowding had cautioned her to give up her adventures into spiritualism, especially the seances, which increasingly occupied her. The seances are evidence of a more and more frantic search into the unknown, the invisible—flights from a visible reality whose strain must have pressed upon her consciousness. It is at this time that she began tearing the bookplates out of her books, destroying those beautiful plates, so much a part of her identity, that had been designed for her by George Plank. She began moving furniture into the hall. Was she preparing for invisibility?

Silvia wished she might then have been there to help H.D. Even after H.D. was hospitalized, Silvia was told H.D. had a physical illness. H.D. was one to concentrate heavily on the person at the period he or she was closest to her, yet the absorption, the intensity would loosen, as it did between H.D. and Silvia. Thus Silvia could not have had warning of H.D.'s true condition. (Their romance, which now had turned into a friendship, would continue until the end. It was to Silvia that Bryher wrote during the last days of H.D.'s life.)

Using all the pull at her command, a determined Bryher, now fully alarmed, seized a chartered plane and flew H.D. to a clinic in Zurich.

Sunday Sept. 29, 1946

My darling Hilda,

You want to know what has happened and why you are at Kusnacht. Last Feb. you were taken very ill and for a time I think you did not know any of us. It was then that Dr Carroll—who is Irish—came to take charge. He wanted to send you to a sanatorium in England but the food and heating conditions had got so much worse that the Bear and I thought the only thing to do was to try to get you to Switzerland.

The Bear and I came ahead to find a place for you. We consulted with a great friend of Professor Freud in Basel and we found See Hof through him. I saw some other places but you would not have been happy in them, for they were like hospitals. We arranged with great difficulty to have you flown out to Zurich. He could not get a whole plane so had to agree to share with a lady who was coming out with her children.

You flew first to Paris where they had to land to re-fuel and then on to Zurich. Dr Carroll brought you out with one of the nurses. They returned to England two days later.

There are no enemy countries now. And no upheavals.

All your friends have been told that you had meningitis and that you are recovering—as indeed you are—in Switzerland, as you had to be in the mountains after the last war. All your letters have reached their destination except for the two you sent to Sir Humphrey Milford who is no longer with the Oxford Press . . .

Everybody—including Perdita—knows that you have been under a terrible strain during the war and all are waiting for you to be quite well again.

You have to make up a lot of weight that you have lost, sleep much better, and listen to all that Dr Brunner tells you—then very soon he will allow me to come and fetch you wherever you would like to go. But until you are recovered no doctor anywhere would let you leave the sanatorium for you might become very ill without proper care.

Philip [Frere] is looking after all your financial affairs, everything is being paid by him for you, the flat and all its contents are being cared for, your papers are locked up, as are your books, till the moment comes when you need them.

I beg of you only to listen to the wise counsel of Dr Brunner, eat well and sleep well, then we shall be re-united sooner. It is no question of sanity or otherwise, it is just that you, like hundreds of other English people, have suffered a terrible strain through the war and lost temporarily your memory. Switzerland is full of people being helped to be well.

Love, Bryher.

PART FIVE

Helen: I never went to Troy. Only a phantom went . . .
Messenger: What's this? Then did we toil in vain there simply
             for a cloud?

                                        Euripides, *Helen*

Deep-girdled, the sun in her hair, with that way of standing,
The print of shadows and the print of smiles
On shoulders, thighs and knees,
The lively skin, the eyes and the great eyelids,
She was there, on the banks of a Delta.
                                        And at Troy?

Nothing. At Troy a phantom.
So the gods willed it.
And Paris lay with a shadow as though it were solid flesh:
And we were slaughtered for Helen ten long years.

                            George Seferis, "Helen" (*Poems*)

CHAPTER TWENTY-FIVE

Lausanne-Lugano 1947–53

As in 1919 following the Great War, after the Second World War Bryher once again became the preserver of H.D. By the winter of 1946, H.D. felt strong enough to want to strike out on her own. Typically, Bryher set out to help her. She decided that nearby Lausanne was the right-size city. International, with historic associations, it also had the advantage of being a short railway ride from Kenwin. She scouted out what she considered was the most comfortable and suitable hotel for H.D., the Hôtel de la Paix.

In December H.D. moved into this handsome hotel, which is located on the upper slopes of the town, not far from the famed cathedral, in the midst of shops and next to the relaxed and dignified park Mon Repos. H.D. would often go to this park. Mon Repos lives up to its name. It shelters exotic aviaries and quiet paths, one of which leads up to the house in which Voltaire, that hero of Aldington, had lived. Bryher had made a wise choice, as the hotel exactly met H.D.'s needs at the time. She would winter there for the next six years. Bryher was only twenty minutes away, yet she was *away*. H.D. held to the illusion, encouraged by Bryher, that she was on her own and not a dependent. Bryher would make elaborate plans to visit H.D., but only on occasions specified by II.D.

H.D. was sixty. Her beauty was yet more bizarre, the jaw a stricken line, the cheekbones gaunt upon the lean skin. Her eyes, seldom soft, were now Cassandra-like. She looked strange. More than ever she was a woman at whom people would stare on the street. Her wizardry was intact.

Now began the prolific years of H.D.'s life, when she would write her most significant work. She wrote that she agreed with Ellen Glasgow, who had said her life began at sixty. Her productivity would be astounding. She had risen from the grave of the war, from a breakdown so serious as to have required a special treatment with injections of a chemical compound, an invention of Dr. Brunner's which Dr. Heydt insists is not to be confused with electric shock treatment. An excellent clinic and careful posttreatment care had restored her to the world. From now on there would be no lapses, if she could prevent them, in her schedule. A confidence descended on her—she believed the worst was past; she had survived to live in a place where her work would be nurtured by a conspiring seclusion.

There were no day-to-day domestic problems such as presented themselves at Lowndes Square. H.D. took her meals at the hotel. She also soon found a pleasant café where she could go for her morning coffee while her room was being straightened. She would go down to the port below the town at Ouchy (near the place where once they had made their films) and sit under a marble plaque marking the spot where Byron had sat while composing "The Prisoner of Chillon." In short, she had nothing to occupy herself with except her own writing. All legal and literary details were to be taken care of by Bryher and Pearson. Bryher even busied herself with ordering clothes for H.D. The responsibility of a daughter disappeared with the departure of Perdita for the United States.

A correspondence with Aldington now sprang up. Having left America, he was living in the South of France at Le Lavandou. In 1951 he would move to Montpellier; from there would be a final move to Sury-en-Vaux. He was just near enough now for H.D. to be aware of his unobtrusive presence; this need became increasingly important to her. Again he was her critic, her friend; the letters began to pass back and forth as if no time or lovers had intervened. Once more they needed one another. Her letters to him illumine her circumstances:

> I am snug enough with old scripts and papers, books, a few friends, the happy sound of tea shops in rain or sun, my eleven o'clock coffee or tea rather a brilliant new Dôme where the music is elegant, candelabra, concealed lighting and masses at present of gladiolus; there were sunflowers and Michaelmas daisies in rotation. There is a really charming shop called Mutrix, with a lively roof, now closed, alas, many bright umbrellas, fish in a pond . . .

Very much a description of a maiden lady's view of paradise, as indeed that section of bourgeois Lausanne still presents.

H.D. was working on "The Sword Went Out to Sea," encouraged by Aldington and Pearson, who believed that it might be the best thing she had written. Aldington suggested that with a few minor changes the book could become a best-seller! He probably based this misjudgment on H.D.'s unreal concept of the book, which shows up in a letter she wrote in January 1947 to Bryher:

> I can not tell you how funny it is, a sort of War and Peace cum the Last Days of Pompeii. It will be one fat Victorian volume, or two or three short or long short novels . . . I am on the second Vol. now I call them WINTERSLEEP AND SUMMERDREAM—sleep and dream and so-called "reality" values contrasted. I did not want to worry you with the war part but later when Cuth [Aldington] sends back the first MSS I will hope that you can find time to read it. It is also the reincarnation but on a

rather mosaic of Bulwer L. Pompeii style, scenes with the players at Delhi worked up from my Stratford experience . . . I just sit down and automatic write. I feel I have a rattling gun in my hands—whatever a rattling gun is. It is a fight to the finish for War and Peace!

H.D.'s wild description is an example of an author's delusion about the written page. "The Sword" was begun on the eve of her breakdown. It is nearly incomprehensible, as Helen Wolff, Bryher's publisher, said (in a conversation with this author) she came to believe when the manuscript was presented to her for possible publication. It is rather like attending one of the London seances. Lord Dowding, here called Lord Howell (although during the war he was Sir Hugh), is one of its heroes, and the story provides a fictional background for his belief in many worlds or "mansions" that presumably dwell beyond our sight. To his credit, Dowding was reluctant to have H.D. publish it, claiming he wished to retain his anonymity.

"The Sword" is a sort of kedgeree of spiritualism that combines H.D.'s concept of Dowding's ideas (based on his book *Many Mansions* and his lectures she had attended in London), in which the dead aviators from World War II continued to remain alive on another plane of existence, together with her own added historical personages, Vikings, Greeks, etc., who enact their fictive lives in worlds heretofore unexplored, outside or beyond the visible. Even Bryher, an opponent of all occult researches, praised it, calling the book not prose, but a series of poems. Honoring the still delicate psychic state of H.D., Bryher may have chosen prudence over criticism. A synopsis of the book is numbing. Those dead Greeks and Vikings are joined by creatures from Oberon's court! So far "The Sword" has remained in its original manuscript form, unpublished. Yet who knows, the world with its rapturous acceptance of extraterrestrial tribunes may now be prepared for H.D.'s earlier servings.

H.D.'s next enthusiasm was for the Pre-Raphaelites. She began to write "The White Rose and the Red." What H.D. really wanted was to concentrate on William Morris, as the Morris table Bryher had bought from Violet Hunt's effects (which had served in the seances) had brought this radiant genius close to her. There was also "the miracle of all that marvelous real Morris period tapestry" that had been purchased. In many ways this Morris period is close to H.D.'s own temperament. Although along with Pound and Eliot she had earlier deserted Dante Gabriel Rossetti as an influence, she had in fact been much influenced by those first purveyors of a contemporary attitude toward art and life, breaking the Victorian and bourgeois traditions of Edward Burne-Jones and his group. After all, hadn't Rossetti written that "a picture is a painted poem, those who deny it are simply men who have no poetry in their composition"? Rossetti, along with his opium, enjoyed a seance with the spirits. H.D. had probably never read Christina Rossetti's *Goblin Market*. This haunting, even terrifying, book of Christina's speaks of hidden worlds without H.D.'s consoling tapestries.

It was the *style* of the Pre-Raphaelites that appealed to H.D., and their Romanticism—she liked their cloudiness, mysticism, concentration of effect. She ignored the Pre-Raphaelite dogmatism, just as rampant as that of the academicians. She was an admirer of Elizabeth Siddal, whom Rossetti had married. Siddal committed suicide; the remorseful poet who helped wreck their marriage had thrown his poems into her grave (although later he retrieved them). The Siddal-Rossetti tragedy appealed to H.D.'s sense of drama.

H.D. while in Lausanne that winter of 1947 asked that two sets of her manuscripts from *Life and Letters Today* be sent her. These would include "Writing on the Wall," her memoir of Freud. She also wanted a pile of notebooks she had written while in Vienna. This request intimated that she wanted to work on some sections of a book she tentatively called "The Professor." H.D. reasoned that she could make use of the material from her private sessions as a patient in a creative way that would keep alive all that Freud had meant to her. Thus began to germinate the "Advent" section of *Tribute to Freud*.

In the spring of 1947 H.D. left Lausanne and moved to the Minerva Hotel in Lugano. This move would initiate a pattern for the next years. So long as she was physically able, she would spend winters in Lausanne and spring and summer in Lugano.

H.D. discovered a Lugano of the imagination. Quoting Petrarch, she wrote to Aldington: "Solitudo transalpina mea jucundissima,"[1] announcing that she subscribed heartily to these words. She thought Lugano, situated on the lake, was without exception the most beautiful place she had ever lived; she could take long boat trips—more beautiful even than the Nile Valley and the Gulf of Corinth! In praise of Lugano she would cite her newly discovered neighbor, Herman Hesse, who loved the place. She now wanted to make translations of his poetry and she needed Schmideberg's help, Bryher's also. It was as if the famous mystic had sent her his blessing for choosing to live in his location. What remains of the translation idea is a poem of Hesse's dedicated to H.D.

Her schedule in Lugano was the same as that in Lausanne: work, posting letters, buying cigarettes and stamps, shopping (she found a "Bloomsbury raffia belt, very V. Woolf"), typing, lunch, then more typing. H.D. was concluding that life was more Greek in Lugano than in Greece. She also had become very India-conscious, and after visiting Campione on the lake was under the illusion that the town of nesting villas was like a Ganges village! Modern Lugano is infested with tourists

---

[1]"The transalpine solitude is most joyous to me."

who, in their haste to reach the gambling casinos, rub off the romance. Yet the site is still beautiful and the hotels retain some of the elegance they once had. Lugano, in a curious way, reflects the Rapallo of Ezra Pound, a combination of provincialism and foreignism, of the rich and the petit bourgeois. H.D. had selected her own place; Lugano was a new "Capri," a Mediterranean town, so she pictured it, yet not too far from the familiar terrain of her earlier Switzerland.

Dorothy Richardson was sent a draft of "The Sword." (Her silence worried and puzzled H.D. Richardson never did comment to her on the book.) Then H.D. completed what she called the "first volume" of "The White Rose and the Red." She had too much material for only one volume and was now considering a second. Although she wouldn't admit it, she had gone too deeply into a subject that would interfere with her other projects, and she soon very sensibly dropped the Pre-Raphaelite book. No matter. She had found as much pleasure in its writing as she did with the needlework of her own tapestry.

Aldington was becoming H.D.'s advisor, just as in their first years together. She had persuaded Bryher to overcome her reluctance to have anything to do with Aldington, and Bryher was now helping him financially. A gift of a secondhand typewriter and much advice went to his daughter, Catha. Bryher, her educational theories still rampant, would have preferred to send Catha to the Sorbonne, inasmuch as Catha had been raised in France. Catha dispensed with this program of Bryher's by marrying a Frenchman in the Camargue, but for some years she was the subject of letters, advice, and money. "Hoping it's enough," H.D. continued to send Aldington cautious sums of money.

In 1949 H.D. was reminiscing about their early days at Mecklenburgh Square, adding that she had always recognized the enormous amount of work Aldington had accomplished. She hadn't minimized it, only she had to do her own work in order to protect herself by keeping "even with Ezra," jostled by her fear of being neglected. Her autobiographical novel had been "on the hob" for thirty years, ever since she had begun to write the story in Cornwall in 1918. She believed, so she told Aldington, that she had written an authentic Lawrence, and it pleased her. The book, which she called "Madrigal," had been rewritten the last summer she was in Vaud (1939).

> I do think I have a very authentic Frederico, [Lawrence] and that pleases me as I did not want to let all that go, without a sort of hail and farewell. I did the book the last summer in Vaud, 1939, but I left the Mss there and was about to destroy it with some other old things, but I could not; so I boiled it down and tightened up the last chapters . . .

Aldington in reply mentioned Lawrence, commenting that he was now out of print. It may have been the presences of Lawrence and Aldington that inspired H.D. by 1948 to complete "Madrigal." Yet it was not until 1953 that she got around to sending Aldington her manuscript. His reply was what she wished to hear:

> It is awfully good, Dooley, really good, authentic and concentrated, better than the equivalent chapters in *Aaron's Rod* where Lorenzo was in one of his fits and guying us all.
>
> You bring out splendidly L's mimicry and you were right to do so. It was something much more than monkey tricks, because he could also do it on paper, when it becomes genius. It was that plus his refusal to take people at their own valuation and his seeing through their self-deceptions which made him so hated . . .
>
> I finished reading Madrigal with a temp of about 101 which accounts for the fact that towards the end I found myself rather exhausted, with the intensity of all those self-absorbed emotionalists.

Aldington suggested turning it into a three-act play. He also told her that his secretary, Alister Kershaw, liked it very much. Then with a typical Aldington emphasis, he went on to discuss price and sales.

After considering the manuscript in a cooler fashion, he next wrote her that he thought it far above her other prose. "It seems to me just as well written as Virginia Woolf, much more interesting and 'human' and truly poetical."

Somehow between 1949 and 1951, H.D. found time to write "The Mystery," a story about the early Moravians and their leader, Count Zinzendorf. This story is a lengthy listing of names connected with Moravians, of castles, nuns, sisters, St.-Germain—a story of a religion; yet if read in its natural cadence, it reveals an early development of the form of her later poetry. The story is so personal, involuted, concerned with people unknown who appear as if from out of ancient walls, that there is no way to clarify the tale in a practical way. Yet it has, despite the confusion, H.D.'s distinctive voice. "The Mystery" is a prelude to *Helen in Egypt* and the final *Hermetic Definition*. H.D. had begun to wrap herself in the medium's scarves and veils that would finally assume the visible and craftsmanlike shapes of her last works.

After completing "The Mystery" in 1951, H.D. went to New York to visit her daughter, now Mrs. John Schaffner. When there, her old friend Mary Herr drove her on to Bethlehem. This was a significant return for her, signaling as it did the completion of two books whose tribal center had been Bethlehem. *The Gift* had been her initial confrontation with Moravianism; it had also included an intimate family portrait. "The Mystery" is the echo of another voice, calling ancestors, as later *Helen* would re-create the ghosts of her past and from a foreign city invoke her ancestors.

Perdita had gone to New York City in 1946, where she took out United States citizenship papers. Bryher had urged her to leave Europe, warn-

H.D. and Perdita, 1952,
on Lake Lugano.
(Beinecke)

Cecil Gray and Norman
Douglas on' Capri, ca.
1948. *(Courtesy of The
British Library)*

H.D., Norman Holmes Pearson, Bryher at Yale, 1956. *(Beinecke)*

Richard Aldington and Netta P
ca. 1940s. *(Beinecke)*

Dr. Erich Heydt with
colleagues at a congress
in Paris. *(Courtesy of
Dr. Erich Heydt)*

Bryher, ca. 1950s, at Anticoli, home of Kenneth Macpherson near Rome. (*Photograph by Islay Lyons*)

H.D.'s copy of her first book, *Sea Garden,* 1916; on flyleaf Frances Gregg has transcribed "Hermaphroditus," one of her own poems in homage to H.D. *(Courtesy of Oliver Wilkinson)*

ing Perdita her life could be smothered by herself and H.D. "We would eat you up!" she told Perdita.

In 1950 Perdita married a literary agent, John Schaffner, for whom she had been working. They proceeded to establish the John Schaffner Literary Agency in their home, one of those rare New York City clapboard houses, now a landmark. "Very Olde New York," wrote Bryher to H.D.

The Schaffner household became one of literary enterprise combined with raising a family of four children, born between 1950 and 1960. Children, manuscript reading, and the entertainment of clients were part of Perdita's day. Having assimilated the work habits of her "two mothers," as she would call them, she set aside a period each day for her own writing. Perdita now is called upon to write prefaces to new editions of her mother's books, while she continues with her own writing.

Two of the sons, Valentine and Nicholas, are published authors. The daughter, Elizabeth Bryher, is an artist. Perdita had repeated, remarked H.D. toward the end of her life, the pattern of her own mother, with three boys and a girl. H.D. would now see in the Schaffner household fresh rewards of her own literary creativity. The youngest son, Timothy, wrote on the walls of the third floor shared by the children in their East Hampton, Long Island, country house: "We are the Sitwells of today!"

H.D.'s "solitudo transalpina" in Lugano was sometimes interrupted by visitors from the outer world. Bryher and the Bear, Schmideberg, would visit her, staying at H.D.'s hotel, now the Bristol. They were cautious not to disturb her precious work schedule, but even their presence, though welcome, was an interruption. Around H.D., everyone was inclined to tiptoe. The little maids silently picked up the breakfast tray she had left outside her door. The waiters in the dining room solicitously took her order. Bryher and the Bear mostly kept to themselves, although there were daily invitations to H.D. for walks and meals. Even Perdita's visits tended to throw H.D. off-center. Perdita was solicitous of her mother, almost overly so. Whatever hours or occupations suited H.D., those Perdita would follow. The oracle would speak first; the others would uphold the silence. When beckoned, they scampered; when dismissed, they turned away. What is so astonishing is that H.D. showed no surprise at this obeisance. Her love existed for others but it tended to show its face only when the lady so wished. It was a sublime sort of selfishness, or dedication, to use a gentler word; it brought no alienation from loved ones. The priestess, "sorceress of words," as Isis is called, held within her presence an allure irresistible to mortals.

After the breakfast tray went outside the door, H.D. would go back to bed. Propped up on pillows, she would lie in a half dream for another hour (very like her heroine in "Murex" in the early *Palimpsest*). "I loved this waking dream in the half-stupor of early morning; I was perhaps in-

clined to over-do this waking-dream state then. I appreciated these little
calls, of Bear and Fido but inwardly resented the interruption. I was
only half-sorry when they left. I began almost at once, the *Helen* sequence."

In 1948 *The Pisan Cantos* had been sent to her by Ezra Pound's publishers, New Directions. There is no doubt that these cantos were the fer-
ment on both the conscious and the subconscious levels of what would
become H.D.'s own book of cantos, *Helen in Egypt*. She wrote to Viola
Jordan that she found Ezra's cantos heartbreaking. There were "really
more lines of sheer beauty in the Pisan than in any of his work."

The influence of those meetings in the British Museum tea shop would
repeat itself in far-off Lugano. The early "Hermes" would change form;
Helen in Egypt would begin to make herself felt. Ezra's unseen hand
would make the corrections on the new page. His genius would challenge
her into competition, his evocation of the past would become a lure.
If Canto LXXIX refers to H.D. as his "dryad," his "lynx," his attendant
at the pools of September (her month), if she was to "guard my vine-
yard," as she believed the canto indicated, then she must prove herself a
worthy inheritor of these duties. (The Pound scholar Wendy Flory does
not believe this canto refers to H.D. She accepts the suggestion that
Pound is writing about his wife Dorothy Shakespear.) H.D., although nowhere is there written evidence from her, only innuendoes, must have
considered herself the inspiration for this canto. She was Pound's "lovely
lynx." Physically, the description suits H.D., to whom such nouns as
"lynx" and "dryad" had been attached, much more than the restrained
Dorothy Pound. Pound in these cantos referred so frequently to Botticelli's "Primavera" that H.D. thoughtfully mailed a book to his publisher, James Laughlin, containing details of the Botticelli painting so
that Pound might have a copy of the original in his room at St. Elizabeth's Hospital, where he was now incarcerated. And H.D. herself was
living a second springtime. More frequently in her classical town she
consulted her copy of Dante. As the several years of writing and rewrit-
ing *Helen in Egypt* passed, Pound would never be out of her thoughts.

There was, nevertheless, another influence that played a primary role
in the writing of *Helen*.

In 1949 H.D. was visited by E. M. Butler. Eliza M. Butler, a discovery
of Bryher's who had sent Bryher a fan letter, has written a unique autobiography, *Paper Boats*. In this book she tells of her upbringing by a
governess, her schooling in Germany, and finally, through her competence, of being made Schroeder Professor of German at Cambridge. On
the surface, the career of a balanced, intelligent woman, but Butler
confessed she would have preferred to have been an explorer. Throughout her life she took trips to exotic places and, at the time H.D. knew
her, was preparing to go off to a remote part of India. She lived with a

woman friend whom she called "Squires," and they kept house in Cambridge. Later, Butler departed Cambridge for the University of Manchester. She wrote biographies of Byron, Goethe (dedicated to H.D.), and Heine. Her underlying interest, however, was psychological in origin and centered on the esoteric. The study of the Faust legend with its attendant rituals of magic and myth was particularly suited to her, and her book *The Fortunes of Faust* is a brilliant consideration of the legend. She also wrote a novel, *Silver Wings*. These two books were to be major influences on *Helen in Egypt*.

When the two women first met in 1949, neither book had been published, but Butler must have discussed with H.D. Goethe's use of the legend of Helen's having fled to Egypt and her double appearing on the walls of Troy. Butler also emphasized the ambiguity of Helen as described by Goethe. In *The Fortunes of Faust* she writes that "the first scene of his Helen-act . . . is one of the most fascinating ghost-stories in all literature; indeed only *The Sense of the Past* by Henry James can be compared with it for subtlety." (Apparently taking her clue from Butler, H.D. decided then to read Henry James.) Butler continues: "The state of mind of Helen is the crux of the situation, a dream-like state of mind, into which doubts of her own reality intrude and bewilder her."

> Can it be memory? Is Illusion seizing me?
> Was I that woman? Am I still the same? Am
> I yet to be
> The dream and terror of city-wrecking men?
>
> Goethe

Then Mephisto in the guise of Phorkyas

. . . begins to recapitulate her past history, slyly insinuating her essential unreality, since she had been seen in Troy and Egypt at one and the same time. She is distressfully uncertain herself as to which of the two she is: the virtuous wife who (according to some Greek legends) remained hidden in Egypt during the Trojan episode, or the fatal beauty . . .

PHORKYAS: And then they say that from hollow Shades
Achilles too was joined in passion to thee,
Who earlier loved thee despite all Fate's decrees.

HELEN: Eidolon I and Eidolon he, yes we were wed;
It was a dream the works themselves proclaim the truth,
I vanish hence, a dream now to myself.

[Butler continues] . . . but the tragic irony of her situation remains: feeling and thinking as a real woman, she is but a shade, and one perhaps who has never had a real existence except in the minds of men, strange, beautiful, mythological being.

It was Butler who taught H.D. how to *realize* the meaning of the *double,* an idea she had already encountered in the Stesichorus version of the legend, which had Helen living in Egypt, not Troy. Following Butler's lead, in reference to Goethe's Helen, H.D. developed in her own poem the ambiguities that pursued and wearied the "strange, beautiful, mythological being" in her search for her identity.

In his introduction to *Helen in Egypt,* Horace Gregory quotes her as expressing "a wish to make real to myself what is most real." Had not H.D.'s sessions with Freud been a search to establish her mislaid identity?

(Whatever the direction of her research, H.D. has, in fact, re-created the scenes and people from her own life—imaginary, suspended, hallucinated, real, or shelled from the unconscious. Of the characters who appear in *Helen,* Achilles is her war hero, Lord Dowding; Paris is the doctor at the Küsnacht sanatorium, Erich Heydt, who would befriend and captivate H.D.; Theseus, who solved the puzzle of the labyrinth, is Freud; Menelaus is Aldington. In "Winter Love," a poem in her last book there is an envoi to *Helen,* in which Ezra Pound appears as Odysseus.)

Butler's influence on H.D. extended into her novel *Silver Wings.* This is a second-rate novel; only a creative eye could recognize its possibilities as a model. *Silver Wings* is one of those literary puzzles in which the parts never fit or come together. Events are executed and explained . . . but is the explanation true? Did the events really occur? One person relates these events and gives his explanation, and thus we proceed through several interpretations of what may, or may not be, the real story. Finally an explanation of what has really occurred is given by someone whom we have every reason to believe. This presumably is the final truth. But is it? Are we not finally returned to a realm, which would be seized upon by H.D., where the dead dream their dreams? And who can read them?

In gratitude, H.D. wrote to Butler that she could not have written *Helen in Egypt* had it not been for *Silver Wings.* Finally in 1953, when she mailed the first completed cantos to Bryher—for H.D.'s book, like those of Dante and Pound, is written in cantos—she tells Bryher that at last in *Helen in Egypt* she has set *Silver Wings* to music.

H.D. confessed that Helen was her alter ego, that only through Helen could she remain alive. She could endure anonymity, solitude, so long as she could stay alive to complete the Helen sequence. Her endurance lasted from 1952 to 1956, through several serious illnesses. In 1953 she considered the book complete, but she wisely realized additional prose explanatory introductions needed to be attached to the separate books that comprise the whole. Curiously, she only realized this necessity for prose introductions after she had made a recording of *Helen in Egypt* in a studio in Zurich. This recording now gives us the pleasure of listening to the cultivated transatlantic voice of the poet.

Helen in Egypt is in certain ways a quest for sexual identity. H.D. is asking herself what her sexual feelings were toward the people who appeared in her life, and what her effect was on others. The interior plot of Helen concerns H.D.'s attempt to explain her relationships with other people. This search turns out to lead to another *Silver Wings*. The myth about Helen is the myth about herself. Had she really lived in America, or in Europe? Troy or Egypt? Where had dwelt the real H.D.? All through the war this question troubled her, the loyalty of an exile, perplexity of a lost nativity. During the war she had attempted to relieve this spatial anxiety by writing about her childhood in America. In *Helen* it was the Greece of her early poetry that she wanted to relate to the Egypt of her maturer intellectual interests.

In *Bid Me to Live* H.D. had announced her determination to tell what had happened to her during the Great War. *Palimpsest* with its separate stories repeats the biographical pattern. She finally summarizes her sexual and emotional difficulties, her wisdom and her loss, in the formidable *Helen*. In each of her former books she had told a different story (as *Silver Wings* does), and yet the plot is the same, but the variations make the difference, and therein lies her talent. *Helen in Egypt,* although difficult, narcissistic, cloudy, obsessive, is high theater. H.D. sets herself up beside Euripides. The book gathers its distinction, apart from the necessary and practical influence of Butler, from the inspired *Pisan Cantos* of Pound.

By instinct, H.D. had found a mature way back stylistically to the "early H.D." Bryher encouraged this return, partly because it was with "the early H.D." that she had fallen in love. (At this time Pound also was searching for his early shadows, letting them fall across his melancholy, late poems.)

That *Helen* is an improvement over the war poetry, *Trilogy*, there is no question. H.D. is returned to the lands that had captured her imagination, and once there she moves with greater surety and control. She is among the scenery and props of her youthful writing—scarves, sheathes, sandals, flowers, islands, sand, and ships. She is on familiar ground, and her writing now shows the rewards of a long apprenticeship. She is an older Helen, wandering in her private haunts, with her sandals securely strapped. When Bryher received the final copy from H.D.'s sanatorium at Küsnacht in 1956 she lovingly wrote: "I think the last poems of the Helen sequence are your major work." H.D. considered that with *Helen* she had repaid her debts—to Freud, Heydt, Pound, Aldington, the men who had helped her create and resolve her own myth.

CHAPTER TWENTY-SIX

The Bryher Path

Bryher, never one to remain long in one place, particularly after a war's confinement, had flown off to America in January of 1947. She was divorcing Kenneth and would receive her decree in February of that year. Bryher adored the flight with all its pleasurable delays. She wrote: "It was almost my ideal of life, flipping up and down all over continents."

She found Macpherson "very young, very slim, but has got chubby cheeks and baby blue eyes like an American, or one of the Erotes on a Greek vase." He was living among Peggy Guggenheim's collection of paintings and sharing a house with her. Peggy Guggenheim has written about him in her autobiography, *Out of This Century*—as with others before her, his charm and sympathy had conquered. She ignored his faults, which included an elegant form of opportunism, and instead enjoyed the spectacles he could provide. Bryher never mentions Peggy. As a survivor she was now interested in food, which she decided was more important than culture. She also commented that old "Alexandrine" New York had departed.

Bryher discovered that Kenneth was, underneath the princely window dressing, "very sad, disillusioned and more mature." He didn't want the divorce and wanted once more to be with her. But Bryher was learning to be independent, both of H.D. and Kenneth. This may well have been because at last she had found herself in writing her historical novels. *Beowulf* would soon be published in Paris. *The Fourteenth of October* was nearly finished, and would be accepted by the distinguished editors Kurt and Helen Wolff, of the Pantheon Press. (Sylvia Beach disliked this book. She said she was sure it was beautiful, but she couldn't read historical novels and the characters weren't real.)

Bryher continued to analyze Kenneth, whom she found profoundly disillusioned with the States. She believed that he lived like a hermit, which to her meant that he wasn't attempting to employ his natural talent. She wrote H.D.: "I don't mind if people have a psychological blockage—it can happen to any of us. It is if it's a conscious rejection of responsibility that annoys me." She also mentioned that Kenneth—from whom H.D. had detached herself, because his ideas and prepossessions no longer interested her, in fact bored her—had spoken of her constantly.

Then there was the traditional meeting with Marianne Moore, the person in the United States (besides Perdita) of whom Bryher was fondest:

> She terrified me, she was so very queer about her mother. The mother was thought to be dying of cancer and in such agony Marianne wanted the Dr. to do something, as the mother could neither eat nor speak, and could eat nothing, because she could not eat if Mother could not eat, and thus got rashes and kidney trouble and pains. Now she will only eat her mother's diet—raw vegetable juice. Really I was frightened about Marianne. But she is upset over the worldliness of her niece!

Bryher also saw Harold Doolittle, whom she much respected. She always got along with businessmen. His finances were "immaculate"—the highest praise. At this time (1947) he was beginning to buy cows and wished to retire to the country to raise them. This he eventually did. His family wanted to remain in Pittsburgh, but Harold "lives for his cows!"

No sooner had Bryher returned to London, to the darkened lonely streets, the sad flat, than she was off to the Caribbean with Robert Herring and Schmideberg. This would be the beginning of nearly ten years with Schmideberg as a companion, hostage, and finally a dependent. Before leaving, Bryher secured the address of a dentist in Jamaica from Dorothy Richardson (as the Miriam of her own *Pilgrimage*, Richardson had worked for a dentist now retired there!).

Herring, ultimately lazy, adored the Caribbean; Bryher liked bits of it, but decided the climate wasn't conducive to work and that there were, which was true, a lot of South of France sort of people around, a comment of opprobrium. The Riviera had never been a "serious" resort for the Kenwinites, nor had any of them in their gilded days felt compelled to join the international society described by Maugham and Fitzgerald. Uniquely, Bryher decided that Barbados reminded her of Cornwall—it may have been the combination of wet weather and tropical sun. She also learned that in Barbados Sir Walter Ralegh's son had been buried, and she wrote a very good poem called "Young Rawley," which she sent to H.D. Had Bryher forced herself to remain longer in the Caribbean, she might have produced another regional historical novel.

Bryher's next piece of news, which caused no comment from H.D., was that T. S. Eliot had been awarded the Order of Merit and Vita Sackville-West had been made a Companion of Honour. Several months later, Edith Sitwell would be made an honorary doctor of literature, and Bryher mentioned that Edith now wished to be addressed as Dr. Sitwell.

During the early 1950s on one of her trips to the United States, Bryher had another of her enjoyable conversations with Harold Doolittle. This time she learned to her surprise that H.D. was a wealthy woman in her own right. Now she chose to speak out to H.D. about money. She had al-

ways paid all bills willingly, but the idea of money idling away in a bank
was too much for her:

> I am afraid I am rather shocked, and almost a little angry with you. I
> heard from your brother. I think you don't realize it but you have over
> £ 50,000 tucked away with him in good American dollars and he is
> worried *because you never spend any of it,* and if anything should hap-
> pen to you, due to death duties, the American government would take
> about half of it. Now you could buy yourself a car and hire a permanent
> chauffeur or have a maid. And you must try to give people a bit more,
> and larger tips. Why you've got almost as much as I have. You can't go
> on asking about cheap pensions and living like thirty years ago as a stu-
> dent. And for heaven's sake, start spending some money, you can't take it
> with you.

Together with Bryher's 1940 settlement on her, H.D. in today's terms
would have been worth several million dollars.

Somehow the idea had been instilled in H.D. that she was impoverished. This dated from the early London days, yet even then an allowance had been given to her by her parents and this continued through
her marriage to Aldington. True, most of her friends at that time had little money, and the Lawrences in particular continually needed help.
From time to time funds from Amy Lowell were arranged for Lawrence
by H.D. The question of money had been raised by H.D. in her sessions
with Freud, though she is not detailed about what Freud did say on this
subject. Her checkbook had been one of the first of her personal effects
H.D. demanded the first time she had been brought to Küsnacht for
treatment after the war breakdown. On her own, she would have lived in
the cheapest of flats and spent meager amounts on food. Cigarettes she
considered to be her extravagance. There was nothing lavish about her—
and yet she showed generosity toward her friends. After H.D. met
Bryher and realized the extent of her riches, there is no doubt she was
impressed. Who could be as rich as the Ellermans? Not even Amy Lowell. After their relationship had been established, it was natural for
Bryher to assume the financial obligations. This, in turn, gave Bryher
more power over H.D., and such an assumption pleased Bryher's own
fondness for handling and dispensing money.

In reality there was this other side to the story. H.D. was in fact extremely well-off. Her brother managed her affairs superbly, and after the
sale of family property in New Jersey she was a rich woman. There is the
ring of the miser when H.D. writes Aldington that as she cannot get
funds through to Switzerland and is only living on an income, which she
implies is small, that she will be able only to send him one hundred dollars
a year. After much hesitation, she continued to do so. Ezra Pound always
thought H.D. lived off Bryher and that was the main reason for her
remaining with Bryher. In fact, Bryher was constantly sending checks to

H.D., which were usually hoarded. At the same time H.D. was very thoughtful about pointing out to Bryher writers who deserved financial aid.

Kenneth had no qualms about spending money. Divorced, by 1949 he had moved to Capri, where he was installed in a villa given him by Bryher. He there attended the aging Norman Douglas, also a Bryher dependent. Perdita visited him on Capri. And she had her brief meeting— the first and last—with Cecil Gray, her father, who would die in a few years. At that time Gray was known as Don Cecilio, the reigning don of music. He lived resourcefully with a former opera singer, dined and drank rather too much.

Later Bryher assisted Kenneth in renting another villa outside Rome and an apartment in Rome near the Coliseum, both of which he shared with his friend, the photographer Islay Lyons. Then, tiring of the Roman environment, with the further help of Bryher, they moved to a villa in the province of Siena, where Macpherson died prematurely in 1971. (Islay still lives there today.) Bryher enjoyed her visits with Islay and Kenneth. "Highlanders have the gift of place," she decided. They existed in a graceful atmosphere she was as incapable of providing for herself as much as she was of feeling any jealousy. Whenever she visited Islay and Kenneth her letters show her to be blissfully happy.[1] She even briefly stopped worrying about the upkeep of Kenwin as she admired Kenneth's improvements on the property she had bestowed.

Bryher's letters all through the 1950s are filled with worry about the expenses of Kenwin. Boiler repairs, heat, a gardener asking for higher wages, a maid leaving. She may have lectured H.D. about her miserliness, but in Bryher the anxiety about money took another form. She was perfectly ready to spend money on anyone but herself, and as she thought continually about money (mainly because money became a game for her, an objective around which her active mind could circle), naturally her peculiar monetary worries must have rubbed off on others, causing a permanent uneasiness. With H.D. it took the form of a constant threat of displacement. Like many manipulators, Bryher enjoyed creating a sense of suspense. There was never any question of impoverishment, but she liked to pretend there was.

Bryher was also hostess now for Dr. Schmideberg, who had an extended invitation to Kenwin. Bryher appreciated and respected him and he was a fellow worshiper of psychoanalysis, about which they could make many conjectures. But the sad truth was that like so many she had cared for, with the exception of H.D., he drank. Bryher's abstemious self

---

[1] "I like this austere and wolf haunted landscape of the Sabine hills . . . And I had a curious feeling that I knew this place centuries before. Perhaps not." So she wrote to H.D. in 1951.

had been curiously dedicated to drunkards. Schmideberg was intelligent, intuitive, amusing, elegant; she admired him enormously. He provided her with treats of conversation and wit. She wasn't lonely at Kenwin when the Bear was in residence.

For a long time the extended visits of the Schmidebergs were anticipated and enjoyed. It is very sad that Schmideberg's wine consumption got out of hand. Bryher began to feel the weight of his problem. She was so concerned about Kenwin and its inhabitants that she finally reached a peak of near hysteria, unusual for her. She threatened to sell the place to Charles Chaplin or Anne Morrow Lindbergh or rich Egyptians, all of whom she learned were looking for property in the vicinity. Then she threatened to cut the place up into flats. Bryher was chasing around her kennel like a maddened Fido. She wanted *out*. After all, H.D. had performed a disappearing act. Bryher was terrified that the responsibilities of Kenwin would prevent her from writing. Pathetically, she wrote to H.D. that she finally had a compliment. "This morning the Protestant-Italian maid from the hills said to me firmly, 'it is Ascension Day, shall you be working?' *No maid has ever asked me if I was working."*

That little maid, Inez, remained with Bryher until Bryher's death. The nagging problems of the household would soon solve themselves. Bear would become ill and go to Küsnacht. Bryher would find research for her books an acceptable reason for her travels. She began to write steadily. Soon she would accept Kenwin and its winter heating bills as a necessity, and her life would go on, until it ceased at Kenwin. The unnecessary battles and worries were postponed.

Although Bryher returned again and again to England and to Cornwall and the Scillies, it was apparent that H.D. never wished to return to London. The memories of the city must have terrified her. And of those who were close to her, Aldington never returned to London, nor did Kenneth. Ezra Pound, after his release from St. Elizabeth's, visited England only once more to pay his respects to Eliot in Westminster Abbey. Lawrence had never returned.

Meanwhile Bryher continued to keep up with her pets, Marianne Moore and Edith Sitwell. From one of her American trips she reported that Marianne said she had taken more pride in passing the test for a driver's license than she had from her poetry. In 1950 Marianne remarked of Eliot's receiving the Nobel Prize that "the humility of his Nobel-ness weighs him down." Marianne had been seeing Ezra, whom she found crazily abusive. In her dress, Marianne was looking "smarter and smarter." She confided to Bryher that she had been interviewed by the "Morgue of Time" (Alden Whitman), who told her that Bryher wasn't as good as she was supposed to be, that is, good in the sense of writing books. Bryher agreed with him.

Edith Sitwell was always material for a story. Bryher reminded H.D.

of the honors bestowed on her contemporaries, thus creating in H.D. a natural arrogance mixed with jealousy. But Bryher needled for a reason. She wanted her beloved Kat, "the Queen of Song," to exert herself and obtain the honors she deserved. Bryher unswervingly promoted H.D.'s cause, as did Norman Holmes Pearson, and they were each successful in the pursuit. But at the time of Edith's elevation to Dame Commander, Order of the British Empire, in 1954, H.D. could only be consoled by Bryher's story about a request for a poem coming to Edith from Marya Zaturenska, and Edith's reply that she should have been addressed as Dame Edith because, "The Queen has made me a Lady." Bryher also continued for H.D.'s amusement: "She has got it AT LAST. Her full title on envelopes is now Dame Edith Sitwell, D.B.E., D. Litt. She is out of her mind with joy. She says it is the happiest day of her life." Then Bryher urged a reluctant H.D. to write Edith, congratulating her.

In 1954 Bryher went off to India with Kenneth and Islay Lyons, departing from Kenwin and its responsibilities. As always, her solution to her own problems was a trip. Bryher had a positive mania for making and unmaking travel plans; India required all her resources, and she responded nobly. She again had a marvelous time buying rugs, shawls, looking at sunsets, mountains, admiring Islay's photographs, and disapproving the Victorian remnants that still littered India. She would have made a splendid travel writer. She knew the history of each place she was in, and yet she never permitted her knowledge to overcome her aesthetic reactions. Like any good travel writer, she was alert to the humor of the situation—she could move rapidly from a description of the beauty of the horned moon to comment on how many hours it took to change money.

Bryher's need was for a life that could be built upon and around personages. As H.D. once said, "she had an uncanny ability for vicarious enjoyment." Since H.D. was no longer available, she turned, among others, to Edith Sitwell. She needed a "family" to take care of. All her life she attempted to establish this family with Kenwin as its base. The difficulty had been that she depended on a circle of intense individualists who would not for long permit themselves to be contained within a "family pattern." It is true that Perdita and her husband and children remained faithful through the years, but the others found themselves in various countries, occupied with their own pursuits and pleasures. Bryher could no longer be her father; she could no longer be master of the ship. However, she was not one to be long deprived of her resources.

Besides Edith, there were the faithful Sylvia Beach and Adrienne Monnier. Bryher went to the 1959 exposition in Paris entitled Les Années Vingt, which celebrated youthful days in Paris and was a terrific success. She wrote to H.D.: "It is most beautifully done with everyone we knew and many we did not. Your picture is up between Hymen and Heliodora with Cummings on top of the board." She went on to say that whenever they walked in the street people murmured, "C'est Mademoiselle Beach!" Sylvia Beach came frequently to visit Bryher at Kenwin. They always got along splendidly, despite Beach's inability to read Bryher's novels.   Their friendship was based on the admiration they shared for women who had done much to help others.

Shortly after her celebratory trip to Paris, Bryher was once again in London. Here occurred one of those frequent incidents in Bryher's life that resulted from her "sensible," unplumaged dress. "I went to Harrods this morning and as I had a suitcase said I would wait for a receipt after buying some towels, in case they asked me to open it. 'Ah well, you see Madam, you dress and talk like we do and they think you are staff shopping in unauthorized hours . . .'" Ever concerned about H.D.'s career, she went on to advise her to send the poet and protégé of the Sitwells, Alberto Lacerda, her books of Selected Poems, as he was going out to Brazil for two months on a lecture tour.

In January 1960 Bryher discovered that Romaine Brooks and Natalie Barney, whom Rémy de Gourmont in 1912 addressed as the "Amazons" in his famous Letters to the Amazon, were in Lausanne, having arrived there from Romaine's retreat on the Riviera. They were both getting on to ninety. "But nothing seems to daunt these old ladies," said Bryher, adding that Romaine's great friend was the octogenarian Somerset Maugham.

> Romaine was wonderful, she looks just the same though she must be well over eighty. She only has a little trouble with her eyes and can't manage books, reads Time as it gives her the news in brief. She refused to leave Fiesole [Romaine had been there all during the war] as apparently she is very naive about politics and poor Natalie refused to leave her and suffered horribly because Natalie likes people and good food and they did not dare to speak to anybody and the food gave out. She has written a description of it all but people were against it as she was a bit muddled over the Mussolini affair . . . I beg her to let me have all her mss.

So much consideration had been given to the work of those whom she admired that a reminder is necessary of the number of books Bryher herself wrote between 1948 and 1972. There are twelve of them. Modest as she always was about her work, she delighted to repeat the bad reviews. She quoted from the London Times, which said of Gate to the Sea (1958): "Bryher does not display the literary gifts to provide the abstract poetic analogy; her language is jerky and unmelodious; her characterisation too thin." H.D. suspected that Bryher wasn't satisfied with her work, and certainly Bryher had to put up with much criticism from her friends who wanted her to add sex to her themes. They even felt that with a little sex in her writing she could produce a best-seller in the tradition of the more popular historical novels. But Bryher stuck to her guns. She was a historian, not a sex queen. And she was quite right. Young people who were finding themselves interested for the first time in history, not fiction, read her books. They are convincing entertainment for an early age group. Historians have remarked how in their youth they got their first taste of the excitement that could be found in history by reading Bryher's novels.

And it must not be forgotten that Bryher had written not only countless reviews for *Life and Letters Today*, but also earlier books printed for the most part privately, which covered a large range of subjects: poetry, literary criticism, autobiography, geography, Russian film.

Thus writing, travel, friendships, philanthropy, and unceasing, if frequently absent, care of H.D. kept Bryher reasonably occupied. She also enjoyed her visits to the Schaffner household and, although not maternally inclined, would see to a new layette, a handsome present for the new child. She considered the children her own grandchildren.

With her life ordered according to her own pattern, Bryher was still prepared for the demands suddenly created by a crisis in the life of H.D. Bryher might complain about life not being an easy place for little dogs, but she had also written: "There is something to be said for confusion and upheaval sometimes: I don't think I like peaceful surroundings very much." She was not to be threatened by peace so long as H.D. needed to be guided through her imaginary difficulties and helped over what now loomed as a very real hurdle.

PART SIX

Kennst du das Land, wo die Zitronen blühn,
Im dunkeln Laub die Gold-Orangen glühn,
Ein samfter Wind vom blauen Himmel weht,
Die Myrte still und hoch der Lorbeer steht,
Kennst du es wohl?
  Dahin! Dahin
Möcht' ich mit dir, o mein Geliebter, ziehn.

      Goethe, *Wilhelm Meister*

You know the realm where citrus blooms,
And golden oranges in dark foliage glow,
A gentle wind blows from blue skies,
Still is the myrtle and the laurel stands high,
You know it well?
  There, there
Would I with you, oh my beloved, go.

    (translated by Richard Wellish)

CHAPTER TWENTY-SEVEN

Küsnacht

The felicitous "transalpine" tenor of H.D.'s days was abruptly interrupted in January 1953 when, now aged sixty-seven, she was taken to the
Clinique Cécile in Lausanne for an operation. It was an abdominal intes-
tinal occlusion, and they removed a section of her intestines; had H.D.
not had the operation, she would have died. After four months she returned to the Hôtel de la Paix; then in May she was back at the clinic for
another operation. She convalesced until July, when Bryher decided to
take her to Dr. Brunner's Nervenklinik in Küsnacht, just five miles out of
Zurich. H.D. had moved backward to 1946. It wasn't until August, after
she had been incapacitated for seven months, that she was up and permitted to take coffee with the other patients. And not a word of complaint, except to request that if another operation were necessary, just to
"let her go."

For another person, the forced retirement to a sanatorium after the
freedom of hotel life would have been disastrous. But for H.D., the painful operation and its prolonged convalescence brought its reward. She
discovered the pleasures of Küsnacht. Years before, she said that had she
been a Catholic she would have chosen to become a nun. She desired a
convent life with its removal from the world, its hours of meditation and
dedication to the exploration of the spiritual self, and at Küsnacht she
found the perfect substitute. H.D., like her father before her, had retired
from the conflicts of a household to the "transit house."

Küsnacht was mainly, as it then was called, a Nervenklinik. Bryher said
its proper title was "microcosm of the world." It cared for drug addicts,
alcoholics, the emotionally disabled, and a few of the physically ill. It
was a refuge for those who could not manage life on the outside. The
fragile H.D., who had heroically labored to establish herself alone in her
various hotels, refusing to live with Bryher at interruptive Kenwin, found
that she was in a sort of "earthly paradise," which in the last section of
the nearly completed *Helen,* she turned into "L'Isle Blanche," the Leuki,
where the happy dead of *Helen* roamed.

Dr. Brunner, the owner of the Klinik, gave H.D. rooms in his own
house, Am Strand, when she first came in 1953; he visited her every day
and held her in special regard. There were five main buildings at the
Klinik: Am Strand, Dr. Brunner's house, which also housed patients on

the second floor; the Sanatorium, a sixteenth-century building on the ground floor of which were doctors' offices, several sitting rooms, and the dining room, where patients and doctors had meals together, and on the top floor of which were patients' rooms; Zur Geduld (connected to the Sanatorium by a glass passageway), which housed administrative offices on the ground floor and Dr. Erich Heydt's apartment on the second; Seehof, another sixteenth-century building, where Heydt had his office and where many of the patients lived (Seehof had once been the home of the famous Swiss writer Conrad Ferdinand Meyer; today it is rented out to the Jung Institut); and Villa Verena, a turn-of-the-century building that housed patients.

H.D. lived first on the second floor of Am Strand, then moved to the upper floor of the Sanatorium, where she was only a short walk away, along the glass passageway, from Heydt's apartment in Geduld; her final quarters at Küsnacht would be on the ground floor of Villa Verena. All the buildings, except Villa Verena, were alongside the lake; Verena was set back in the grounds, within the large park. The young psychiatrist-doctor Erich Heydt, a staff doctor, visited her daily, in what would become less a doctor-patient relationship and more one of friends who engaged in explorative conversations on literature, and the life of the unconscious. Dr. Heydt revives the H.D. of Küsnacht in this letter to the author:

> With H.D.'s deep interest in the mind's working, her knowledge of psy-
> chodynamics, her love for the unusual, eccentric, even strange person-
> alities, she was fascinated by the problems (psychiatric and otherwise) of
> the guests, and she took a lively interest in the Sanatorium community.
> She was sought out regularly by patients as a "wise lady," as a
> confidante, and as an auxilliary therapist . . . She always remained calm
> and kind . . .
> Her world of English poetry, and my world of German poetry (and lit-
> erature in general) touched each other . . .

He also mentions the regular afternoon tea meetings, which were such important events for her, where they could talk about literature and exchange their ideas on Greek mythology, German poets, and finally the writers whom she had known personally.

H.D. was happy, almost euphorically so. And, as formerly when elated, she wanted to get down to work. The Freud material (so in key with the atmosphere of Küsnacht and her conversations with Heydt), "Writing on the Wall," was sent to her. She would tell the story of her analysis, or discipleship, whichever attitude she chose to take, in her own way. H.D. writes a story of a woman who came to a far-off place in search of a self she had lost. We are not convinced that she found this self. Her encounter with Freud is more a fable, or story, than the account of an analysis. The book came to be called *Tribute to Freud*. In describing him as she saw him each day, his physical characteristics, the atmosphere of his "office," she gives us literature, rather than a clinical account. She also manages to write extensively of her emotional self. She becomes a combination of the tender Ophelia, her psyche fractured by events beyond her control, and Artemis, the tough goddess of the hunt. Freud is "the little Professor" with whom she often, in her role of Artemis, engages in a mental battle; as Ophelia, she needs him to dry her tears and free her from the threats of her neurosis.

Writing this book at Küsnacht during 1954 and 1955 (it was published in 1956), she was in the very atmosphere of working psychiatry. It is surprising that she is able to stay so aloof from the clinical world in this book. Although her book has been extensively read by psychiatrists in their search for an insight into the personality and methods of Freud, it should be recognized that what she leads us to is another thread in the long skein of her autobiographical writing.

Kenneth Fields, in his introduction to the Godine edition of *Tribute to Freud*—a book he has read closely, and which he takes as an opportunity to discuss symbolic analogies in H.D.'s poetry—writes that he prefers the earlier title *Writing on the Wall*. This is because, as he correctly sees it, her book is not, properly speaking, a tribute to the professor, it is a presentation of the events of her own life. True, Freud's interpretations are presented, yet they are overshadowed by the psychic personage of H.D. Fields makes the important point that her *Tribute* "is as close to a memoir as we are likely to get, and it gives us a better sense of her life than *Bid Me to Live*, her autobiographical novel. It is so much a memoir, in fact, that the title is somewhat misleading . . ."

Küsnacht, isolated from the world, a "magic mountain," (Thomas Mann lived just opposite across the lake) encouraged the introspection that could lead to autobiography.

In a letter to Viola Jordan written during the early days of her stay, H.D. describes her life at Küsnacht:

Here we are deep in snow. I have a glassed-in balcony room and each window gives a scene out of Jap prints; I cannot get over it and keep jumping up, I feel it may vanish. This room has a beamed ceiling, rather Japanese too, looking out on lake and opposite shore. There are white swans like lumps of snow AND the snow and all around huge pine and cedar trees, now heaving with snow.

. . . as Br. has closed Kenwin until March I will stay on a bit, as I have made such interesting contacts with people in Küsnacht and Zurich; we have over thirty five cinemas too, such good films, saw Julius Caesar, a few days ago. I have had charge of a reading group, English, but we are doing French and German in rotation. *I have not been so* active for years, I mean these readings and trips to Zurich to films; there are concerts too and a wonderful exhibition of the old Dutch painters. I have rarely had such a full and exciting Xmas, Bryher was here in the house with me . . .

I am so well, the food is good here and I was tired of Hotel life and they seem to like to have me here in Doctor Brunner's private house, Am Strand.

She was preoccupied with the people within the Sanatorium, especially Dr. Heydt. He would become the Paris of her Helen sequence, completed finally at Küsnacht. He was the Germain of her yet unwritten *Hermetic Definition*. She called him her latest "Hermes."

H.D. was grateful for her illness. If it had not been for the operation, she would never have left Lausanne; she would never have found her spiritual home. She emphasizes she would never have met Erich Heydt, now added to her list of "initiators," following upon Freud and Schmideberg.

The unpublished "Majic Mirror," written during her first years at Küsnacht, is the mirror within which she views her daily life at Dr. Brunner's. There is Heydt's apartment with his piano, music, tea, and talk; the still important breakfast tray; her observations about the other patients. The figure of H.D. moves across the glass-enclosed passageway that connected her suite in the Sanatorium with Geduld, the administration building, above which was the apartment of the resident doctor. She is going to tea with Heydt, or she is joining the patients, breaking up the solitude of her day.

H.D. writes of herself, whom she calls "Rica" in "Majic Mirror," sitting in the "Rosier":

It is a comfortable ground floor room, or rooms, with the large glass or winter room. There were many things to talk about, London, New York, but they were more concerned with this small republic, this microcosm . . . in microcosm, this small world in a world already as small as it could be, not the country of Luxembourg which hardly counted. They did not want to spread wings over the mountains. What was there outside?

Further along she writes:

"You can't wear green with blue," he said. She remembered fabulous Scotch scarves—can't go into schoolgirlish discussions.

His treatment is harsh, then chocolates, cigarettes.

She thought, I am completely identified with the story, the romantic game we [she and Heller-Heydt] play. He knows that I am not dangerous to him as a woman. I know that he is professionally concerned and really cares about me, as a patient, a case history of some interest, connections. He pretends to disregard the "classic Freudian technique," but he is always eager for gossip of those very far off days and people . . . Maybe he just likes me, a perfect mother-symbol.

But she thought to herself I am not his mother. I have gone over that ground, she thought, I have accepted the years and the years do not concern me. Between us is a light—no vision—warmth—no hallucination, no cerebral exaltation. My brain flowers. It is not thinking what it will make of this or anything. It is created rather than creative.

As Heydt stands in the doorway, wearing his velvet jacket, H.D. has a vision of his double, who is the Rosenkavalier. Is H.D. the Marschallin who falls in love with her Rosenkavalier, in the opera sung by a mezzo-soprano? She makes a connection between Erich Heydt and Cecil Gray. She had a dream (this was after Gray's death in 1951) that "Cecil Gray took off his pearls before we started on our beach walk." She believed the dream was caused by Heydt's remarking on some pearls she had been wearing. *"What makes the dream important is that I felt that Gray was Erich and I felt that some barrier would be down if I could tell Erich this."* (my italics) On she rambles, describing her room with a photograph of Freud in a frame over her dressing table. "There is my book on the *Blameless Physician;* I am so much younger than I was in Vienna more than twenty years ago."

She writes further of the "three graces," the lonely women who stand outside Heller's (Heydt's) window to watch his lights from the garden.

Interrupting the hypnotic spell of Küsnacht, H.D. would make a yearly summer trip to Lugano until 1956. She recognized that "the world of reality and of myth or imagination were superimposed here. She would lose both, if she broke bounds and made a dash for some sort of freedom. Freedom from what: *She needed the ties of reality to control or sustain the dream."* (my italics)

Soon she would be back at Dr. Brunner's, drawn by "a vibration, an intoxication in the air," or so she would write in her exalted moments. Along with "Majic Mirror" she started "The Compassionate Friendship," which is a journal of reminiscences, fragmentary speculation about the patients and her own past.

In 1953 at Christmas, Schmideberg came to Dr. Brunner's. He was seriously ill and needed treatment. Weak, yet alert, he and H.D. strolled in that "William Morris garden," as Bryher called the paths of the sanatorium, gossiping about the doctors and the patients. They decided Heydt and his friends, who visited him from the outside world, were like "early Conrad Veidt."[1] H.D. had known Schmideberg since 1935, when

[1] Here H.D. returns to the German era of "Filmland." Veidt, like Werner Krauss, would be part of the group of actors she had known in Berlin in 1927. Veidt starred in *The Student of Prague* (1926), a film concerned with the question of identity. Veidt

he first helped her through her difficulties. She was so attached to him that Bryher, wishing to spare her Kat, suggested she leave early for her trip to Lugano before his condition worsened. While H.D. was in Lugano, Schmideberg was diagnosed as suffering from cancer of the pancreas. He survived the operation, but died shortly after in 1954.

H.D. said, "his death marked the end of a period as certainly, too, the Helen sequence did." She then added, "I feel I have made my peace with Freud, with God, with poor Schmideberg."

Chance, which rules filmdom, brought a motion picture company to Küsnacht. They were filming F. Scott Fitzgerald's *Tender Is the Night*, photographing Dr. Brunner's clinic as the clinic where Dick Diver, the psychiatrist-hero of the book, first meets a patient, Nicole Warren, who will become his wife. In the film, the character, based on Brunner, describes his sanatorium "as a rich man's clinic." Fitzgerald wrote:

It was a damp April day, with long diagonal clouds over the Albishorn and water inert in the low places. Zurich is not unlike an American city . . . In Zurich there was a lot besides Zurich—the roofs upled the eyes to tinkling cow pastures, which in turn modified hilltops further up—so life was a perpendicular starting off to a postcard heaven. The Alpine lands, home of the toy and the funicular, the merry-go-round and the thin chime . . .

Professor Dohmler's plant consisted of three old buildings and a pair of new ones, between a slight eminence and the shore of the lake. At its founding ten years before, it had been the first modern clinic for mental illness . . . two buildings were surrounded with vine-softened walls of a deceptive height. Some men raked straw in the sunshine; here and there as they rode into the grounds, the car passed the white flag of a nurse waving beside a patient on a path.

One day in 1956, after her return from a visit to America, H.D. was in the Geduld building. She was downstairs, just outside an office door, when she slipped on a rug lying on the polished floor. She fell, breaking her hip. She was rushed to the excellent Klinik Hirslanden in Zurich, noted for the charm of its surroundings, the refinement of its upper-middle-class patronage, and the expensive solicitude of its staff. Again she was uncomplaining during the four months she was there. On the contrary, she viewed the accident as a blessed intervention. Incapacitated, she would not be forced to decide whether or not she should return per-

---

is a student whose mirror image is claimed by the devil. Another Faustian-Helen legend. This film had been preceded by the famed experimental *The Cabinet of Dr. Caligari* (1919) with its Freudian overtones and in which Veidt also starred.

manently to America. "I am so happy now I do not have to stay in America," she told everyone.

While she was at the Klinik H.D. received from Melitta Schmideberg a fascinating book, *The Cat, In the Mysteries of Magic and Religion.* Reading it, she asks herself:

> Was the Cat Ra responsible for her tripping on the rug, putting out an experienced, expert paw? I found no possible explanation for this accident— Ra, Fate, Destiny . . .
>
> > Sacred cat possessing 'the head of Ra,
> > the eyes of Uraens, the nose of Thoth,
> > the ears of Net-emtcher, the mouth of
> > Tem, the neck of Nehab-ka, the breast of
> > Thoth, the heart of Ra, the hands of
> > the Gods, the belly of Osiris . . .
>
> He did not want me to get "lost."

She decided that Melitta's book had been a message from the Bear himself, to give her an explanation for her accident and to protect her from suffering.

Returned to Dr. Brunner's and installed at Villa Verena, H.D. was permitted to recover in the way best suited to her temperament, as well as her physical needs. Once again she rejoiced in the long meditative hours in bed. Heydt (in a letter to the author) suggests that Dr. Brunner's fulfilled the concept of a sanatorium as "a healing place, healing the wounds of life, a comfortable mixture of hotel, rest home and hospital." The view from her rooms through the trees over the lake would have been healing, also. Her "meditation" he calls "self-analysis," which "she had continued (like every good analysand, but more intensely and more in depth)." This exploration of her psyche tunneled its way into her writing, as evidenced by "Majic Mirror" and "The Compassionate Friendship," besides her published work.

Also therapeutic, because it lent a dimension to her life, was the friendship now intensified between H.D. and a newcomer, Joan Waluga. Joan soon became an inseparable part of H.D.'s life at Küsnacht. Joan was the niece of the former Doris Banfield. Doris and Bryher were co-owners of Trenoweth, the farm in Cornwall. "Co-owner" may have been a euphemism, as Bryher probably owned the farm, but Doris ran it.[2] Joan

---

[2] At Trenoweth, Doris, according to John Schaffner, "soon had a flourishing business, not only supplying early spring flowers for London wholesalers, but for their counterparts in the low countries. She eventually became known as 'The Daffodil Queen.' The farm was no ordinary farm . . . a sort of mini-manor which had been designed by . . . Sir Edward Lutyens." It had a beautiful little pavilion in the Palladian manner and on clear days a view of the Channel. This, then, was "the farm" to which H.D. would reluctantly travel during the war years, and where she refused to take refuge among its (then) rabbits and vegetables.

had been born in India, the daughter of a brigadier. Her parents divorced and she married a Pole named Waluga, who not only deserted her, but disappeared without trace. Joan and her father, who now occupied the family home, quarreled bitterly; soon Joan was in a shattered emotional state. Bryher generously reached out to help her and sent Joan to Dr. Brunner's clinic. Joan proved a great release for H.D., who soon adopted her as a confidante. Their age difference was no obstacle. H.D. and Joan in the rarefied atmosphere of the Klinik duplicated the self-absorption and intimate conversations of the youthful Frances and Hilda.

H.D., stomping along with her "sticks" like skis that helped her to walk, managed pain and inconvenience. She liked to be alone in her room to dream. Those in the outside world—Bryher, Pearson—managed the chores of her profession. In 1956 Pearson arranged for the BBC to broadcast an hour-and-a-half program of H.D.'s *Ion*.

At the clinic, H.D. was surrounded by people who were charmed by her. She had several golden years: there was the music, so necessary to these Europeans; there were her sessions with Erich Heydt, continued after his marriage to another psychiatrist. Fortunately for H.D., Heydt was himself cultivated and literary. He introduced her to that sweetest of German poets, the Mozartian Eduard Mörike, whose poems were set to music by Johannes Brahms, Hugo Wolf, and Robert Schumann. He found the Mörike poem "Erinna to Sappho" appropriate to her. Erinna was a highly praised young poetess, a friend and disciple of Sappho. She died at nineteen.

> "Many are the paths to Hades" the ancient song
> proclaims. "And do not doubt that you your-
> self are treading one!"
> Who, sweetest Sappho, doubts?
> Speaks not each day of this?
> But lightly cling such words to the living
> and he who has dwelled by the sea since
> childhood, through blunted ear no longer
> hears the surf's pounding . . .
>
> And so I weighed my manner of death;
> at first with a dry eye,
> until I thought of thee, Sappho,
> and of all female friends
> and the cherished art of the muse
> and then my tears welled up.
>
> (Translation courtesy of Richard Wellish)

In such a civilized place, even if there were near lunatics about—"Don't call it an insane asylum," cautioned Bryher—H.D. found the necessary encouragement for her work. Heydt, intrigued by this patient of his who had known so many literary figures, and realizing that Pound was very much on her mind after his arrest and incarceration in St. Elizabeth's, suggested she write her memoirs of Pound. She wrote Pearson that Heydt "absolutely dragged Ezra out of me and sustained me at a distance in the Helen Sequence."

It was her youth H.D. was returning to, even after having written so extensively about it. Her youth meant Pound and their ambivalent relationship. When Bryher visited her, she would hide the Pound books that were piled on her desk. He represented her life in America before she met Bryher. She wrote: "I feel so violently American in the pro-Ezra sense . . ." Yet it was Bryher who believed that Pound would go "up" (in reputation) as Eliot went "down." Bryher never underrated Pound as a poet. She did believe that the *Cantos* should be cut, and felt if that took place, he would be considered one of the world's greatest poets. It was Pound's politics and anti-Semitism that so enraged her.

Aldington sent H.D. a copy of "A Weekend with Ezra Pound," published in *The Nation* in 1958, along with a poem on Pound by Ramon Guthrie. This article gave her the needed impetus to write the book about herself and Pound. The twenty-year-old David Rattray, a classics student at Dartmouth, who had read Pound in high school, had decided with the encouragement of his professor, Guthrie, to visit Pound in Washington. In a conversation with the author he described Pound as warm, friendly, funny—marvelous. A woman, Sheri Martinelli, was present during their conversation. Rattray recalls that he had never met anyone like her. She was "pre-hippy," he said. Rattray believed that Pound was in love with her. She had all the attributes Pound required. She was beautiful, intelligent, and adoring. Rattray's description of Martinelli brings to mind H.D. when Pound first knew her and made her his disciple. It is not surprising that H.D. later would come to identify with Martinelli when she learned more about her. She was, like H.D., an "undine" and a "dryad." And H.D. would become attracted to the beatniks, of which Martinelli was an early female member. Without the firm intellectual guidance of a Pound, H.D. might well in another era have become one of the hippies in a rebellion against Philadelphia and the parental world.

She wrote her book and called it *End to Torment*. H.D. explains that she was searching in this book for "the feel of things rather than what people do. It runs through all the poets, really of the world." Written in a variation of a diary form, the book again is as much about H.D.'s past and present world as it is about the Pound days. Pound is the image. H.D. is the theme.

When finally H.D. sent her book to Pound after he was released and had returned to Rapallo, his only comment was that the title was "a bit optimistic." Harkening to Aldington's advice, she laid aside the book, fearing the opprobrium of the press. *End to Torment* was not published until 1979, by which time New Directions was able (gracefully) to include the poems Pound had given H.D. in "Hilda's Book," written in the first years of their friendship, 1905. H.D. always believed this precious book had been "lost" during the last war; happily, it found its circuitous way to the Houghton Library at Harvard.

End to Torment was only a book. Pound and H.D. went on talking in their letters to one another until the end of her days. They corresponded from Küsnacht and St. Elizabeth's. After Pound returned to Europe in 1958 he asked her if he and Sheri Martinelli might visit her at Küsnacht. Bryher's foot might be small, but it could put itself down firmly. No Pound under a roof for which she was paying.

H.D. wrote to Pound explaining that where she now lived, although called Villa Verena, is "really part of the Klinik Brunner. I wanted to disguise the fact that I was not *free*. I have not been away for two years and am having some special massage all takes time and energy . . . I would like to have seen you, her, any or all of you!"

Pound was not fooled by H.D.'s equivocations. From Rapallo he wrote: "Despite yr / being invalided it is better to have a busted leg than a wormy conscience / Old Marianne wd / be better off as a catholic then cd / confess to have accepted too MANY lies because it wd / have been inconvenient to examine them. You took up for reasons of convenience with the murderer's daughter." He told her that he hadn't known what had gone on in her head for the past forty years and would have liked to have seen her. Then: "While we are at it, might as well face fact that Miss Ellerman has sabbotaged my work for forty years along with that snivel about my helping others. Of course it has been a hard life for her, cursed with that parentage . . ."

H.D. was writing "Winter Love," which would be dedicated to Pound. She speaks of it, when she answers Pound's letter, as a sort of coda to her long Helen sequence, in which she now brings in Odysseus, who is Pound himself. She tells him that she is fearful of his criticism of her "altmodisch" manner. Later she wrote him that she might send him this coda as a "little *divertissement* for you to slash it to pieces and return it or not." She offers him another "Hermes" to edit.

Pound's wise response to her when finally he had read "Winter Love" was that it was the best thing she had ever written, despite himself as a subject. As usual, it is difficult to disagree with Pound. The coda is Helen or H.D. speaking to herself on the enchanted Isle of the Dead. The poetry wears an unnerving stillness and sadness. This atmosphere is missing from the poetry of her Pound-inspired youth. Once again she is in her Greek homeland and when there she writes her best. The associations of her poetry need the bridle of Greek mythology, otherwise they become either too personalized, or too esoteric. "There was a Helen before there

was a war" is a refrain within the poem intended for Pound, for Aldington, for herself.

Earlier in 1957 she wrote "Sagesse." The idea for the poem came from
a photograph of a caged owl. The owl is the bird of Athena, the bird of
Virgo. The owl is the caged Pound in Pisa and St. Elizabeth's in Washington, D.C. Pound in Rapallo had been too obstreperous for his neighbor, Sir Max Beerbohm. "He seems to be out of place here," said Sir Max
to Phyllis Bottome. "I should prefer to watch him in the primeval forests
of his native land wielding an axe against some giant tree. Could you not
persuade him to return to a country in which there is more room?"

The owl represents the caged H.D. at Küsnacht. But the bird is only a
point of departure for her readings in the esoteric Ambelain with his list
of presiding angels, three for each hour. It is a hermetic poem, torturous
(as were her own nights) and difficult. Erich Heydt appears in the person of Germain, and the poem's lines read as the contents of their conversations.

> . . .
>
> and Germain says, "Your weakness and your nerves
> are due to apprehension; if you write like this,
> create, you must expect reaction . . ."

Her reactions lead to word associations that become tiresome; to a nam-
ing of the angels of the hours, which becomes tedious. What relieves this
long poem of boredom is its symphonic gloom, the near madness of its
exhausted visions, and the compulsiveness, which becomes hypnotic, of a
mind that is determined to reach the end of its thoughts. H.D. in
method reflects Dante, her great predecessor, whom she so often consulted, when he speaks of *"the secret need to be veiled in a lonely
deceit."* (my italics)

"Sagesse" finally appeared in *Hermetic Definition,* but before that it
was published in *Evergreen Review,* whose editors, Barney Rosset and
Donald Allen, were sympathetic to new writing in America, especially
that of "the Beats," and their associates. "Sagesse," or "Wisdom," returned H.D. to the world of the young.

H.D. exchanged letters with Denise Levertov in New York, who was
an admirer of her poetry. Robert Duncan sent her the manuscript of *The
Opening of the Field,* later published by Grove Press in 1960. She corresponded with him, finding him "stimulating and exciting." She began to
compile her mythology of life in San Francisco. When Erich Heydt
visited San Francisco, she sent him to see Duncan and his friend, the artist Jess. In Duncan she had found a young poet with whom she could di-
vide her mystical shares. An audience was opening up that excited her;
she would willingly exchange the foehn of Zurich for the fogs of San
Francisco. Martinelli (to whom she had given the money from her Har-

riet Monroe Prize award in 1956) had been the first voice from the Bay area. Duncan, as if to impress upon her the regard in which she was held, sent her his long paper "Towards a Study of H.D." This "study" would eventually evolve into what the poet calls his yet unfinished "H.D. Notebooks." Just as H.D. regarded Duncan's poetry in a subjective relation to her own poetry, so it may be that Duncan has considered H.D. as a departure for his own ideas of the art of poetry.

By 1959 H.D. had obtained, with much urging by Bryher and Pearson, an American passport, for the first time since her marriage to Aldington. This declaration of her American citizenship did not signal a break with Aldington. If anything, the two were closer each year. She was always known legally as Mrs. Hilda (or H.D.) Aldington. Ever since 1946 letters had passed between them, more frequent as the years went on, about work, about dreams fulfilled, or scattered. Neither she, Aldington, nor Pound were social creatures. They had avoided the world of parties and dining out. There was time for letters. She sent Aldington the manuscript of *End to Torment,* which he read carefully and cautioned her not to publish while the battle over Pound's guilt continued—he believed the attendant publicity would be bad for her. He advised her on her writing, and she in turn consoled him about life.

Aldington, after the success of *Death of a Hero,* had written an unfavorable biography of T. E. Lawrence. This brought the critics and the publishing world down on him; for the public, Lawrence of Arabia was a legendary figure. From that time on, Aldington's star dimmed. It was gossiped that he had "wasted his life." *Literary Lifelines,* the recently published correspondence between Lawrence Durrell and Aldington, reveals him in reduced financial circumstances, a neglected writer living scrappily in Provence. Durrell, to whom Aldington had been a hero, found himself in the same position as H.D., bolstering Aldington's ego, praising him. It is an entertaining correspondence.

Aldington wrote H.D. from Sury-en-Vaux, where he lived with his daughter, that he was ill, tired, burned out. H.D. responded with an invitation to Küsnacht. When he arrived for a physical examination, Joan was vastly impressed. Heydt privately thought he looked old. Heydt's reaction surprised H.D., who found Aldington "mature, worldly, amusing" —a far different reaction from the "Cuthbert" days, or that time in Florence when she caught sight of him and decided he looked "fat and déjà vu." Rather pathetically, he brought her a copy of a review with his *Des Imagistes* article of 1940 praising H.D.

The examination showed that Aldington had no serious illness. It was decided he was suffering from a depression brought on by a sense of failure and the departure of his wife. Aldington needed to work, but that drive to work had left him. (Once in 1930 he told a journalist in an interview that he could turn out an article between tea and dinner.) More and more he relied on the loyalty of his dependable secretary, Alister Kershaw; Bryher lent financial aid. Bryher gave presents to Catha: a car, a trip to Rome. Aldington, reversing the stance of his post-World War I years, was now grateful to H.D. for "l'autre." At Küsnacht the prognosis of Aldington was far too sanguine; they prescribed that he lose weight and practice Yoga to relax. There may have been no organic disease, but Aldington lived only a year longer than H.D.

Aldington did introduce her to the work of Durrell, which she feasted on; she became an addict of the *Alexandria Quartet*. H.D. also read Nikos Kazantzakis, thoughtfully selected by John Schaffner. And she could discuss her latest attachment, Heydt, with Aldington. Aldington had always understood her "crushes" and had encouraged them. Heydt and Aldington were closest to her in Europe; in America there was Pearson. These men supported her. Without these people (and of course, Bryher) in whom she could confide, who would guide her with literary and psychological advice, she could never have written as she did to Aldington: "I sometimes wonder why I should be so happy—I wish I could share out some of it with others of my 'lost generation.' I feel so entirely un-lost—could do with a good chunk of sheer physical stamina, otherwise I feel another 'miracle' (like Dunkirk)."

CHAPTER TWENTY-EIGHT

Medals of Honor

A series of publications and awards that would culminate in 1960 with the Gold Medal given by the American Academy of Arts and Letters began in 1956. First, Pearson arranged for H.D. to come to Yale for a seventieth-birthday celebration of her work. At the same time Oxford University Press, the original publishers of *Tribute to the Angels*, gave Grove Press permission to print the book in the United States with an introduction by the poet Horace Gregory, now an editor with Grove. Bryher's publishers, Kurt and Helen Wolff, published *Tribute to Freud* in 1956 with an introduction by the poet-psychoanalyst Merrill Moore. The following year Grove Press printed an edition of *Selected Poems;* a year later came Edith Sitwell's anthology, *Atlantic Book of British and American Poetry*, which included H.D.'s poetry and praise from Sitwell. In 1960 *Bid Me to Live* was published, again by Grove Press. In 1961, the same press published *Helen in Egypt*.

Along with the publications came the honors: the Harriet Monroe Prize in 1956, at the same time as the celebration at Yale; in 1959 the Brandeis Award and the Longview Award; in 1960 a citation from Bryn Mawr (a ceremony H.D. did not attend, but where she was represented by Mary Herr); then in the same year the Gold Medal Award from the American Academy of Arts and Letters, which officially crowned the "Queen of Song."

The awards were fine, but receiving them in person was another matter. H.D. was still difficult about travel. Pearson was persuasive enough to get her to Yale, but she refused to leave Küsnacht to go to Brandeis for an award, and Pearson represented her there. With a firm push from Bryher, H.D. appeared to receive her American Academy Gold Medal in 1960.

It was a struggle for H.D. to contemplate the 1956 trip to Yale, in New Haven. She suffered advance travel pains. Bryher promised to accompany her, and made all the arrangements, including tranquilizers for H.D. Bryher needed no encouragement—travel was her ambrosia. They were an amusing pair: the one, anxious and brooding; the other, exhilarated and bouncy. They arrived in New York and put up at the Beekman Towers near Perdita, where Bryher had formerly stayed.

There was a visit with the Schaffners, where H.D. was introduced to the newest child, Elizabeth Bryher, who most resembled H.D. physically. And there was the pleasure of hearing English spoken. For a moment H.D. began to look at Switzerland as an "ingrowing" country.

Pearson had intended H.D.'s visit to Yale to be a historic occasion, and so it was. She was greeted as a celebrity by students and the press. H.D. may have been fearful about making the trip, but once there, she was able to exert her considerable magnetism on whomever she met. An interview with the New Haven *Register* ("Poet Hilda Doolittle, on Yale Visit Assails Imagist Label Used to Describe Her Work") reported that "H.D. has denounced the label used to describe her work. She emphasized that the term cannot be applied to describe her work written since World War I." H.D. had then gone on to say that "I don't know that labels matter very much. One writes the kind of poetry one likes. Other people put labels on it." In its own way this is a true statement. Pound had "labeled" the poem she had shyly showed him in the tea room. When asked what was meant by Imagism, she answered, "Something that was important for poets learning their craft early in this century. It is still important to any poet learning his craft. But after learning his craft, the poet will find his true direction, as I hope I have."

H.D. certainly understood that she was vastly indebted to the Imagist movement. Her renown had come through her connection with the movement and her designation as the purest Imagist of them all. By now Imagism, as a literary term, had entered into literary history. But it was 1956, and she had just completed *Helen in Egypt*. She believed that the "early H.D.," the poet of *Sea Garden*, had matured with this later (still unpublished) book, and she had been looking for a way to magnify the label "Imagism," much too indefinite and microscopic a term for her later work. Despite her equivocations at Yale, after H.D. returned to Europe, she did an about-face and to Aldington, who also decried Imagism in a letter to her, answered: "How sad I am that you so regret having to do with the Imagist sign. I have been bored with it, too. But at seventy-two it is part of my youth."

Bid Me to Live (earlier called "Madrigal"), the story of the Mecklenburgh Square days and H.D.'s 1918 sojourn in Cornwall, was finally published in 1960. H.D. wished to use the pseudonym "Delia Alton"; most fortunately she was dissuaded by everyone—Horace Gregory, Bryher, Aldington, Pearson. They insisted that the public would only want to read the book if it appeared under H.D.'s own name.

The book owed its publication to Horace Gregory, then an advisor to Grove Press. Five years previously Aldington had unsuccessfully attempted to interest British publishers, and the manuscript had been turned down by Rupert Hart-Davis, to whom it had been shown, on the grounds that nobody would want to read it. After its favorable reception in America, the book was published the following year in England. Aldington wrote that "on the day of her death the Times Literary Supplement published an appreciative and almost fulsome review."

Lionel Durand, a Haitian who recently had covered the Algerian war, was sent from the Paris office of *Newsweek* to interview H.D. in Switzerland in April 1960. This interview, which came to mean so much to her, nearly did not take place. It was a close call, due to H.D.'s fear of meeting people, or of any intrusion on her privacy. Bryher put a stop to H.D.'s equivocations. She wrote to H.D.:

> Yes, I fear you have to see Newsweek, they are awfully nice people and not aggressive. I or much better Unser [Heydt] can be there. If necessary I will come over for the day . . . *You can take a pill* [Bryher's italics] . . . And we will rally round, but if you insist on writing poetry you owe it to the book and the poetry to stand up to these little attentions. Don't squeal so. I am thoroughly delighted and enthusiastic that they want to come.
>
> I wired "Understand you wish to contact Mrs. H.D. Aldington . . . please write first as she has influenza and cannot receive visitors . . . signed Aldington."

Bryher congratulated H.D. on "Madrigal," pointing out that it evoked the very feeling of the 1914–18 war. She also singled out the Cornish bits and the passage H.D. wrote about her feeling for Greek words. As in so much of H.D.'s prose, Bryher claimed to find underneath the prose structure the rhythms of a poem.

Lionel Durand arrived at Küsnacht in April 1960. H.D. stood at the top of the stairs to receive him. Walking up to her, he held out his hand. His gesture, as she interpreted it, was one of reassurance. Among the subjects they discussed was the current writing of the beatniks. H.D. said, "I must confess I have a little affectionate feeling for those beatniks. I have heard some bitter comments on them, but people shouldn't ride them down. I feel they are looking for something. I think they need understanding." She also went on to say that she had become, from her recent reading, fonder of Faulkner and Hemingway.

In his interview printed in *Newsweek*, Durand wrote:

> In a large, brightly lit and book-filled room in the quiet resort of Küsnacht near Zurich Hilda Doolittle Aldington, an expatriate from her native America since 1911, has been living for the past three years in the silent company of swans weaving their way on the Zurichsee. Suffering from a bone illness the tall, gaunt woman of 73 uses metal canes to move about between her room on the first floor of a clinic and the terrace that overlooks the water.

He found that despite her physical difficulties, H.D.'s mind was aflame, her thoughts provocative, her opinions strong. Pulling eagerly on her cigarette, she said, "I have a pretty secluded life, you see. My idea is to get away. Get away! Like that." About *Bid Me to Live* she confided to Durand:

> They like to think that I wrote it very recently, but I really did it all after World War II. I was in a villa near Vevey when suddenly everything came back to me. In a sort of intense state I wrote it off. I think they [the publishers] liked it because I have D. H. Lawrence in it. Half the book is devoted to him. I started *Bid Me to Live* as a tribute to him. He was such a cult, and everything he said or did was considered perfect. I became bored with that image and I thought it was not the Lawrence I used to know.

She admitted readily that the book was a *roman à clef*. She didn't discuss with Durand the possibility that the title, despite its being a quotation from Herrick, had been inspired by Lawrence's injunction to "kick over your tiresome house of life!"—a command she had obeyed.

The review of *Bid Me to Live* when it appeared in May in *Newsweek* was called "Life in a Hothouse." It is not a pleasing review; the writing is called "quivering impressionist prose." It does mention the highlights of poetic writing, of descriptions of sky, flowers, teacups, wineglasses. The conclusion is that the book "is interesting as history, and if you can stand its preciousness, it has its fascinations as a novel." *Newsweek* at that time used a device called "Summing Up" tacked onto the end of the article, which for H.D.'s book read: "Through crystal glasses." Not exactly a sympathetic review after the obvious rapport of the Durand-H.D. meeting. H.D. accepted the criticism, as she had accepted all criticism of her work, with little comment. Yet she must have experienced some disappointment at its belittling tone. What she did not know was that *the book review had not been written by Durand*. Durand had sent in his copy, which was solely the interview at Küsnacht, to the magazine in New York. The review of the book was written by a *Newsweek* staff member.

If she was upset by the review, she did not mention it. Obeying her impulses, H.D. had claimed Durand as one of her imaginary loves. She was now set loose to wander over a new romantic terrain. Durand was placed in her pyramid of "initiators," and he would even briefly supplant Heydt. He became a star in her heavens.

From this meeting and from the one other which took place when she was in New York that same May, H.D. created a legend. In her last book of poems Durand became the "Star of the Day." There is, of course, no logic in this. It all came about through vibration and the magic of stars and mystic associations that made up the world of H.D. Since she was old and he so young, there was no sexual threat. Still there was that tremor of sexual ambivalence with which she helplessly threatened her loves. This was not a foolish old woman's last ardor—that was not H.D.'s

way. She could never view any event or any person as a single occurrence. Everything must be part of the infinite particles that made up the
whole. Durand, for the brief period he existed in her life, was as important to her as anyone she had known for years.

After their interview he had written to her: ". . . allow me to tell you
how much I have enjoyed both the visit and the book. Both are the sort
of 'white stone' which, as the French say, should mark one's path in
life . . ."

Instantly she wrote back to him:

> You speak of "white stones," I think more of the lodestones, that magnet.
> I feel, even if I do not see you, that you could draw me to America or
> even draw me back . . . It would be good to see you [in America] if you
> have a minute to spare [she was going over for the Academy Award]. I
> would love to see you but am, as you can imagine rather "psychosomatic"
> over the whole thing . . . in any case, whether there or here or only in
> the "white stones" that you speak of or in my own phantasy.

There were other repercussions from her book. A review, irritating yet
amusing, appeared in the Geneva newspaper *Die Tat*. It was called "A
Novel About D. H. Lawrence." In translation it went something like this:
"This Hilda Doolittle wishes to clear up her situation as described in
Richard Aldington's openly autobiographical novel. After the separation
and his death she loses all control or hold. She traveled a good deal, always with a pretty large brandy flask and had more lovers than were
good for her or them." She was angry, then she laughed and decided sensibly to content herself with a "dignified" note to the Geneva paper. She
wrote to Aldington: "I must ask you to be good enough to refute this
'error' sort of thing." Then she added: "To me, this peepshow seems as
innocuous as Alice in Wonderland."

The last sentence of the review is a direct, if scrambled, quotation
from Aldington's *Death of a Hero*. Had the reviewer not wished to be
malicious he would have understood that Aldington, like most authors, is
here drawing a composite picture of his character taken from several
types of women whom he had known. Elizabeth, the widow of the dead
war hero, who is identified as H.D., is described by him as a vaguely "artistic" sort of woman of the 1930s, self-destructive and promiscuous. She
is passing her time with a clever and famous young novelist. Aldington
should have taken it upon himself to correct the reviewer. Did he hesitate, because now in his lean years he throve on a mention even if in-
direct of his past novel? The texture of H.D.'s existence did not dissolve
itself in brandy, as Aldington well knew.

Voices were heard from the past. A letter arrived from a furious John
Cournos, now living in New York. He had read her little book, "not
without pity." He chided her maliciously for having permitted Lawrence

to have placed her in the position of "a woman scorned." He ended with: "I trust your Greek occupations do not involve you with the ghosts of Clytemnestra, Medea and other murderesses on the Greek scene who had the good fortune to exist before Freud could analyze them . . ." He signed off with: "Semper idem, Ivan Korshoon [his name in her book], John Cournos." Bryher considered the Cournos letter "simply insane."

Cournos was still frustrated by H.D.'s personality. He wrote to the librarian at the Houghton Library to whom he had sold his H.D. and Aldington correspondence: "Between ourselves H.D.'s novel, 'Bid Me to Live,' is, according to my knowledge of events, rather a whitewashing operation (of self I mean) at the expense of others, and of one person in particular; not myself, for, as good luck would have it, I was in Petrograd at the time . . . The letters you have of H.D.'s will throw additional light, not recorded in the novel." He accompanies his letter with a list of the real names of the personages in the book, and a list of "mistakes" made by H.D. in her account. This list is largely spiteful, but no doubt contains a few truths.

The person Cournos had referred to as having been sacrificed in the novel was "Arabella," or Dorothy Yorke, with whom the angry Cournos was now in touch. Dorothy was in a nursing home in New Jersey and would never have heard of the book if Cournos had not written to her. Some of his wrath was reflected by her, but her innocent and rather unworldly character was incapable of a strong hatred.

In an interview in 1964 at her nursing home, Dorothy was questioned about the scenes H.D. had described. Her replies show her to have been very much in love with Aldington, although intelligent enough to be aware of the difficulties in his character. She had been close to Lawrence and Frieda and they were attracted to her touching combination of innocence and affection. In the interview she described her life with Richard and Brigit at Port-Cros. The visiting Lawrences made life difficult enough, but Richard added an additional drama. He would leave Dorothy's room to go to Brigit, yet all the time, said Dorothy, he was so in love with Nancy Cunard that he wore the beads she had given him around his neck when he went to the several beds in the night.

Dorothy insisted that *Bid Me to Live* was "entirely false." Dorothy, in making such a statement, was moved by what she believed was H.D.'s inference about herself, that she had "many operations." Dorothy angrily declared that she never had an abortion, in fact had never had a child. She admitted that H.D. had been in love with Aldington, "Inasmuch as she was capable of loving anybody." Reversing herself, she noted H.D. had been generous to her in taking no rent from her at Mecklenburgh Square and in giving up her bed so that she and Richard might share it. Forgetting her pique, Dorothy went so far as to say that H.D. was a "good poet and wrote some beautiful things." Aldington had told her that H.D. was "the only one of the Imagists who was a real Imagist. He thought she was a great poet and always thought so."

The Dorothy Yorke interview reflects much pathos. Anger, pathos, self-justification, remembrance were the reactions out of which *Bid Me to Live* was conceived. H.D. had the final word: *"True, I have lived too much, seen too much, travelled too much, been too cerebrally aware of events . . . that was, the recrudescence of memories with the Lawrence, the 'other' Lawrence whom I knew at one time and I think adequately portrayed in my own novel, Madrigal."* (my italics)

On the final journey to New York in 1960 when she was to receive the Gold Medal from the American Academy of Arts and Letters, H.D. once more saw Durand at her hotel. "Very romantic and correct," she judged him. Neither of them could foresee that he would die nine months later of heart disease.

Before this trip, as usual, H.D. had gone into a spin over the prospect of leaving Küsnacht. For one precarious moment she had considered asking Aldington to accompany her. This suggestion was turned into a rumor that H.D. was ailing and wanted her one-time husband to take care of her. H.D. laughingly denied the rumor: didn't people know that elderly men never took care of elderly women; wasn't it the other way around? Aldington may have been a panicky choice, but her turning to him at this time shows that she did in these years rely upon the correspondence that had drawn them together again. She must have been quietly aware that—as Harry T. Moore, the Lawrence scholar and authority, believed—"Richard was *always* in love with H.D." (Moore's italics, in a letter to the author.) To the end, as her letters illustrate, it would be Bryher and Aldington in whom she would most often confide.

Bryher, well aware of H.D.'s trepidation, wrote her that "Zurich-New York-Zurich should blend, as Heracleitus said into a smooth continuous line." Reflecting on Greek philosophy was no help to H.D. She remained fearful. This time Bryher sounded a firmer note with the sage advice:

> Du calme. Giving up pills won't help you to emerge, you should rather double them . . . Don't repeat, you are too good a Freudian now not to examine yourself very closely for the reasons for repetition. You are not cutting yourself off from R.A. or anyone else. This is life and it flows, quietly and continuously. You may stay in America, you may come back to Brunner, let it be unspecified. It will mean work there with a physiotherapist and it will be up to you to decide whether that work or your leisure is the more important. Meantime, du calme, double your pills and take life quietly.

It was then that Bryher added that she saw no reason why the Queen of Song should not travel in regal manner, taking along a companion, in this case Blanche, Dr. Brunner's granddaughter, his son Dr. Rudolph Brunner's daughter.

After tears and trepidation the flight turned out to be marvelous. Once in New York, H.D. found her family waiting to greet her with flowers and champagne and the new baby, Timothy ("thank heaven it isn't a Hilda!"). She settled into a comfortable suite at the Stanhope Hotel. (Much too handsome for her, she said. Bryher told her to stop fretting, she would pay for it!)

The Stanhope was a most fortunate choice. Situated on upper Fifth Avenue at Eighty-first Street, it is just across from the Metropolitan Museum. At the Stanhope, H.D. proceeded to hold court. Friends came for tea. Poets Denise Levertov and Robert Duncan arrived to pay homage. Her descriptions of her schedule led Bryher to write that it sounded as if she were living on champagne and peaches. Pearson was there. Perdita and John were in constant attendance. It was well on the way to becoming a royal welcome.

One of her favorite excursions was to walk unassisted across the street to the museum. H.D. was at home looking at the Pompeian alcove and frescoes, the archaic Greek statues near the museum restaurant, which is bordered by a long, refreshing pool where she was in the habit of lunching (on apple pie and vanilla ice cream) and entertaining her friends. Just as on her travels in Greece or Europe, she bought postcards—this time at the museum shop. The museum became her focus. Although she seems never to have gone to its upper European galleries, she was comforted by the Greek and Egyptian sculptures near the restaurant. It was her atmosphere.

On the 1956 visit to America she and Bryher, when they returned from New Haven, had stopped briefly at the Stanhope. In the hotel elevator the operator then had whispered to Bryher, "Who is that beautiful lady?" Bryher cherished this remark, as well as the remark of Herman Hesse, who had said to Bryher, "I am so glad I saw her before the accident [when she broke her hip], so beautiful, so gracious, like a beautiful English woman of Lord Byron's time with such lovely hands." What a pleasure it was to hear these words, reflecting Bryher's own romantic feeling about H.D., from the famed Hesse, who was an international figure.

There is the inevitable question of why Bryher did not accompany H.D. on this celebratory 1960 trip. The answer is that Bryher deliberately chose to remove herself from the scene; remaining at Kenwin was a conscious act of selflessness on Bryher's part. She would have adored to have been there. But it was H.D.'s moment of triumph and she wanted H.D. to prove to herself that she needed no one to assist her in receiving the tributes that would follow. From a distance, Bryher followed H.D.'s reported movements. She set her clock to New York time. Each day she wrote to H.D. and a letter was waiting for H.D. on arrival. One of Bryher's most thoughtful and loving letters said:

First thought as the twenty-fifth draws near, I am so truly happy that your genius is recognized at last. I hope the day will be a very happy one, like the reading in London with the attendant queens. I shall be thinking of you all day and hoping that everything is going just as you wish it. It is a flowering but not the final one. We all long for more books, poetry, and prose.

In another letter she had told H.D.: "I think so very much about you. Thinking too of picking up *Sea Garden* in 1918. I must say they have taken their time but I suppose that is the way of the world." "They" had taken their time, indeed, and without the continual support of Bryher and her exposure of H.D.'s work, the Queen may never have had her day. (Although, it must be assumed, a now powerful Pearson had been hard at work behind the scenes.)

The day of the great event arrived. Not even Dame Edith could have been more careful or chosen more conscientiously what she should wear. H.D. wrote Bryher: "My dress was lovely with pearls and a little hat. Perdita sent a lovely little shoulder bouquet and I wore one white glove and carried the other—and felt completely right!" There spoke the correct Professor's daughter in her Bryn Mawr treble.

It was an occasion on which H.D. would rejoin old friends, her peers. She was excited about meeting the other poet who would be awarded the medal, St. John Perse. In advance of their meeting she had been reading and admiring his poetry, noting that many of his poems were inspired by the coast of New Jersey and Casco Bay, scenes used in her own early poems. She was now an enthusiastic admirer of *Amers* and *Exil*. It is surprising that, as a contemporary of Eliot, she had never read Eliot's translation of the Perse *Anabase,* nor had she been aware of the influence of Perse on Eliot. There would be a brief, for her historic, personal contact, when leaving the reader's desk on the platform, she "staggered—no swayed," and the courteous Léger Léger (as she called him) reached out to help her. This moment would be magnified by her into a poem.

It is best to rely on H.D.'s own description of the Day:

Thank heaven all went well. I was stunned with the H.D. acclaim . . . Elizabeth Bowen—she lectures at Vassar—Glenway Wescott (Master of Ceremonies) was delightful, Djuna Barnes, Kay Boyle talked of Paris. I did not recognize Flossie Williams so old, so very delapidated, flung at me and Wm. C. was himself almost speechless. Thornton Wilder was heavy and great screams. Mark van Doren was my "god father" and read the old violet poem of H.D. so beautifully. He was supposed to come first but in getting to the desk we mixed places and I read my little piece before the introduction—it was lovely as he said he would have the "last word" and the violets became a sort of offering to H.D. St. Léger kissed my hand on the platform after my little speech and he kissed my hand earlier in the day—so—we had a wild party last night with Shaffs and champagne. Norman insisted on taking the bill though I struggled for it.

This she had written to Bryher. In a letter to Aldington: "May 25th passed off miraculously. There were 3,000 and Norman tells me about one hundred were turned away. My god father, Mark van Doren who read my old violet poem said: 'H.D. to you these lines, these violets and this mead; whose gift honoring us we think quite as richly as it honors you.'" She then went on to tell him that she had some very fine *Bid Me to Live* reviews and some silly gossip-column ones.

H.D. saw her old friends Viola Jordan and Mary Herr, who brought her the Bryn Mawr citation. Mary Herr would die shortly after; H.D. wrote her obituary in the form of a tribute to her for the Bryn Mawr magazine. There was her brother Melvin and his wife; Melvin, who had "some sort of cancer of the bone." She must have seen Harold; it would be her last meeting with the brother who had looked after her monetary affairs and property. The brother who loved cows.

H.D. gave herself time to enjoy being in New York again. Even if the weather was hot and sultry, she could take it or "almost anything for the sake of the people and the English spoken." How she must have longed for just that "English spoken" at the sanatorium. One can speculate that the sound of those foreign voices may have driven her further into herself, where she heard the sound of her poetry. The foreign speech may thus have been an asset.

But now she watched TV, shamelessly. She sat through "two Westerns, a mid-ocean luxury liner 'mystery' and another 'low mystery' all in one go, before, during and after dinner. I forced myself to switch off at ten P.M."

Stephen Guest, who had been in America since before the war, telephoned; he wanted to see her. She decided that it would be best to include him with the Gregorys at lunch at the Metropolitan. She was no longer really interested in Stephen, only curious as to what he had done with his life. Her real interests were with Marianne Moore and the younger poets, Robert Duncan and Denise Levertov. She left no record of who else came to call, except to note that Bowen wanted to arrange a reading for her at Vassar; the Poetry Society of America wished to arrange a special celebration in her honor. She declined both offers. The doctor, whom she had consulted on a previous visit, was called in. He told her there was nothing wrong with her. Privately, he then confided to Blanche that H.D.'s physical condition was very bad. Her heart was extremely weak. It was the same Dr. Prutting whom Bryher would go to later, who told Bryher that she had too much energy and gave her tranquilizers. He suggested to Bryher that perhaps Switzerland was too healthy a place for her to live in!

Then it was all over. H.D. returned to Villa Verena at Küsnacht to finish *Hermetic Definition*.

CHAPTER TWENTY-NINE

"Write, Write or Die"

H.D. once again assumed the role of a recluse surrounded by her court. Joan was still the favorite. Bryher had been asked to limit her visits by Dr. Heydt, who decided that H.D.'s equilibrium was upset by Bryher's energetic, and frequently disruptive, "dog-runs," as Bryher would call her padding back and forth from room to garden, fetching books, returning notebooks from Kenwin, a faithful, if overly efficient, Fido. There was the telephone, which was used to keep them in touch as much as the economical Bryher would allow. Here is a typical cautionary note to H.D. about their telephone conversations from one of Bryher's letters of this late period: "Always hang up the long distance telephone at first of three pings. Otherwise they charge you even if you do not go on speaking. They ping three times, if you can hang up between 1st and 2nd ping all is well, if you are still holding at 2nd ping they charge. It is complicated."

Although Heydt for nearly seven years had been the court wizard, H.D. was preoccupied with new luminaries, St. John Perse and Lionel Durand. Also as Heydt—ever aware of her states of mind—observed, intellectually she was shifting away from her strict Freudianism. Pearson shows he was also aware of this shift by calling her "quasi-Jungian" in his introduction to *Hermetic Definition*.

Jung had always acknowledged the need for religion; for him its myths and rituals were essential. He would have encouraged her instinctive turning back to her earlier religious beliefs. Freud, although he wrote in immaculate prose about *Moses and Monotheism,* had rejected the Judeo-Christian God—he had invented a new religion.

Geographically, there was Jung's near presence on their shared Lake of Zurich at 228 Seestrasse. H.D. could watch the new buildings on his Bollingen property being constructed. Although still observing her daily ritual of Freudian self-analysis, in the poetry she was writing H.D. was drawing closer to the Jungian orbit. In spirit she was closer to Jung's Egypto-Hellenic orientation while writing *Helen in Egypt,* in spite of the appearance of Freud as Theseus and her verbal homage to him.[1]

---

[1] According to Vincent Brome, in his biography of Jung, Marie Jolas recommended to James Joyce that he send his daughter, Lucia, to Dr. Jung. In September 1920, Lucia Joyce entered the private sanatorium of Dr. Brunner at Küsnacht, where Jung was then the chief consultant.

Freud—exploring the unconscious, in order to lighten the recesses of the mind, methodically experimenting in order to arrive at a scientific diagnosis of the mystery of the human microcosm—would not have encouraged H.D.'s forays into mysticism and Hermeticism. H.D. was still in search of that place in which Freud did not believe, life after death.

Seeking the numinous wherever it was concealed, she read Robert Ambelain's (she constantly misspells his name "Amberlain") *In the Shadow of the Cathedrals,* where Ambelain writes of a secret code the stonecutters of Notre Dame had left to instruct the decoder in the mystery of the church. She sought the hidden meanings of the Cabala. There was Jean Chaboseau with his occult bases of tarot and alchemy, which he believed were part of the tradition of Hermeticism. Hermeticism, as he defined it, was "the more subtle side of philosophy, the more mysterious if you wish. It incorporates the totality of 'secret' spoken knowledge, ending in a 'conquest of divine knowledge.'"

Esoterism, mysticism, Hermeticism, what H.D. was on the watch for was her religious self. Closer to her in spirit—she called *Love in the Western World* her "textbook"—was Denis de Rougemont's book, printed first in 1940 and again in 1957. De Rougemont wrote about the fierce, inhuman religious wars of the Middle Ages. The Albigensians—like the Catholics and the Lutherans of the time of the persecuted Moravians—set out to destroy the Cathars, the dissenters. The Cathars held a doctrine of the love of Christ, and "the radiance of love." H.D. could identify with de Rougemont's subject. Such persecution had been endured by the Moravians, who believed in the illumination of the love of Christ. De Rougemont wrote, and it could have been meant for H.D.'s ears alone: "What should be looked for in courtly rhetoric is not rational or precise equivalent of dogma, but the lyrical and psalmodic development of the fundamental symbolism." He also wrote that the *erotic and mystical speak the same language.* (my italics) It was that courtly civilization of Languedoc that the Albigensian Crusade devastated, scattering the last of the troubadours.

De Rougemont further explains that the Church of Love, as he calls the Cathars, went underground, just as the Moravians had done. They split into different sects, but all professed a doctrine of "radiant joy." All were anticlerical, cultivated an egalitarian spirit, almost a complete communism. (Here, once more, was the Rananim of Lawrence—and those fragments of the troubadours Pound had reinterpreted.)

The poetry H.D. was writing in the late 1950s until 1960 may well have relied on "Ambelain's categories of the stars, or the cabala, astrology, magic, Christianity, classical and Egyptian mythology, and personal experience into a joint sense of Ancient Wisdom," but wherever her reading led her, H.D. was returned to herself. She was returned to Bethlehem, Pennsylvania, to the Moravians, and to the night watchers at Hernnhut, whether she gave them biblical or Egyptian names. The al-

chemical poetry she called "hermetic definition" was a name she used for
her interpretation of her own life.

From August 1960 to February 1961, H.D. wrote the poems that would
open *Hermetic Definition:* "Red Rose and a Beggar," "Grove of Academe," "Star of Day." The first poem is about her meeting with Lionel
Durand. It is a love poem from a woman of over seventy to a man not
quite forty. She compares this poem with her earlier *Red Roses for
Bronze.* The bronze now would be the skin of Durand, the Haitian, together with that of a "bronze" U.S. decathlon star. They would be beautiful late runners beside the love poems of *Red Roses for Bronze,* which
celebrated Kenneth Macpherson, another beautiful young man who had
run gracefully through her life.

When H.D. wrote about Durand, she believed he had "brushed aside"
her verse in his review, pointing out her "preciousness" (we know now
that the review had not been written by him). She apologizes for this
necessary "preciousness." Despite his disapproval she commands herself
to "write, write or die."

> It was April that we met,
> and once in May;
> I did not realize my state of mind,
>
> my "condition" you might say,
> until August when I wrote,
> *the reddest rose unfolds,*
>
> I did not realize that separation
> was the only solution,
> if I were to resolve this curious "condition,"
>
> you were five months "on the way"
> I did not realize how intimate
> the relation, nor what lay ahead;
>
> I did not know that I must keep faith
> with something, I called it writing,
>
> write, write or die.

She "carries" this startling suggestion of their meeting, bringing about
his conception as the Durand of her imagination, a literary child who
reached "full term" in the last poem, "Star of Day."

> but I went on, I had to go on,
> the writing was the un-born
> the conception.
>
> Now you are born
> and it's all over,
> will you leave me alone?

> whether you have gone to archangels and lovers
> or to infernal adventures,
> I don't know,
>
> I only know
> this room contains me,
> it is enough for me . . .

"Grove of Academe" is about her encounter with St. John Perse. She had been hypnotized by his poetry, which she continued to read after she returned from the American Academy of Arts and Letters awards. She quotes in her own poem from his perfect lines: "l'odeur solennelle des roses," "lois de transhumance et de dérivation," and many, many others. Seldom has a poet so incorporated into her poem the lines of another poet. She recalls his courtesy at the hour of the acclaim they shared:

> you are my own age,
> my own stars;
> I accepted acclaim
> from the others,
> for the honour,
> unexpectedly thrust upon me.
>
>   .   .   .
>
> and I might have fallen
> but your hand reached out to me,
> and it was the *grove of academe.*

These three poems with the earlier "Sagesse" and "Winter Love" completed *Hermetic Definition.* When Hugh Kenner reviewed *Hermetic Definition,* he wrote:

> A voice from the past, a ghost in fact, still defining itself. She cut her name down to two letters a long time ago, sixty years ago now; and her sense of herself became a few glimpsed pictures, the quester on the shore, the supplicant, the weaver of spells.
> Unlike most ghosts, she had the guts to keep coming back and her hour may be here at last . . .

Without warning, Dr. Brunner's son, who had inherited the sanatorium on the death of his father, decided in the spring of 1961 to sell the Nervenklinik. H.D. at seventy-five was faced with eviction from her "haven or heaven." Physically her health was so precarious the move made little difference. Emotionally she suffered intensely. The sanatorium had been her home, with interruptions, ever since her breakdown in 1946. She was a nun forced from her cloister. She was Helen pursued by the Eumenides.

Bryher once again located a hotel, the Sonnenberg, in Zurich. H.D.'s room had a splendid view of the town and mountains, yet it was not a consoling one. For consolation she turned to what she called her "Diary to Durand." The diary is a record of terrible night sweats, of sleeplessness, gasps for breath. She thinks obsessively of Durand and asks him if his suffering was like hers before the heart disease killed him. With longing, she remembers the half-wakeful, meditative nights in Küsnacht. She attempts to read Robert Graves' *The Anger of Achilles*. Suddenly she wants to reedit the stacks of manuscripts piled around her.

One morning in July she was speaking to Heydt on the telephone. Suddenly her voice broke and he heard her moan. When she would not answer him when he called out to her, he realized something serious had happened. He rushed to the hotel, where he discovered she had suffered a stroke. She was paralyzed and unable to speak. She was then taken to the Klinik Hirslanden; when she first arrived there they did not believe she would last the night.

Then began a repetition of the emergency of 1918. By the time Bryher arrived, it was believed H.D. was slipping away. Bryher went into her old emergency routine. She demanded more medication for H.D. She insisted on "injections" being given. She did her best to organize the Klinik around H.D. Bryher wrote to Silvia Dobson that she didn't trust any of them at the Klinik unless she was "all the time on the spot to control." There was one significant difference this time. In 1918 the young untried Bryher was hovering over the great writer, H.D. In 1961 Bryher wrote gloomily to Silvia, that if she remained there "in control," and it was necessary she should do so, then, "I can't do my own work."

It was apparent when H.D. was in New York on that last visit, that however much she enjoyed the applause and meetings with friends and relatives, she was very, very frail. When she had returned to Zurich, the loss of her haven at Küsnacht had been a shock. At the hotel the phantom spirits of Durand and Perse had been an occupation, not a consolation. Her endurance had been of the spirit, not the body. She had received her honors, then like an aged seabird she had found her way back across the Atlantic. The physical agony, due to the ministrations of Heydt, was comparatively moderate; the spirit suffered more. At the Klinik Hirslanden she may have been semiconscious. She died there on the twenty-seventh of September 1961. The day before she died, H.D. received her publisher's copy of *Helen in Egypt*, which Bryher placed in her hands. It is doubtful if she could recognize the book.

H.D. once said "serenitas"
(Atthis, etc.)
at Dieudonné's
in pre-history.[2]

---

[2] Ezra Pound, Canto CXIII.

When Aldington learned of H.D.'s death he wept. It was as if he were finally subdued. He only outlived her one more year. Aldington's letters to Lawrence Durrell after he had learned of her stroke, and even before that, contrary to the usual complaints about his own health and public neglect, had been filled with reports of H.D.'s physical condition. The first words in his October 1961 letter to Durrell were, "H.D. is dead." Mistakenly, but heartbreakingly, he believed she had been cremated on the anniversary of their marriage, October 18, 1913. The actual cremation had taken place on October 2.

Durrell, who cared for Aldington and had supported his failing morale, must have written as soon as he received Aldington's letter. He reminded Aldington that "a poet's death is never wholly sad, in the sense of a life unlived—because the work is there, like the after-taste of a wine of high vintage."

There is a phrase H.D. used in her dedication of another of her books, *The Gift:* "l'amitié passe même le tombeau." These words may have been a consolation to Bryher. A letter reached her from Romaine Brooks soon after, reminding Bryher of "the little scented candles" H.D. had given her. In 1965 her old friend Romaine again wrote Bryher thanking her for a photograph of H.D. and one of her books. Romaine wrote: "What a beautiful head H.D.'s. Thank you dear Bryher. The inner life of those strange poems needs an inner depth to read them."

H.D. was buried on Nisky Hill in Bethlehem, where Mamalie had taken her and her cousins to look at the family graves and sit under the shade trees. There she had stood on the sidewalk outside the picket fence that encloses the graveyard, listening to the trombones, the special musical instrument of the Moravians, sound their notes as the newly dead were buried: one high, one low, male, female, married, widowed. The children could guess from the trombone call which member of the congregation had died.

There was the golden haze of sun through trees, burning off the mountain cold; the soft air of Indian summer, the nurtured houses, some nineteenth century, like the now demolished house on Church Street of the Doolittle and Wolle families; some remaining buildings of the Moravian founders; the tended cemetery. Stones marking the graves were there placed flat, as was the Moravian custom, so that no marker should stand higher than the other, no stone signify greater attainment or wealth in this communal graveyard. H.D. returned, a daughter to an orderly house. A safe place where sentinels keep the watches of the night.

A few years before her death, H.D. had written to Norman Holmes Pearson from Küsnacht words that could be her own epitaph:

"I think I did get what I was looking for from life and art."

BIBLIOGRAPHY

Books by H.D.

NOTE For a list of H.D.'s periodical contributions, and H.D.'s contributions to books by other authors, see Bryer, Jackson R., and Roblyer, Pamela. "H.D.: A Preliminary Checklist." *Contemporary Literature* 10, no. 4 (Autumn 1969).

Sea Garden. London: Constable & Co., 1916; Boston and New York: Houghton Mifflin, 1916.

Choruses from Iphigeneia in Aulis. London: Egoist Press, 1916; Cleveland: The Clerk's Private Press, 1916.

The Tribute and Circe, Two Poems by H.D. Cleveland: The Clerk's Private Press, 1917.

Choruses from the Iphigeneia in Aulis and the Hippolytus of Euripides. The Poets' Translation Series. London: Egoist Limited, 1919.

Hymen. London: Egoist Press, 1921; New York: Henry Holt & Co., 1921.

Heliodora and Other Poems. Boston: Houghton Mifflin, 1924; London: Jonathan Cape, 1924.

Collected Poems of H.D. New York: Boni & Liveright, 1925 and 1940.

H.D. Edited by Hughes Mearns. The Pamphlet Poets. New York: Simon & Schuster, 1926.

Palimpsest. Paris: Contact Editions, 1926; Boston: Houghton Mifflin, 1926. Revised Edition: Carbondale and Edwardsville: Southern Illinois University Press, 1968.

Hippolytus Temporizes. Boston: Houghton Mifflin, 1927.

Hedylus. Boston: Houghton Mifflin, 1928; Oxford: Basil Blackwell, 1928 and 1929. New Edition: Redding Ridge, Conn.: Black Swan Books, 1980.

Red Roses for Bronze. New York: Random House, 1929.

Borderline—A Pool Film with Paul Robeson. London: Mercury Press, 1930.

Red Roses for Bronze. London: Chatto & Windus, 1931; Boston and New York: Houghton Mifflin, 1931. Extended edition.

Kora and Ka. Dijon: Imprimerie Darantière, 1934.

The Usual Star. Dijon: Imprimerie Darantière, 1934.

Nights. Dijon: Imprimerie Darantière, 1935. (Written under the pseudonym "John Helforth.")

The Hedgehog. London: Brendin Publishing Co., 1936.

Euripides' Ion. London: Chatto & Windus, 1937; Boston: Houghton Mifflin, 1937; Toronto: Macmillan, 1937.

What Do I Love? London: Brendin Publishing Co., 1944.

The Walls Do Not Fall. London and New York: Oxford University Press, 1944.

Tribute to the Angels. London and New York: Oxford University Press, 1945.

The Flowering of the Rod. London and New York: Oxford University Press, 1946.

By Avon River. New York: Macmillan, 1949.

Tribute to Freud. New York: Pantheon, 1956; Toronto: McClelland & Stewart, 1956.

Selected Poems of H.D. New York: Grove Press, 1957; Toronto: Collins, 1957.

Bid Me to Live (A Madrigal). New York: Grove Press, 1960; Toronto: McClelland & Stewart, 1960.

Helen in Egypt. New York: Grove Press, 1961.

Hermetic Definition. New York: New Directions, 1972.

Trilogy. (The Walls Do Not Fall, Tribute to the Angels, The Flowering of the Rod.) New York: New Directions, 1973.

Tribute to Freud. ("Writing on the Wall," "Advent".) Boston: David R. Godine, 1974.

End to Torment. A Memoir of Ezra Pound. Edited by Norman Holmes Pearson and Michael King. With the poems from "Hilda's Book" by Ezra Pound. New York: New Directions, 1979.

HERmione. New York: New Directions, 1981.

The Gift. New York: New Directions, 1982.

Notes on Thought and Vision & The Wise Sappho. San Francisco: City Lights Books, 1982.

Collected Poems 1912–1944. Edited by Louis L. Martz. New York: New Directions, 1983.

Selected Bibliography

NOTE The editions cited are those used; they are not necessarily the first, or the latest, editions.

Ackroyd, Peter. *Ezra Pound and His World.* New York: Charles Scribner's Sons, 1980.
Aeschylus. *The Complete Plays of Aeschylus.* Translated by Gilbert Murray. London: George Allen & Unwin, 1952.
Aiken, Conrad. *The Great Circle.* New York: Charles Scribner's Sons, 1933.
———. *Modern American Poets Selected by Conrad Aiken.* New York: Modern Library, 1927.
———. *A Reviewer's ABC.* New York: Meridian Books, 1958.
———. *Ushant.* New York: Oxford University Press, 1971.
Aldington, Richard. *All Men Are Enemies.* Garden City, N.Y.: Doubleday, Doran, 1933.
———. *Death of a Hero.* London: Penguin Books, 1936.
———. *D. H. Lawrence, Portrait of a Genius But . . .* New York: Duell, Sloane & Pearce, 1950.
———. *Life for Life's Sake.* London: Cassell, 1968.
———. *Literary Studies and Reviews.* New York: Dial Press, 1924.
———. *The Poems of Richard Aldington.* Garden City, N.Y.: Doubleday, Doran, 1934.
———. *Soft Answers.* Carbondale and Edwardsville: Southern Illinois University Press, 1967.
Aldington, Richard, and Durrell, Lawrence. *Literary Lifelines. The Richard Aldington–Lawrence Durrell Correspondence.* Edited by Ian S. MacNiven and Harry T. Moore. New York: Viking, 1981.
Allen, Donald, and Tallman, Warren, eds. *The Poetics of the New American Poetry.* New York: Grove Press, 1973.
Allen, H. R. *Who Won the Battle of Britain?* London: Arthur Barber, 1974.
Ambelain, Robert. *Dans l'ombre des cathédrales.* Paris: Éditions Adyar, 1939.
Anderson, Margaret. *The Fiery Fountains.* New York: Horizon Press, 1967.
———. *The Little Review Anthology.* New York: Horizon Press, 1953.
———. *My Thirty Years' War.* New York: Horizon Press, 1969.
Bair, Deidre. *Samuel Beckett.* New York: Harcourt Brace Jovanovich, 1978.
Barry, Iris. "The Ezra Pound Period." *The Bookman* 74, no. 2 (October 1931).
Beach, Sylvia. *Shakespeare and Company.* London: Faber & Faber, 1956.
Benét, Laura. *When William Rose, Stephen Vincent and I Were Young.* New York: Dodd, Mead, 1976.
Benét, Mary Kathleen. *Writers in Love.* New York: Macmillan, 1977.
Benét, William Rose, ed. *Fifty Poets.* New York: Duffield & Green, 1933.
Bittinger, Lucy F. *German Religious Life in Colonial Times.* Philadelphia: Lippincott, 1906.

Black, E. L. [John Ellerman] *Why Do They Like It?* Territet, Switzerland: Pool Editions, 1927.

Bogan, Louise. *A Poet's Alphabet.* New York: McGraw-Hill, 1970.

Boll, Theophilus E. M. *Miss May Sinclair: Novelist.* Rutherford, N.J.: Fairleigh Dickinson University Press, 1973.

Bonaparte, Marie. *Female Sexuality.* New York: Grove Press, 1962.

Bovet, Félix. *The Banished Count; or, The Life of Nicholas Ludwig Louis Graf Von Zinzendorff.* Translated by the Reverend John Gill. London: Nisbet, 1865.

Bowra, C. M. *Ancient Greek Literature.* New York: Oxford University Press, 1960.

Brewster, Dorothy. *Virginia Woolf's London.* London: George Allen & Unwin, 1959.

Brome, Vincent. *Jung.* New York: Atheneum, 1978.

Bryher, Winifred. *Amy Lowell: A Critical Appreciation.* London: Eyre & Spottiswoode, 1918.

——. *Beowulf.* New York: Pantheon, 1952.

——. *Civilians.* Territet, Switzerland: Pool Editions, 1927.

——. *The Coin of Carthage.* London: Collins, 1964.

——. *The Colors of Vaud.* New York: Harcourt, Brace and World, 1969.

——. *The Days of Mars: A Memoir, 1940–1946.* New York: Harcourt Brace Jovanovich, 1972.

——. *Development, a Novel.* London: Constable, 1920.

——. *Film Problems of Soviet Russia.* London: Pool Publications, 1929.

——. *The Fourteenth of October, a Novel.* New York: Pantheon, 1952.

——. *Gate to the Sea.* New York: Pantheon, 1958.

——. *The Heart to Artemis: A Writer's Memoirs.* New York: Harcourt, Brace and World, 1962.

——. *The Lament for Adonis.* Translated from the Greek of Bion of Smyrna. London: A. L. Humphreys, 1918.

——. *Paris 1900.* Translated by Sylvia Beach and Adrienne Monnier. Dijon and London: Pool Publications, 1930.

——. *The Player's Boy, a Novel.* New York: Pantheon, 1953.

——. *Roman Wall, a Novel.* New York: Pantheon, 1954.

——. *Ruan.* New York: Pantheon, 1960.

——. *This January Tale.* New York: Harcourt, Brace and World, 1966.

——. *Two Selves.* Paris: Contact Publishing Co., 1923.

——. *Visa for Avalon.* New York: Harcourt, Brace and World, 1965.

——. *West.* London: Jonathan Cape, 1925.

Bush, Douglas. *Mythology and the Romantic Tradition in English Poetry.* New York: W. W. Norton, 1963.

Butler, E. M. *The Fortunes of Faust.* Cambridge: Cambridge University Press, 1952.

——. *Heinrich Heine. A Biography.* New York: Philosophical Library, 1957.

——. *Paper Boats.* London: Collins, 1959.

——. *Silver Wings.* New York: G. P. Putnam's Sons, 1953.

Butts, Mary. *The Crystal Cabinet.* London: Methuen, 1937.

Callaghan, Morley. *That Summer in Paris.* New York: Coward-McCann, 1963.

Cardozo, Nancy. *Lucky Eyes and a High Heart. The Life of Maud Gonne.* New York: Bobbs-Merrill, 1978.

Carnevali, Emanuel. *The Autobiography of Emanuel Carnevali.* Compiled by Kay Boyle. New York: Horizon Press, 1978.

Carswell, Catherine. *The Savage Pilgrimage.* London: Secker & Warburg, 1951.

Carswell, John. *Lives and Letters.* New York: New Directions, 1978.

Cecil, David. *Max. A Biography.* London: Constable, 1964.

Chaboseau, Jean. *Le Tarot.* Paris: Éditions Niclaus, 1946.

Chesterton, G. K. *Autobiography.* London: Hutchinson & Co., 1936.

——. *Orthodoxy.* New York: Dodd, Mead, 1908.

Chisholm, Anne. *Nancy Cunard.* New York: Alfred A. Knopf, 1979.

Colette. *The Pure and the Impure.* London: Secker & Warburg, 1968.

Contemporary Literature 10, no. 4 (Autumn 1969). Special number on H.D.

Cooper, Diana. *The Rainbow Comes and Goes.* London: Rupert Hart-Davis, 1958.

Cournos, John. *Autobiography.* New York: G. P. Putnam's Sons, 1935.

——. *Miranda Masters.* New York: Alfred A. Knopf, 1926.

Crosby, Harry. *Shadows of the Sun. The Diaries of Harry Crosby.* Edited by Edward Germain. Santa Barbara: Black Sparrow Press, 1977.

Damon, S. Foster. *Amy Lowell.* Boston: Houghton Mifflin, 1935.

Deighton, Len. *Fighter. The True Story of the Battle of Britain.* London: Jonathan Cape, 1977.

Delany, Paul. *D. H. Lawrence's Nightmare. The Writer and His Circle in the Years of the Great War.* New York: Basic Books, 1978.

Delavenay, Emile. *D. H. Lawrence. The Man and His Work.* Translated by Katharine M. Delavenay. Carbondale and Edwardsville: Southern Illinois University Press, 1972.

Donoghue, Denis, and Mulryne, J. R., eds. *An Honored Guest. New Essays on W. B. Yeats.* New York: St. Martin's Press, 1966.

Dowding, Hugh. *Many Mansions.* London: Rider & Co., 1943.

Drake, William. *Sara Teasdale. Woman & Poet.* New York: Harper & Row, 1979.

Dunan, Renée. *The Love Life of Julius Caesar.* Translated by Arabella Yorke. New York: E. P. Dutton, 1931.

Ede, H. S. *Savage Messiah. Henri Gaudier-Brzeska.* New York: The Literary Guild, 1931.

Elborn, Geoffrey. *Edith Sitwell: A Biography.* Garden City, N.Y.: Doubleday, 1981.

Ellis, Havelock. *The Fountain of Life.* Boston: Houghton Mifflin, 1930.

——. *My Life.* Boston: Houghton Mifflin, 1939.

Ellmann, Richard. *James Joyce.* New York, London, and Toronto: Oxford University Press, 1965.

Elwin, Malcolm. *The Life of Llewelyn Powys.* London: John Lane, The Bodley Head, 1946.

Euripides. *Four Plays about Women. The Medea. Helen. The Trojan Women. Electra.* Edited by David Greene and Richmond Lattimore. New York: Washington Square Press, 1973.

——. *Ten Plays.* Introduction by Moses Hadas. New York: Bantam Books, 1977.

Faris, John T. *Old Churches & Meeting Houses in and Around Philadelphia.* Philadelphia: Lippincott, 1926.

Fielding, Daphne. *Emerald & Nancy—Lady Cunard and Her Daughter.* London: Eyre & Spottiswoode, 1968.

Fitts, Dudley, trans. *Poems from the Greek Anthology in English Paraphrase.* New York: New Directions, 1956.

Fitzgerald, F. Scott. *Tender Is the Night.* New York: Charles Scribner's Sons, 1962.

Flacelière, Robert. *Literary History of Greece.* Chicago: Aldine Publishing Co., 1964.

Fletcher, John Gould. *Life Is My Song.* New York: Farrar & Rinehart, 1937.

Ford, Ford Madox. *Memories and Impressions.* New York: Harper & Row, 1911.

Ford, Hugh, ed. *Nancy Cunard: Brave Poet, Indomitable Rebel 1896–1965.* Philadelphia, New York, and London: Chilton Book Co., 1968.

——. *Published in Paris. American and British Writers, Printers & Publishers in Paris, 1920–1939.* London: Garnstone Press, 1975.

Friedberg, Anne. "Approaching Borderline." *Millenium Film Journal*, nos. 7 / 8 / 9 (Fall-Winter 1980–81).

Friedman, Susan Stanford. *Psyche Reborn: The Emergence of H.D.* Bloomington, Ind.: Indiana University Press, 1981.

Fromm, Gloria G. *Dorothy Richardson.* Urbana and London: University of Illinois Press, 1977.

Gates, Norman T. *A Checklist of the Letters of Richard Aldington.* Carbondale and Edwardsville: Southern Illinois University Press, 1977.

Glassco, John. *Memoirs of Montparnasse.* London: Oxford University Press, 1970.

Glendinning, Victoria. *Edith Sitwell: A Unicorn Among Lions.* New York: Alfred A. Knopf, 1981.

——. *Elizabeth Bowen. Portrait of a Writer.* London: Weidenfeld & Nicolson, 1977.

Goldberg, Isaac. *Havelock Ellis. A Biographical and Critical Survey.* New York: Simon & Schuster, 1926.

Goldring, Douglas. *Trained for Genius. The Life and Writings of Ford Madox Ford.* New York: E. P. Dutton, 1949.

Gould, Jean. *Amy. The World of Amy Lowell and the Imagist Movement.* New York: Dodd, Mead, 1975.

Grant, Joan. *Far Memory.* New York: Harper & Brothers, 1956.

——. *Winged Pharaoh.* New York: Harper & Brothers, 1938.

Graves, Robert, and Riding, Laura. *A Survey of Modernist Poetry.* London: Heinemann, 1927.

Gray, Cecil. *The History of Music.* New York: Alfred A. Knopf, 1931.

——. *Musical Chairs.* London: Home & Van Thal, 1948.

——. *Predicaments.* London: Oxford University Press, 1936.

Greene, Graham. *Ways of Escape.* New York: Simon & Schuster, 1980.

Gregory, Horace. *The House on Jefferson Street.* New York: Holt, Rinehart & Winston, 1971.

Grosskurth, Phyllis. *Havelock Ellis. A Biography.* New York: Alfred A. Knopf, 1980.

Guggenheim, Peggy. *Out of This Century. Confessions of an Art Addict.* New York: Universe Books, 1979.

Hahn, Emily. *Lorenzo. D. H. Lawrence and the Women Who Loved Him.* Philadelphia and New York: Lippincott, 1975.

Hale, Nancy. *Mary Cassatt. A Biography of the Great American Painter.* Garden City, N.Y.: Doubleday, 1975.

Hall, Donald. "Ezra Pound: an Interview." *Paris Review*, no. 28 (Summer-Fall 1962).

Hamilton, Edith, trans. *Three Greek Plays.* New York: W. W. Norton, 1937.

Hamnet, Nina. *Laughing Torso.* London: Constable, 1938.

Hassall, Christopher. *Edward Marsh, a Biography.* London: Longmans, Green, 1959.

Hemingway, Ernest. *Selected Letters.* Edited by Carlos Baker. New York: Charles Scribner's Sons, 1981.

Holloway, Mark. *Norman Douglas.* London: Secker & Warburg, 1976.

Howarth, Herbert. *Notes on Some Figures Behind T. S. Eliot.* Boston: Houghton Mifflin, 1964.

Hughes, Glenn. *Imagism & the Imagists. A Study in Modern Poetry.* New York: Biblo & Tannen, 1972.

Hunt, Violet. *The Flurried Years.* London: Hurst & Blachett, 1926.

Hutchins, Patricia. *Ezra Pound's Kensington. An Exploration 1885–1913.* London: Faber & Faber, 1965.

Huxley, Aldous. *Antic Hay.* New York: George H. Doran, 1923.

Jones, A. R. *The Life and Opinions of Thomas Ernest Hulme.* Boston: Beacon Press, 1960.

Josephson, Matthew. *Life Among the Surrealists.* New York: Holt, Rinehart & Winston, 1962.

Joyce, James. *Letters.* Edited by Stuart Gilbert, New York: Viking, 1957.

———. *Selected Letters.* Edited by Richard Ellmann. New York: Viking, 1975.

Kenner, Hugh. "Hermetic Definition." New York *Times Book Review,* December 10, 1972.

———. *The Pound Era.* Berkeley and Los Angeles: University of California Press, 1971.

Knight, Arthur. *The Liveliest Art. A Panoramic History of the Movies.* New York: Macmillan, 1957.

Knoll, Robert E. *Robert McAlmon. Expatriate Publisher and Writer.* Lincoln: University of Nebraska Press, 1959.

Kreymborg, Alfred. *Troubadour. An American Autobiography.* New York: Liveright, 1925.

Lawrence, D. H. *Aaron's Rod.* London: Heinemann, 1922.

———. *The Collected Letters.* Edited by Harry T. Moore. New York: Viking, 1962.

———. *Kangaroo.* London: Heinemann, 1923.

———. *Lady Chatterley's Lover.* New York: Grove Press, 1959.

———. *The Man Who Died.* New York: Alfred A. Knopf, 1931.

———. *Women in Love.* New York: Viking, 1933.

Lehmann, John. *Virginia Woolf and Her World.* London: Thames & Hudson, 1975.

Lewis, Wyndham. *The Letters of Wyndham Lewis.* Edited by W. K. Rose. London: Methuen, 1963.

Lidderdale, Jane, and Nicholson, Mary. *Dear Miss Weaver. Harriet Shaw Weaver 1876–1961.* New York: Viking, 1970.

"Life in a Hothouse." *Newsweek,* May 2, 1960.

Lowell, Amy. *The Complete Poetical Works.* Boston: Houghton Mifflin, 1955.

———. *Poetry and Poets. Essays.* Boston: Houghton Mifflin, 1930.

———. *Tendencies in Modern American Poetry.* New York: Macmillan, 1917.

Lucas, F. L. *Greek Poetry for Everyman.* London: J. M. Dent, 1951.

McAlmon, Robert. *Being Geniuses Together 1920–1930.* Revised and with supplementary chapters by Kay Boyle. Garden City, N.Y.: Doubleday, 1968.

———. *A Hasty Bunch.* Carbondale and Edwardsville: Southern Illinois University Press, 1977.

———. *McAlmon and the Lost Generation. A Self-Portrait.* Edited with a Commentary by Robert E. Knoll. Lincoln: University of Nebraska Press, 1962.

McGreevy, Thomas. *Richard Aldington.* London: Chatto & Windus, 1931.

McMillan, Dougald. *transition. The History of a Literary Era 1927–1938.* New York: George Braziller, 1975.

Macpherson, Kenneth. *Rome. 12 Noon.* New York: Coward-McCann, 1964.

Martin, Jay. *Conrad Aiken. A Life of His Art.* Princeton, N.J.: Princeton University Press, 1962.

Meyer, Bernard C. *Joseph Conrad. A Psychoanalytic Biography.* Princeton, N.J.: Princeton University Press, 1967.

Mizener, Arthur. *The Saddest Story: a Biography of Ford Madox Ford.* New York: World, 1971.

Monnier, Adrienne. *The Very Rich Hours of Adrienne Monnier.* Translated by Richard McDougall. New York: Charles Scribner's Sons, 1976.

Monroe, Harriet. *A Poet's Life.* New York: Macmillan, 1938.

Monroe, Harriet, and Henderson, Alice C., eds. *The New Poetry. An Anthology.* New York: Macmillan, 1918.

Moore, Harry T. *The Intelligent Heart. The Story of D. H. Lawrence.* New York: Farrar, Straus & Cudahy, 1954.

——. *The Priest of Love. A Life of D. H. Lawrence.* Revised Edition. New York: Penguin Books, 1981.

Moore, Marianne. *The Complete Poems.* New York: Macmillan and Viking, 1967.

——. *Predilections.* New York: Viking, 1955.

Muggeridge, Malcolm. *Chronicles of Wasted Time.* London: Collins, 1972.

Murry, John Middleton. *Reminiscences of D. H. Lawrence.* New York: Henry Holt, 1933.

Norman, Charles. *Ezra Pound.* New York: Macmillan, 1960.

Orage, A. R. *The Art of Reading.* New York: Farrar & Rinehart, 1930.

Patmore, Brigit. *My Friends When Young.* London: Heinemann, 1968.

——. *No Tomorrow.* New York and London: Century Co., 1929.

——. *This Impassioned Onlooker.* London: Robert Holden, 1926.

Patmore, Derek. *The Life and Times of Coventry Patmore.* New York: Oxford University Press, 1949.

——. *Private History.* London: Jonathan Cape, 1960.

Pearson, Hesketh. *The Man Whistler.* New York: Harper, 1952.

Pearson, John. *The Sitwells, a Family's Biography.* New York: Harcourt Brace Jovanovich, 1978.

Perse, St. John. *Letters.* Translated and edited by Arthur J. Knodel. Princeton, N.J.: Princeton University Press, 1979.

Pound, Ezra. *A Lume Spento.* New York: New Directions, 1965.

——. *The Cantos.* New York: New Directions, 1979.

——. "A Few Don'ts by an Imagiste." *Poetry: A Magazine of Verse,* March 1913.

——. *The Letters of Ezra Pound.* Edited by D. D. Paige. New York: Harcourt Brace, 1950.

——. *Personae. The Collected Shorter Poems of Ezra Pound.* New York: New Directions, n.d.

——. *Poems 1918–1921.* New York: Boni & Liveright, 1921.

——. *Pound / Joyce. The Letters of Ezra Pound to James Joyce, with Pound's Essays on Joyce.* Edited by Forrest Read. New York: New Directions, 1967.

——. *Selected Poems.* A New Edition. New York: New Directions, 1957.

——. *Selected Prose, 1909–1965.* New York: New Directions, 1973.

——. *The Spirit of Romance.* New York: New Directions, n.d.

Powell, Anthony. *Agents and Patients.* New York: Periscope-Holliday, 1936.

——. *Casanova's Chinese Restaurant.* London: Heinemann, 1960.

——. *Messengers of Day.* New York: Holt, Rinehart & Winston, 1978.

Powys, John Cowper. *Autobiography.* New York: Simon & Schuster, 1934.

Powys, Llewelyn. *The Letters of Llewelyn Powys.* Selected and edited by Louis Wilkinson with an Introduction by Alyse Gregory. London: John Lane, The Bodley Head, 1943.

——. *Skin for Skin.* New York: Harcourt Brace, 1925.

Pratt, William, ed. *The Imagist Poem.* New York: E. P. Dutton, 1963.

Quinn, Vincent. *H.D. (Hilda Doolittle).* New York: Twayne, 1967.

Rachewiltz, Mary de. *Discretions.* Boston: Little, Brown, 1971.

Ramuz, C. F. *When the Mountain Fell.* New York: Pantheon, 1947.

Rattray, David. "Weekend with Ezra Pound." *The Nation,* November 16, 1957.

The Record of the Class of Nineteen Hundred and Five of Friends' Central School 1900–1905. Philadelphia: Friends' Central School, 1905.

Riding, Laura. *Lives of Wives.* New York: Random House, 1939.

——. *A Trojan Ending.* New York: Random House, 1937.

Rougemont, Denis de. *Love in the Western World.* Garden City, N.Y.: Doubleday, Anchor Books, 1957.
——. *Passion and Society.* New York: Pantheon, 1956; Garden City, N.Y.: Doubleday, 1956.
St. John, Christopher. *Ethel Smyth. A Biography.* London: Longmans, Green, 1959.
Salter, Elizabeth. *The Last Years of a Rebel. A Memoir of Edith Sitwell.* Boston: Houghton Mifflin, 1967.
Satterthwaite, Alfred. "John Cournos and 'H.D.,'" *Twentieth-Century Literature* 22, no. 4 (December 1976).
Schaffner, Perdita. "Merano, 1962." *Paideuma* 4, nos. 2, 3 (1975).
The Second American Caravan. A Yearbook of American Literature. Edited by Alfred Kreymborg, Lewis Mumford, and Paul Rosenfeld. New York: Macaulay, 1928.
Secrest, Meryle. *Between Me and Life. A Biography of Romaine Brooks.* Garden City, N.Y.: Doubleday, 1974.
Seferis, George. *Poems.* Boston: Little, Brown, 1960.
Seyffert, Oskar. *Dictionary of Classical Antiquities.* Revised and edited by Henry Nettleship and J. E. Sandys. Cleveland and New York: World, 1964.
Sieburth, Richard. *Instigations. Ezra Pound and Rémy de Gourmont.* Cambridge: Harvard University Press, 1978.
Simon, Linda. *The Biography of Alice B. Toklas.* Garden City, N.Y.: Doubleday, 1977.
——. *Thornton Wilder: His World.* Garden City, N.Y.: Doubleday, 1979.
Simpson, Louis. *Three on the Tower. The Lives and Works of Ezra Pound, T. S. Eliot and William Carlos Williams.* New York: William Morrow, 1975.
Sinclair, May. *Mary Olivier: a Life.* New York: Macmillan, 1919.
——. *Tree of Heaven.* New York: Macmillan, 1917.
Sitwell, Edith. *Collected Poems.* New York: Vanguard, 1954.
——. *Fanfare for Elizabeth.* New York: Macmillan, 1946.
——. *The Queens and the Hive.* Boston: Little, Brown, 1962.
Sitwell, Sacheverell. *The Hunters and the Hunted.* New York: Macmillan, 1948.
Smoller, Sanford J. *Adrift Among Geniuses. Robert McAlmon, Writer and Publisher of the Twenties.* University Park and London: Pennsylvania State University Press, 1975.
Spender, Stephen, ed. *D. H. Lawrence. Novelist, Poet, Prophet.* New York: Harper & Row, 1973.
Stapleton, Laurence. *Marianne Moore. The Poet's Advance.* Princeton, N.J.: Princeton University Press, 1978.
Stauffer, Donald Barlow. *A Short History of American Poetry.* New York: E. P. Dutton, 1974.
Stein, Gertrude. *Gertrude Stein on Picasso.* New York: Liveright, 1970.
——. *Look at Me Now and Here I Am. Writings and Lectures 1909–45.* Edited by Patricia Meyerowitz. Baltimore: Penguin Books, 1967.
Stevens, Wallace. *The Letters of Wallace Stevens.* Selected and edited by Holly Stevens. New York: Alfred A. Knopf, 1966.
Stock, Noel. *The Life of Ezra Pound.* New York: Pantheon, 1970.
Swann, Thomas Burnett. *The Classical World of H.D.* Lincoln: University of Nebraska Press, 1962.
Symonds, John Addington. *Studies of the Greek Poets.* London: A. and C. Black, 1920.
Talbot, Daniel, ed. *Film: An Anthology.* Berkeley and Los Angeles: University of California Press, 1972.

Tuohy, Frank. *Yeats.* New York: Macmillan, 1976.

Untermeyer, Louis. *American Poetry Since 1900.* New York: Henry Holt, 1923.

Wagner, Geoffrey. *Wyndham Lewis. A Portrait of the Artist as the Enemy.* New Haven: Yale University Press, 1957.

Weigall, Arthur. *The Paganism in Our Christianity.* New York and London: G. P. Putnam's Sons, 1928.

Weinberg, Herman G. *Saint Cinema. Writings on the Film 1929–1970.* Second Revised Edition. New York: Dover Publications, 1973.

Whitall, James. *English Years.* London: Jonathan Cape, 1936.

White, Eric W., and H.D. *Images of H.D. / From The Mystery.* London: Enitharmon Press, 1976.

Whittemore, Reed. *William Carlos Williams. Poet from New Jersey.* Boston: Houghton Mifflin, 1975.

Wickes, George. *The Amazon of Letters. The Life and Loves of Natalie Barney.* New York: G. P. Putnam's Sons, 1976.

Wickham, Anna. *The Contemplative Quarry.* New York: Harcourt Brace, 1921.

Wilkinson, Louis. *The Buffoon.* New York: Alfred A. Knopf, 1916.

——. *Swan's Milk.* London: Faber & Faber, 1934.

Williams, William C. *The Autobiography of William Carlos Williams.* New York: New Directions, 1967.

——. *Imaginations.* New York: New Directions, 1970.

——. *I Wanted to Write a Poem.* Reprinted and edited by Edith Heal. Boston: Beacon Press, 1958.

——. "A Letter from William Carlos Williams to Norman Holmes Pearson Concerning Hilda Doolittle and Her Mother and Father." *William Carlos Williams Newsletter* 2, no. 2 (Fall 1976).

——. *The Selected Letters.* Edited with an Introduction by John C. Thirlwall. New York: McDowell, Obolensky, 1957.

——. *A Voyage to Pagany.* New York: Macaulay, 1928.

——. *The William Carlos Williams Reader.* Edited with an Introduction by M. L. Rosenthal. New York: New Directions, 1966.

Wolff, Geoffrey. *Black Sun. The Brief Transit and Violent Eclipse of Harry Crosby.* New York: Random House, 1976.

Wolle, Francis. *A Moravian Heritage.* Boulder, Colorado: Empire Reproduction & Printing Company, 1972.

Woolf, Virginia. *The Diary of Virginia Woolf.* Edited by Anne Olivier Bell. Vol. 2, 1920–24. New York: Harcourt Brace Jovanovich, 1978.

Wright, Robert. *Dowding and the Battle of Britain.* London: Macdonald, 1969.

Unpublished Sources

NOTE Conventional footnotes have not been used in this book. Instead, published sources quoted or cited in the text are listed in the Bibliography, those people who contributed personal papers or information are listed in the Acknowledgments, and institutions holding major collections of unpublished materials are described below.

I. The Beinecke Rare Book and Manuscript Library, Yale University, New Haven, Connecticut.

Beinecke Library is the major repository for H.D.'s and Bryher's papers. Correspondence in these vast collections include letters from H.D. to Richard Aldington, Gretchen Baker, Bryher, Lionel Durand, Viola Jordan, Robert McAlmon, Norman Holmes Pearson, George Plank, Walter Schmideberg, and Eric Walter White, among others. Also included are letters to H.D. from Richard Aldington, Sylvia Beach, Bryher, Helen Doolittle, Robert Duncan, Lionel Durand, Cecil Gray, Viola Jordan, Robert McAlmon, Kenneth Macpherson, Brigit Patmore, Norman Holmes Pearson, Ezra Pound, Dorothy Richardson, and Edith Sitwell, among others.

Unpublished manuscripts by H.D. in the Yale Collection of American Literature include, among others:

> "Asphodel" (1921–22)
> "Autobiographical notes"
> "The Compassionate Friendship" (1955)
> "Diary to Durand" (1961)
> ["Diary"] (Paris, 1912)
> "The Gift" (1941–43)
> "Her" (1927). Published in 1982 as *HERmione*, but consulted in its manuscript form.
> "Hirslanden Notebooks" (1957–59)
> "Majic Mirror" (1955)
> "Majic Ring" (1943–44)
> "The Mystery" (1949–51)
> "Notes on Thought and Vision" (1919)
> "Paint It Today" (1921)
> "Pilate's Wife" (1924, 1929, 1934)
> "The Sword Went Out to Sea" (1946–47)
> "The White Rose and the Red" (1948)

Also in the Beinecke Library are the following separate collections:

The Ezra Pound papers, which include letters from H.D. to Ezra Pound, and from H.D. to Mrs. Homer Pound.

The Norman Holmes Pearson papers, which include correspondence between N. H. Pearson and Bryher, H. P. Collins, Robert McAlmon, Victoria McAlmon, and Margaret Snively Pratt, among others.

The Robert McAlmon papers, which include the typescript of his unpublished novel "Some Take Their Moments."

II. The British Library, London.
The Manuscripts Department holds the Cecil Gray papers, which include a letter from H.D. to Cecil Gray, and letters from Philip Heseltine to Gray.

III. Bryn Mawr College, Bryn Mawr, Pennsylvania.
The College Library holds H.D.'s and Bryher's letters to Mary Herr.

IV. The State University of New York at Buffalo.
The Poetry Collection of the University Libraries holds letters from H.D. to William Carlos Williams.

V. Houghton Library, Harvard University, Cambridge, Massachusetts.
The Manuscripts Department holds the H.D.-Amy Lowell, Bryher-Amy Lowell, and Richard Aldington-Amy Lowell correspondences, as well as the correspondence from John Cournos to H.D. and from John Cournos to Richard Aldington.

VI. The New York Public Library.
The Berg Collection holds correspondence from H.D. and Bryher to May Sarton, and from May Sinclair to Charlotte Mew.

VII. The Rosenbach Museum and Library, Philadelphia, Pennsylvania.
The Marianne Moore Collection includes the correspondence between H.D. and Marianne Moore, and between Bryher and Marianne Moore.

VIII. Southern Illinois University, Carbondale, Illinois.
The Richard Aldington Papers in the Morris Library include letters from H.D. to Richard Aldington, and from Richard Aldington to Alec Randall.

IX. The Huntington Library, San Marino, California.
The Huntington Library holds letters from H.D. to Conrad Aiken.

INDEX